HATING EMPIRE PROPERLY

Hating Empire Properly

The Two Indies and the Limits
of Enlightenment Anticolonialism

SUNIL M. AGNANI

Fordham University Press
NEW YORK   2013

Copyright © 2013 Fordham University Press

All rights reserved. No part of this publication may be reproduced, stored in a retrieval system, or transmitted in any form or by any means—electronic, mechanical, photocopy, recording, or any other—except for brief quotations in printed reviews, without the prior permission of the publisher.

Fordham University Press has no responsibility for the persistence or accuracy of URLs for external or third-party Internet websites referred to in this publication and does not guarantee that any content on such websites is, or will remain, accurate or appropriate.

Frontispiece: Jacob Lawrence (1917–2000), *General Toussaint L'Ouverture*, 1986. From the Toussaint L'Ouverture Series. Silk screen; image: 28 1/4 x 18 1/2 inches; paper: 32 x 22 inches. © 2012 The Jacob and Gwendolyn Lawrence Foundation, Seattle / Artists Rights Society (ARS), New York. Image courtesy of DC Moore Gallery, New York.

Fordham University Press also publishes its books in a variety of electronic formats. Some content that appears in print may not be available in electronic books.

Library of Congress Cataloging-in-Publication Data

Agnani, Sunil M.
  Hating empire properly : the two Indies and the limits of Enlightenment anticolonialism / Sunil M. Agnani.
    pages ; cm
  Includes bibliographical references and index.
  ISBN 978-0-8232-6739-2 (cloth : alk. paper)
  1. Imperialism—History. 2. Imperialism—Philosophy. I. Title.
JC359.A55 2013
325'.3—dc23

2012046396

Printed in the United States of America

15 14 13   5 4 3 2 1

First edition

A book in the American Literatures Initiative (ALI), a collaborative publishing project of NYU Press, Fordham University Press, Rutgers University Press, Temple University Press, and the University of Virginia Press. The Initiative is supported by The Andrew W. Mellon Foundation. For more information, please visit www.americanliteratures.org.

The being of something is determinate; something has a quality and in it is not only determined but limited; its quality is its limit and, burdened with this, it remains in the first place an affirmative, stable being. But the development of this negation, so that the opposition between its determinate being and the negation as its immanent limit, is itself the being-within-self of the something, which is thus in its own self only a becoming, constitutes the finitude of something....

The finite not only alters, like something in general, but it *ceases to be*; and its ceasing to be is not merely a possibility, so that it could be without ceasing to be, but the being as such of finite things is to have the germ of decease as their being-within-self: the hour of their birth is the hour of their death.

—HEGEL, *SCIENCE OF LOGIC* (1816)

Contents

List of Illustrations ix
Acknowledgments xi
Prologue: Enlightenment, Colonialism, Modernity xv

Introduction: Companies, Colonies, and Their Critics 1

PART I Denis Diderot: The Two Indies of the French Enlightenment

1 *Doux Commerce, Douce Colonisation*: Consensual Colonialism in Diderot's Thought 23
2 On the Use and Abuse of Anger for Life: *Ressentiment* and Revenge in the *Histoire des deux Indes* 46

PART II Edmund Burke: Political Analogy and Enlightenment Critique

3 Between France and India in 1790: Custom and Arithmetic Reason in a Country of Conquest 69
4 Jacobinism in India, Indianism in English Parliament: Fearing the Enlightenment and Colonial Modernity 109
5 Atlantic Revolutions and Their Indian Echoes: The Place of America in Burke's Asia Writings 133
    (a) Reflections on the Revolution in St. Domingue/Haiti 133
    (b) Compensation in the East, or, From Virginia to Hindostan 162

Epilogue. Hating Empire Properly:
European Anticolonialism at Its Limit   177

Notes   191
Bibliography   249
Index   267

Illustrations

1 "Les Anglois demandent pardon à Aurengzeb qu'ils ont offensé." From Guillaume Thomas Raynal, *Histoire des deux Indes*.   8

2 James Gillray, "The Political Banditti Assailing the Saviour of India."   76

3 James Gillray, "The Impeachment, or 'The Father of the Gang Turned King's Evidence.'"   129

4 Anne-Louis Girodet, *Le Citoyen Jean-Baptiste Belley, Ex-Représentant de colonies*, 1798.   151

5 [William Dent]: "Thunder, Lightning and Smoke, or the wind shifted from the North to the East."   164

6 "Toussaint Reading the Abbé Raynal's work." From J. R. Beard, *The Life of Toussaint L'Ouverture, the Negro Patriot of Hayti*.   178

Acknowledgments

The longer one takes to complete such a project, the lengthier the list of debts becomes. In its early forms, Gauri Viswanathan, Gayatri Chakravorty Spivak, Nicholas Dirks, Talal Asad, Emma Rothschild, Jenny Davidson, and Seamus Deane all provided helpful comments and criticism. I benefited more broadly from a range of scholars who were at or passed through Columbia University. The memory of Edward Said's seminar remarks and casual asides is unavoidably with me when I recall this group of people. The widely divergent manner in which they conducted their intellectual lives was itself instructive. As much a part of this world were friends and colleagues Sanjay Krishnan, Milind Wakankar, Tim Watson, Qadri Ismail, Aamir Mufti, Colleen Lye, Sanjay Reddy, Teena Purohit, Chenxi Tang, Nauman Naqvi, Nermeen Shaikh, Jonathan Magidoff, Ninon Vinsonneau, and Clarisse Berthezène.

A range of individuals and research institutions assisted my work through fellowships: a Fulbright for study at the Institut für Kulturwissenschaft at Humboldt University in Berlin allowed me to read widely (my thanks to Hartmut Böhme there and to Andreas Huyssen for his assistance); a William Reese Company fellowship from the John Carter Brown Library, directed by Norman Fiering, gave me tactile access to *Histoire des deux Indes*; the Princeton Society of Fellows (then ably directed by Leonard Barkan, whom I must thank) enabled me to expand the scope of this project; an Ahmanson-Getty Fellowship from the Clark Memorial Library at the University of California–Los Angeles put me in touch with intellectual historians of empire (I thank Peter Hanns Reill, Anthony Pagden, and Sanjay Subrahmanyam for this opportunity); and, finally, the Newberry Library in Chicago, where I attended a National Endowment for the Humanities summer seminar on the French and Haitian Revolutions, led by Jeremy Popkin (I must also acknowledge my discussions with Emmanuel Chukwudi Eze here, now sadly passed away). The Newberry also graciously provided me with research space as a scholar in residence for several years.

During the two years I spent at Princeton, Gyan Prakash, Michael Wood, Claudia Johnson, Hans Aarsleff, and Mary Harper were all generous with their time and support. I would like to thank my colleagues in Ann Arbor while I was in the English Department at the University of Michigan, especially Patricia Yaeger, Jonathan Freedman, Sidonie Smith, Lincoln Faller, David Porter, Dena Goodman, Sumathi Ramaswamy, Scotti Parrish, Adela Pinch, Lucy Hartley, Yopie Prins, Barbara Metcalf, James I. Porter, and Sean Jacobs.

Since joining the University of Illinois at Chicago in 2008, it has been my pleasure to interact with faculty in both the Department of English as well as History. Their encouragement and the intellectual diversity (if my colleague noted below will permit me the word!) of their opinions and interests has taught me the worth of provocative critique. I must particularly thank Mark Canuel, always ready with advice and gentle nudges to move forward with this book. Beside him were many others who were supportive (or productively challenging) interlocutors: Lennard Davis, Lisa Freeman, Robin Grey, Laura Hostetler, Jim Sack (an especially careful reader!), Astrida Orle Tantillo, the late James Searing (his sudden passing is still a shock), Walter Benn Michaels, Joseph Tabbi, Ellen McClure, Nicholas Brown, Deirdre McClosky, Alfred Thomas, Dwight McBride, John Huntington, Gerald Graff, Stephen Engelmann, Rachel Havrelock, Ainsworth Clarke, Anna Kornbluh, and Corey Capers.

Along the way, others allowed me to present parts of this work or provided comments and suggestions: Margaret Cohen, Srinivas Aravamudan, Uday Mehta, Ato Quayson, Sankar Muthu, David Armitage, James E. G. Zetzel, Jennifer Pitts, Ajay Skaria, Ranajit Guha, Isabelle Clark-Decès, Jim Clark, Sudipta Kaviraj, David Bromwich, Akeel Bilgrami, Betty Joseph, Pauline Lavagne, Isabelle Gadoin, Marie-Élise Palmier-Chatelain, Pratap Bhanu Mehta, Susanne Greilich, Carla Hesse, Bhikhu Parekh, Ann Thomson, Thomas Metcalf, Kapil Raj, Matthew Smith, John Mowitt, Siraj Ahmed, and the late Yves Benot. Suvir Kaul provided detailed suggestions. I am very aware that some of those named may not agree with the arguments of this book; misreadings and mistakes that follow are most certainly my own, but I hope in the spirit of discussion (I will not say the public use of reason) that they will momentarily indulge the work.

In addition to the Modern Language Association and the American Society for Eighteenth-Century Studies, portions of this book were presented at the following research forums or conferences: the Bloomington Eighteenth-Century Workshop, organized by Fritz Breithaupt, at Indiana University (thanks to Jonathan Sheehan and Kenneth R. Johnston for comments); the Irish Studies Seminar, University Seminars at Columbia University (arranged by Mary McGlynn and Martin Burke); the American Conference for Irish Studies, Princeton University (my thanks to Abbey Bender); the International Society for Eighteenth-Century Studies, hosted by the University of Genoa; Religion and the English Enlightenment, organized by Sophie Gee of the English Department and the Center for the Study of Religion, Princeton University; the International Society for Intellectual History, organized by Marco Sgarbi and hosted by the University of Verona; Atlantic Enlightenments, Center for the Humanities, University of Miami (Frank Palmeri provided helpful comments); Caribbeanscapes, the Annual West Indian Literature Conference, held at University of the West Indies–Mona, Jamaica; the American Comparative Literature Association (Vancouver); L'Inde des Lumières, organized by Ines Zupanov and Marie Fourcade, L'École des Hautes Etudes en Science Sociale, Paris; the Fourteenth International Conference of the Forum on Contemporary Theory, organized by Lewis Gordon (Temple University) with Prafulla Kar (Institute for Contemporary Theory, Vadodara) and held in Jaipur, India.

An earlier version of chapter 1 was published as "*Doux commerce, douce colonisation*: Diderot and the Two Indies of the French Enlightenment," *The Anthropology of the Enlightenment*, ed. Larry Wolff and Marco Cipolloni (Stanford: Stanford University Press, 2007), 65–84. Similarly, an earlier version of chapter 4 appeared as "Jacobinism in India, Indianism in English Parliament: Fearing the Enlightenment with Edmund Burke," *Cultural Critique* 68 (Winter 2008): 131–62.

I consider myself lucky to have worked with Helen Tartar and her assistant Thomas Lay at Fordham University Press; they steered this work to completion and were exceedingly efficient. I would also like to thank Tim Roberts at the American Literatures Initiative. The cover illustration and frontispiece to this book are by the noted painter Jacob Lawrence, associated with the Harlem Renaissance. Lawrence produced a series of forty-one paintings on the life of Toussaint Louverture and the Haitian Revolution in 1938, the same year in which C. L. R. James published his history of the event, *The Black Jacobins*. The silkscreen I have chosen from 1986 is Lawrence's revisiting of that work from very early in his career, when he was only twenty-one. The full series—especially his descriptive captions—bristles with the contradictions of anticolonial and antislavery sentiments of the Enlightenment against a backdrop of French ambivalence. I would like to thank the Jacob and Gwendolyn Lawrence Foundation, the Artists Rights Society, and DC Moore Gallery for allowing me to use this most fitting image.

If it were possible to thank civic entities or neighborhoods, I should like to express my gratitude to Morningside Heights, Fort Greene, and Park Slope in New York and Lincoln Square in Chicago for providing the random street encounters and phatic everyday conversation that mitigates the unavoidable isolation of scholarly work.

My "little platoon," as Burke might say, is one group I know I cannot thank enough: Rama Mantena, most of all; Anish and Maya for warmth and entertainment (and for putting, nearly every day, *Émile* to the test); Karuna Mantena; Anasuya and Raju Mantena; and, finally, my sister, Seema, and parents, Mohan and Jasvanti Agnani.

Prologue: Enlightenment, Colonialism, Modernity

Enlightenment, *les lumières*, *Aufklärung*: What does it mean to invoke this term, with its evident and often-examined root metaphor of light? Does placing it alongside *colonialism* immediately mark a turn to its inversion, a shift in metaphors from light to dark (for example, the "dark side" of the Enlightenment and similar variations on this theme)?[1] And in response to the complicity suggested by such a turn, must one then undertake a full exculpation of Enlightenment thinkers, extricating their work from the lapses and moments of failure that allow their ideas to lend support or underpin projects growing out of colonialism (a hierarchy of peoples, the civilizing mission, etc.)?[2] This book proposes to do neither; indeed it seeks out the moments of inconsistency and contradiction in a thinker preeminently associated with the French Enlightenment, Denis Diderot, and in another who famously attacked these "magpies of philosophy,"[3] the British writer and parliamentarian Edmund Burke. But even this remark must remain unsatisfactory for some, given the variety of the critiques of the term *Enlightenment*, whether from historically minded writers such as J. G. A. Pocock, who urge us to replace the singular enlightenment with plural enlightenments, or from thinkers associated with postmodernism who have allegedly impugned it.[4] A reflection on some varieties of Enlightenment, and more broadly eighteenth-century anticolonialism certainly obliges one to examine critically the organizing terms that are used. More robustly, since I am interested in this inaugurating question as a component of colonial modernity, how does one situate this particular form of historical understanding, its relation to the past, present, and future?[5] This book continues a set of questions enabled by postcolonial thought, though I use the term as a shorthand to indicate the persistence of the problematic of empire in relation to the emergence of modernity (rather than a reference to an institutionalized discipline within literary studies).[6] What this book shares with key works from that field is the sense of an inevitable entanglement of the modern West with the history of colonialism.[7] However, what might be called another species of Eurocentrism actually indicates a quite different understanding, namely, an awareness that European modernity has been critically shaped and defined by colonialism. (The reverse, that former colonies have been shaped by Europe, need not even be said; the course of nineteenth-century history made this explicit.) In that sense, this book holds true to the spirit of Kantian critique, if we understand Kant's work (especially his essay "What Is Enlightenment?") as an instance of philosophical thought reflecting on its own present. It was, manifestly, Michel Foucault's influential reading of Kant's essay that laid stress on this element, one that I would like to invoke as a means to ground the method, the reading practices, and occasional forays into historical interpretation which are elaborated in the chapters that follow.[8] In his essay on Kant, Foucault refers to the "attitude" of modernity, which he provisionally compares to the Greek notion of an *ethos*. Modernity as an attitude (a mode of relating to contemporary society) rather than as a period of history, he remarks, is a more significant distinction to consider rather than the premodern "era" in contrast to a postmodern one. The philosophical ethos is then the permanent critique of our historical era, a view that enables one to avoid what he appropriately calls the "blackmail" (*chantage*) of the Enlightenment.[9] By invoking the notion of blackmail, by refusing it, Foucault characterizes and dismisses an either/or relationship to the Enlightenment: either accept its rationalism or escape from its principles of rationality—a concise way of understanding the arguments against the Enlightenment in some of the early texts of postcolonial thought.

Critique of this kind exists only, Foucault writes, in relation to something other than itself and is therefore an instrument.[10] If critique is indeed associated (to invoke his deeply striking phrase) with the "art of not being governed," then it must inevitably encounter and consider notions of conquest and colonialism—the very instances where sovereignty would appear to be the least present. In an observation that couches within itself a strong interpretation, he asserts that critique is the examination of "voluntary inservitude" and is therefore not far from Kant's own definition of *Aufklärung*.[11] More broadly, critique is a component of the examination of the governmentalization of society, which must inevitably lead us to *colonial* society since it undertook (or was subjected to) this governmentalization in an accelerated manner under the specific forms and modalities of colonial power.

There have been others who have developed components of Foucault's argument, such as François Hartog, who makes the case for understanding modernity as characterized by a certain "regime of historicity" that locates the present as a focal point in the representation of time and instrumentalizes the categories of past and future.[12] But for some time, the relevance of Foucault's argument for understanding areas beyond Europe was made clear by David Scott in his essay "Colonial Governmentality," which cautioned that "the critique of European hegemony in the construction of knowledge about the non-European world" ought to be distinguished from "programmatically ignoring Europe, as though by seeking to do so one would have resolved the problem of Eurocentrism."[13] The readings of Diderot and Burke in this book are part of a similar effort at a "conceptual repositioning" of Europe, one that resolutely does not argue for programmatically ignoring it but rather making Europe's internal plurality a starting point.

In this sense, I should make clear my understanding of that crucial word affiliated with the notion of Enlightenment: *modernity*. Foucault's rich sense of the concept, traced in such texts as "What Is Enlightenment?" and "What Is Critique?," laid stress—particularly in the examples he gives from Baudelaire's *The Painter of Modern Life*—on the practices of *askesis*, or asceticism (an exercise over the self); modernity for Baudelaire was a mode of relating to oneself in a *transfigurative* manner.[14] The dandy, for example, takes himself to be an object of elaboration and makes himself into a work of art. This constitution of the self as an autonomous object is, argues Foucault, rooted in the Enlightenment.[15] I would, however, like to supplement and modulate Foucault's understanding with the expressive phrase invoked by Talal Asad and developed by David Scott to identify the nature of subject-formation for many colonized subjects or those otherwise touched by empire; these are neither passive subjects nor the fully autonomous subjects Foucault seems to identify through Baudelaire's figure of the dandy or the painter of modern life. They are, rather, "conscripts of modernity."[16] What Asad's iteration of the notion of modernity in this descriptive phrase enables is (as Scott notes) less a focus on the "actor's volitional subjectivity (his or her agency) than the conditions of possibility for that subjectivity to be and act."[17] For Scott, it is Toussaint Louverture who illustrates the significance of this; indeed it is one way of understanding what C. L. R. James meant by taking Toussaint to be the paradigmatic figure of the colonial intellectual, and why, for Toussaint, "the modern is confronted as a tragic condition."[18]

James may be mentioned as one early proponent of the significance of slavery and empire in understanding modernity generally—both European modernity and colonial modernity. (For James, the plantation was an inaugural moment of modernity in the Caribbean.)[19] If it is from thinkers such as Foucault and Reinhart Koselleck that one can understand the subject formation and temporal awareness that underlie a definition of modernity, then it is from a very different intellectual such as James—and more recent scholars such as Asad and Scott—that we can adjoin to these elements an awareness of the conscript's entanglement with European thought: "Toussaint Louverture is most usefully understood as a conscript—rather than a resisting agent—of modernity; moreover ... his self-fashioning relation to the abbé Raynal's *Philosophical and Political History* is best read in this light as the inaugural negotiation of the colonial conscript's relation to the modern west."[20] Although a passing reference to Raynal, it is an apt emblem for the reading practice and interpretative aims of this work: to correlate from the other side in what way one might read pivotal texts from European authors in light of this understanding of colonial modernity, and to embed this within an understanding of European modernity itself. The notion of the conscript enables one to avoid a presumption of outright resistance—to the modern, to Europe—and instead understands this relation as modulated, turning to the forms of engagement with the modern and with Europe.

That one needs a revised understanding of modernity is a position I take as evident, in part persuaded by a range of recent writings on this subject but also by the immanent evidence of a reading practice that is attuned to the contemporary co-emergence of a species of the modern in colonial spaces (rather than the "lateness" of the modern in those spaces as suggested by a conventional understanding of European modernity, and more obviously in the modernization theory that reigned for a time in some social sciences).[21] Sudipta Kaviraj has noted how the theory of modernity originating in Europe was extended to settler colonial societies such as the United States, Canada, and Australia on the premise that they originated as "extensions" of the Western world. But he also remarks upon the awareness in authors as early as Tocqueville that the presence of the "three races of America" (native peoples, European settlers, and the enslaved of African descent) made American modernity distinct from that of Europe.[22] If we are to take seriously Kaviraj's suggestion that we reject an "easy diffusionist teleology," which he argues emerged most saliently in the theories of modernity proposed by Weber and Marx, then this also requires an evaluation of the manner in which we situate the remarks about the non-European and colonial world by Enlightenment and (more generally) eighteenth-century writers such as Diderot and Burke. It is in this manner that we might undertake—adapting a phrase from Dipesh Chakrabarty—to provincialize the Enlightenment.[23] This does not mean relegating it to the margins but rather considering in what way a revised or broadened sense of the modern might alter our view of the preoccupations with the colonial world that these writers patently exhibit.

As may be clear from some of the theoretical and methodological texts cited here, I have found it indispensable to include in my purview of the late eighteenth century the works of scholars associated with the study of South Asia and the Caribbean, or with postcolonial thought more generally. If a justification for this is needed, one answer would be quite simple: it is literally unthinkable for someone who reflects on the modernity of any eighteenth-century colonial space not also to incorporate in a very profound and indeed structural way a consideration of Europe and its internal complexity. Unfortunately until recently the reverse has not been true. It is easy to find examples of studies of European modernity that simply relegate Europe's former colonies to a theoretical periphery or historical footnote; the neglect of the Haitian Revolution in the established historiography of the French Revolution can serve as one example.[24] Indeed, as I explore in chapter 5, even when St. Domingue was mentioned by name in Burke's parliamentary speeches, later collections of these speeches simply omit to mention the entanglement of his references to St. Domingue in the midst of a discussion of the then ongoing revolution in France.[25] The modernity of these spaces was, in the words of Sybil Fischer, explicitly "disavowed."[26]

In the opening pages of *Ancien Régime and the Revolution*, Tocqueville writes of the opportune (we might say felicitous) moment to evaluate the French Revolution: he seized a window of interpretative opportunity that was limited and would pass,[27] able to still enter the feelings of those who undertook it (because it was not so far distant) yet far enough away to evaluate it. Perhaps it was this awareness that enabled him to remark on the manner in which revolutionary discourse relied upon and created a new notion of the past—and thereby a new relation to that past—expressed by the phrase *ancien régime*. François Furet, the eminent historian of the French Revolution and eventual gadfly against the French left (or at least of its influence on historiography), developed this observation to argue that the *ancien régime* formed part of an "indissoluble pair" with *revolution* and that this thereby distinguishes the French (idea of) revolution from the English.[28] For Furet, the term *ancien régime* was used to denounce a range of targets—feudalism, monarchy, the Middle Ages—yet, crucially, this contrast is what created (in another disciplinary language, one might say "constructed") the ancien régime as an "almost palpable reality," an idea so widely accepted as to not require any further comment. In his examination of the emergence of the phrase, Furet observes that it was first applied to monarchical government and that it is tied to the idea of a "fresh start" so characteristic of the French Revolution. All this leads to his critical remark that *ancien régime* ultimately signified anything that was antagonistic to the revolution, so much so that it became "the Revolution's antithesis." The polemical thrust of his argument is that *ancien régime* might be a more hollow phrase than is often granted, produced and constituted in tandem with revolution. In a parallel manner, Daniel Gordon observes that the bias against the Enlightenment in postmodern thought was due to a similar structural opposition: "'Enlightenment' is to postmodernism what 'old regime' was to the French revolution."[29] Gordon argued that the series of derogatory clichés that represented the Enlightenment (such as "the elimination of cultural diversity" and a belief in "infinite progress") enabled the false idea that "enlightenment symbolizes the modern that postmodernism revolts against."[30] He is surely correct to note the status of the Enlightenment among some thinkers associated (rightly or wrongly) with postmodernism, and his observation is kindred with what I have alluded to in some varieties of postcolonial thought. (This was, however, a moment now incorporated into a larger debate and needs to be contextualized within it.) By virtue of its links with Eurocentrism, the Enlightenment was subject to the same withering critique implied by texts such as *Orientalism*.[31] Hence the significance of including those moments when Enlightenment thinkers attempt to unthink, to critique their location within Europe and to demonstrate the latent interpretative possibilities of avoiding the view that all forms of thought in the period form a single, unified, Enlightenment "project."

Furet's point about the French Revolution's creation of a new temporality ironically brings to mind Ranajit Guha's argument regarding the way time was colonized by imperial historians. This affinity between historians of the left and right comes out of a critique of the way narratives of conquest restructure time: in the one case, the Jacobins in France; in the other case, the British and European historians of the British Empire in India.³² Each remade the *telos* of the nation (or, as Burke might have said, of the "country of conquest"). As Guha notes, although the Battle of Plassey is commemorated as a victory by the East India Company that inaugurates "colonial" India, the actual British conquest of India took well over "a hundred more years of war, intrigue, and piecemeal annexation . . . to be consummated."³³ And yet, in spite of this, colonial histories produced within two decades of the battle already "foretold" of conquest. There is a future-directedness to the process of conquest, one that requires the mediation of symbolic forms and narrative to establish itself. My point here is to emphasize that in such a context, we may well speak of a "conscripted modernity" (to adapt that phrase) in the colonial space to indicate the manner by which it was incorporated—with a mixture of willing agency and coercion—into modernity at large. The problem is precisely that most accounts of the modern claim its European face and disavow these mixed forms, believing that the history of Europe or the West (not to mention the Enlightenment) can be written without reference to them.³⁴ If, however, one can demonstrate that the thought of writers and intellectuals like Diderot and Burke is profoundly formed and even, if I may be permitted the phrase, deformed by reflection upon slavery and conquest, then it ought to be possible to reconfigure the relationship between enlightenment, colonialism, and modernity in a more proximate and productive manner. This *ethos* (to return to Foucault's point) or attitude of several key writers in this period is the object of my examination more than the application of a predefined approach or hermeneutic denominated by the term *postcolonial*; rather it is the problem space opened up by the structuring questions in this field that are vital to an understanding of the Enlightenment in a global frame.

A brief word on the context of this work and the methods it deploys. Some readers may find that, much like Burke's own image of the French nation after the revolution, this book brings together elements that do not sit well beside one another, that it shifts registers between the theoretical and the historicist, the rational and the affective, and that it is thereby (to recall Burke's image of the revolution) a monster beyond nature, neither human nor animal. It was formed in the crucible of literary studies (both the comparative and Anglophone variety), and my path to this subject went first through a course of study of twentieth-century decolonization; from there it tracked back to the imperial zenith of nineteenth-century British and French history and found its object only in the closing decades of the eighteenth century.

It is my hope that these are productive tensions, since if one is to contribute to a reconsideration of a postcolonial present, this involves disentangling and pursuing contradictory discourses initiated—both in Europe and in former colonies such as Haiti and India—in an Enlightenment past. However, pluralizing this Enlightenment past, in a manner compatible with but different in approach from suggestions made by scholars such as Pocock, Jonathan Israel, and the like, ought to make this legacy a partial opportunity. Not a "gift" in the ambivalent sense (both that which is given and a "poison," as Derrida once outlined it, or as Dipesh Chakrabarty seemed to provocatively invoke at the end of his study in referring to the "gift" of European thought),[35] but a partial opportunity since reconceiving anticolonial thought in the Enlightenment might allow for a more complex understanding of the negotiations with it later taken up by thinkers such as (to name but a few from the modern Indian context) Naoroji, Ambedkar, and Gandhi. Not that they carried it forward, but it might allow us to understand what their object of critique was, what they disliked, even "hated" in this legacy, in addition to what they preserved, retained, or redeemed.

One consequence of this scholarly trajectory through literary interpretation alongside historically inclined readings is that it is my aim precisely *not* to erase, cover over, or resolve the contradictory and ambiguous moments that arise while examining the works of authors such as Diderot and Burke. (Indeed some of these tensions are even immanent to a disciplinary subfield like the literary study of colonialism, if one considers the profound differences in style between a critic like Gayatri Spivak alongside Edward Said's predominant mode of analysis.) If one is to take seriously the remarks by Foucault noted earlier on the need to refuse the blackmail or *chantage* of the Enlightenment, then this translates also into a reading practice: to refuse to read Burke, for example, as either straightforwardly reactionary (commonly presumed) or pro-Enlightenment (an unusual position, but one that has been recently argued).[36] Effectively, this dichotomy lines up with the neat divisions between two views of the Enlightenment: either it is a flawed project bound up with racism, dominance, and conquest (as some early readings in postcolonial thought argued), or it is a valiantly liberatory movement that lays the groundwork for the very overturning of many of these categories of race and empire (as some recent readings of a "radical Enlightenment" or an "Enlightenment against empire" have argued).[37] I am sympathetic to and persuaded by both facets of this view of Enlightenment thought, but would it not be more suited to the complexity of the object instead to recover the richness of the contradiction and to place one's focused gaze upon it? It is with this in mind that I turn to these inconsistent critics of empire, asking what this inconsistency may tell us, what these momentary windows of opportunity (putting a company or a whole empire on trial, abolishing slavery in French colonies) meant, and how these brief outbursts of radicalism or indignation (Diderot's encyclopedic tirades) might be understood.

Understanding how reason—or rather colonial reason—operated requires that we reconstruct and replicate its own vacillation between two different modes of inquiry and critique: both the moments of abstract universalism one finds in Diderot and the emphasis on particularity in Burke's view of custom or colonial knowledge. These reflect distinct forms of understanding difference, and it is only by examining them side by side that we can illuminate the insights and limitations of each.

Introduction: Companies, Colonies, and Their Critics

> *Falstaff:* O! she did so course o'er my exteriors with such a greedy intention, that the appetite of her eye did seem to scorch me up like a burning-glass. Here's another letter to her: she bears the purse too; she is a region in Guiana, all gold and bounty. I will be 'cheator to them both, and they shall be exchequers to me: they shall be my East and West Indies, and I will trade to them both. Go bear thou this letter to Mistress Page; and thou this to Mistress Ford. We will thrive, lads, we will thrive.
> —SHAKESPEARE, *THE MERRY WIVES OF WINDSOR*, ACT I, SCENE 3

Little could be further from the rage of an angry French philosophe or the moral gravitas of a British parliamentarian with a view to the judgment of history than the comic narcissism of Shakespeare's Falstaff. In his efforts to woo two mistresses at once—a cheater to them both—he loses both. And yet, unlike Falstaff, many European countries did indeed trade at once, and very effectively, with two Indies, east and west. The early modern imagination of these regions would develop in color and specificity a great deal before the figures discussed in this book wrote their treatises regarding possible avenues for trade and their considerations regarding the transformation of Europe and the Indies which might result from such traffic. As here in Falstaff's remark, the reader will find that in the late eighteenth century there continued to be a sexual component to the many schemes proposed for settlement and colonization. (The two valences are brought together in Shakespeare's pun, with "cheator" carrying both the sense of an escheator or exchequer as well as, more obviously, sexual infidelity.) At times these writings conformed to the now familiar figuration of the land to be possessed as female and the explorers male. Mistress Page and Mistress Ford, however, had already spoken to each other and could conspire together to mock and defeat the intentions of their portly seductor. Our analogy, therefore, perhaps ends there. Falstaff may have failed, but in his exclamation "We will thrive, lads, we will thrive," he was not so far off the mark. Just as he duplicated a love letter for his two would-be mistresses, several European monarchs gave exclusive charters to trading companies in America, Africa, and

India in the hope of gold and bounty, and often these paid off.[1] The story told in this book deals incidentally with one of the problems of Falstaff's faulty courtship technique: in wooing more than one person at the same time, the singularity of his praise and devotion is lost.

It would be wrong to make the ethical relationship between individuals similar to the forms of colonial knowledge that were beginning to be compiled in such an extensive manner throughout the eighteenth century. Nonetheless at play in this episode is a helpful distinction regarding the particularity of the archive of colonial knowledge—which I take as a form of singularity and distinctiveness—in tension with the often discussed impulse toward an outline of universalistic principles and tendencies in the Enlightenment. "Enlightenment universalism" and "colonial knowledge" are therefore a means to arrange a set of oppositions which I also intend at times to place in question. To be open about the significance of this pair of terms, I examine the idea of enlightenment universalism as it emerges out of an encyclopedic impulse in France, mainly taking Diderot's contributions to the *Histoire des deux Indes* (after his efforts in the *Encyclopédie*) as my object. Burke himself wrote some pieces early in his life that bear comparison to these, such as his contributions to *An Account of the European Settlements in America* (1757),[2] though in this study I focus on his later writings and correspondence. It is in the speeches that Burke gave in Parliament and in his letters to acquaintances (some expanded and intended for publication, such as *Reflections on the Revolution in France*) that one finds an illustration of the effects of colonial knowledge in the late eighteenth century.

Although I have mentioned Falstaff's speech comparing his dual courtship with the two Indies, by the mid- to late eighteenth century these ties between Europe and the Indies would already be more greatly developed. Mistress Page would be much more than a region in Guiana providing "gold and bounty"; there would be the more mundane but no less profitable list of sugar, coffee, cotton, and so on. With these commodities, some of them tracked by works such as the *Encyclopédie* and the *Histoire des deux Indes*, came the necessity to gather and accumulate knowledge. But more than knowledge was at stake, for there was also a set of debates initiated into the basis and legitimacy of colonial rule, on how the sovereignty of the British Crown might extend to such far dominions.[3]

It was, in fact, the frequent presence of these debates in Parliament in the mid-eighteenth century, concerning the rights and limits upon the East India Company, that prepared the ground for a staging of Burke's later arguments on the reform of this relationship between Britain and its territories in India,[4] which are in part the focus of the second half of this book. Though the question of direct influence on Burke would be hard to trace, one ought also to place Diderot's fiery contributions to the 1780 edition of the *Histoire des deux Indes* within the forum of texts composing the debate on territorial and settler colonialism in the period. If these are predecessors to the discourse on colonialism at the end of the century, historians of South Asia have also indicated what distinguished Burke's prose from what followed after. In attempting to periodize the ideologies of the Raj, Thomas Metcalf points to the awareness of a complicity with the notion of oriental despotism which appeared in both the structure of rule established by Hastings and Cornwallis and in the indictments of the company from Burke and Philip Francis. This awareness was to wither away and be replaced by the idea of absolute difference, which became essential to underwriting the righteousness of the British conquest of India.[5]

Chapters 1 and 2 concern Diderot and elaborate the manner in which he illustrates elements of Enlightenment universalism. This is due to both the enterprises in which he participated—most famously the *Encyclopédie* but also the *Histoire des deux Indes*—and to the style of thinking these works make manifest. I explore how these works, expressive of a larger encyclopedic impulse in the period, if considered with other texts, such as the *Supplément au voyage de Bougainville,* reveal a supple and playful thinker who vacillates between an emphasis on the universalistic character of human behavior and one aware of the irreducible singularity of cultural practices as well. These latter singular characteristics I associate with colonial knowledge, more salient in the thought of Burke—and visible in key terms in his lexicon, such as manners—which are examined in the second half of the book (chapters 3–5). These particular manners—a term that can incorporate both social practices inherited by custom and the political institutions that instantiate them—work against an aggregative universalistic system of thinking, which Burke identified as a core flaw of the French philosophes, and an impulse within Jacobinism more largely. In this sense, I could well have elected to focus on someone like Jean-Jacques Rousseau, whom Burke once rather memorably (if exaggeratedly) called "the insane Socrates of the National Assembly."[6] I address Burke's venom toward Rousseau in a section of chapter 4; the question of their relation merits greater investigation since it forms a larger part of the story of the circulation of French thought and its reception in Britain. But Diderot's contributions to the *Histoire des deux Indes* are a more interesting foil than the work of Rousseau to explore elements of Burke's political thought on Europe's relation to its incipient colonies. There are some admirable works on Burke's India writings (most notably Uday Mehta's *Liberalism and Empire*), and yet these studies beg the question of how to bring the readings of India back (as it were) to his writings on France; I illustrate how the intermingling of these two issues in his late correspondence justifies such a move.[7] To that end, and to situate Burke's thought in a spectrum of writing about empire, Diderot's strident anticolonialism in the 1780 edition of the *Histoire* bears some natural resemblance to Burke's language in, for example, "Speech on Fox's East India Bill" (1783). And yet it is startling to consider just how different their respective motivations for such an attack may have been. Here are two major figures, each perhaps among the handful who might be called the most important thinkers of the period, who had extensive writings on the question of colonialism—one from the "left" and the other from the "right" (though to use these terms is make use of an anachronism; it relies upon the very political languages that were formed in the wake of the revolution controversy in France and Europe more generally).[8] In any case, the conceptual contrasts (to leave alone the political ones) are illuminating enough to merit their consideration alongside one another and preclude the delimitation of this work to only one national context. To invoke another influential schema for understanding these two thinkers together, we might think of Burke as closer to what Jonathan Israel characterizes as the "moderate" Enlightenment (bearing the influence of Locke, Hume, etc.), while Diderot is more proximate to the radical Enlightenment.[9]

Thriving in the Indies: Trading Companies and the Contours of Empire

Anglo-French colonial rivalry, which so marks the writings of these years, calls for a comparative examination of discourses and debates from each national frame. And yet many studies of this period, if they take one national context into their purview, often lose sight of the very different ways the same problems and aporias of the legitimacy of colonization and settlement were resolved in another. The period this book delimits as its main focus, broadly the last three decades of the eighteenth century, is still covered by the long shadows cast by the French and Indian War in North America and the Seven Years' War in Europe (1756–63) that placed the importance of colonial territories at the center of dispute. Whether it was over who should gain control of the Ohio River Valley (in the case of the former) or Hanover (in the case of the latter), this tension quickly spilled out to mingle with confrontations occurring between these powers in colonial theaters of war such as India and the West Indies. By the time of the Franco-British Treaty of Paris (1763), Britain had won from France claims to North America east of the Mississippi, and France further renounced all conquests made in India or the East Indies since 1749. Yet the barter and swapping of all corners of the Earth is more extensive than this: France ceded Grenada, Saint Vincent, Dominica, and Tobago; Britain restored to France the islands of Guadeloupe and Martinique and the West African colony of Gorée (Senegal). Even this is necessarily only a partial list.[10]

This give-and-take of an imperial calculus indicates another aspect regarding the similarity between the writings of Burke and Diderot examined here: they take as their object the people and actions of the various European trading companies and forts that had been established around the globe. The most important of these in the case of South Asia, the (English) East India Company, was founded in 1600 (around the year that Shakespeare wrote the lines cited in the epigraph to this chapter) as a monopolistic trading body, which aimed to gain a share in the spice trade that was proving so profitable to Spain and Portugal. Indeed in its initial stages, these two nations were its rivals along with the Dutch, though this was to change with the Company's defeat of the Portuguese in India in 1612, an event that allowed them to extract trading concessions from the Mughal Empire.[11] The Company's monopoly aroused opposition within England and even provoked the creation of a rival company, though the two were fused in 1708 under the official title of the United Company Merchants of England. It was this entity that was to play a historic role in shaping the Indian Subcontinent, particularly through the English settlement of eastern India (later the Bengal presidency). The twenty-four directors of the United Company, in London, were elected annually by a Court of Proprietors who were shareholders. This proved to be a critical flaw after the Company gained control of Bengal in 1757, since shareholders' meetings dictated Indian policy, and votes at these meetings could be bought with the purchase of shares. Alongside this was the spectacle of returning Company servants with their amassed fortunes; much of this was made in the lucrative private trade done on the side by Company officials. In his capacity as governor-general, Warren Hastings sent diamonds home from central Indian mines, while his investigations into his opponent, Philip Francis, showed the latter to be sending home remittances of £45,000 on a salary of £10,000.[12] It is telling that the only term devised to describe those who had engaged in this preeminently mercantile form of accumulation was one that drew on the language of feudalism, namely *nabobs* (from *nawab*, most immediately from Urdu, though it is the Persian term in the Mughal Empire for a ruler of a district). They play a large role in the public discussions of trade and incipient empire in the period, and correspondingly in this book when I discuss Burke's writings on the Company and its servants.

It was in this context that Hastings was appointed first governor-general in 1772, with a mandate to reform policy dictated by simple shareholder imperatives or runaway Company servants out to make private fortune. It is important to note this, for this reform mandate is not the lens through which Burke came to view him. The year of his appointment occurred soon after the Bengal famine of 1770, which killed fully one-third of the population of the region and was aggravated by the Company's monopoly over rice and other commodities.[13] And yet Hastings was stepping into the initial great hopes for profits raised by Robert Clive (governor from 1765), which had been completely reversed by the Company's request for a loan in 1772 of £1 million to avoid bankruptcy.[14] The following year the British government gave a loan exceeding this amount, but its terms included the Regulating Act, which limited the affairs of the Company and effected important institutional changes (the creation of a supreme court and the establishment of the governor-generalship in Bengal with supervisory control over other Indian settlements). The other watershed event in this period of the Company's history that deserves mention is William Pitt's India Act of 1784, which marked a further step toward Parliament's influence over Company affairs through the creation of a new Board of Control superintending the directors. In spite of all these reforms, the drain of wealth from Britain to India has been calculated at £1.3 million annually from 1783 to 1793.[15] Contrary to many existing understandings of the East India Company as a mere private corporation with rule over eastern India, it is important to keep in mind that the company's institutional shape and influence already represents a certain form of "state formation."[16] Although the language used to name these entities—*state* versus *company*—appears to contradict this possibility, it is perhaps one of the ruses accomplished by remaining with this opposition to efface this very obvious fact.

The effort to establish a French equivalent of England's East India Company began not long after the latter's foundation, in 1604, when the letters patent were granted by Henry IV. This went nowhere, and a second effort began in 1611, only to meet a similar end. La Compagnie des Indes was formed in 1642, but this too was eventually superseded by an entity created by Jean-Baptiste Colbert, finance minister of France, in 1664. The great difference to be noted with the French company is that it was a state-controlled organization from the outset, unlike those of

England and Holland.[17] The French company's expedition first reached India in 1688, at Surat (in contemporary Gujarat), and over the course of the following century it was able to make the most of internal disputes within the various regions. Offering support to slighted noblemen, the French rivalry with the English was to become most manifest in the 1740s. In part the rise of this rivalry as a real factor in the region was due to the death of Aurangzeb in 1707 and the unraveling of the Mughal Empire as a counterweight to these interests. In the case of India, what began in Surat would end only with the last of the three Carnatic Wars (1760–61), when the contest between the French and the British was effectively settled with the predominance of the latter. Pondicherry and two settlements on the Malabar coast, Jinji and Mahé, were taken by the British (though Pondicherry was restored to the French in 1765 after a peace treaty). To many the French effort along the western coast of India was doomed as long as Bengal and control of the sea belonged to the British, effectively the case from the Battle of Plassey (1757) onward.[18] After the Seven Years' War and France's losses in the region, government support for the Company declined in favor of potential profits in the West Indies. Its monopoly over trade with India ended in 1769, and the Company itself ceased to exist after the French Revolution in 1789.[19]

With these brief sketches of the respective Company histories in mind, the significance of the period discussed in this book becomes clearer. The gradual acquisition of territory by the East India Company was to bring the question of sovereignty into sharp relief. Who was to rule over whom in a period of such transition, and under which set of laws? These uncertainties, once settled in clear favor of the Company, were to make the question of despotism and its oriental varieties pertinent and pressing. Hastings began his governor-generalship with the sense that he was to reform existing abuses, but he was to end up—in large part due to Burke's efforts—becoming a shorthand for these very practices. We can see why both Burke and Hastings sought to claim the legitimacy (or its lack) for the transformations being effected in India with regard to custom, tradition, and so on. In each case, these concepts have a dual history as they circulate between discussions in a European context (particularly in relation to France and England) and a colonial one—and here one would include not only India but also the West Indies and North America. The acquisition of territory in this manner should certainly cast doubt on the observation that the British Empire was acquired in a "fit of absence of mind," as J. R. Seeley famously put it—though his aim was perhaps to remind listeners of their "imperial responsibility" and not to condone a larger public's forgetfulness.[20] The state at home

FIGURE 1. "Les Anglois demandent pardon à Aurengzeb qu'ils ont offensé." From Guillaume Thomas Raynal, *Histoire des deux Indes* (Genève: Jean-Léonard Pellet, 1783), vol. 2, frontispiece. Courtesy of the John Carter Brown Library at Brown University. The *Histoire des deux Indes* reflects French and British interimperial rivalry as much as anticolonial sentiments. There is a certain pleasure in the depiction of several Englishmen prostrate before the Mughal emperor.

may officially have been absentminded, but its subjects abroad certainly were not. Nonetheless these circumstances do certainly go some way to explaining just why Burke and many others in the period were ambivalent about taking over other lands and territories without reflection. And ultimately it is precisely as a goad to such reflection (provocative reflection) that the *Histoire des deux Indes* opens with its famous question, "Europe has everywhere founded colonies; but does it know the principles upon which one ought to found them?"[21] The foregoing paragraphs have made more mention of Burke while discussing the British and French East India companies in the period because the very organizational structure and form of the *Histoire des deux Indes* owes so much to the existence of the trading companies (or *établissements*, as they are referred to in the full French title of the work), and it thereby requires less justification for being tied to this historical context. Diderot's contributions are dispersed throughout this work, which finds its narrative logic in tracing the national trading companies as a way to address the larger question of the legitimacy of colonialism and slavery as such.

On Antithetical Pairs

The one took his stand outside the received opinion, and surveyed it as an entire stranger to it: the other looked at it from within, and endeavored to see it with the eyes of a believer in it. . . . From this difference in the points of view of the two philosophers, and from the too rigid adherence of each to his own, it was to be expected that Bentham should continually miss the truth which is in the traditional opinions, and Coleridge that which is out of them, and at variance with them. But it was also likely that each would find, or show the way to finding, much of what the other missed. —JOHN STUART MILL, "COLERIDGE" (1840), COLLECTED WORKS OF JOHN STUART MILL

Though diametrically opposed to one another on so many issues of politics and philosophy, Diderot and Burke reward the critic willing to think through the categories each employs with a significantly enriched understanding of the period. Burke is attuned to the emotional pull of the "little platoon" (akin to what Raymond Williams would call a knowable community),[22] while Diderot is an articulate proponent of a cosmopolitanism that was to underpin so vitally many calls for justice from the conquered and the colonized. As writers, both ranged over a variety of literary genres, addressed the relation of aesthetics to politics, and held distinct views on the possible transformation of human society in an age of revolutions (only Burke was famously to witness the French; Diderot reveals his favorable views of the American Revolution throughout the

Histoire des deux Indes). Both also, later in their lives, expended a great deal of ink (or air) discussing Europe's colonies in a manner that ought to alter any limited conception of their interests; in Burke's case fully three of the nine volumes of the authoritative edition of his collected writings and speeches concern India.[23] He himself remarks in his correspondence that *Reflections on the Revolution in France* was written in part to take his mind off the impeachment trial he had instigated against Warren Hastings of the East India Company. In both instances, for different reasons, many readers of these authors pay scant attention to their writings on empire.[24] Too often Diderot is known primarily for his *Salons*, selected entries from the *Encyclopédie*, his novels, and dialogues, while Burke appears mainly in discussions of the Sublime and reactions to the French Revolution—or so at least was the case until recently within literary studies.[25] (There is an irony in this, given the popularity of some of his parliamentary speeches in the nineteenth century, testified to by the numerous editions and anthologies of his work from that period.) If one shifts to the field of history or the history of political thought, where empire is indeed discussed, one finds several studies of the significance of Burke's writings on India, but often in isolation from other engagements (such as France). There have been works that address this disjuncture, whose unintended consequence was to hygienically seal off Europe from these colonial spaces, and this book is one contribution to that effort.[26]

John Stuart Mill's remark on the poet associated with Romanticism (Coleridge) and the philosopher rigorously associated with Utilitarianism (Bentham) comes from a period when these two areas of experience and reflection were at a further remove from each other; nonetheless the aim of Mill's essay is to emphasize the dialectical need for each, to indicate the blindness and the insight that each system of viewing the world generates when on its own. It is with this aim—to "survey as a stranger" *and* to see with "the eyes of a believer"—that this book primarily proceeds on its way, and not as an investigative biography of the direct relations between Diderot and Burke. Nonetheless, since they were contemporaries, for some the question may arise: Did Diderot ever meet Burke, and what influence did one have on the other? There are some enticing links. Not Diderot himself, but the abbé de Raynal, editor of the *Histoire des deux Indes*, on one occasion sent a letter to Burke for information on English colonies and paid a visit to him in 1777.[27] In the other direction, Burke's name nowhere appears in any of Diderot's writings, though scholars have argued that he certainly had read Burke's *A Philosophical Enquiry into the Origins of Our Ideas of the Sublime and Beautiful* (1757), which appears to have influenced passages from the *Salons* of 1765 and 1767.[28] Indeed one of the few efforts directly to compare Diderot and Burke has been on the question of aesthetics. Gita May, author of this article, goes beyond what has been noted above and asserts, "There is no reference to Diderot in Burke's works, and . . . the converse is also true. Nevertheless, Burke's biographers generally allude to a possible meeting between the two men in Paris in February, 1773."[29] John Morley, a disciple of Mill and later secretary of state for India, in addition to being a prominent Victorian scholar of the eighteenth century, also speculates about this meeting (perhaps at Mademoiselle Lespinasse's salon) in one of his books on Burke.[30] However, more recent scholarship on Diderot, though still limited to speculation, asserts that although he interacted with David Hume a great deal (during the latter's stay in Paris from 1763 to 1766), "there were also some Englishmen who had deliberately avoided him," including Dr. Johnson and perhaps Burke.[31]

We cannot blame these Britons for avoiding the fractious salons in which Diderot moved; their differences with him were indeed great. Diderot and Burke responded to the ferment of the decades covered in this book in profoundly different ways, whose dates must serve as only a rough delimitation. This book is organized around the start of a decade, 1770, which saw the publication of the first edition of the *Histoire des deux Indes* in Geneva, witnessed a massive famine in Bengal that drew attention to the region, and perceived the rumblings of a revolution in the American colonies soon to come (about which both Burke and the contributors to the *Histoire* had much to say). Moreover the whole decade follows a watershed year, 1763, which is decisive in determining the shape of the British and French imperial frames—their rivalry in the two Indies, the Americas and Asia.[32] Diderot's death in 1784 (before the French Revolution but after the American) is a reminder of how much of his intensive work on the third edition of the *Histoire* of 1780 occupied the final years of his life, whose contours are defined by the ancien régime. The emergence of the cipher of the modern inaugurated by the events of 1789—which was to so shock Burke—and that regime's eventual demise compelled him to intertwine his reflections on India and France (and America and Ireland) in such unusual ways in his later writings and correspondence. Many of these letters are among his final writings, dating to 1796. He was to die in July of the following year, occupied by his thoughts of Jacobinism and "Indianism" (more on this term shortly). Confirmed in his early prognostications on the former by the events of the Terror in France, and in his fear of the latter by the acquittal of Hastings alongside continuing abuses of power by the East India Company in its colonial outposts, the phenomena he named by these words were expressive of the evisceration of existing human character and the gutting of working structures of governance—two effects that Diderot would have been pleased to push further along provided the right circumstances. To see with the eyes of one is to witness with horror what the other might have perceived with delight; in every way we can therefore agree with Mill's remark on a similarly antithetical pair, that "each would find, or show the way to finding, much of what the other missed."

> ACT III
> *The Antiquarian Society*
> *Secretary.* Sir Matthew Mite, preceded by his presents, will attend this honorable Society this morning.
> *1 Antiquarian.* Is he apprised that an inauguration-speech is required, in which he is to express his love of vertu, and produce proofs of his antique erudition?
> *Secretary.* He has been apprised, and is rightly prepared.
> *2 Antiquarian.* Are the minutes of our last meeting fairly recorded and entered?
> *Secretary.* They are.
> *1 Antiquarian.* And the valuable antiques which have happily escaped the depredations of time ranged and registered rightly?
> All is in order.
> —SAMUEL FOOTE, THE NABOB (1769), THE WORKS OF SAMUEL FOOTE, ESQ. IN TWO VOLUMES

Every good drama must have an interplay of voices that makes up its dialogue and a plot to drive it forward. Like the Antiquarians who will evaluate and inaugurate Sir Matthew Mite, a recently enriched Nabob returned to London modeled loosely on Robert Clive (leader of forces at the Battle of Plassey and famously the recipient of a *jaghire,* an annual grant paid to him from taxes assessed on local villages in Bengal), the reader will suitably adjudge the "valuable antiques" presented in this work as evidence for (or against) erudition antique and modern. The rage for order that the Antiquarians display, fairly recording their minutes and correctly preparing those who are to speak to them, demand a minimum demonstration of persuasiveness. The characters in this dialogue, assuming their various voices, are obviously Diderot and Burke; the plot I have threaded together in the manner described below.

Part I of this book, "Denis Diderot: The Two Indies of the French Enlightenment," comprises two chapters and takes as its main object the aforementioned encyclopedic work edited by abbé de Raynal titled

Histoire philosophique et politique des établissements et du commerce des Européens dans les deux Indes (Philosophical and Political History of the Settlements and of the Commerce of Europeans in the Two Indies [1780]). This multivolume series, published over the course of several decades, counted Diderot and Baron d'Holbach among its contributors. Diderot anonymously authored the more radical parts of the text—antislavery and anticolonial in their international views, antimonarchical in their domestic interventions—upon which my discussion concentrates. Although, as Robert Darnton has noted, it was a best seller in its day, it has until recently escaped the notice of interpreters of the Enlightenment (Koselleck's *Critique and Crisis* is a notable exception).[33] I consider how the *Histoire des deux Indes* allows us to fundamentally revise prevalent views of this period by examining forms of anticolonialism in the Enlightenment and relate this to Diderot's allegedly relativist moral position.

The thinkers of the eighteenth century, in their effort to make sense of the massive international flows of peoples and goods between several continents that went into so mundane an act as the consuming of coffee (from Arabia) with sugar (from the West Indies) diluted with milk (locally obtained in Europe), were more aware of this global network than may be apparent from a cursory examination of the period. "You see, madame," as the economist abbé Baudeau once wrote, "in a simple Breakfast, united before your eyes and in your hands the productions of all climates and of the two hemispheres."[34] They were implicitly and explicitly reflecting both upon the practice of slavery and upon incipient multiethnic empires whose contours (and fissures) are much more visible today, an age of obvious globalization and mass migration (economic and political).

How such an argument was advanced, veering between universal schemas (such as theories of world history moving from primitive society to modern commercial ones) and particular examinations of individual cultures, accounts for the different genres made use of by a writer such as Diderot. In chapter 1, I consider the failure of communication dramatized between a mischievous Tahitian native and a French priest by means of a parodic and philosophic dialogue, *Supplément au voyage de Bougainville*, which exists in apparent tension with his empirical efforts at detailed description undertaken in the *Histoire des deux Indes* and the *Encyclopédie*—the latter most famously evincing an aspiration to global knowledge, to its collection from all the "scattered" corners of the earth. In one place the effort to gather knowledge with infinite aspiration is asserted, while in the other—through the figures of the cleric and colonial native—there is great emphasis on the incommensurability of one culture with another. This part of the work considers a double movement in the French Enlightenment: an encyclopedic impulse that aims to incorporate and comprehend alongside a sometimes contrary impulse emphasizing cultural and ethical singularity or uniqueness. One aim, discussed in the prologue, is to avoid understanding the Enlightenment exclusively as an inherently imperial project by examining Diderot's contributions to the *History of the Two Indies*. In a sense, this is a problem that can be traced to the multiple ways Edward Said understood orientalism to operate. Though he qualified that orientalism was not "reflected passively by culture, scholarship," and the like, his positive argument received greater attention, namely that "it is rather than expresses, a certain will or intention to understand, in some cases to control, manipulate, even to incorporate, what is a manifestly different (or alternative and novel) world."[35] Based on the antislavery works and tracts of period, and in partial agreement with one recent and justly influential reading of Diderot, I examine how Diderot argued against empire.[36] Yet I would add, tacking in the other direction, that Diderot's radicalism placed him in a bind that could be resolved only by turning to political fantasy: unwilling to fully accept the legitimacy of colonial dominance, he imagines what I name "consensual colonialism," a soft colonization, in which the interests of settler and native are unified and the dominance of the settler is established with the voluntary consent of the colonized. In certain passages, Diderot goes so far as to speculate on how biologically breeding a docile subject has enabled the successful settling and peopling of colonial spaces. What is produced is an odd conjunction of beliefs that aims to be both liberal (by relying on consent) and imperial (by colonizing and civilizing the native). At this moment at the end of the eighteenth century, I suggest, the centrality of the idea of consent reveals a complicity between the languages of liberal political thought and the imperatives of empire and gives us an inkling into nineteenth-century political forms such as liberal imperialism.

Whereas the first chapter examined the uses of *douceur*, or sweetness, chapter 2 turns to the contrary set of passions or affects, namely those of *ressentiment*, revenge, and anger—modes of address that are surprisingly prominent in a text ostensibly about European settlements and trading companies. I explore the nature of Diderot's angry call to the reader and elaborate a distinction between anger and *ressentiment*. I suggest that the *Histoire des deux Indes* provides an instance when one can supplement the examination of commerce and history in eighteenth-century thought with the inclusion of affect, which is in part the management of a response to a perceived injustice. Diderot links the absolution of hatred (the anger of the colonized) to the question of justice, and it is one intention of this chapter to read these "outbursts" in relation to the larger question of global justice, or justice in the colony. The examples I analyze in this chapter come from several sections from the *Histoire des deux Indes* that geographically span the Southern Cape of Africa, to Goa, Jamaica, and the island of Guam (part of the Mariana Islands). In each, the response of the colonized vacillates between anger and revenge. I conclude by examining an episode that elaborates what I identify (using a term from the text itself) as the "double advantage." Once again, the *Histoire des deux Indes* searches for an alternative to the structuring antagonism and conflict inherent in the colonial context, and it is the double advantage that is meant to describe this mutual benefit. The advantage, to be clear, is doubled because the Mariana Islands—where this example is drawn from—would be a lucrative colony and (ideally) possess happy subjects, thus commingling an ethical language with the language of commerce and value so common in the period. One finds additionally throughout, that where Diderot attempts to imagine this alternative he has recourse to the mode of the historical counterfactual: What if it had been otherwise? What if colonization had taken place in this other manner?

The second part of this book, "Edmund Burke: Political Analogy and Enlightenment Critique," is composed of three chapters. Famous in literature departments as a theorist of the Sublime and in political theory for his concept of the ancient constitution, Burke had a range of political thought that extended far beyond the confines of his justly well-known *Reflections on the Revolution in France*. What underlying logic made possible his eventual support of the decision of the American colonists to secede in 1776, his scathing attack upon the Jacobin revolutionaries in France in 1790, and his even more passionate denunciation of Warren Hastings and the East India Company, which he undertook long before, during, and after the attacks on the revolution in France that seem to mark such a definitive break in his political thought? Chapters 3 and 4 provide one set of answers to these questions.

Chapter 3 examines closely key terms in Burke's lexicon such as *custom, sympathy, despotism,* and *arithmetic reason*. I consider the relation between his writings and anticolonial thought and delineate how to read his writings on British colonialism in India and the French Revolution as related and even deeply intertwined concerns, rather than as merely chronologically contemporary ones. Burke's underlying disquiet had to do with the question of societies undergoing a complete transformation and whether this was an upheaval to be desired or dreaded. I argue that in both the Indian and the French case (which is more widely known), Burke's response was one of fear. Part of this fear was based on the emergence of a rapid class mobility, uninhibited and unfettered by the regulating social customs of Europe, a mobility enabled by the space of the colonies. These India-returned Britons would easily mingle with the gentry of England, exhibiting what Burke elsewhere referred to as the capacity for burghers in a society to be "miscible." Significantly, one of the striking qualities that ties together Burke's reading of France and India is that he views each as having suffered from a conquest. What this means in the French case is that he views the Jacobins as treating France as a country of conquest virtually indistinguishable from a colonial occupation. The parallel implied between India and France leads me to explore the possible parallels between the French and the American revolutions in Burke's thought and to consider why it was that many in Britain and France expected Burke to be in favor of the French Revolution. Conceptually, this chapter explores a surprising link in Burke's thought between his critique of French Enlightenment thought, expressed in such terms as *arithmetic reason* (used disparagingly by Burke), and his image of the colony. Modernity, embodied for Burke in certain aspects of the French Revolution, involves a degree of estrangement, which I relate to his argument against defining the notion of the citizen in the abstract. Through this one can understand why he argued against an emerging colonial modernity in India that he saw being created by the East India Company and the estranged, placeless modernity he argued the Jacobin order was establishing in France.

Chapter 4 develops the relation between Burke's concerns in France and India but turns in another direction: I suggest the manifold ways we can see how Burke's writings on the East India Company anticipate and give shape to the type of critique he will make against the Jacobins and the events of the French Revolution. I begin by examining several components of the *Reflections* that reveal an imbrication with Burke's writings on India and discuss the circumstances of its composition; it was written in the midst of the impeachment trial against Warren Hastings in 1790. Theoretically, I also suggest that, should this argument be true, we must learn from it to avoid viewing revolutions as occurring first in Europe and then—in yet another methodological expression of a "colonial lag time"—appearing later in the colonies. Rather what Burke's writings express, in such striking phrases as "Jacobinism and Indianism are the two great evils of our time," are the coeval transformations taking place in Europe and such spaces as colonial India. I therefore organize my argument around a reading of the *Reflections* and recuperate the global vision that Burke's notion of Jacobinism implied in tandem with his later concept of Indianism (his own neologism). Jacobinism, for Burke, is preeminently linked with a particular definition of the idea of prejudice. It was this that the Jacobins wished to erase, to make anew, treating the human persona and character, with all its messy inheritances through custom and mores, as a tabula rasa. I discuss the manner in which Burke argued for a link between the violence of the gesture of wiping this slate clean (to stay with the image of the tabula rasa) and the necessary political violence which he felt would follow. If this was his understanding of Jacobinism, then we may adjoin to that the operation of the other nefarious force (from his perspective) that was waxing in the colonies and would come to threaten Britain itself, namely Indianism. The latter involved the despising of the rule of law, and its effect was to delegitimize the use of force by the state, which in turn could jeopardize the very undertaking of the imperial project. The "rich delinquents of India," as he once contemptuously referred to the British Nabobs—the very Nabobs who would return to London to profess their love of *vertu*, as Samuel Foote would have it—were an example of the "breakers of law in India" coming home to become the "makers of law" for England. I suggest that, from this evident circularity, we can see that the emergence of a colonial modernity is not simply a peripheral element helpful in understanding the beginnings of modernity in Europe (marked by many through the event of the French Revolution) but is also constitutive of the very language used to describe and name that modernity.

Chapter 5 extends Burke's notions of Jacobinism and Indianism to other domains by exploring the link between Britain's loss of the Americas and a rising interest in Asian conquests. I have two Atlantic revolutions in mind: the Haitian and the American. The first part of the chapter attempts to locate the significance of the Haitian Revolution within Burke's thought through a consideration of St. Domingue (Haiti after its revolution) in his letters and speeches to Parliament. My intention is also a comparative one: to explore a possible limit in Burke's sympathy for the colonized, which seems so expansive in his Indian writings, by looking at the more complicated case of St. Domingue, a neglected participant in the great revolutions of the late eighteenth century. The second part of the chapter returns to some of Burke's earlier writings from the late 1770s and early 1780s to illustrate how the shifting imperial focus from the Americas to Asia is articulated at times as a "compensation in the East." It is prompted by his own truly striking formulation, when reflecting on the extent of the British Empire at this period, which disavows an attempt to bring the "natives of Hindostan and those of Virginia" under one purview.

In the first part of the chapter I argue that the horror Burke expresses in response to the violence he reads about coming from St. Domingue confirms his view of French Jacobinism and his explicitly stated fear of the "rights of man" being exported to the colonies. St. Domingue, further, becomes a figure for a racial violence but also reveals something about what is discursively possible when Burke speaks on behalf of the oppressed in India; in that latter space, it is the discursive (not literal) absence of an insurgent native group that allows for his speech. I then turn to his "Letters on a Regicide Peace" and explore his discussion of the West Indies within it, particularly his fear of the Jacobins establishing what he provocatively calls a "transatlantic Morocco," a space of brigandage and piracy, to undermine British power in the region. Burke goes so far as to impugn the possibility of a "man of colour" in some future colonial assembly, and I juxtapose his words with one such example, General Belley, who speaks to the National Assembly in France against the institution of slavery. By counterpoising Burke's words alongside those of Belley (and also, briefly, Danton), I mean to bring out more sharply the availability of other possibilities in the period that Burke unwisely foreclosed. The second part of the chapter contrasts Burke's response to insubordination in America with that by East India Company officers in Madras. The episode is part of his "Speech on Restoring Lord Pigot" (1777), which is punctuated with comparative references to India and America. What becomes gradually visible is the idea that the irrecoverable loss in the West, most immediately the North American colonies, is to be compensated for in the East—but by means of the cultivation of certain qualities absent in the management of the former. In turning to the speeches that reveal this, my intention is to illustrate the intimate relation of the loss of the American colonies and of events in the West Indies with the policies formulated for India. The conceptual difficulties that begin to arise for Burke have to do with the difference between seeing America as a place of settlement and seeing British outposts in India as managed by a small number of European residents. This, in turn, affects his notion of what constitutes "rebellion" in each space. I conclude the chapter by proposing that one understand Burke's intellectual movement across different geographical spaces as a kind of concatenation—a political concatenation or linking of analogical events which serves to bring together productively an ensemble of locations (India, France, Ireland, North America, Haiti) that later nineteenth-century considerations will prize apart.

The contradictory elements of Diderot's and Burke's arguments against empire serve as an illustration of European anticolonialism at its limit, upon which I speculate in the epilogue. I draw on the thought of C. L. R. James and Theodor Adorno to work through some legacies of Enlightenment in the mid-twentieth century. So proximate in some manner (as readers of Hegel) and yet so different intellectually (in their education, certainly, and also on the question of populism, for example), they provide a more contemporary divergence on the possibilities of critique. I discuss the context of Adorno's often-cited quip in *Minima Moralia* that one must "hate tradition properly" and explore his misrecognition of the historical significance of intellectual formations associated with third-worldism and the politics of decolonization in the 1940s and 1950s. In the case of James, I consider what the figure of Toussaint Louverture tells us about his view of Enlightenment critique. Toussaint does not represent pure oppositionality but rather is able to understand the radical implications of Enlightenment thought from within, and he thereby serves as a model for the type of engagement with a (radical) tradition for which James hoped.

PART I

Denis Diderot: The Two Indies of the French Enlightenment

1 / *Doux Commerce, Douce Colonisation:* Consensual Colonialism in Diderot's Thought

> *Let us stop here and place ourselves back in the time when America and India were unknown. I address myself to the most cruel of Europeans, and I say to them: there exist many regions which will furnish you with rich metals, with appealing clothing, with delicious dishes. But read this history and see at what price this discovery is promised to you. Do you, or do you not want it to take place? Does one believe that there could be a creature so infernal as to say: I WANT THIS. Well! There will be no single moment in the future where my question would have the same force.*
> —DENIS DIDEROT, "REFLECTIONS ON THE GOOD AND EVIL WHICH THE DISCOVERY OF THE NEW WORLD HAS DONE TO EUROPE" (1780)

> *What do these forts you have garrisoned all the beaches with attest to? Your terror and the profound hatred of those who surround you. You will no longer be fearful, when you are no longer hated. You will no longer be hated, when you are beneficent. The barbarian, just like the civilized man, wants to be happy.*
> —DENIS DIDEROT, "PRINCIPLES WHICH THE FRENCH SHOULD FOLLOW IN INDIA, IF THEY SUCCEED THERE IN REESTABLISHING THEIR ESTEEM AND PRESENCE" (1780)

First the traveler, then the *philosophe*: this couplet is as important to the story of eighteenth-century intellectual history as is the revolutionary and the philosopher or the soldier and the statesman.[1] As a variation on this I would also add the administrator and the philosophe as another vital pair of complementarities and antagonisms. This chapter considers two texts by Diderot with a view to investigating the significance of some of these doubles. The first text is rather well known, although it has of late sparked or been reilluminated by scholarship with a greater degree of historical specificity.[2] I refer to *Supplément au voyage de Bougainville*, which is set in the South Pacific (though it is a South Pacific of the mind as much as of the seas, and this will be part of my consideration). What one finds when looking at the writings of the philosophes is in part a lucid demonstration of the now widely recognized but still debated thesis of *Orientalism*: the traveler and the administrator undertake to gather and collect information, and this in turn plays a vital role in informing the technologies of management and government.³ But this goes straight to the apparently menacing outcome of an initially rather innocent or pure act: I mean the desire, as Diderot remarked in the *Encyclopédie*, to note down and to "collect all the knowledge that now lies scattered over the face of the Earth."⁴ It is here that we may locate many of the secondary reflections, as one could call them, on the initial reports from the field: the famous considerations of natural man by Rousseau in his *Discourse on Inequality*; the various footnotes throughout the work of Kant, even in his aesthetic works, to the Caribs, Africans, and others; and Diderot's peculiar and parodic remarks on Tahiti in the *Supplément*.⁵ But all along there are interruptions in this smooth continuum that connects the traveler or administrator to the philosophe, disrupting the apparent imperatives for empire, land acquisition, or trade.

One of the primary flaws of the debate around orientalism, at least within the discipline of literary studies, may have been to lay too much emphasis solely on the question of representation. It is fair to say that for Said, orientalism was not merely about the question of representation; it was also a discursive field (an effect of power, a productive effect, etc.). "Indeed, my real argument is that Orientalism *is*—and does not simply *represent*—a considerable dimension of modern political-intellectual culture, and as such has less to do with the Orient than it does with 'our' world."⁶ Nonetheless, constrained by the terms of this debate, I too will begin by commenting upon the question of representation in Diderot's work. I hope, however, to attach these observations to a set of keywords in the political lexicon of the period that circulate among the writers of these works. I must first reiterate one link between the question of representation, in this case of the native or of native society, and political analysis which pertains, more specifically, to the concept of hegemony.⁷ In order to operate, hegemony requires constant repetition and reiteration; in one formulation it depends upon coercion and consent (and it is the presence and importance of consent that make it amenable to some forms of liberal political thought). I introduce this idea primarily to illustrate what one finds throughout Diderot's later political writings: unwilling to accept the necessity of coercion as an element of colonization, he both attempts to imagine in many different formulations how this project could be undertaken by means of consent, participating in a set of representations that legitimize dominance of one kind, and frequently fractures this image. In the *Supplément* this is evident by his undermining of the truth claims of Antoine de Bougainville's original text and in his use of an imagined Tahitian Other to flay the priest and cleric in France.⁸

Composed around 1772 (soon after the original publication of Bougainville's work in 1771), Diderot's *Supplément au voyage de Bougainville* was short and relatively coherent, not widely available in his lifetime, and circulated as an underground manuscript (perhaps because of its sexually scandalous nature).[9] By contrast, the second text under consideration is much more scattered, was anonymous in its initial editions, and only in the mid-twentieth century was Diderot's authorship conclusively verified. I refer to his contributions to the immense and fascinating work known as the *Histoire philosophique et politique des établissements et du commerce des Européens dans les deux Indes*.[10] The ten-volume work was edited by the abbé de Raynal and went through three editions (1770, 1774, and 1780). This much one can learn from reading the brief selection of material present in a modern English edition of Diderot's *Political Writings* (1992).[11] But there are several other aspects of this massive work that are hardly visible from the excerpts presented there. Diderot's involvement in the three editions increased with each publication, and he was said to have thoroughly rewritten the third edition by spending as much as fourteen hours a day at the task.[12] By many estimations, his contributions amount to approximately a third of the 1780 edition.[13] It is clear that Diderot had some doubts whether his contributions, even if eloquent, would be of any worth. Raynal's reply in a letter was admirably frank about the respective talents of each author: "Non, non . . . faites toujours ce que je vous demande. . . . Je connais un peu plus que vous le goût du public; ce sont vos lignes qui sauveront l'ennui de mes calculs éternels."[14] Although Raynal may have felt he could serve up a work to suit public taste, this does not lessen Diderot's own commitment to the work, as illustrated by a dispute he had with Friedrich Melchior Grimm. Grimm had criticized Raynal for the third edition of the *Histoire* (1780), and this enraged Diderot. Arthur Wilson, Diderot's biographer, cites a letter discovered in the twentieth century (probably unsent), in which Diderot rails against Grimm for becoming an "antiphilosophe" of the most dangerous variety. Grimm, Wilson argues, became more and more conservative, while Diderot increasingly lost faith in the possibility of political reform and became by contrast more revolutionary.[15] In May 1781 the Parlement of Paris condemned the *Histoire* to be burned and the author to be imprisoned, while the abbé Raynal was prudently away.[16]

The subtitle to part 1 of my study emphasizes the notion of the "two Indies," extending a thought implied by the structure of Raynal's work, which moves at times from Occident to Orient, from North to South. Indeed the two are not identical images of each other, not exactly twin Indies, not *les Indes jumelles*.[17] Yet the affinity suggested in such a work between *les Indes occidentales* and *les Indes orientales*, in conjunction with a shift between *l'Amérique septentrionale* and *l'Amérique méridionale*, brings out a quality that is quite striking to the contemporary reader: the link between the old colonies and the newer ones in this colonial encyclopedia, or—to put the matter in other terms—the relation established between the New World and the Old. One sees the same distinction at work in Burke's writings on India, which are fundamentally shaped by events in the New World; by this I mean events both in North America and in the West Indies. In the writings of both Diderot and Burke there is ample evidence to sustain Anthony Pagden's helpful distinction in this period between the "new" and the "old" colonies.[18] The old or first colonies refer to those in North and South America, while the new or second colonies refer to the growing importance of Asia to European colonialism in the eighteenth century. We see this axis of comparison everywhere in the *Histoire des deux Indes* (beginning with the organization of the contents of the ten volumes), in travelogues from the period, in administrators' memoirs, and in the movement of such military figures as Charles Cornwallis, leaving Yorktown in Virginia for Bengal. (Indeed this conjuncture of Virginia and "Hindostan" will recur in Burke's thought.) In addition to this axis of comparison is a second between North and South America within the New World; one could attempt to enumerate the typologies of this discourse in order to understand their various functions.[19]

This second opposition between North and South America will become increasingly important as comparative reflections of the fate of societies and man in the various regions of the New World proceed in the nineteenth century. It is this comparison that is at work in some of Tocqueville's reflections in *Democracy in America* when he wonders why "no nations upon the face of the earth are more miserable than those of South America" in spite of its enjoying an isolation from enemies and a geographical richness akin to North America.[20] Often this distinction between North and South America becomes a shorthand for several other oppositions having less to do with geography than with religion. One could mention here Voltaire's positive evaluation of the behavior of the Quakers in North America for winning over and persuading the Indians by commerce, in contrast to the methods commonly used, in his view, by the Jesuits in South America.[21]

There will be two foci to my examination. The first concerns Diderot's exploration of the possibility of a colonialism that is consensual; I refer to this as *douce colonisation* or "soft colonization." (The phrase is my own, coined on analogy with *doux commerce*.)[22] The second theme is related to this by the transposition of reciprocal consent to the intimate sphere, where it thereby pertains to *métissage*, or breeding. The two elements are also both related to issues of population and settlement. The discussion of procreation, and of population as a form of wealth in the *Supplément*, derive from the larger consideration of the settlement of colonies (part of *douce colonisation*). The *Supplément* supplies the occasion to introduce these topics, while the *Histoire* allows for their elaboration and contextualization.

Doux Commerce and Breeding

As a word on its own, breeding has many divergent valences, to which the title of this section refers (from manners to animal husbandry to biology).[23] One comes upon the notion frequently when examining the *Histoire des deux Indes*, which is caught in the whirl of discussions around the possibilities of commerce in the period. Yet tied in with this economic debate is an essential relationship to sexuality, and this occurs via a notion of wealth as it is yoked to the emerging idea of *population* in the period. To summarize: an empty continent, or empty island, to use the example given by the Tahitian native in Diderot's *Supplément*, obviously needs someone to labor upon it. (So it was argued, following a logic stated in its clearest form in Locke's *Second Treatise of Government*—the "agricultural argument," as it is sometimes named.)[24] Wealth, both in the *Histoire* and in the *Supplément*, is often explicitly understood as population—an idea not surprising to scholars of the French eighteenth century, where one finds many writers concerned with the depopulation of one continent (North America) in a manner linked with the depopulation of another (Africa). On the one hand was the accidental ethnocide of disease alongside the intentional effects of conquest (as popularly reported, whether accurately or not, by de Las Casas in the sixteenth century); on the other hand was the concomitant forced migration of Africans as slave labor.[25] Two continents' native populations, it was argued, were thereby jeopardized.[26]

There are two or three different ways in which breeding operates in Diderot's work, which may hold more generally in related late eighteenth-century French Enlightenment thought (keeping in mind that this forms a part of the plural Enlightenments discussed in the prologue—a more apt way of understanding this period). The questions I would like to consider are, schematically, the following: What role does breeding play in Diderot's understanding of consensual colonialism? How does Diderot understand the figure of the Creole? What is the relation of wealth to population, and of these two terms to breeding? Finally, how does Diderot understand the idea of "directed breeding" or "rational breeding"? In addressing these questions it is also important to speculate on how the larger issues of political economy and population are tied into Diderot's thoughts on the intimate relations that are possible between colonizer and colonized.

The Supplement to the Voyage of Bougainville

With other eighteenth-century writers and thinkers, it is often easy to push aside questions of sexuality. Though Burke's language and rhetorical presuppositions are everywhere dependent on sexual difference, particularly in his *Philosophical Enquiry into the Origin of Our Ideas of the Sublime and Beautiful*, but even in *Reflections on the Revolution in France* (as Wollstonecraft was quick to point out in her rather prompt reply, *Vindications of the Rights of Men*), it is rare that one finds more explicit political pronouncements on these matters in his work. This, however, is impossible to avoid when one turns to Diderot, who everywhere bears some oblique and at times more direct relationship to the theme of libertinage in the French Enlightenment. It should not be surprising that someone whose first novel, *Les bijoux indiscrets*, concerned physical bodies, sexuality, and the exotic in a humorous and bizarre mixture should return to the question later in his writerly life. (Perhaps it was for this reason that Foucault declared in *History of Sexuality*, "The aim of this series of studies? To transcribe into history the fable of *Les bijoux indiscrets*.")[27]

Indeed what is striking about the *Supplément* is the centrality of sexuality and gender. Any reading that focuses only on the exotic and the anthropological elements without considering in some cursory way their relation to these aspects will miss what is both most distinctive and most peculiar about the work. The *Supplément* is sometimes read as proto-feminist, or at the least as a hymn to the more free sexual ways of Tahitian society in relation to Europe.[28] Other critics have considered it an expression of Diderot's "anarchic" strain of thought.[29] We should, however, be wary of calling it either feminist or anarchic, while recognizing that the text raises important issues pertaining to colonialism and gender.

The sexual liberation that Diderot presents is part of a male fantasy structure, which in addition relies upon an underlying heterosexual matrix.[30] (Another illustration of this matrix, grounded in nature, in

Diderot's text: a Tahitian male instinctively detects the cross-dressed female disguised as a male crew member. The natives' natural heterosexuality does not rely on "surface appearances" which have successfully deceived the European crew members during the length of the journey.)[31] Men are still the sexual keepers of women; what is described is a social structure in which women are passed to men for breeding. What might be seen as liberation is actually the use of female labor and procreation for the "wealth" of society, and we can thereby tie together several terms in this work. The emphasis in the text on the circulation of human bodies as commodities should be linked to the language of French political economy in the period.[32] The focus on bodies may be a contrast with prevailing Physiocratic views of land as a source of wealth, though Diderot's relationship to that school was changing over the course of his life.[33] Is Diderot proposing that labor power in the form of human bodies capable of work are in fact a truer source of labor? If so, this is why such a view should be connected with the colonial fantasy of open land (i.e., land to be labored upon), which is central to the text. One instance of this is when Orou rhetorically asks the chaplain why people place such an emphasis on population. He answers himself: "If you wish to judge its value [the value of the French male visitors' mating with Tahitian women], imagine that you had still two hundred leagues of coastline to navigate, and that every twenty miles the same tribute [of mating] was collected from you. We've vast tracts of untilled soil; we lack hands and asked you for them."[34] The open coastline and vast tracts that must be settled demand a populace to exert labor upon them; that these hands are "asked" of the European visitors is also significant.[35] Thus in a preliminary way we can argue that there is some link between population, sexuality, and colonial fantasy, and all of these fit into Diderot's theory of political economy.[36]

One should take note of the form of the text, namely the role of parody and comedy in undercutting what otherwise would be a too serious effort at the gathering of knowledge. Here we can recall the full title of the work: *Supplement to the Voyage of Bougainville, or Dialogue between A and B on the Inappropriateness of Attaching Moral Ideas to Certain Physical Actions That Do Not Accord with Them*. The prying apart of the moral idea from the physical action—primarily the negative pall cast upon human sexual activity by Christianity—is the aim of Diderot's critique. He also contrasts the empirical effort of the scientific ethnography and his parody of it in the form of a pseudo-ethnography. However, if it is overstating the case to call the original an ethnography, it would be more accurate to say that the object of his parody is Bougainville's traveler's tale, with its claim to a truth beyond fiction (though often the genre of the traveler's tale made use of novelistic techniques).

I would also call attention to the genre of the work, the philosophical dialogue, familiar since Plato's establishment of the form. Thematically too the *Supplément* echoes the *Republic*'s discussion regarding the design of the *kallipolis*. There Plato argued for the common ownership of women and children, the elimination of notions of "mine and thine"; in Diderot's *Supplément*, these efforts are apparently realized.[37] Tahiti as an actual historical referent is bracketed, as it were, by Diderot's clever and humorous use of the traveler's account. The dialogue contains within itself the critique of its claims to veracity, as when Diderot cuts from the conversation between Orou and the Chaplain back to A and B. After the chaplain discusses his lapses of restraint with several of the Tahitian women, A and B comment to each other:

- A: I warm to this polite chaplain.
- B: And I much more to the manners of the Tahitians and remarks of Orou.
- A: Though they show a rather European influence.
- B: I don't doubt it.[38]

This appears to be a humorous sign of the self-awareness of the work, a wink to the reader that Diderot knows he is making fast and loose with Tahiti as a place and Orou as its spokesperson. This is also why there is a great emphasis on the many levels of mediation in the text: Orou is said to translate the old man's speech from his vernacular to Spanish, which he knows, and this is transcribed into French.[39] Thus there are two filters between the text we read and the original speech. The original recedes and at times is fully inaccessible, as when one speaker says to another, "The chaplain remarks in a third fragment which I've not read to you that the Tahitian doesn't blush."[40] What B has not read to A, but apparently has in his possession, is the *absent* original text.

Nature, the term really under investigation, is what Diderot self-consciously makes the center of his philosophical dialogue. For him, the layers of civilization that have accreted in civilized societies over natural man may fall away when he reaches the colonies. The savage and the monk, the natural man and the artificial, Tahiti and Europe—all these are used to lead to the idea of relativism. Or so it seems. It may be that the question—as to which of these oppositions may be better—is itself being thematized in order to interrogate the basis for such a cultural critique. In contrast to later writers on exotic locales, although Diderot emphasizes the heightened physicality of the Tahitians, he does not seem to argue that this comes at the expense of rationality. The dialogue opens with the Tahitian seeming to be fully other-directed, altruistic, sexually free and uninhibited, to be working basically within a gift economy.[41] But then there is a moment in the dialogue where Orou says, "However savage we are, we know just how to scheme." This follows his explanation for their apparent generosity: "While more robust and healthy than you, we saw at once that you surpassed us in intelligence, and we immediately marked out for you some of our most beautiful women and girls to receive the seed of a race superior to ours. We tried an *experiment* which may still bring us success."[42] This passage depicts a kind of self-improving native who works by directed breeding. Though eugenic in its etymological sense (seeking to produce "fine offspring"), it is a self-willed or collectively undertaken decision and not imposed externally from above; the role of the state is certainly much more central to the twentieth century's understanding of the term. This is Diderot's fantasy of a controlled experiment in interbreeding, in a directed *métissage*, a theme that will recur in the *Histoire des deux Indes*. The idea of a calculating native may be part of a standard stereotype, inasmuch as with the oriental or savage there was always the possibility of an inversion: the passive oriental suddenly is represented as wily and conniving, the lazy savage as menacing. Nevertheless, in these passages from Diderot, the native, while healthy and vigorous, is also represented as fully rational. Orou is rather the very picture of a philosophe himself.[43]

With regard to the masculine domination of Tahitian society as portrayed by Diderot, the idea of women as the property of men is addressed directly in the dialogue by A and B: it is in consequence, they remark, of the early introduction of the idea of property that many ill effects follow. The end of the dialogue, where Diderot initiates a characteristic "call to arms," is a key passage in part because it illustrates a style of expression that appears often in the *Histoire des deux Indes*. Diderot presents a lengthy list of the wrongs of European society in the mouth of B: "Orou explained it ten times over to the chaplain.... It's the tyranny of man which converted the possession of woman into property."[44] This critique of woman as property allows Diderot to declaim against the unnecessary practices of modesty and constancy; his genealogy shows these to have been formed as virtues and vices only as a consequence of this flawed beginning. All of this is due, once again, to the falling away from nature: "How brief would be the codes of nations, if only they conformed rigorously to that of nature."[45]

As noted earlier, Diderot, perhaps unsurprisingly, does not question the heterosexual relation between man and woman. This obvious remark yields more insight when we relate it to the political economy that he envisions, wherein sexual activity must be productive, like any other labor. In order to be a man, it is implied, one must procreate. Thus the chaplain, in Orou's eyes, is emasculated because he refuses to mate. When he does succumb, Orou tells him, "My first thought was that Nature . . . had deprived you of the ability to reproduce your kind. . . . But, monk, my daughter told me that you are indeed a man, and robust as any Tahitian."[46] Confirmation of his heterosexual masculinity is provided by his "ability to reproduce."

L'Histoire des deux Indes

In shifting from the *Supplément* to the *Histoire des deux Indes*, we move from a literary *conte* to a work that does not operate by these conventions but itself makes some of the same claims to truth as the text that Diderot parodied and drew upon, Bougainville's original *Voyage autour du Monde*. Nonetheless many of the themes and questions that animate the *Supplément* appear in this work; questions merely latent in that work regarding the relation of the economy to sexuality and population are explicitly discussed in the *Histoire*. One of these is the question of interbreeding with an indigenous population. We therefore find in the *Histoire* several examples that attempt to conceive of an alternative to the outcome of depopulation (of the New World by the activities of the Spanish, and of Africa by the slave trade) and yet that carry on the imperative to colonize. Suggesting that European colonizers arrive and intermarry with local populations thus seemed a more "humane" way to civilize and settle a territory. In the *Supplément*, as we have seen, the solution imagined is one in which this activity would be undertaken with the *consent* of the colonized. The Tahitians realize the superiority of their visitors in certain domains and hope to benefit from this, as we learn in the surprise revelation of their crafty calculations, turning the economy of the gift into the self-interest of the exchange. (Indeed in the character of Orou can be seen many of the "naturalist" attitudes toward sex defined by the physician Charles Vandermonde in *Essai sur la manière de perfectionner l'espèce humaine*, published in 1756.)[47]

The motif of population within Diderot's thought is rather widespread and brings together many disparate areas of his thinking. Although I focus on its relation to his views on the ideal form colonialism could take, we see it even in relation to his views on the Church. On reforms that should be undertaken to ensure the Church's subservience to the state, Diderot writes in the *Histoire*, "The vow of chastity is repugnant to nature and diminishes the population; the vow of poverty is only that of an inept or lazy person. The vow of obedience to some other power than to the dominant one and to the law is that of a slave or an outlaw."[48] He decries the vows the clergy must undertake; his argument against the vow of chastity is based on the naturalist idea of sexuality already discussed and its effect on diminishing the population. The core of his views on the matter of population are, however, most clearly expressed in a passage added to the 1780 edition within a discussion of national character (*esprit national*). Diderot presents a theory of national character as deriving from both variable and constant causes, and further distinguishes the national character from the code of behavior that determines the actions of individuals, who generally will not hesitate to build their "own prosperity through public ruin." On the one hand, he correlates national character with the nation's capital city in particular; on the other hand, he takes as his figure of the quintessential individualist the person who has traveled farthest from this metropolitan capital. This is the colonist, who loses any trace of national character when he passes "beyond the equator." Instead he is capable of "whatever crime will lead him most quickly to his goal." Diderot concludes, "This is how all the Europeans, every one of them, indistinctly, have appeared in the new world."[49] The opposite, therefore, of the *esprit national* is manifested on an almost mathematical inverse ratio of distance from the capital; in fact it is this theory that enables Diderot, unlike most other thinkers of this period, to account for the contradiction of the fine phrases regarding liberty at home and the despotic practices undertaken abroad.

But what solution to this contradiction does Diderot propose? We are brought back to the recurring fantasy: "Would it not have been more useful and humane, and less costly, to have taken to these distant regions a few hundred young men and women? The men would have married the women of the country, and the women the native men. Ties of blood, the strongest and most immediate of bonds, would soon have formed a single family out of the natives and the foreigners."[50] The argument operates by an appeal to self-interest alongside a claim to greater moral good (e.g., "more useful *and* humane, and less costly"), which is characteristic of the political language of the period (compare Burke's notion of "graft[ing] benevolence even upon avarice").[51] Here this idea is joined to Diderot's idea of rational breeding, undertaken by the colonizer with the colonized. But rather than posing the opposition of the parties to this encounter in dichotomous terms, "the foreigners and natives of the country," Diderot imagines that "a single and uniform family" will be produced by consanguinity.[52] The consequence of this encounter is described in terms demonstrated by the narrative of the *Supplément*. The intimate relationship (*liaison intime*) would lead the primitive inhabitant (*l'habitant sauvage*) to realize that the arts and knowledge that are brought to him (*qu'on lui portait*; the original brings out the form of address more strongly) are superior and would lift him from his state. The manner used by these soft colonizers, or imploring and moderate teachers (*instituteurs suppliants et modérés*), would lead the natives to submit themselves to them "sans réserve." This absence of reserve can serve as an index of the degree of dominance *with* hegemony that Diderot imagines is possible.

What is the outcome of this *douce colonisation*? Out of the "heureuse confiance" peace would emerge, impossible with the "ton impérieux" normally employed by masters and conquerors. That this event would be fully compatible with the mercantile aims of empire Diderot had no doubts: "Commerce establishes itself without trouble between men who have reciprocal needs, and soon they become accustomed to seeing as friends and as brothers those whom interest or another motive leads to their country."[53] (Note the importance of introducing the language of kinship in order to legitimate such an order.) Though the different editions of the *Histoire* express conflicting degrees of optimism on the role of commerce in the development of *les mœurs*, overall it is striking how pervasive this sentiment is. To adduce but one example, consider this moment, which combines a classic panoptical view (perhaps that of one rising up in a hot-air balloon, an icon to become so popular in the visual culture of the French Revolution), with an expression of the civilizing process:

> In dealing with subjects that are important for human happiness, your first concern and duty must be to rid your soul of all hope and fear. There, lifted up above all human considerations, you float above the atmosphere and look at the earth beneath you. . . . There, finally, as I see at my feet these beautiful lands where the arts and sciences are flourishing, and which lay for so long under the darkness of barbarism, I have wondered: who is it who dug these canals, drained these plains, founded these towns, brought together, clothed and civilized these people? And the voices of all enlightened men among them have answered: "It is commerce; it is commerce."[54]

It may seem unusual in hindsight to see commerce as unambivalently furthering the progress of *lumières*, especially after the nineteenth century, the Industrial Revolution, and Marx's language used to describe the extraction and drain that characterize (in some analyses) the colony-metropole relationship.⁵⁵ However, it is a familiar echo of Montesquieu's language of *doux commerce* and the Scottish Enlightenment's discussion of commercial society as a culmination of the four-stage theory. Moreover it should be understood within the context of the burdensome structure of French absolutism in the 1770s; in relation to this, commerce is equated with a kind of liberty.⁵⁶ It also may owe something to Diderot's response following a visit to Holland in 1773, when he initially expressed the widespread admiration held by many philosophes in the period for the small merchants of that country—an enthusiasm tempered in his later reflections.⁵⁷

Let us return to the passage cited earlier to examine a second consequence which Diderot imagines follows from *douce colonisation*, one that is perhaps surprising given the tenor of his other writings on the subject of religion: "The Indians would adopt the religion of Europe, for the reason that one religion becomes common to all the citizens of an empire when the government abandons it to them, and when intolerance and the madness of preachers does not become an instrument for discord."⁵⁸ This view does not seem as relativistic as that presented in the *Supplément*, since both the civilization and the religion of Europe are assumed to be self-evidently superior but *tainted by their mingling with force*. Civilization, as he says in the next line, will be adopted by inclination so long as one does not demand it be adopted "par la force." Though this passage does not by any means present us with a consistently anticolonial position, I would nonetheless argue against the view taken by many scholars of Diderot's political evolution that this greater pessimism about the claims of alterity represents his abandonment of "primitivism" for a more "realist" view. In trying to relate these fascinating writings from Diderot to contemporary scholarly discussions on colonialism, we should at least take note of his awareness that modernity arrives with colonialism and is thereby tainted in a manner that is quite different from the experience within Europe. *Douce colonisation*, or the fantasy of a noncoercive colonial encounter, is a response to this awareness. Laurent Versini, the editor of an important recent edition of Diderot's works, neglects the elements of a genuinely radical critique that appear throughout Diderot's corpus of writings.⁵⁹ Versini argues that in the later editions of the *Histoire des deux Indes* Diderot became more and more convinced by Hobbes over Rousseau, and he cites several lines from the *Réfutation d'Helvétius* in support of this, concluding, "Diderot est profondément, résolument et religieusement l'homme de la sociabilité et du progrès."⁶⁰ This seems too strongly to negate the ferocity and irony of the early Diderot regarding clerics, the destruction of primitives as a result of their encounter with Europeans, and so on. Moreover it overlooks the fact that Diderot, perhaps unlike Rousseau, already mocked the idea of a wholly innocent natural man, which many readers accuse Rousseau (rightly or wrongly) of vaunting.[61] Diderot was never fully persuaded by this illusion and revealed this awareness in other discursive forms, such as the *Supplément*. In this sense it is crucial that he turned to these other mixed genres. In a strictly philosophical or political treatise, he might not have been as flippant, humorous, or incautious. Literature, however, is that medium which allows "one to say everything, in every way." "The space of literature," writes Jacques Derrida, "is not only that of an instituted fiction, but also a fictive institution which in principle allows one to say everything."[62] It is precisely this fictive and free quality of the literary that frequently leads it, as in the case of Diderot, to defy the law of the encyclopedic impulse, of the information-retrieval function of colonial knowledge as a verifiable archive. In literature, that form of writing in which anything can be said, Diderot is willing to take a thought to its extreme, even when it negates his initial impulse. (This is one example of thinking at a conceptual limit.)

It is for this reason—the internal contradictions—that Michèle Duchet, influenced by French structuralism of the 1960s and 1970s, introduced the term *écriture fragmentaire* to describe the *Histoire des deux Indes*. Further, and more to the point for my argument here, she notes that it is precisely these inconsistencies of the work that should interest us as much as the statement of a consistent political position. By dismissing the philosophes' evident curiosity about the primitive and their concern for various colonies, others have argued that "by the final edition the colonies had become something of a pretext; any Frenchman reading the *Histoire* in the tense political atmosphere of the 1780s could not fail to realize that he was being called upon to recognize the fact that a radical turning point had been reached in the destinies of France and Europe, and that this active participation was required to usher in a new order."[63] This argument unnecessarily reduces the implications of the *Histoire* by reading it in an exclusively European context. To assert that all ten volumes are merely coded ciphers for a critique actually directed against French absolutism is unpersuasive. This would presume precisely what should be examined, namely a political perspective that makes a claim to liberty in the European context but does not see it as necessary that this critique should be extended or applied in a more genuinely universal manner—that is, in Europe's colonies as well. It may have been exactly this excessive focus on internal European debates that contributed to a lack of interest in the *Histoire des deux Indes*. For example, I disagree with the judgment that Diderot, when asked by Raynal in 1765 to contribute to the *Histoire*, "at first ... seems to have taken no great interest in it and his contributions to the first edition ... are generally unremarkable; they are mostly concerned with the bad effects of colonization and religion, the injustice of slavery and reflections about *sauvages*."[64] By contrast, what is after all striking about such a work as the *Histoire* (with its numerous contributors) is that so many figures in the 1780s and 1790s were beginning to conceive of *the globe*, of the movements of commodities and populaces in this larger frame of analysis, and with their movement the concomitant movement of ideas and cultural practices. And this reflection was undertaken not in a peripheral work of the period, but in fact, as Robert Darnton notes, in one of the period's veritable best sellers.[65]

Certainly the implications of such an *écriture fragmentaire* are everywhere apparent, even, or rather particularly, in the modern edited collections and translations of the *Histoire* that have been made. There is, for example, a final paragraph in the section I have been discussing that is left out of the English selection of Diderot's *Political Writings*.[66] After the claim that the Indians would accept the religion and ways of the Europeans provided they were not tainted by force, Diderot writes, "Such would be the happy effects which *the most imperious attraction of the senses* would produce in a colony which is being born. Absolutely no armaments, no soldiers, but plenty of young women for the men, and plenty of young men for the women."[67] In an incipient colony the imperious tone (*le ton impérieux*) of the masters (Diderot's phrase in the earlier passage) is here turned into the most imperious attraction: an overwhelming reciprocal sensual attraction: arms and soldiers replaced by an abundance of young women for men, and vice versa. Note that Diderot here does not imagine a shipload of male conquerors arriving on this primal scene who would mate with native women (closer to what occasionally did happen), but rather both European men and women pairing off with native men and women. It is as if he wishes to mitigate the force associated with conquest by replacing the antagonism between colonizer and colonized with physical, sexual attraction between male and female on both sides. By recourse to this libidinal economy he is able to elaborate a more consensual model of colonization. Thus even his "principles of colonization," as the English title for this excerpt would have it, are tied to his idea of rational breeding.

38 / DENIS DIDEROT

On Colonial Imitation

Why Diderot felt compelled to answer this question concerning the legitimate basis for colonization is clear to anyone who has read Raynal's general introduction to the ten-volume edition. Raynal writes, "Europe has everywhere founded colonies; but does it know the principles upon which one ought to found them? ... Can one not discover by what means and in which circumstances [one ought to]?"[68] Once Diderot felt he had come upon a consistent principle (and perhaps here one could make a link between Diderot's earlier novels on sexual themes and his straightforward proposed "solution" to the dominance involved in the colonial encounter), he was not hesitant to apply it in many contexts. His dealings with Russia and with Catherine II were quite extensive (including his visit in 1773 to Saint Petersburg), but some remark should be made on the amusing scheme he devised to spread the spirit of freedom among the Russian people, who were then too accustomed to the despotism under which they labored. In fact this may be one source of the views he expressed in the 1780 edition of the *Histoire des deux Indes*. In the opening pages of his *Observation sur le Nakaz*, Diderot writes, "The Russian empire occupies an area of 32 degrees in latitude and 165 degrees in longitude. To civilize such an enormous country all at once seems to me a project beyond human capacity, especially when I travel along the border and find here desert, there ice, and elsewhere all kinds of barbarians."[69] The scale of Russia leads Diderot to make several proposals. First, to move the capital to the center of this land mass; second, to appoint someone to civilize one district within it.[70] The third proposition, of particular interest to my argument here, is related to the second: "The third thing would be to introduce a colony of Swiss people, and situate it in a suitable region. Guarantee it privileges and freedom, and grant the same privileges and freedoms to all subjects who entered this colony. The Swiss are farmers and soldiers; they are loyal. I know by heart all the objections that can be raised against these methods; they are so frivolous that I shall not take the trouble to reply to them."[71] This passage fits more clearly with Diderot's general principle of a noncoercive persuasion of the native which one finds dispersed throughout his writings on the primitive. This facet of the passage just cited is clearer if we read it alongside section 38 of *Mélanges pour Catherine II*, which is titled "A Systematic Idea for the Manner of Leading a People to the Sentiment of Liberty and to a Civilized State." There Diderot writes:

> If I had to civilize savages, what would I do? I would do useful things in their presence, without saying or prescribing anything to

them. I would maintain an air of working for my family alone and for myself.

If I had to build up a nation to [the sentiment of] liberty, what would I do? I would plant a colony of free men in their midst, very free ones, such as (for example) the Swiss, whose privileges I would protect very securely. And I would leave the remainder to time and to the force of example.[72]

This passage points to a more complex question regarding the problem of freedom in Diderot's late political thought, which he believes relies on the principle of imitation, as here with the imitation of the Swiss. Can the former primitive ever be original, or is he or she condemned to only the *imitation* of the free? In this sense, the colonized are in a state not much different from one Rousseau observes among certain animals. Though the context is different, recall the moment when Rousseau presumes that pongos, an "anthropomorphic animal" seen in the Congo, push wood into a fire more to *imitate* the action of a man than from any deeper knowledge.[73]

Yet in order to return to the question of breeding in relation to an envisioned noncoercive colonial encounter, I should here cite one of Diderot's most explicit considerations of the racial implications of such a policy, found in his discussion "Sur les créoles" (in the 1770, 1774, and 1780 editions). The arguments he gives in favor of this practice explain the striking analogy with the family noted earlier, when he remarks that "consanguinity" produces one "large family."[74] Regarding the Créoles he writes, "The physical advantage of crossing races between men as between animals, in order to retard the bastardization of the species, is the fruit of a secondary experience, one which comes after the utility recognized in uniting families in order to cement the peace of societies."[75] Indeed earlier his argument that the European male and female settlers should mate with their counterparts was made from the point of view of utility. That argument provided a sociopolitical reason for interbreeding, which is here supplemented by a biological argument in favor of it. "The Creoles are in general well made. Hardly does one see a single one afflicted with the deformities so common in other climates. History does not reproach them with any of the cowardices, betrayals or baseness which soil the annals of all peoples. Hardly could one cite a single shameful crime which a Creole has committed."[76] Thus in the improvement of the race is also produced a docile colonial subject, one unlikely to rebel. What better harmonization of interests could one hope for?

Commercial *Philosophes*?

This gentle colonialism coexists in the *Histoire des deux Indes*—often on the very same page—with passages that excoriate the crimes of Europe and rail against slavery. (Indeed it must have been the mingled presence of these two views that enabled a later reader such as Napoleon to overlook Diderot's tirades and, we are told, carry the *Histoire* with him on his conquest of Egypt; the polyphonic authorship of the ensemble clearly interpellated different types of readers.)[77] Diderot's voice seems to find its most forceful expression from within the security of anonymous authorship, which allows him to adopt a strong, hortatory tone. The countless passages where he switches to the second person, addressing the reader as *tu* or *vous*, enable him to accuse and to speak in a prophetic mode. If we keep these in mind alongside the arguments proposed in favor of *douce colonisation* then we can attend to the contradictory nature of this work (as Duchet urges). But I do not make this remark simply to indicate a formal, epiphenomenal aspect of the *Histoire des deux Indes*. It also seems to me that we can thereby examine this work within the complex field of texts and authors which has been addressed by such important studies as Uday Mehta's *Liberalism and Empire*.[78] In the French context, Duchet, for example, writes about "humanitarianism and anti-slavery," and, considering the policy of interbreeding, she argues that wherever there was a crisis in labor—a labor shortage because of the impossibility or impracticality of slavery—interbreeding with the natives was suggested.[79] Interbreeding, in this sense, is one answer to the crisis caused by the growing antislavery movement. Humanitarianism in France is akin to liberalism in Britain, slavery akin to the coercive aspects of empire. Just as arguments against slavery are shown to have a more practical basis in political economy, so do the arguments against empire (e.g., Adam Smith's anticolonialism moved between a moral argument and an argument concerning efficiency). Both humanitarianism and political liberalism served as alibis for empire by providing a degree of moral legitimacy.

Within this period, as one would expect, the arguments put forth for the abolition of slavery often took on a moral or even religious character. The *Histoire*, however, had something to say about this effort at explanation, arguing against those who would "give honor to the Christian religion for the abolition of slavery. We will dare not to be of his opinion. It is when there is industry and wealth in the people that the princes value them as something significant. It is when the wealth of people can be useful to kings against the barons that the laws improve the condition of the people."⁸⁰ And so we begin to close the unusual circle connecting the terms we have traced in the *Supplément* and the *Histoire des deux Indes*; it is commerce that should be extolled for spreading wealth among people and for bringing about the abolition of slavery. This view of commerce, in turn, should be connected with the critique of absolutism implicit in the above observation. It is this which provokes Diderot to bring together his argument regarding commerce with the primary subject of the *Histoire*, namely colonialism: "In these mercantile societies, the discovery of an island, the importation of a new commodity, the invention of a machine, the establishment of a trading post . . . the construction of a port will become the most important transactions, and as a result the annals of peoples will need to be written by *commercial philosophers*, just as they were formerly written by speaking historians."⁸¹ These future commercial *philosophes* who take the place of "speaking historians" indicate Diderot's search for a kind of writing and insight that would match the radical transformations wrought by these discoveries and innovations. From the language of this passage one might be tempted to think that Diderot had Smith's *Wealth of Nations* in mind; the paragraph opens with the words "A spirit of trucking and exchanging is being established in Europe,"⁸² which recall the famous lines about man's proclivity to truck and barter. However, this passage dates from 1774, before the publication of Smith's work; in fact Smith frequently cites the *Histoire* as his source in his chapter "Of Colonies."⁸³ It seems therefore that what we have here is an example of the prophetic voice in operation.

The *Histoire des deux Indes* itself, I would suggest, attempts to fulfill the very desire that Diderot expresses in the work. Faced with the scale of the discoveries for European science, Diderot dreams of a method that some would later identify with the modern discipline of anthropology:

> The discovery of a new world can alone furnish the food for our curiosity. A vast land lying fallow, humanity reduced to the animal condition, open country without harvests, treasures without possessors, societies without civilization [*police*], men without mores: How could such a spectacle not be full of interest and instruction for a Locke, a Buffon or a Montesquieu! What reading could be as surprising, as moving, as the narrative of their voyage! But the image of raw and wild nature is already disfigured. One must make haste in gathering the half-erased traces, after having described and delivered over to contempt the greedy and ferocious Christians which an unfortunate chance led first to this other hemisphere.⁸⁴

In retrospect, one can see in this statement many of the notable achievements and constitutive flaws of modern anthropology. The *Histoire des deux Indes* is at times an attempt to be this reflection of Locke, had he actually visited North America and seen the Indians of the Carolinas, or of Montesquieu had he actually visited Persia and China. And like the later *tristesse* that would strike Claude Lévi-Strauss, there is also an urgency and a haste to undertake this project before the traces of the primitive fade away, only to become objects of nostalgia for European society. This temporal relation to the future is apparent throughout the work; it is that of the future anterior, the will-have-been, in this case the will-have-been-destroyed, and accounts for the haste.[85] Hence in posing the question to the European (cited in the first epigraph), whether you still wish that the Americas had been discovered, Diderot writes, "There will be no single moment in the future where my question would have the same force." Natural man was discovered, and in his discovery was lost. The "philosophical fiction" for a moment entered indicative prose, only to vanish back into the imagination.

"These New Hercules": Toward a Traveling Philosophy

That the dream was not Diderot's alone is clear from another passage to which, it strikes me, the philosophe was responding, perhaps directly. In 1754, tucked away in a lengthy ten-page footnote to an essay that made an effort to answer a question posed by the Academy of Letters at Dijon (the very same academy through which Raynal would later pose his question on the settlement of the New World), a citizen of Geneva complained:

> For the three or four hundred years since the inhabitants of Europe have inundated the other parts of the world, and continually published new collections of voyages and reports, I am convinced that we know no other men except the Europeans; furthermore, it appears, from the ridiculous prejudices which have not died out even among men of letters, that under the pompous name of the study of man everyone does hardly anything except study the men of his country. In vain do individuals come and go; it seems that philosophy does not travel.[86]

So wrote Jean-Jacques Rousseau in the *Discourse on Inequality* as he reviewed the achievements of European travelers, which he asserted were limited mainly to the study of natural sciences. Rousseau wishes that two men, one of great wealth and the other a scientist, would undertake a voyage to study "not always stones and plants, but for once men and morals,"[87] which rather directly corresponds to Diderot's call for a "philosophe commerçant" or commercial philosopher. That the primary discovery of such travels thus far was also circumscribed by the vision of the one who sees, as Rousseau here asserts, perhaps also informed the witty aside by one of the speakers in the *Supplément* concerning Orou's remarks that "they show a rather European influence." Yet more interesting, to my mind, than any play of mirrors (between self and self as other) is Rousseau's criticism that philosophy did not travel, which Diderot's "traveling philosophy," described in the passage cited earlier from the *Histoire*, was meant to supply. Rousseau notes that virtually all the information one has on the two Indies derives from unreliable sources, since "there are scarcely more than four sorts of men who make voyages of long duration: sailors, merchants, soldiers, and missionaries."[88] The first three, according to Rousseau, cannot be relied upon as good observers, while the fourth (missionaries) are more concerned with their "sublime vocation."[89]

For all of these reasons, Rousseau wishes that those who voyaged were of another disposition; in fact he wishes that Diderot himself (among others) might undertake to travel "as Plato did":

> The academics who have traveled through the northern parts of Europe and the southern parts of America intended to visit them as geometers rather than as philosophers.... We know nothing of the peoples of the East Indies [*des Indes Orientales*] who have been frequented solely by Europeans more desirous to fill their purses than their heads.... Let us suppose a Montesquieu, Buffon, Diderot, Duclos, d'Alembert, Condillac, or men of that stamp traveling in order to inform their compatriots, observing and describing, as they know how, Turkey, Egypt, Barbary... the Malabars, the Mughals, the banks of the Ganges... then, in the other hemisphere, Mexico, Peru.... Let us suppose that these new Hercules, back from their memorable expeditions, then at leisure wrote the natural, moral, and political history [*l'Histoire naturelle Morale et Politique*] of what they had seen; we ourselves would see a new world [*un monde nouveau*] come from their pens, and we would thus learn to know our own.[90]

It is difficult to ascertain whether this passage had any direct effect upon Raynal as he formulated the *Histoire Philosophique et Politique... des deux Indes* (here we should note the similarity and variation of the more complete title from the one Rousseau proposes) or Diderot in his capacity as contributor; it is more striking, to my mind, to remark upon the sentiment expressed. In its desire to mix philosophy and travel, to produce a more comprehensive and encyclopedic account of "the new worlds" to be seen, these citations attest to the global vision of much eighteenth-century prose and the desire of many to undertake this "Herculean labor." But, one might ask, to what end?

Consensual Colonialism as a Conceptual Limit: The *Histoire des deux Indes* and the Contradictions of Liberal Thought

The line cited in the first epigraph to this chapter, "There will be no single moment in the future where my question would have the same force," is an example of the *production* of nostalgia, an affect that necessarily contains within it a temporal element. It is linked to the operation of a future anterior: not simply the will-have-been but rather (morosely) the will-have-been-destroyed. In this case, the will-have-been-destroyed refers to the tribal cultures of the primitive which Diderot foresees disappearing completely from the Earth with the expansion of Europe.

Diderot's views on the possibilities and limits of colonialism as *douce colonisation* can be more keenly imagined and hoped for by him precisely because it precedes the classical period of imperialism in the nineteenth century. What is more on his mind is the reform of the methods employed by Spanish colonists in the New World. Thus arises a turn to breeding, by means of the concept of population, itself derived from debates on political economy in the period. Not only is breeding, or interbreeding, a kind of libidinal sublation of the political conflict presented between colonizer and colonized, but it is also presented as a rational decision on *biological* grounds, whose end result is imagined to be a docile colonial subject—a docility inscribed in biology. It is in this earlier period that mixture of this sort can be solely considered from a biological viewpoint (to the exclusion of a focus on the psychology of colonialism, more clearly a legacy of modern movements of decolonization). If we are not, however, presented with a glimpse of the interior experience of the colonized, we are given an exterior vision that perceives a fragility, a vulnerability of the societies that Europe is encountering.

It is this vulnerability that is expressed as nostalgia, a nostalgia in the future anterior. The newness of this sentiment, of the vulnerability of societies and ways of life—many of which have indeed ceased to exist—should be seen as the impetus behind the call for the new genre of prose for which Diderot had no name. In seeking this worldly prose, was Diderot dreaming of anthropology in the modern sense? In any case, one finds here the same paradox that Walter Benjamin noted in his essay on the "oral" tales of Nikolai Leskov: the very possibility of the appreciation of their oral quality was already a sign of the demise of orality itself.[91] Only in its passing away did the shimmer of a fading aura become visible. And so it is here, only when the possibility (glimpsed so early, in 1780) of the complete obsolescence of these manifold societies was imagined, that the birth of an anthropological imagination was possible; it was also underwritten by a vision of the globe constructed from the geography of many European empires, whose contours are traced in the very form of the *Histoire des deux Indes*: the Dutch, the Portuguese, the Spanish, the French and English colonies. The *Histoire* is therefore a testament to and key document in the prehistory of the modern concept of globalization, in that it envisions both a global form of hegemony and gives inklings of global forms of counterdominance that were to emerge, such as the famous prophetic lines on an imminent rebellion led by a black slave incarnating the figure of Spartacus: "Where is he, this great man, which nature perhaps owes to the dignity of the human race? Where is he, this new Spartacus, who will not anywhere meet a Crassus? Thus will disappear the *Code Noir*."[92] Toussaint Louverture was in fact rumored to be one such reader of the *Histoire*.[93]

How ironic this fact is: the very same work that is said to have inspired anticolonial figures like Toussaint also stirred Napoleon's "zeal" for conquest. This effect of the *Histoire des deux Indes* is worth keeping in mind and seems overlooked by some revisionist readings of Enlightenment documents. One may make the case for an Enlightenment against empire, for example, but then why exactly did Napoleon carry this book with him in his pursuit of the latter? And what made it possible for Toussaint (whether in rumor or reality; either suits our case) to hold the very same book in his cell in his final years, imprisoned by Napoleon?

This should be connected with a primary thesis concerning the relationship between liberalism and empire: empire was the *historical space* from which liberalism as a *political practice* and coherent set of political beliefs emerged. What does one do with this apparent contradiction? Is this a contingent historical overlap, or is there some more immanent constitutive flaw to political liberalism? This reading of Diderot has aimed to trace one set of linkages between consent, hegemony, and dominance, particularly the fantasy of a dominance *with* hegemony, a submission "without reserve." Consensual colonialism, the expression of this fantasy and also of a conceptual limit, is thus a political formulation that can exist *within* liberalism, and we may thereby have a better sense of the evolution of that other peculiar institution of the nineteenth century: liberal imperialism.[94]

2 / On the Use and Abuse of Anger for Life: *Ressentiment* and Revenge in the *Histoire des deux Indes*

> Le spectacle de tant de vastes contrées pillées, ravagées, réduites à la plus cruelle servitude reparaîtra. La terre couvre les cadavres de trois milles d'hommes que vous avez laissé ou fait périr, mais ils seront exhumés, ils demanderont vengeance au ciel et à la terre, et ils obtiendront.
> —DIDEROT, "LE PRIVILÈGE DE LA COMPAGNIE, SERA-T-IL RENOUVELÉ?," HISTOIRE DES DEUX INDES (1782)

> Vous êtes fiers de vos lumières: mais à quoi vous servent-elles? de quelle utilité seroient-elles à l'Hottentot!
> —DIDEROT, "ETABLISSEMENTS DES HOLLANDAIS AU CAP DE BONNE-ESPÉRANCE," HISTOIRE DES DEUX INDES (1782)

Anger, hatred, revenge, *ressentiment*: this chapter begins a preliminary consideration of this set of closely related if distinct terms.[1] Not, perhaps, a happy collation, but one important layer that recurs frequently in the thick and varied strata of the *Histoire des deux Indes* under the covered earth to which Diderot refers. To some it must serve as a bilious and dense schist beyond which they cannot, or desire not, to dig any deeper. But as we will see, it is a mineral not evenly distributed. That one finds it in two or three locations gives no guarantee that it will appear in the fourth. More than that, and outside of the natural variation of geology, there are indeed reasons why it—revenge and its cognates—should appear in some but not other places. There are rival elements competing for predominance in the explanations given in the *Histoire* regarding how colonization has been and can be undertaken. Affect, I will argue, is one index to the movements and rumblings of this debate, a debate over past and present colonial enterprises. If we have already been well trained by astute readings in this period to watch for the constellation of terms gathered in the phrase *virtue, commerce, history*, I will argue we can supplement this and thereby attune ourselves to the prose of occasional insurgency that arises by considering affect, commerce, history.[2]

The role of the first term of this trio, *affect*,[3] is in part the management of a response to a perceived injustice. The second term, *commerce*, is built into the form of this *encyclopédie* we are considering. Commerce provides the methodology of the work and one organizing principle; its routes laterally outward in four directions from a port city lead the *Histoire* to its next regions for discussion. Rather than discrete national entities, in the *Histoire des deux Indes* one is constantly given a glimpse of the globalized set of economic exchanges that haphazardly connect, say, the coast of Mexico to the Mariana Islands, and these islands to Southeast Asia. The third and final term, and perhaps the grandest, is the idea of *history* which this *Histoire* discusses directly and obliquely; in both cases what is most striking about the work is its dependence on the idea of a *historical counterfactual*. What if the colonization of the Americas—to take Raynal's own question—had been different, or not occurred at all? Revenge and *ressentiment* become more legitimate and real to Diderot in the work the more one admits the validity of posing a counterfactual. For Diderot, it is linked to an openness of history dimly perceived and quickly fading. The more one acknowledges the contingency of history, the more one has the *right to be angry*. Is anger hopeful or despairing? Does it goad one onward or retard genuine reflection on the cause of a historical malaise? These are some of the questions behind the uses and abuses of anger for life.[4]

* * *

Throughout the *Histoire des deux Indes* one comes upon passages that express hatred or revenge; at times this is extended to a language of haunting, invoking the unmourned dead. Much has been written about this topos in another context, characteristic as it is of many contemporary postcolonial novels, but it is remarkable that the sentiment is seldom considered within the Enlightenment itself.[5] Indeed many striking passages on this theme from Diderot—certainly no marginal figure to any history of European letters in the eighteenth century—have not even been translated into English under his name. Whether it is Santo Domingo, South America, or, as in the first epigraph, the Indian subcontinent, we find Diderot deploying what I have referred to as a prophetic voice. The prophecy of reappearance makes use, once again, of the future perfect, the will-have-been, though here it is to proclaim the certainty that "il faut que, tôt ou tard, la justice soit faite."[6] As with other references to justice in the text, the question remains as to what constitutes justice in the sphere of colonial conquest, though often the rhetoric of such passages leads Diderot to declare that, in effect, blood must be paid for blood (the sanguine language is his own).

As noted in chapter 1 on Diderot's contributions to the *Histoire des deux Indes*, the force of these remarks have led many readers to believe that Diderot's anger is a displacement of his critique of the *ancien régime*, in other words, that his pessimism regarding the possibilities of political reform in France in the 1770s find an outlet by such remarks on the colonies. One of the clearest suggestions that this may be the case is to be found at the end of a chapter titled "Etablissements des Hollandais au cap de Bonne-Espérance."[7] It is also to this passage that one must turn in order to consider the relationship between the language of haunting and vengeance with the key affective thematic of hatred in the work. There, at the end of a chapter describing the Dutch settlement and its effects upon the Hottentots (now usually referred to as the Khoikhoin), Diderot writes, "Si mon discours vous offense, c'est que vous n'êtes pas plus humains que vos prédécesseurs, c'est que vous voyez dans la haine que je leur ai vouée celle que j'ai pour vous."[8] Hatred, in this context, refers to the hatred which the voice of the *Histoire* evokes against the colonizer. This is an imagined, empathetic hatred, where Diderot speaks, as it were, on behalf of the colonized. It is, however, a hatred possible only because of Diderot's intimacy with the corruption of "les sociétés policées" (civilized societies). The other kind of hatred he employs is one based on a kind of symptomatic reading of the colonizer. Recall the passage cited in chapter 1, when Diderot writes, "What do these forts you have garrisoned all beaches with attest to? Your terror and the profound hatred of those who surround you.... You will no longer be hated, when you are beneficent [*bienfaisant*]."[9] As is so often the case in the colonial context, one is returned to the underexamined theme of *ressentiment*. However, what is different here from both Nietzsche's use of the term and Fanon's is that it is not based on the inner psyche of the subjugated or colonized.[10] In a historical sense, it is too early for that, or at the least too early for Diderot based on the sources of which he makes use. One might venture the speculation that it is, in fact, the absence of these first-person narratives of the colonized that heighten the importance of the *imagined* voice of the other. Diderot links the absolution of hatred, in both cases, to the question of justice: "You will no longer be hated, when you are *bienfaisant*" and "La justice soit faite." There is in his declaration of hatred also a more immediate and literal meaning: "If this discussion [of the Dutch in southern Africa] offends you, it is because you [French reader] are no better." Certainly this is a connection—from the earlier

Dutch and Spanish to the later French and English settlements—which the *Histoire* is keen to make evident.[11]

The Cape of Africa, or the Enlightenment's Utility for the Hottentots

As I will propose, the language of anger and hatred is part of a specific affective economy and will help to explain many of the observations made in chapter 1, particularly in relation to the central role played by *douceur*. Earlier I made reference to the manner in which Diderot's vacillating rhetorical position in the work was perhaps indicative of a set of contradictions within liberal political thought. For some readers, such a critique of liberalism may not seem novel since there already exists Marx's own highly developed analyses of the hidden ideological work behind liberalism's language. Michèle Duchet's discussion of "humanitarisme et antiesclavagisme," and its parallel with more current reflections on liberalism and empire, gives a functional reason for why the interbreeding of settlers with a native population was suggested at various moments. These had to do with the impracticality or impossibility of slavery. This is consonant with many Marxist accounts of the demise of slavery as an institution, which debunk a liberal claim that a growing respect for the rights of man—or of the idea of the universality of freedom—had anything to do with emancipation. Instead what is emphasized is how slavery was simply discovered to be an inefficient system for the expenditure of capital.[12] Rather than seeing the abolition of slavery as a result of philanthropic efforts, in the writings of the Physiocrats one finds many practical reasons for its abolition. As Duchet writes, "Humanitarianism and political economy were thus one and the same thing: the quantity and quality of work furnished depends necessarily upon the condition rendered to a man.... More than a crime, slavery was an *error*, and the economic error was doubled."[13] If humanitarian thought came to its conclusions regarding slavery based on economic reasons, as so many of the administrator's memoirs analyzed by Duchet attest to, then we might see in some of Diderot's proclamations a troubled reflection on this fact. What good is the Enlightenment? Returning to the very same passage where Diderot declares his hatred to the reader, we find him asking, a few paragraphs before this, "Vous êtes fiers de vos lumières: mais à quoi vous servent-elles? de quelle utilité seroient-elles à l'Hottentot! est-il donc si important de savoir parler de la vertu sans la pratiquer! Quelle obligation vous aura le Sauvage, lorsque vois lui aurez porté des arts sans lesquels il est satisfait, des industries qui ne seroient que multiplier ses besoins &

ses travaux, des loix dont il ne peut se promettre plus de sécurité que vous n'en avez?"[14] With so many contemporary reflections on the Enlightenment in the colony, it is important to note that it is not solely an obsession of the present to pose the question in this manner. The very author of one of its indisputable central works—*l'Encyclopédie*, which aimed to gather together arts and material techniques of many varieties—wonders what its worth is when viewed from the state-of-nature colony. It is a query that many others after him would also pose. The question undoubtedly relies upon a presupposition quite different from the critique which one would make in the present; his presupposition is that the state-of-nature colony is in a sense more innocent than the corrupt metropole. The inhabitants of the latter, however, simply do not have a language to read the corrosive words inscribed on their society. While the dawning of Enlightenment might have caused many to view native customs as so many irrational superstitions, this is surprisingly *not* the militant philosophe's opinion. "You laugh with contempt," Diderot writes, "at the superstitions of the Hottentot. But do your priests not poison you by engendering prejudices which form the torture of your life, which sow division in your families, which arm your countries one against the other?"[15]

We have seen this mixture of anticlericalism and a defense of purportedly primitive custom before in the *Supplément*. It is important to remark that this is not a critique of the very category of superstition; it is primarily a reminder of the incomplete project proclaimed in Voltaire's famous dictum, "Écrasez l'infâme!"[16] However, where others would only rebut the claim to a more rationalized society that a European might make by indicating the irrationality that persists within Europe, Diderot goes the further step of demonstrating how even the most alien of systems contains its own very clear logic. Having presented a brief description of the Southern Cape and of the social structure of the Hottentots, Diderot turns quickly to a peculiar observation which many previous European travelers to the region have reported. "But it is very true," he writes, "that the Hottentots have but one testicle. This has been often remarked upon."[17] Rather than the curiosity that such a form of bodily mutilation might provoke (a curiosity connected, John Morley might have remarked, to the absence of a "scientific" study of race),[18] Diderot presents the practice as a form of vital communication between those who belong to a faction or tribe. Like a shibboleth, like circumcision (Diderot's own analogy), this practice speaks only to those who *already ought to know*. "It is thus that in revolutions," he elaborates, choosing a suggestive analogy, "the factions have *signs* by means of which they recognize each other, in spite of the tumult and in the midst of the fighting.... It is the sound of an instrument which awakens those to whom it is addressed, while it leaves those who do not possess the key to it in the torpor of sleep or security."[19] We do not have here relativism for relativism's sake, or something akin to Montaigne's observations on cannibals.[20] Instead we have an early if undeveloped effort at seeing the practice in a semiotic manner. "Such is, according to all appearances, the first origins of the majority of the singular [*singulier*] usages which one finds among savages, and even in civilized societies [*sociétés policés*]."[21]

It would be folly, however, to take too far this similarity with semiotic anthropology, for Diderot alternates these moments of detached analysis with moments of unmitigated affect hardly suited to that discursive style. Anger, as I have begun to argue, is one of these affects deployed throughout the *Histoire*. Often in tandem with it is the hortatory mode, usually addressed to the European reader. There are also moments when Diderot makes an impossible address or appeal in directing himself to voices lost from history. It is a moment that holds out the poignant hope implied in a historical counterfactual: What if it had not happened this way? What if the Hottentots had defeated the Dutch settlers? "Run, unfortunate Hottentots, run. Drive yourselves deep into your forests. The ferocious beasts which inhabit them are less frightening than the monsters of the empire you are going to fall under."[22] Here the address is not to the European reader but rather is directed to the Hottentots—but of course one knows that it can be so only rhetorically and not literally. The absence in the *Supplément* of an original text, of the speech of the Tahitian native that recedes behind the many mediators finds its analogue here in the absence of a native *reader* to this recounted episode of a defeat. Rhetorically the defeated are the absent but desired readers; the anger present in the work may itself be a kind of mourning for them. Without carrying my speculation too far, one finds that the impossibility of a native reader (Toussaint's eventual rumored readership notwithstanding) is one of Diderot's anxieties while writing this work. Referring to the arrival in the seventeenth century of the founder of the Dutch colony on the cape, Diderot writes, "It is time, Riebeck approaches.... Neither the Hottentot nor the inhabitant of the countries which are left to you to devastate will hear or understand [*s'entendront*] this."[23] His earlier comment to this recurrent figure— "cruel Européen"—observed ominously, "There will be no single moment in the future when my question would have the same force" and thereby expressed a certain haste which one also finds here, though in this instance the haste is demanded of the indigenous peoples to arm themselves as much as it calls for a reform of European behavior.[24] Because we are still in that earlier part of the *Histoire* which is a narrative up to the present, the address here is to a ghost in the past; the cry "Flee, Hottentots!" is thus necessarily a pathetic (pathos-ridden) cry because it is a failure foretold.[25]

Anger, therefore, when deployed in the work alternates with other counterpoising affects, such as pathos and *douceur*. Pathos limns the words addressed to the Hottentot, and anger those addressed to the European. So, having explained in what way the life of the Hottentot is in fact closer to the idea of virtue than that of a corrupted member of civilized society, Diderot asks, "Do you therefore believe that the corruption in which you are plunged, your hatreds, your perfidies, your duplicity do not *revolt my faculty of reason* more than the impropriety of the Hottentot revolts my sense?"[26] Whether it is an example of hatred ("la haine . . . que j'ai pour vous") or revulsion, as here, the aim is to break a complacence expected of the reader. What this angry, anonymous voice does urge at one extreme is *anticolonial violence*. "If you feel within yourself the courage," this unobjective spectator to history urges the Hottentots, "take up your hatchets, pull tight your bows, and rain down upon these foreigners your poisoned arrows. Let there remain not a single one to carry back to their citizens the news of their calamity!"[27] The extremity of this sentiment must have struck many readers; it was in fact for this reason that so many later critics, in a post factum manner after the French Revolution, wished to read these remarks as *allegory*, a speaking about European colonists that was really about French absolutism. (I have said enough about why in the end I find this very unpersuasive.)

Goa: Complicity and Its Disavowal?

No discussion of the idea of anger in this work could overlook a passage that exceeds even the one already cited and makes patently visible the connection I have made between such passages and the call to violence. It occurs in the first book of the *Histoire* in a chapter titled "Corruption of the Portuguese in India."[28] Having already discussed in previous chapters the natural wealth of the various regions under their control (Goa, Daman, Ceylon, and others), the *Histoire* details the causes of Portuguese decline: the "fanaticism of their religion," "criminality in their finances," and the fact that their commanders take in "a crowd of singers and dancers, of which India has many."[29] Often this *Histoire* reflects upon the rise and fall of great empires, and it was perhaps for this reason that the work is seen as an influence on Edward Gibbon (who praised it highly).[30] In observing the decline of the Portuguese, the narrator returns to this theme and remarks, "It would be sad to rest one's gaze upon the decline of a nation . . . that might have enlightened the world . . . without being a scourge to its neighbors or to distant regions."[31] This, however, is not the case here; instead "it is sweet to foresee the fall of this tyranny."[32] Where the foreseeing of injustice causes despair, the foreseeing of the decline of tyranny induces pleasure; because there is not even a claim to an ethical basis for this empire, there is no sadness in seeing its decline. Even after presenting a critical description of these settlements, however, the narrator worries that he is himself jaded by the received accounts of plunder, "led on by habit,"[33] and not conveying the "indignation" which the event merits. Whipped up to this frenzy, we are presented with one of the most violent yet remarkable passages in the *Histoire*:

> Barbares Européens! l'éclat de vos entreprises ne m'en a point imposé. Leur succès ne m'en a point dérobé l'injustice. Je me suis souvent embarqué par la pensée sur les vaisseaux qui vous portaient dans ces contrées lointaines; mais descendu à terre avec vous, et devenu témoin de vos forfaits, je me suis séparé de vous, je me suis précipité parmi vos ennemis, j'ai pris les armes contre vous, j'ai baigné mes mains dans votre sang. J'en fais ici la protestation solemnelle; et si je cesse un moment de vous voir comme des nuées de vautours affamés et cruels, avec aussi peu de morale et de conscience que ces oiseaux de proie, puisse mon ouvrage, puisse ma mémoire, s'il m'est permis d'espérer d'en laisser une après moi, tomber dans le dernier mépris, être un objet d'exécration![34]

Strong words, these; it certainly is not surprising that many readers wished to isolate this anger, which is in part a self-hatred, to the *ancien régime* as its isolated object. The hope was that it would bear the brunt of these charges. I say that these words are in part self-hatred in order to express the idea of *complicity* which Diderot (identified as the author of this passage) both acknowledges and then performs a disavowal of. The disavowal takes the form of a spectral figure: the seditious shadow of "la pensée" follows the trading vessels to the colonies. Once there, this insurgent, "bearing witness" to atrocity, joins with the natives who make an effort at violent revolt.[35] In writing this philosophical and political history, the narrator becomes aware that the retelling of a conquest can become reaffirmation and legitimation. The solemn profession, or *protestation* in French, is also a vow to *remain* angry, to remember: "If I cease to view such activities as heinous," one might paraphrase his remark, "then I call upon you to execrate myself and my legacy." For an atheist philosophe, this was perhaps the best way one could call upon oneself to be condemned in an afterlife for betrayal.[36] If anger has a use for life, Diderot seems to have found it to be a glue for memory and conviction.

Jamaica, or Intractable *Ressentiment*

"Righteous anger!" many would say of such remarks, particularly the more moderate eighteenth- and nineteenth-century British readers of this work who foresaw in such emotions the affective (if not the ideological) origins of postrevolutionary violence, and even the Terror.[37] (Certainly Edmund Burke, whose comments on Rousseau and the philosophes are discussed in part 2, would have been the first to denounce such gory prescriptions for revenge.) Yet throughout this chapter on Diderot's contributions to the *Histoire des deux Indes*, I have made an effort to show why the attempt at displacing the anger aimed against European colonialism expressed in the work cannot be adequately understood if one takes French absolutism or the *ancien régime* as its primary object. If there are political displacements in the work, however, these are to be found within the shifting *internal* contexts of the colonial theater. So, for example, the *Histoire* contains lengthy descriptions of slave revolts in the English colony of Jamaica in a chapter titled "Dangers Which Threaten Jamaica from Within,"[38] passing quietly over those in the French colony of St. Domingue. My discussion of Jamaica will be the third and final example—after the first on the Hottentots in the chapter on the Cape of Good Hope and the second on the Portuguese settlements in Asia—to be considered in relation to the question of the uses of anger in the *Histoire*. After the consideration of these three, I turn to another passage in the *Histoire* (not by Diderot) that concerns the island of Guam. The section on Guam will serve to demonstrate how the anger of the more anticolonial passages is managed and how proposals for the containment of *ressentiment* are elaborated.

But even in the description of the revolts in Jamaica, there are already proposals of how to address the intransigence of the hatred of the dominated.[39] The passage opens with a description of black and mulatto former slaves who take to the hills after the colony passes from the Spanish to the English in order "to protect in the mountains a liberty which seems to offer them a sanctuary from their defeated tyrants."[40] There is throughout a sympathy for the runaway slave within the *Histoire*, though the consequences of this—when this leads to violence against settler communities, for instance—is also the very motivation behind the project for a reformed colonialism which elsewhere appears in this work.[41] Yet for the group of philosophes who authored the *Histoire* this set of political concerns engenders a more general reflection upon human nature (the soul, the roots of evil, etc.) in relation to fury and anger. "The *ressentiment*," it is observed, "of a nature violated by a barbarous policy [i.e., the practice of slavery] places so much fury in the soul of the blacks bought by the whites that the latter, in order to cut the evil at the root (so they say), resolved in 1735 to make use of all the fierceness [*féroces*] of the colony to destroy an enemy who had become justifiably implacable."[42] This passage is quite central to understanding what is meant by *ressentiment* in the *Histoire*; *ressentiment* is an incurable state of being and something directly caused by slavery. *Ressentiment* and slavery are thus linked very closely. What is the immediate consequence of this desire to "cut the evil at its root," to wipe out the slaves? "Immediately after, *military* laws took the place of all civil administration."[43] What the *Histoire* is beginning to connect in this narrative is an observation that could be made only of the English and not of the Spanish; the focus on the conquest and conversion which the latter undertake in the *Histoire* seldom allows for a consideration of their civil policy. In the gradual erosion of this civil policy among the British, and its replacement by military law, the *Histoire* maps out the unraveling hypocrisy of a liberal imperialism. And the trigger (or perhaps we should use Montesquieu's language and say "spring" or *ressort*) for this whole process is the "implacable hatred" of the fugitive former slave.[44]

As elsewhere in the period, even or especially in Burke's description of Warren Hastings, one common rhetorical technique often made use of is inversion.[45] For an internal critic of Europe such as Diderot and many contributors of the *Histoire*, inversion involves the reassociation of a weave of words normally sewn onto the rough clothing of the despised and outcast. "If they," the *Histoire* refers to the rebellious blacks and mulattos of Jamaica, "were defeated, it was not without vengeance. Their blood was at least mingled with that of their *barbarous* masters."[46] Barbarians are often at the gate in this work, but they tend to emerge from Europe.[47] (Savages, however, do not hail from there, *sauvage* in French having a stronger association than its English translation with the idea of wild, natural, e.g., "les fleurs sauvages.") In the line cited earlier, the cause of the fury was also described as "une police barbare," a barbarous policy on the part of the English. Conjoined to this reassociation or reinscription of terms such as *barbarous* and *barbarian* is also a sympathy with the slave in revolt, indicated by the naming of the slaves' anticolonial violence as vengeance rather than as a sign of their unruly behavior or congenitally violent nature. This sympathy is even more present in the unflinching way the work often refers to *blood*; to say "at least" (*au moins*) the blood of the defeated was mingled with that of English reveals quite nakedly where the author's preferences lie.

In the midst of this entry on Jamaica, there is a one-paragraph intervention by Diderot that characteristically sharpens the focus of the paragraphs that precede it. From current defeat and retreat into the hills of Jamaica, the reader is instead given a prophetic description of likely revenge. Nature itself is said to feed and support the runaway slaves who take to the hills. If they are brave enough to run away rather than to submit to the yoke of foreign rule, then they are likely to await their time, until the moment arrives when they will chase out the foreign invader who has become lazy. Of such a person Diderot writes "that he cedes the plains to the multitude of troops, to the paraphernalia of armaments ... to the munitions and hospitals, and ... pulls back into the heart of the hills, without baggage, without shelter, without provision. Nature knows well how to nourish and defend him."[48] As Duchet argues in her study of colonial administrators' accounts, and of the philosophes' writings on these, it is not the slave and his or her bondage that captures the political imagination of the philosophe, but rather the *slave in revolt*. This fugitive figure, the runaway slave, confirms the concept of freedom for the philosophes; indeed the figure may be central to the claim that such an impulse to freedom is "natural" or in man by nature.[49] The maroon, *marronage*, represents the negation of slavery, a theme Duchet sees entering the historical scene around 1730, precisely as a consequence of the slave revolts in Jamaica and in French Guyana.[50] It is certainly this quality that Diderot emphasizes in the passage he inserts into the account of Jamaica. Yet he goes further in acknowledging the power of *naming* in rendering or removing legitimacy from the slave in revolt. Such a person must "brave in the end the injurious names of brigand and assassin which a great nation will put upon him [*lui prodiguera*] without shame, a nation so cowardly as to fully guard itself against a handful of hunting-men and so weak as to be unable to defeat them."[51] The account that follows details the efforts of Trelaunay, "this wise governor,"[52] at bringing the rebellious slaves to heel; an agreement is reached with the renegades, promising them their freedom in exchange for leaving peacefully with the English. Nonetheless in 1760, taking advantage of a European war occurring in America, "the black slaves also resolved to be free."[53] The real importance of this phrase, "d'être libre aussi," lies in the *aussi* because it indicates the consistent application of a more universal and complete liberty and is consonant with the language employed to describe the mobilization and failure of the enslaved: "But the *impatience for liberty* rendered unstable the unanimity of their conspiracy."[54] The plot is foiled and the slaves take to the hills; a shameful bounty is paid by the British for the head of any who are caught, and thus (in the language of the passage) they are defeated by their own race. If I have spent so much time summarizing the sequence of events in this entry, it is to bring out the manner in which a gradually forming ensemble of key terms in the lexicon of the period—and of this work in particular—begins to form a conceptual sentence. Such a sentence, figuratively speaking of the ensemble and literally speaking of the account, occurs in the description of the English punishment of these renegades. In their cruelty, these punishments are reminiscent of descriptions from de Las Casas on the Spanish (not incidental given the sequence of the volumes of the *Histoire*): men shackled alive in gibbets and left to die slowly in the hot sun. "However," it is written of this event, "their tyrants [the English] savored with eagerness the torments of these wretched people, whose sole crime had been to have desired to recover by vengeance the rights which avarice and inhumanity had taken forcefully from them."[55] To introduce the idea of *droit*, or right, in this context is itself an extension of a political vocabulary beyond the common confines of its use; to conjoin the word *right* with vengeance is even more startling. Though the phrase is not a *right to vengeance*, it is a right to recover what "inhumanity" had taken away. The "impatience for liberty" mentioned earlier is this desire to recover what, it is implied, it is only natural to possess. The cruelty of the punishments meted out, the way these are "savored," all indicate a deformation. The *Histoire* is able to detect this and to link it with inconsistencies in English political life—inconsistencies made all the more glaring because of the particularly high esteem in which England was held among the French philosophes. "Thus it is that the English, a people so jealous of their liberty, *play* with that of other men."[56] To play with the life and death of others, but to guard fiercely one's own sovereignty—the difficulty of sustaining logically this disposition was not lost upon the authors of this work. A more perfect line demonstrating a contradiction between liberalism and humanism in the domestic space and brigandage and despotism in the colonial territories could hardly be found. The intelligence of the *Histoire* lay in its ability to both praise the English love of liberty and also to hail its purported enemies, as in the case of the American Revolution or in Jamaica, when it undertook a policy discrepant from this belief. We certainly also find in the *Histoire* an illustration—at the risk of speaking in overly general terms—of how each colonial power will blame another one. Perhaps, aware of this hypocrisy, anger for Diderot is the sign of an unavoidable complicity, unavoidable because the anger itself is a disavowal of the act described but bears within it an acknowledgment that this proclamation is not expiation enough. The seditious ghostly thought of the philosophe may part ways with the settlers and traders once the ship is at shore, but the spirit will only be put to rest through vengeance. Did the humanism of the *Histoire* allow for a right to revenge?

* * *

We are given a reprise of the negative answer to the question which Raynal himself had sponsored at the Académie de Lettres à Dijon, and with it a reflection on its implications for the very self-conscious idea of *lumières* in the period. The question, once again: Was the discovery of America an event beneficial to humankind? Implicitly answering this, in the entry on Jamaica is a short sketch of the causal chain of disasters that has taken place in the New World and in Europe. "It is to this excess of barbarism which the traffic [*commerce*] and enslavement of the blacks necessarily must have led the usurpers [i.e., the British]. *Such is the progress of injustice and of violence.* To conquer the New World, it was necessary without a doubt to purge it of inhabitants. In order to replace them, it was necessary to purchase blacks—the only ones suited to the climate—for work in the Americas."[57] Not only does one detect here the kind of inversion referred to earlier regarding the use of such terms as *barbarism*, but there is also a conceptual inversion expressed through irony in the second sentence: such is the *progress* of injustice and violence. The irony does not, however, take on as bleak a form as it might; the true corruption of a word such as *justice* would have been expressed had it been written "such is the progress of justice" (not *in*justice). The progress of violence which is here referred to is in fact the set of causal connections, or consequences, that connect the colonization of the New World with the emergence of despotic forms of governance. The logic, according to the *Histoire*, is simple. The New World is colonized. The indigenous inhabitants being killed, new laborers and workers are now needed. Thus they are taken from Africa. In order to make them work without giving them ownership, slavery is instituted. Thus there are revolts, and so come into existence bad laws ("des lois atroces").[58] The Jamaica example suggests the possibility that if unchecked one unintended consequence of the discovery of the New World might be the corruption of the spirit of the laws in Europe—in this case, in England, since the *Histoire* obviously did not hold the *ancien régime* to be a defender of freedom. If Burke feared that "Indianism" would overtake the English Parliament, the authors of the *Histoire* have some inkling of the basis for this.[59]

Unlike Burke, however, the French philosophes were not loath to suggest arming angry slaves against their masters. Referring to the "cruelty" of British rule of the island, the *Histoire* observes, "In the end even [this] cruelty in its destructive nature has its own set course. One moment suffices: a felicitous descent to Jamaica could enable the conveyance of arms to men who have embittered [*ulcérée*] spirits and arms raised against their oppressors."[60] There was, however, a reflection similar to Burke's in the understanding that instability would bring with it a violence that might not lead forward in any way. Thus an argument is made against France's exploiting this advantage for its own benefit, with a fear analogous to Burke's concept of Indianism that such unrest had the potential to spread far beyond its initial confines. "The Frenchman who dreams of nothing but vanquishing his enemy [the British] without foreseeing that the revolt of the blacks in one colony could spark unrest in all of them hastens a revolution in the midst of the war."[61] It is here that one certainly sees an oblique reference to St. Domingue and thereby an example of the displacement *within* the colonial theater I argued for earlier. One must also place this statement within the context of the Seven Years War between Britain and France, the source of the lingering rivalries underlying this observation. The unusual mélange one finds in this section between decrying the inhumane treatment of Africans in the slave trade and considering how best to manage a colony demonstrates the fact that the political aim of seeking colonies in this period was not incompatible with calls for humanitarian reforms and improvement of the lot of slaves. As one scholar has noted, even when the French Parlement condemned the *Histoire* in 1781, no particular mention was made of the chapters that deal with the slave trade.[62]

The argument against an action based on imperial rivalry finds its justification within the general conclusion which Diderot appears to have appended to the Jamaica entry. This returns to the question of violence, but here the response is more modulated than the one expressed in the passage concerned with the Hottentots of southern Africa. "The Englishman put between two fires [i.e., French support and native unrest] would lose his force, his courage, and would leave Jamaica to the prey of those slaves and conquerors who would dispute over it with new horrors. Here is the unfurling [*enchaînement*] of injustice."[63] As we shall see, this sentiment is certainly closer to a Burkean observation in its fear of unrest and violence. How such a conclusion is reached, however, differs from the latter parliamentarian's reasoning. What is described is indeed a spiraling and accumulating violence, but there is an original injustice which gives rise to the cyclical growth. "Voilà l'enchaînement de l'injustice" recalls, in closing this chapter on Jamaica, the inaugurating remark "Tels sont les progrès de l'injustice et de la violence." And when it—the progress or unfurling of injustice—is indeed presented it reads like a catalogue of the self-perpetuating violence between colonizer and colonized. "It [injustice] attaches itself to man by bindings which cannot be broken without iron. Crime engenders crime; blood attracts blood, and the earth remains an eternal theater of desolation, of tears, of misery and mourning, where generations come successively to be bathed in the carnage, to gather [s'arracher] the entrails and toss around in the filth."[64] This vision of a violence that persists over many generations is the obverse of the responsibility that Burke will posit between generations in his effort to reinscribe the language of the social contract within his lexicon.[65] This passage also makes quite a different use of the image of "bathing in blood" which an angrier Diderot had deployed with less restraint and in greater anger. In the passage on the Hottentots, the narrative voice (Diderot's anonymous rage) had proclaimed, "I separate myself from you [the settler]. . . . I have bathed my hands in your blood."[66] Here instead one finds a passage lending some credence to those readers who emphasize Diderot's pessimistic vision in his late years: an anger mingled with *despair*.

Mariana Islands and Guam: How the Savage Conquered His Anger

As if in direct response to Diderot's pessimism in the passage on Jamaica, with its observations on the intractability of *ressentiment* once engendered, one finds a quite contrary diagnosis of the same problem within this compendium of comparative colonialism. There is an entry on the island of Guam that occurs in a chapter titled "Description of the Mariana Islands. Singular Qualities Observed There."[67] Having discussed three passages that each implicitly ask the question of what role anger and *ressentiment* play in colonization (the examples of the Portuguese in Goa, the Dutch in the Southern Cape of Africa, and the English in Jamaica), I turn now to an example of the Spanish in the Pacific. These pages were not written by Diderot, and this perhaps will account for the optimism of some of its prescriptions (though there is a resemblance to elements of the writings I examined in chapter 1). In one sense, the entire episode is recounted in order to lend credence to the idea that one sure means toward the development or civilizing of the island is to encourage the concept and practice of private property within a society that did not know it. Guam is understood in relation to its larger archipelago, Les îles Mariannes, or the Mariana Islands, from which much of its population is said to derive. "The Mariana islands were discovered in 1521 by Magellan," begins the account. "This celebrated navigator named them the Thieves' Islands because their wild [*sauvages*] inhabitants, who did not have the slightest idea of the right of property (unknown in the state of nature), took away from his ships some trinkets which attracted their curiosity."[68] That their thievery is due to a kind of innocence is thereby declared at the outset, as is the idea that the right of property does not exist in nature. The archipelago, we are told, was neglected because there was initially very little there to attract the Spanish. It wasn't until 1668 that the ships "which put into port there from time to time while going from Mexico to the East Indies left behind several missionaries."[69] The description of this trade route also gives us an explanation of why the discussion of these islands in the Pacific Ocean should be discussed in the middle of book 6 of the *Histoire*, which is ostensibly devoted to "the discovery of America; the Conquest of Mexico. Spanish settlements in this part of the New World."[70] The rationale for placing a discussion of this archipelago in this section becomes clearer if one bears in mind that the chapter preceding this one is titled "Mexico's Relations with the Philippines."[71] Having discussed Mexico in depth over the course of many chapters (book 6, chapters 8–20), the final chapters illustrate the typical effort of the *Histoire* to trace its links by sea and land to the East (chapters 21–22: Philippines and Mariana Islands), North (chapter 23: California), and South (chapters 24–25: Peru, Guatemala, and Honduras).

The discussion of the settlement of the Mariana Islands holds onto the perspective, common enough throughout the *Histoire*, of the cruelty and perfidy of missionary activity: "Ten years after [the arrival of the missionaries in 1668], the Court of Madrid judged that the means of persuasion did not give it enough subjects, and it enforced by soldiers the sermons of its apostles."[72] The shift from persuasion to force is the cause of a counterreaction that has also already appeared in the *Histoire*, as in the example of Jamaica: "The majority of them [the natives of Mariana Islands] would rather be massacred than subjugate themselves."[73] As with the runaway slaves, the instinctive drive toward freedom reaffirms the argument that slavery is contrary to nature; here those who survive the aggression of the Spanish took the "desperate measure" of inducing abortions in the women of the island "in order not to leave behind them enslaved children."[74] Those who survived the diseases that swept the islands and these events were few and were gathered together on the island of Guam, "the unfortunate leftovers of a formerly abundant people."[75] Having established the origin of the populace, the *Histoire* turns to a naturalist description of the physical aspect of the island and the animals in the wild that inhabit it. A dwindling population on a fertile island whose denizens nonetheless sustain themselves only by hunting: witness to this, "an energetic man, humane and enlightened" realizes that this declining state can be corrected only if "he succeeds in making his island agricultural."[76] With this insight we come upon the primary significance of this chapter and its contrast with the previous three examples I have examined, both in regard to the question of *ressentiment* and in relation to the general possibility of the incorporation of a colony within the political culture of the metropole.

In the proposals for establishing a Swiss colony in the midst of Russia—part of an effort to gradually civilize that land—Diderot had described his hope that the mere example of an efficient, freedom-loving people would cause others to follow and imitate their ways. We see the same principle at work in this episode. "This lofty idea," observes this chapter on Guam, referring to the settler's insight that the island be made agricultural, "made him become a cultivator himself. By his example, the natives [*les naturels*] of the country cleared the lands whose ownership [*propriété*] he had promised to them."[77] The mere force of an example, however, is here augmented by the incentive which the right to property encourages. Once this principle is developed, rocky soil is cleared, formerly wild lands are tilled, and so on; the effects of this extend beyond the physical to the social landscape. There is, in fact, a seamless transition from the one to the other: "Their fields were covered with rice, coco, corn, sugar, indigo ... whose use, for the last century or two, they had been left in ignorance of. Success had increased their docility."[78] Here again we begin to detect the components of an optimism I described earlier by the phrase *douce colonisation*. My emphasis had been on Diderot's biological thought and the way docility was inscribed in the body of the *métisse* or *créole*. None of these biological concerns is present here, but rather the possibility of creating a settlement that would be prosperous for the colonizer and be undertaken with the consent—more than the consent, even the enthusiastic support—of the colonized. I cite the passage in full in order to show the logic by which this chapter of the *Histoire* combines a discussion of docility with happiness:

> Success had increased their docility. These children of a raw nature, in whom tyranny and superstition had accomplished the degradation of man, had practiced in the workshops several arts of primary and frequent necessity.... Their joys were multiplied with their increased occupations, and they were happy in one of the best

countries in the world. So true is it that there is nothing that one cannot bring about with sweetness [*douceur*] and with kindness [*bienfaisance*], since these virtues can extinguish *ressentiment* even in the soul of the savage."[79]

This passage is the culmination of an implicit thesis on the use of *douceur*. In order to indicate the possibility of progress, the natives are here described as children of a raw nature, which is nevertheless contradicted by the arts and techniques they quickly develop; the possibility of this transformation is one of the classic preoccupations of the philosophes, namely the overcoming of the burdens of tyranny (in the realm of politics) and superstition (in the realm of reasoning and belief). The "multiplication of joy" is a phrase that will recur in various formulations; here it expresses the commonly held thesis regarding the achievements of commercial society. Whereas with Adam Smith the diversification of occupations enables more complex forms of society (culminating in commercial society), the emphasis in this passage is on the relation of joy (*jouissance*) to their being happy (*heureux*). There is a fairy tale quality to the passage, in the extremity of its observations and the simplicity of the moral lesson it aims to convey. Not only are the natives now happy; they are happy in one of the *best countries in the world*. What is the end to this tale, which might be given the title "How the Savage Defeated His Anger"? The virtues of *douceur* (sweetness) and *bienfaisance* (kindness) overcome and extinguish a resilient ressentiment. Although before, in the passage on Jamaica, *ressentiment* was a state that appeared irreparable because of past crimes, in the Mariana Islands episode this is a curable state. Perhaps this is the fulfillment of Diderot's taunt (referred to earlier) to the reader whose "fear" would subside only when "you are no longer hated." The solution prescribed there: "You will no longer be hated when you are *bienfaisant* [kind or beneficent].""[80]

One can now establish a clearer relation between the three examples cited earlier and this example on Guam regarding the structural couplet of *haine / douceur*. If *douceur* occupies such a central place in Diderot's conceptual lexicon and in the language of the *Histoire*, it is in part because he allows for the importance of *la haine*. Is it a contempt for the reader? In the schizophrenic performance of both the colonizer and the colonized, the voice of Diderot must turn to both *douceur* and *haine* in order to maintain an adequate expression of each position. Like the haunting bogey Diderot would like to conjure up, these are words expressed either as a loud warning to an imaginary native or an eerie whisper in the ear of the European reader. If to the native Diderot yells

"Fuyez, Hottentot," to the potential or actual settler colonial he blows the windy susurration "J'ai pris les armes contre vous. J'ai baigné mes mains dans votre sang."[81] However, in the reformist colonial project suggested in the chapter on the Mariana Islands, it is *douceur* which outweighs its antonym. And in this utopic example, all ends well.

The Double Advantage

There remains much to be said on the transformation of native society undertaken in the account of the Mariana Islands. The multiplication of happiness was only one of the effects achieved by the Spanish governor of the colony, Tobias, the enlightened individual who introduced the right of property to the islands and thereby brought about the changes described earlier. Once hatred has been extinguished, Tobias has "the consolation of seeing the diminution of the passion of his dear children [the natives of Mariana] for palm wine, and seeing the growth of their taste for work!"[82] From wine to work, from the idleness of food fallen from the breadfruit tree to the productivity of clearing land, this is a fairy tale whose end fulfills the transition from the state-of-nature colony to an efficient center of production for the European metropole. The success of Tobias's plan leads the authors of the *Histoire* to turn, once again, to a historical counterfactual: What if it had been otherwise? "If from the beginning the Spanish had had the reasonable views of the wise Tobias, the Mariana Islands would be civilized and cultivated. This *double advantage* would have procured for the archipelago a security which a garrison of a 150 men concentrated in Guam could not guarantee."[83] In the Southern Cape of Africa, the counterfactual gave a glimmer of what might have continued to exist if the Hottentot had defeated the Dutch; here what is imagined is instead a greater consonance, the double advantage of the aims of the settler with those of the Mariana natives.

Through the notion of a double advantage one can elicit many concepts that underwrite the reformist view of this passage. The advantage, to be clear, is doubled because the Mariana Islands would be a lucrative colony *and* possess happy subjects. (More often than not when the second of these could not be obtained, the first would usually suffice.) The security of their dominance established, the anxiety so often associated with ruling over a foreign territory would, in this fairy tale, also vanish. "Peaceful [*tranquille*] in their possessions, the conquerors could give themselves over to the love of discovery, which was after all the dominant genius of the nation."[84] The dominant genius spoken of here refers to the islander's singularly developed navigational skills.[85] The paradox here is that the colonizers' ability to enjoy the genius of the nation over whom they preside can take place only after its subordination. However, within the understanding of this chapter in the *Histoire*, this alternative form of colonization is a means for the dissemination of the benefits of the Enlightenment and its material advancements in arts and techniques, whose effects are described in quasi-religious terms: "Supported [*Secondé*] by the talent of their new subjects for navigation, their activity would carry useful arts and the spirit of society to the numerous islands that cover the Pacific ocean, and even further still. The universe would, so to speak, be enlarged by such glorious work."[86] If the discussion of this term *double advantage* does not seem to fit with the general question of anger and *ressentiment* that I have raised, it should be clear that what is proposed here is an alternative to the formation of antagonism based on the assumption of mutual gain. At the individual level *douceur* and *bienfaisance* extinguish *ressentiment* in the soul of the savage, while at the social level it is prosperity and the production of happiness: "Without a doubt all the commercial nations would gain, with the passing of time, some utility from relations formed with these regions—heretofore unknown—since it is impossible that one people would enrich itself without the others participating in their prosperity."[87] Mutual prosperity, mutual gain: the double advantage would ensure the transmission of knowledge of the "spirit of society" and benefit from local skills such as navigation. Once again one finds a picture of the perfect harmonization of interests more keenly hoped for than achieved. The policy advocated is much closer to a modern argument for "development" rather than treating the islands as a mere point to resupply passing ships. "If we are not mistaken," the chapter concludes, "this order of things would be better for Spain than a situation which reduces the Marianas to furnishing supplies to the ships which return from Mexico to the Philippines."[88] The double advantage serves as an illustration of the effort to break up the affective economy set up between anger and sweetness; it is yet another example of the effort to imagine the management of a contradiction set up between the imperative to empire along with the claim to a higher ethical position involved in the creation of happiness for a subject people.

* * *

Writing against the idea of a discrete domain of knowledge removed from the realms of affect that have occasionally been the focus of this chapter, Nietzsche quoted Goethe approvingly in a manner that parallels the spirit of Diderot's labor on the *Histoire des deux Indes*: "'Moreover

I hate everything which merely instructs me without increasing or directly quickening my activity.' These were Goethe's words with which, as with a boldly expressed *ceterum censeo*, we may begin our consideration of the worth and worthlessness of history. Our aim will be to show why instruction which fails to quicken activity, why knowledge which enfeebles activity, why history as a costly intellectual excess and luxury must, in the spirit of Goethe's words, be seriously hated."[89] These words open Nietzsche's work and authorize the critique of pure knowledge which he elaborates in the later pages of his essay. True, it is enmeshed in his preeminent concerns for "life" as a type of health or vitalism in its desire for "quickening activity." But by "hating" history of the antiquarian variety (used in his sense as that which "mummifies" and seals off from the present),[90] his thought lends support to the active engagement of critical consciousness with the significance of the past, especially with regard to its transformation for some futural end. Given the variety of images (some literal and drawn from the visual culture of the period, others figural and drawn from the imagination of writers like Mercier and Diderot) that pertain to the active use of the *Histoire* by someone like Toussaint Louverture (and here again the rumor of his reading may be as relevant as the unprovable fact, since it indicates a disposition or *ethos*), it seems only appropriate, indeed it seems hard to avoid thinking of the Haitian case when Nietzsche concludes his thought thus: "Certainly we need history. But our need for history is quite different from that of the spoiled idler in the garden of knowledge [*Garten des Wissens*], even if he in his refinement looks down on our rude and graceless requirements and needs. That is, we require history for life and action, not for the smug avoiding of life and action."[91] The urgency he gives to this relation, a need for history, is distinguished from the humanist's ideal of the garden of knowledge. We need not go so far as to impugn this humanist as a "spoiled idler" in order to take away the insight of Nietzsche's description. "Hating" this disposition, this form of knowledge was a means to ground the situated critique, the genealogical method that other readers of Nietzsche (such as Foucault) have elaborated and which may serve as an apologia for Diderot's aims during the furious final years of his life spent writing these passages for Raynal's work.

PART II

Edmund Burke: Political Analogy and Enlightenment Critique

3 / Between France and India in 1790: Custom and Arithmetic Reason in a Country of Conquest

> *For whoever has restricted their studies and observations only to France will, I venture to say, understand nothing of the French Revolution.*
> —ALEXIS DE TOCQUEVILLE, *THE ANCIEN RÉGIME AND THE FRENCH REVOLUTION* (1856)

Forget the Condorcets and Raynals

Let us cross over the English Channel and follow the current of popularity of the *Histoire des deux Indes* as it spread from France to one particular reader in Britain. This reader, already a noted member of Parliament and in the midst of his engagement with American affairs, found much to admire in that work. Indeed it may have aided him only a few years later in framing his indictment of the East India Company. If previous chapters examined Diderot's anticolonialism and its limits, here I turn to Edmund Burke's position regarding similar questions. This shift to Burke's critique of the East India Company considers what relation that critique bears to Diderot's contributions to the *Histoire des deux Indes*, a text Burke had in all likelihood read. There may in fact be a circularity to this reading since evidence suggests that Burke was himself the recipient of a *questionnaire* sent by the abbé de Raynal as he was compiling information regarding the English colonies for the *Histoire des deux Indes*.[1] We know for certain that Burke entertained Raynal at his home in Beaconsfield during the latter's visit to England in 1777 since he refers to the abbé in a letter to a friend.[2] Additionally Burke composed what appears to be a letter of introduction for Raynal during this visit and refers to the work that brought Raynal fame: "The person who will deliver you this [letter] is one of the most curious men and the best authors of this Age. It is the Abbe Raynal, who has written the celebrated Histoire philosophique et politicque des etablissemens Europeens aux Indes [sic]. Pray shew him, whilst he stays at Bristol, that attention, that his merit deserves, and you are so well disposed to pay to merit wherever you meet it."³ In spite of this praise, Raynal was in fact to let down his hosts by his very *lack* of curiosity.⁴ Years later Burke's disdain for the abbé was, however, made even more plain; soon after the publication of the *Reflections*, he wrote in a letter in 1791 to Claude-François de Rivarol of the situation in the Austrian Netherlands. With dire warnings for the future of the monarchy there, he observed:

> Would not prudence rather dictate to that great Sovereign, the surest mode of fortification? Would not prudence direct him . . . to fortify himself in the heart of his people, by repairing rather than by destroying those dykes and barriers, which prejudice might rise in his favour and which cost nothing to his treasury. . . . It were better to forget once for all, the *Encyclopedia* and the whole body of Economists and to revert to those old rules and principles which have hitherto made princes great and nations happy. . . . He will not care what the Condorcets and the Raynals, and the whole flight of the magpies and Jays of philosophy may fancy and chatter concerning his conduct and character.⁵

Raynal has become one among many intellectuals and philosophes, including Diderot and Condorcet, a flock of noisy birds whose calls for the implementation of various schemas and other forms of abstract thought would serve only as a failed counterpoint, as Burke saw it, to the "practical principles of a practical policy" (as he put it elsewhere in the same letter).⁶ Better to forget the *Encyclopédie* and the economists and follow the "those old rules" that were so soundly guided by prudence and allowed a sovereign to win over "the heart of his people."

In retrospect, Burke's long involvement with the affairs of the East India Company was a prominent component of his reputation in late eighteenth-century London, generating reports in the press, political cartoons, and several scandals. My focus is more on the logic of Burke's attack on Warren Hastings, head of the East India Company, who served as his object of legal and rhetorical ire, and how it sits beside the larger context of Enlightenment anticolonialism rather than these public and social aspects of what became Burke's impeachment effort. Nonetheless since it is the *Reflections on the Revolution in France* for which he is unfortunately most famously remembered, one often finds a flat and one-dimensional picture of Burke presented, featuring the *Reflections* as the clearest statement of his horror at the fate of the *ancien régime* in France.⁷

Burke, it is true, rarely argued against empire as such; instead he argued for the end of the East India Company's rule as it was then organized and for parliamentary oversight of its territories.[8] In Burke we find a conservative basis for a radical critique of the kind of imperialism being conducted under the auspices of Company rule—and perhaps this is another way to understand and extend Novalis's compelling observation of Burke: "There have been many anti-revolutionary books written for the revolution. Burke, however, has written a revolutionary book against the revolution."[9] Indeed, *mutatis mutandis*, one might say that there have been many revolutionary books written against colonialism, Burke, however, wrote a conservative book against it.

The French Revolution and India

It has been asserted by several scholars that Burke's uniqueness derives in part from his being a witness to the transition from an aristocratic to a bourgeois social order.[10] The unpredictability—as it was seen in his time and recurrently ever since—of his political judgments regarding the American Revolution, the revolution in France, and the abuses of the East India Company reflect his own precarious relationship to the elites in Britain at the time. Himself a product of the possibilities of a meritocracy opened up by transformations in British society, it is not surprising that we should find him expressing contradictory opinions on the social transformations occurring in the societies to which he gave his attention. However, it is crucial to ask how his status as a witness to the changing social transformations in France and England affected his writings on India and vice versa, since the *Reflections* is an eminently comparative text (and without question merits the epigraph I have culled from Tocqueville). The *Reflections*, after all, was written in 1790, in the middle of an impeachment trial conducted from 1787 to 1795 (over seven years). During the very same period Burke witnesses in India a transformation akin to the one he saw in France. I consider later in this chapter whether there are grounds to say that Burke misreads the Indian social order, seeing as aristocratic (in a reformed sense, based on his understanding of the Glorious Revolution in Britain) what is actually feudal. Drawing a parallel between the diverse kingdoms in India and the European aristocracy, does he end up defending the old order in India? Or perhaps he is forced to do this as a result of his desire to argue for the reform of Company rule in India.

My initiating question is a political and ideological one: What consistent set of beliefs, if any, allowed Burke to simultaneously hold the following views (and, I presume, not in bad faith): to lend eventual support to—or certainly express profound sympathy with—the decision of American colonists seeking their independence, to condemn the revolutionaries in France, and to attack the East India Company and its abuses in India? As a prologue to answering this larger question, I begin by considering an ensemble of three broad variables in Burke's thought from this period: his concern with the rapid social transformation of a society; in relation to this, the significance and meaning of the events of the French Revolution; and finally, how he assessed the transformation wrought by British colonialism in India. *Reflections on the Revolution in France* expresses one famous critique of Enlightenment rationalism, yet how does his apparently antirationalist stance derive from his reading of the political situation in France? Further, does this help explain his understanding of the Indian situation vis-à-vis the East India Company? In answering these questions I return to well-known moments in Burke's writings on France but which take on new valences when considered alongside his interest in India, such as the following passage from the heart of the *Reflections*:

> Society is indeed a contract. Subordinate contracts for objects of mere occasional interest may be dissolved at pleasure—but the state ought not to be considered as nothing better than a partnership agreement in a trade of pepper and coffee, callico or tobacco, or some other such low concern, to be taken up for a little temporary interest, and to be dissolved by the fancy of the parties. It is to be looked on with other reverence; because it is not a partnership in things subservient only to the gross animal existence of a temporary and perishable nature. It is a partnership in all science; a partnership in all art; a partnership in every virtue, and in all perfection.[11]

It hardly needs mentioning that this quip is at the heart of his disagreement with Rousseau's *Social Contract* (1762), written nearly three decades earlier; Burke is not fully willing to concede the validity of contractarian theories of society, if these imply that the foundation of the state rests upon them. The counterexample to the state that he gives, of a subordinate concern, is in effect a *colonial* one, which is "nothing better than a partnership agreement" in the commodities of pepper, coffee, calico, tobacco, and so on. Significantly, pepper and calico evoke the East Indies most immediately ("spice islands" and Calicut, etc.), while tobacco brings to mind the colonies in the New World (the Carolinas, Virginia).[12] We see compressed in one rhetorical flourish a theme I will explore in chapter 5: the conceptual proximity of the loss of the American colonies with the emerging importance of India and Asia more broadly to British interests.

Much of what Burke delved into regarding the East India Company's affairs in India was the gradual transformation of these "little, temporary interests" (many of which meant a great deal economically) into a territorial empire. Yet in his terms, this emphasis on commodities to be traded accounted for the absence of an analogue for the quality of "reverence" in the means of its governance. The opposition in Burke's language here is one between mere "contract" (regulating commercial society) and a higher "partnership" (governing the state), "fancy" and "reverence," mere animality and the higher human qualities of art and virtue. This is what Burke himself calls, in the paragraph before this, the "consecration of the state," which is greater than a mere system of consensual economic benefits for participating individuals at any given moment. His remarks relate to his interest in the "moral" project of empire.[13] It is moreover in this passage that Burke links his rejection of a social contract theory of society with his arguments concerning reverence by shifting the contract to an "intergenerational" one. Developing the idea of such a "partnership," he writes:

> As the ends of such a partnership cannot be obtained in many generations, it becomes a partnership not only between those who are living, but between those who are living, those who are dead, and those who are to be born. Each contract of each particular state is but a clause in the great primaeval contract of eternal society, linking the lower with the higher natures, connecting the visible and invisible world, according to a fixed compact sanctioned by the inviolable oath which holds all physical and all moral natures, each in their appointed place.[14]

From the observations on trade we have moved to the crux of Burke's argument against the revolutionaries in France and entered the web of terms he uses to weave this edifice together. By redefining the "partnership" (his preferred term) as one between generations, he diminishes the all-encompassing priority given to the intention and will of the revolutionaries, and he reinserts this within the "great primaeval contract" of an "eternal society." The "dead" and yet to be born, the "primaeval" and "eternal," the "higher" and the "invisible," all of these designations serve to push the discussion out of the realm of the immediate, to reduce the exclusive focus on the agency of "the living." Certainly they form part of the ideological structure that Burke famously puts in place to hold "each in their appointed place," as contemporary readers such as Wollstonecraft were quick to note.[15] The invocation of the "dead," however, also relates to the importance of the model of property inheritance upon which Burke relies to establish the foundation for the "ancient constitution."[16] Just as the constitution is inherited in a primeval manner, so too is the partnership. By introducing this temporal element, Burke breaks the implicit synchronic aspect of contract.[17] However, this diachrony actually trails away from the historical and into a shrouded antiquity. The *Reflections* thus relies on a set of keywords that form part of Burke's larger argument against Enlightenment universality and rationality; "reverence" and the "primaeval" are only two of a wider array of terms in this lexicon, some of whose other elements, such as "wisdom," are discussed below.

Where else does one find Burke's concern with India intruding upon his discussion of the French Revolution? If the passage cited earlier touches upon the colonial question through its reference to trade, an earlier question arises as he frames his attack on the unlimited powers that have been granted to the National Assembly in France, which he compares to the more balanced state that obtains in England's House of Commons: "The power of the house of commons, direct or indirect, is indeed great; and long may it be able to preserve its greatness, and the spirit belonging to true greatness, at the full; and it will do so, as long as it can keep the breakers of the law in India from becoming the makers of law for England."[18] These "breakers of the law in India" of course include Warren Hastings, in whose impeachment trial Burke was then engaged. (I develop his remark in the next chapter.) However, Burke's assertion also relies on a large body of anti–East India Company writing circulating in the British public sphere for several decades, whose staple figure is a greedy Nabob making his fortune in India and returning to Britain as a sort of contagion from the East. (Recall here the satiric sketch of Sir Matthew Mite by the playwright Samuel Foote cited in the introduction.)[19] Within the argument of the *Reflections*, therefore, Burke is making several points. First, the House of Commons is given as an example of an institution that embodies, in Burke's terms, a certain amount of inherited or "latent wisdom" (as he calls it elsewhere). The paragraph preceding the cited passage begins, "We know that the British house of commons, without shutting its doors to any merit in any class, is, by the sure operation of adequate causes, filled with every thing illustrious in rank, in descent, in hereditary and in acquired opulence, in cultivated talents . . . that the country can afford."[20] One fundamental difficulty Burke faced throughout his career was this tension between the notion of "merit" and the belief in the intrinsic value of inheritance or "descent," and this of course related in part to his own reliance on the idea of merit to achieve the station he had. The same difficulty arises in relation to the East India Company, since it too functioned primarily on the basis of merit and enabled a class mobility which Burke elsewhere criticizes. The possibility of success based on merit within Britain is, in fact, linked with Burke's analysis of why the revolution that took place in France is unlikely to occur in Britain. This unlikelihood derives from the fact that the Whig order in England has allowed for a greater "miscibility" between landed and monetary properties.[21] Whereas in this context that quality is mentioned as a source of strength for England, clearly too much "miscibility" may come to undermine England in the long run; it is precisely this social mingling that he attacks elsewhere when excoriating the dubiously enriched "boys" who return from India and marry into the old families of England.[22]

A Class on Probation?

Burke's primary discussion of the question of talent versus inheritance comes soon after his description of the House of Commons cited earlier. With the Earl of Holland in mind, he refers to "men of rank" who "sacrifice all ideas of dignity to an ambition without a distinct object." He has in mind the members of the gentry who, contrary to their "natural" interests, choose to ally themselves with a usurping class. Burke's first interest is to show in what way the Glorious Revolution in England was not like the French Revolution. In the English case, "these disturbers were not so much like men usurping power, as asserting their natural place in society. Their rising was to illuminate and beautify the world."[23] By describing the events in this manner, he shows that the social transformation is in fact a kind of restoration inasmuch as it is harmonious with a "natural order." In contrast, the revolution in France is frequently described as out of or beyond nature, even monstrous. It is a mere attempt at leveling a natural inequality. As he puts it, "Those who attempt to level, never equalize. In all societies, consisting of various descriptions of citizens, some description must be uppermost. The levellers therefore only change and pervert the natural order of things."[24] The natural order for Burke involves the recognition that certain tasks and vocations, certain types of labor render entire classes of people unfit for rule. His rationale is that only those with a certain degree of "leisure" can develop "wisdom." On this point he seems most frank: "The occupation of an hair-dresser, or of a working tallow-chandler, cannot be a matter of honour to any person—to say nothing of a number of other more servile employments. Such descriptions of men ought not to suffer oppression from the state; but the state suffers oppression, if such as they, either individually or collectively, are permitted to rule."[25]

FIGURE 2. James Gillray, "The Political Banditti Assailing the Saviour of India." Published May 11, 1786, by Willm Holland, No. 66 Drury Lane, London. Courtesy of The Lewis Walpole Library, Yale University. Warren Hastings, depicted in Oriental garb sitting serenely atop a camel, is attacked by Edmund Burke (with gun and a leather pouch labeled "charges"), Lord North (on whose scabbard are the words "American Subjugation" as he reaches for a bag of "Lacks of Rupees added to the Revenue"), and Charles James Fox (holding a dagger)

These were the statements that lay at the core of the Revolution Controversy in England.[26] Burke cites two verses from Ecclesiastes in support of this observation, and from this citation we can discern his definition of wisdom: "The wisdom of a learned man cometh by opportunity of leisure: and he that hath little business shall become wise"; and "How can he get wisdom that holdeth the plough, and that glorieth in the goad; that driveth oxen; and is occupied in their labours; and whose talk is of the bullocks?" It is important to note that by the time of this 1790 text, he had altered his view of leisure. In his 1757–59 text, *A Philosophical Enquiry into the Origin of Our Ideas of the Sublime and the Beautiful*, the prevalent view of leisure pertained to its corrupting effects, to the sloth and lethargy it could induce. These were in opposition to the manly vigor associated with the experience of the Sublime.[27] It was perhaps this implicit alteration that led him to his more complicated notion of merit. Anticipating the charge that he was defending the straightforward exclusion of entire classes, he writes, "You do not imagine that I wish to confine power, authority, and distinction to blood, and names, and titles. No, Sir." His alternative is then proposed as the median of two extremes: "Woe to the country which would madly and impiously reject the service of the talents and virtues... that are given to grace and serve it.... Woe to that country too, that passing into the opposite extreme, consider a low education, a mean contracted view of things... as preferable title to command. Every thing ought to be open; but not indifferently to every man."[28] In a sense, Burke is describing himself. "If rare merit be the rarest of all rare things," he writes, "it ought to pass through some sort of probation." This idea of a *class on probation* catches Burke's own ambivalent relation as an anglicized Irishman to the elite order in Britain, as well as elucidating the ideological compromise he seeks to lay out between the people of "ability" and those of "property." It was the latter who were under siege and needed to be protected from the prowess and power of the former: "But as ability is a vigorous and active principle, and as property is sluggish, inert, and timid, it never can be safe from the invasions of ability, unless it be, out of all proportion, predominant in the representation."[29] The masculine associations of Burke's description of ability in contrast to the vulnerable state of property parallel the descriptions of the violation of Marie-Antoinette at the hands of the revolutionaries, and this is indeed what he has in mind. It is part of my argument that what disturbs the text of the *Reflections* is a double anxiety, of which most commentators generally notice only one or the other component: the first is the fundamental and obvious anxiety regarding the spread of revolutionaries in France upon a volatile English population represented by Dr. Price; the second is a fear of the upstart English men of ability who (and this is another connection to empire in his thought) bypass the natural restrictions they would face if they remained in England by going to the colonies to amass their fortunes and influence. If, as Disraeli would later famously write in his novel *Tancred*, "the East is a career," then empire already provided in Burke's view a pivotal field for these dangerous men of ability to emerge.[30] The vulnerability of property, *outnumbered* by the vigor and activity of ability, is another reason why Burke formulates his critique of the tyranny of number. Number in this case implies a political principle expressed by one-to-one representation, between one citizen (to use the French term about whose meaning Burke worried) and his right—his, for this is before the period of universal suffrage—to express his view through a representative in some political body. When Burke argues that property must therefore be represented in such political bodies "out of all proportion," that is, to a far greater degree than the numerical number of citizens who happen to hold this property would suggest, we are already being given a version of what he will with aspersion call "arithmetic reason." I will return to this concept shortly, but here I note the more direct disagreement with the idea of numerical representation which Burke asserts.

A separate point I would like to make concerns the idea of merit in Burke's thought. His aim in this passage, and in his interpretation of the meaning of the Glorious Revolution in England, is to demonstrate how the "threat" of men of ability is defused by their incorporation within the landed classes. This diminishes the possibility of a revolution in England, Burke argues. Yet when he addresses the abuses of the East India Company, he becomes much less favorable toward the defense of merit and men of ability. He is far more critical of the effects of this upstart class, as his exclamation of fear regarding their entry into the House of Commons indicates. The same contradiction applies to his critique of natural right and law. Regarding the "declaration of the rights of man" he is famously dismissive of the idea of abstract right. Yet in relation to Hastings's crimes in Bengal, he is fervent in his pursuit of the idea (to paraphrase him) that a crime in Bengal is no different from a crime in England. We see here a tension between the universalism he disavows and attributes to the French philosophes in the case of rights and its subsequent reinvocation in the Hastings trial as regards the question of justice. This is but one instance of how Burke walked along the treacherously thin line between Enlightenment universalism and the particularities of colonial knowledge.

One comes upon, then, one of the central contradictions of Burke's thought. As already noted, part of his praise for English society is based on the "miscibility" he finds between the landed and propertied wealth.[31] He argues that one motive for the revolution in France was the desire by certain elements to turn money into landed property, from which they were excluded because of the closed nature of the French landed classes. But miscibility is also the cause of the problem when he examines the impact of the colonies on British society, and he is at pains in that context to limit its effects.

Inheritance is not incidental to this argument and ties it to one of the primary themes of the political prose of this period, namely the relationship between property and "virtue."[32] Burke argues that the possibility of passing on, of transmitting property within a family is a goad to virtue and turns the energies that are expended in accumulation toward sounder aims. "The power of perpetuating our property in our families," he writes, "is one of the most valuable and interesting circumstances.... It makes our weakness subservient to our virtue; it grafts benevolence even upon avarice."[33] Virtue is sustained by the knowledge that one can accumulate or make good gains, and then pass these gains on. Burke's relationship to debates in political economy more generally in the period can account for why he should ground his moral theory of action within the order of a property regime. (Indeed political economy was not sharply distinct from moral speculations.)[34] But the easy compatibility between virtue and greed, the grafting of benevolence upon avarice—this thesis would be put under strain in Burke's examination of the abuses of the East India Company. As this chapter examines, what he is willing to concede—or even posit as a basic framework for his analysis—in the European context of the Glorious Revolution he is unwilling or unable to grant in relation to the merchant's operations in India.

Custom and Sympathy in Burke's Writings on India and France

Manners

In an influential reading of Burke's analysis of the French Revolution, J. G. A. Pocock has argued for the priority of the category of "manners" in understanding the uniqueness of Burke's intellectual position. In attempting to name the nature of Burke's analysis, Pocock chooses to employ the term *political economy* as it was used in the period "to denote a more complex, and more ideological, enterprise aimed at establishing the moral, political, cultural, and economic conditions of life in advancing commercial societies."[35] Burke's concern, then, is to defend "a commercial humanism" represented by a Whig aristocratic government that guarded over its development. Contrary to other understandings of the Whig regime, Pocock argues that it was founded on an "assumed identity of interests between a managerial landed aristocracy and a system of public credit, in which rentier investment in government stock stimulated commercial prosperity, political stability, and national and imperial power."[36] Commerce was understood to refine the passions of the citizen and polish his or her manners. Manners, in turn, were understood to be a bulwark against the explosive power of "enthusiasm," which was associated with revolutionary sentiments.

It is important to understand Burke's reliance on the concept of manners in order to see the basis of his stance against the revolutionaries in France. In 1785 Burke had visited Glasgow as lord rector of its university and met with John Millar and later with Adam Smith in Edinburgh. It is likely from them that he took on the four-stage theory of development, in which the human race was understood to progress through the diversification of labor leading to the refinement of its manners.[37] Linked to the specificity of European feudalism, manners emerge as a revolution within the rise of chivalry by which "barbarian warriors had begun to civilize themselves, to acquire more polished and humane modes of conduct towards the weak, the female and one another, and to promote the increased circulation of material goods and the skills entailed in producing them."[38] However, where the Scottish thinkers imply that manners are dependent on commerce, Burke in effect argues the opposite, namely that manners are prior to and a foundation for the possibility of commerce: "If, as I suspect, modern letters owe more than they are always willing to own to antient manners, so do other interests which we value full much as they are worth. Even commerce, and trade, and manufacture, the gods of oeconomical politicians, are themselves perhaps but creatures; are themselves but effects, which, as first causes, we choose to worship."[39] Commerce and other fundamentals are here reduced to epiphenomena of a deeper cause. The preconditions for the growth of commerce that Burke identifies (in contrast, certainly, with most French philosophes' thinking on the subject of commerce) are clerical learning and feudal chivalry. Thus overthrowing the clergy and the nobility undermines the very possibility of commerce. The effect of the revolution is the destruction of "civility," which has more than cosmetic implications. It is by means of this progress of manners that Burke builds his narrative of Enlightenment, and it is a consequence of this belief that he has a much different relation to the idea of tradition than the French philosophes, since manners, custom, habit, and so on are one repository for a society's collective memory—superstitions in the eyes of some, but vital components in the arts of memory for another.

The primary importance of this reading of Burke is the stress it puts on the idea of manners in his thought and how one can understand his differences from Scottish thinking on the same topic at the time. It also accounts for why Burke argued against the transformations intentionally or accidentally effected by the East India Company upon Indian society. Since manners are fundamental and connected with two institutions (the church, the feudal order), he argues against their abolition in France. The advancement of commerce is seen to rely on the progress of manners, and not vice versa, as the Scottish thinkers asserted. Because commerce is viewed as having a refining and polishing effect on society, it can consequently be argued that Burke was not merely defending feudal interests in India and hoping to preserve an indigenous elite but saw this defense as the only means to preserve the customs and manners of this society—essential not only on culturalist grounds but also perhaps for economic reasons in enabling commerce. With France in mind he writes, "Manners are of more importance than laws.... According to their equality, they aid morals, they supply them, or they totally destroy them. Of this the new French legislators were aware."[40] Manners are thus central to Burke's defense of "commercial humanism," which he poses against the aims of the revolutionaries. Commercial Britain was to be the bulwark against this tendency.[41]

Custom as Supplement to Nature

However, it is also clear that manners and custom serve another function in Burke's thought, aside from their imbrication within a larger set of discourses in the period. I shift the discussion here from "manners" to "custom," but these serve similar purposes in supplementing Burke's reliance on the idea of reason or nature. One study of the *Sublime and Beautiful* in relation to the *Reflections* argues, "In the *Reflections*, in order to protect the hegemonic alliance in Britain between money and land, Burke habitually resorts to second nature, custom, manners, and so on, as 'happy auxiliaries' to nature or reason. Although he tries to ground his ideological claims in nature, he also stresses the necessity of supplementing nature with a custom and habit which will yet, as 'second nature,' become a part of nature."[42] Custom is a supplement to the idea of nature and is itself part of a series of terms that operate in opposition to a category that is understood to be more objective, such as reason or nature. Tom Furniss, the author of this passage, interprets this in terms of the ideological debate in which Burke is involved. Like his radical antagonists, Burke is caught "between two desires or needs: he seeks to establish a 'natural' foundation (labor, physiology, land, etc.) for validating or stabilizing the new historical role of the middle class, but this opens up his thought to dangers which compel him to have recourse to a system of conventions (taste, custom, the law, and so on) which would seem to undermine the 'natural' ground of his position."[43] In the case of Burke's involvement with Indian affairs, we must ask: Does he increase his reliance on custom to defend indigenous society against the East India Company? Or does he ground his arguments in a natural foundation or on a more empirical basis?

Cosmopolitan Sympathy and Custom

A central strategy of Burke's writings on India relies on evoking the sympathy of Parliament for a faraway land, though he was well aware of the difficulty of this gesture. "We are in general," he wrote, " . . . so little acquainted with Indian details, the instruments of oppression under which the people suffer are so hard to be understood, and even the very names of the sufferers are so uncouth and strange to our ears, that it is very difficult for our sympathy to fix upon these objects."[44] The necessity of a "sympathy for the stranger" underlies both his "Speech on Fox's East India Bill" and his later writings during the impeachment trial of Warren Hastings. The trial is an exercise in an *interested*, partisan effort in what we might call "cosmopolitan sympathy." Earlier I showed the centrality of custom in Burke whose effect is twofold: it leads him to defend a feudal order in India, but it also makes him take on an anti-Company position, at times verging on an anticolonial one. Since part of my aim is to explore what the possibilities *and limits* of an anticolonial position in this period were, the enigma of this twofold effect will recur.

Manners and custom in Burke's thought therefore need to be thought of in relation to cosmopolitan sympathy. Both terms are in themselves categories that designate difference: they indicate what is proper, what is *singular* about a people. In fact they are precisely about the utter singularity of a "culture."[45] Culture, in these terms, is understood as an ensemble of customs. This exists in tension with Enlightenment universalism, which aims at assimilating the various singularities into one larger narrative of progress, as the thinkers of the Scottish Enlightenment seemed to propose. Manners relate to cosmopolitan sympathy in the following manner: sympathy, an aesthetic faculty, is required and made use of to overcome the utter singularity of manners. This is at work in Burke's "Speech on Fox's East India Bill" in the moments of translation of all foreign elements into the familiar. The speech presents a series of analogies in its efforts to render familiar what lies outside Europe. This is accomplished by resorting to geographical data that make up Burke's picture of the Company's possessions in India. Burke writes:

> In the northern parts it is a solid mass of land, about eight hundred miles in length, and four or five hundred broad. As you go southward, it becomes narrower for a space. It afterwards dilates; but narrower or broader, you possess the whole eastern and north-eastern coast of that vast country, quite from the borders of Pegu.—Bengal, Bahar, and Orissa, with Benares, . . . measure 161,978 square

English miles; a territory considerably larger than the whole kingdom of France. Oude, with its dependent provinces, is 53,286 square miles, not a great deal less than England. The Carnatick, with Tanjour and the Circars, is 65,948 square miles, very considerably larger than England.... Through all that vast extent of country there is not a man who eats a mouthful of rice but by permission of the East India company.[46]

The square mileages allow Burke to commensurate the Indian territories with European counterparts (France, England, and—rather interestingly—Germany) and to remind the listener of the great extent of these possessions.[47] The reference to the man who eats the mere "mouthful of rice" within this "vast extent of country" introduces the representation of the East India Company as the despot, a fundamental part of Burke's rhetorical arsenal against Hastings and the Company. Significantly, the image also resonates with another moment in the *Reflections* where Burke decries the carving up of France by the revolutionaries into new *départements*, ignoring the long-existing historical regions. Even in the French case, however, he may have had in mind the radical effects he had already observed in Bengal with the imposition of new districts, new forms of assessing property taxes, and so on.

"The Vessel of the Commonwealth"

It is only apt that Burke should turn to a nautical and maritime language in his figuration of the British state, whose interests in colonial and mercantile operations were to expand so greatly in this period. In this language he expresses an ideological resolution of the contradiction between the "sluggishness" of property referred to earlier with the principle of a steady forward movement. The volatility of the House of Commons that prompted him to make his remark concerning the "breakers of law in India" leads him to turn to the House of Lords as a further validation of the principle of inheritance and the transmission of property. "It is wholly composed of hereditary property and hereditary distinction," he writes, and returns to the other house: "The house of commons too, though not necessarily, yet in fact, is always so composed in the far greater part. Let those large proprietors be what they will, and they have their chance of being amongst the best, they are at the very worst, the ballast in the vessel of the commonwealth."[48] Following the logic of Burke's earlier remarks on the compromise struck between "men of ability" and "men of land," the quality of "sluggishness" ascribed to land earlier is metonymically displaced to the quality of weightiness in this passage. Whereas earlier landed wealth was slow and heavy, here it is transmuted into the "ballast" in the "vessel of the commonwealth." Its demerit in the earlier case is transformed into a virtue in the present use. To be clear regarding the suggestion made earlier about the possible biographical implications of Burke's pronouncements, in this passage he is not describing himself but rather the large property owners who, at worst, provide a degree of inertia and stability to the "course" of the state. It is an image that lends credence to a passing observation made by Foucault in his discussion of the transformation of the idea and aims of government in the eighteenth century: "The fact that government concerns things understood in this way, this imbrication of men and things, is I believe readily confirmed by the metaphor which is inevitably invoked in these treatises on government, namely that of the ship."[49] Burke's remark is, however, not the only appearance of this image in the text, and the second usage contains some revealing differences. It is to be found, significantly, in the ultimate paragraph of the *Reflections*, which also contains the only other indirect reference to Burke's involvement in the impeachment proceedings.

The *Reflections*, it will be remembered, were prompted by a letter from "a very young gentleman at Paris, who did him the honor of desiring his opinion upon the important transactions, which then, and ever since, have so much occupied the attention of men."[50] Periodically throughout the text and at the end, the reader is reminded of the original circumstances of this composition, which Burke chose to retain even when he became aware that such a lengthy reply and "full discussion" would warrant its being published.[51] The final paragraph, then, turns away from the object of inquiry and to the one conducting it, namely Burke himself. The *Reflections* is both the prose of an ending and of someone "reflecting" not just on the revolution in France but on himself late in his life. How does Burke characterize his own life? First he makes a contrast between the addressee and addressor of the *Reflections*. He establishes a prophetic element to his writing by alluding in the penultimate paragraph to the recipient as witness to a future he himself will not see: "You are young; you cannot guide, but must follow the fortune of your country. But hereafter they [the *Reflections*] may be of some use to you, in some future form which your commonwealth may take." Burke's self-characterization follows upon this:

> I have little to recommend my opinions, but long observation and much impartiality. They come from one who has been no tool of

power, no flatterer of greatness; and who in his last acts does not wish to belye the tenour of his life. They come from one, almost the whole of whose public exertion has been a struggle for the liberty of others; from one in whose breast no anger durable or vehement has ever been kindled, but by what he considered as tyranny; and who snatches from his share in the endeavors which are used by good men to discredit opulent oppression, the hours he has employed on your affairs; and who in so doing persuades himself he has not departed from his usual office ... from one who wishes to preserve consistency by varying his means to secure the unity of his end; and, when the equipoise of the vessel in which he sails, may be endangered by overloading it upon one side, is desirous of carrying the small weight of his reasons to that which may preserve its equipoise.[52]

There are two aspects of this passage that merit further examination. First, the reference to himself as one who "has been no tool of power" may refer to the difficulties he brought to the Whig Party in undertaking the highly unpopular impeachment. Among his "last acts," this was the one for which he hoped to be remembered. The unifying element in his various engagements he names as a battle against "tyranny." More specifically he refers to himself as taking time away from the impeachment trial—against the instigator of an "opulent oppression"—to write about French affairs, both of which relate to his "struggle for the liberty of others." However, he adds that in doing this he has not departed from his "usual office." The apparent contradiction of impeaching the head of the East India Company for its abuses in India and his prior sympathy with the decision of American colonists to revolt—these two positions may seem "inconsistent" with his unambiguous condemnation of the revolutionaries in France. It is this charge to which Burke is replying when he writes that he wishes to "preserve consistency by varying the means to secure the unity of his end." It is here, perhaps more than anywhere else in the *Reflections*, that the proximity of these two events—the revolution in France and the British involvement in India—are yoked together. The third term, superadded to this dyad, is certainly England itself. In effect, one could argue that the real concerns with social transformations in France and India are derived from his more primary worry over British society. The title of the *Reflections*, after all, on the cover page of the first London edition was *Reflections on the Revolution in France, and on the proceedings in certain societies in London relative to that event*. To my mind what this indicates is not that Britain exceeds the other two places in importance as sources of Burke's concern but rather that he is able to grasp the emergence of a set of *common* transformations in each of these contexts not apparent at first glance.

The second aspect worth noting from the passage is the transformation of "the ballast" that Burke had invoked much earlier in the text. The first use arose, as noted, in his discussion of merit and of the benefits of property inheritance. The interests of landed wealth, of the propertied classes who become so by inheritance, are represented as the ballast in the vessel of the state. Burke does not identify himself with the ballast; rather it is the class of property owners who are identified with it. Yet in the second reference to the "vessel" that appears in the final paragraph, Burke locates himself as the counterweight that preserves the vessel's "equipoise." In the former reference, "property" is the "weight," whereas in the latter, reason (Burke's reasoning) serves as a *counterweight*. The operation of the latter expresses the ideological resolution of his relationship to the propertied class and the revolutionaries both in Britain and France: he serves as the counterweight that works in conjunction with the ballast to guide the ship of the state. This reading, interpreting the image as an allegory of class alliances, brings out Burke's fraught relationship to the idea of "liberty" which he claims as his guiding principle.[53] That this image should appear alongside his discussion of India is neither coincidence nor the result of fortuitous juxtaposition. It shows that the sudden acquisition of property in Britain by India-returned company officials was also a threat to the "equipoise" of the vessel, for the way to money has been made too easy. There is no longer any real period of testing or "probation." One of the causes of the French Revolution Burke identifies is the desire of the revolutionaries to convert their newly acquired wealth into land, and in India (as it relates to Britain) Britain is producing a class with the same impulse. The *Reflections* fears both the Nabobs and the auditors of Dr. Price's radical sermons, both the overly eager men of ability and the restive urban laboring classes.

All of the images of weighty ships in Burke's texts, the "vessels of the commonwealth," are in contrast to the weightlessness of France after the revolution.[54] The "firm ground of the British constitution" contrasts with "the desperate flights of the aëronauts of France."[55] These oppositions at the level of rhetoric also align with his economic analysis regarding the paper money printed by the revolutionaries in contrast with the solidity and weightiness of (aptly named) English pounds.[56] Burke's bias in terms of the political economy of the period was the Physiocratic one: in the end the wealth of England is validated by the ownership of land, or property. Land is a more authentic source of value. Returning to Disraeli's observation on the East as a "career," one finds that it was a space that

Burke saw as producing a class of people not unlike the revolutionaries in France: enfranchised in the economic sphere, endowed with ability, and likely therefore to threaten the delicate balance in England between these two elements and the interests of property.

A Colonial Occupation of France?

If it still seems unpersuasive to claim that Burke saw a similarity between the revolutionaries in France and those who worked for the East India Company, I would point to a distinct argument he made that also supports this linkage: he depicts the revolutionaries' siege of France as a *colonial occupation*. There is repeatedly a shift in the *Reflections* between the French-British axis of comparison to a French-Indian one, or perhaps it would be more accurate to say more generally a French-colonial axis. Taking issue with the principle of division used by the National Assembly to demarcate the different departments within France, Burke writes, "It is impossible not to observe, that in the spirit of this geometrical distribution, and arithmetical arrangement, these pretended citizens treat France exactly like a country of conquest. Acting as conquerors, they have imitated the policy of the harshest of that harsh race."[57] It is striking that he should choose to portray the revolutionaries as illegitimate conquerors. Certainly this comparison was made to reply to readers who would have expected him to defend the revolutionaries—he who had after all written so passionately for conciliation with the Americans in their revolt against England.[58] In this figuration, the French revolutionaries are analogous to the English army, understood as imposing by force on America what ought to be accomplished politically or diplomatically. The other implicit parallel is that the *ancien régime* is intentionally allowed to blur with the occupied territory and people, in America represented by the various settler communities. This element of the comparison is manifestly less persuasive since it depicts the monarchy as a group wronged in the same manner as the European settlers in America.

That many contemporary readers felt Burke, if anyone, would have supported the French revolutionaries based on his previous opinion of the American Revolution can be gauged from one famous response to his work. "Had you been a Frenchman," Mary Wollstonecraft wrote, "you would have been, in spite of your respect for rank and antiquity, a violent revolutionist. . . . Your imagination would have taken fire. . . . And, for the English constitution, you might not have had such a profound veneration as you have lately acquired; nay, it is not impossible that you might have entertained the same opinion of the English Parliament, that you professed to have during the American war."⁵⁹ This sense of betrayal was expressed in *The Vindication of the Rights of Men* (1790), where she perceived an apparent contradiction that many of Burke's readers must have felt on the appearance of the *Reflections*. Thomas Paine's fascinating letter from January 17, 1790, also reflects a presumed sharing of views with Burke regarding France. Paine, who had met Burke in 1787 in England in relation to his proposal to construct an iron bridge of his own design, begins his letter with a description of one such bridge before discussing his perception of politics in France during his visit. "The revolution in France," he writes without awareness of Burke's worries, "is certainly a Forerunner to other Revolutions in Europe.—Politically considered it is a new Mode of forming Alliances affirmatively with Countries and negatively with Courts.—There is no foreign Court... that could now be fond of attacking France; they are afraid of their Armies and Subjects catching the Contagion." It was precisely against the contagion of Jacobinism that Burke was to direct his efforts. Paine also refers to a discrepancy between reports on France within England and his own sense: "The English Newspapers continue to hold out the probability of a Counter-Revolution in France.—Where the Power is to come from that is to work this counter-Revolution, I have no idea of." In Paine's estimation, the calculation of those made content by the transformations in France outweigh those discontented; it is striking that Paine should turn to the very type of arithmetic tabulation whose basis Burke was to attack in his *Reflections*. "That there are many who are discontented, such as the high Clergy and Pensioners; and other of that Stamp is very certain," Paine writes, "but as the measures which discontent them take away their power of doing Mischief, and gratifies at least twenty for every one that it displeases... their discontents amount to nothing." Twenty gratified for one discontented, and that one a rogue in Paine's eyes. "Almost every thing related in the English papers as happening in Paris is either untrue or misrepresented," began this engineer in explaining to Burke that what "the English papers call Military Law" was actually "somewhat similar to your Riot Act."⁶⁰ I mention these examples from Paine's letter of 1790 to emphasize how pivotal the break announced by Burke in his *Reflections* was to many English readers.

In the American Revolution, Burke eventually agreed with the less dominant American settlers in their demands to establish a regime or government of their own, independent of the British Empire; in fact he went so far as to see this impulse for autonomy in American settlers as a manifestation of the English love of freedom. One might expect him to therefore view the *ancien régime* in France with the same suspicion that he viewed British actions in America (as militaristic and inflexible). However, for Burke the *ancien régime* in France is actually more akin to the American settler communities, and the revolutionaries in France are in fact aggressors, an occupying army. It was for this apparent "inconsistency" in his views that Burke was mocked in the press and to which he was replying (in the final paragraph from *Reflections* cited earlier) when he defended his "opinions" as issuing from one "who would preserve consistency by varying his means to secure the unity of his end."[61]

For a moment, let us ask the question his adversaries must have asked. Is it not the case that rather than seeing the revolutionaries as laying siege like a band of outsiders to a territory, the *ancien régime* before them too was merely an occupier? Why was the *ancien régime* any better? Burke gives a manifold answer to this question. Again, it is tempting to see here that Burke's vision of India shapes his view of France, though it will be more exact to consider what other examples of "conquerors" he has in mind aside from the English in America and India in formulating this example.[62]

"Colonies of the Rights of Men," or Arithmetic Reason in the Colony

Why the *ancien régime* is superior to the revolutionaries in France in respect of governance has to do with their relation to "custom." Burke's fixation with geometry and arithmetic throughout the *Reflections* forms a part of the same argument. What in fact prompts his comment on the revolutionaries' treatment of France as a country of conquest is the "arbitrary" and mathematically grounded creation of distinct "cantons" (to use Burke's disparaging term, evocative both of the Swiss confederation but also the more primary if obsolete association with angle and angularity) into which France is divided by the revolutionaries. This is the "spirit of geometric distribution" to which he refers. Unfailingly, whenever he refers to arithmetic terms it is always pejorative. The tyranny of number is in some cases one of Burke's ways of containing an electoral argument for democracy: "It is said, that twenty-four millions ought to prevail over two hundred thousand. True; if the constitution be a problem of arithmetic."[63] In this passage, the "twenty-four millions" refers to the population of the country of Britain as a whole, while the "two hundred thousand" refers to the small number of propertied families. Against such overwhelming odds, it is not surprising that Burke took no refuge in numbers. But there is also the tendency in his thought to reduce the fundamental impulses of democratic thought to such hyperrationalist reasons in order to occlude the other grounds upon which such claims for greater enfranchisement may have been made. As in his analysis of the French Revolution, the initially dominant group (those associated with the *ancien régime*) is depicted as vulnerable, threatened by a mob of 24 million, or as he uncharitably calls them elsewhere, the "swinish multitude."[64] Here he aims to protect the British constitution from arithmetic, but the same principle (an opposition to arithmetic rationality) refers to the land and geography of Britain. Land, for Burke, is one of the ways a society "remembers."[65] The previous citation on the constitution and the following one both come from the first part of the *Reflections*, where Burke is primarily responding to Price and is therefore more focused on the implications of the revolution for the state of affairs in Britain. He asks, "Is our monarchy to be annihilated, with all the laws, all the tribunals, and all the antient corporations of the Kingdom? *Is every land-mark of the country to be done away in favour of a geometrical and arithmetical constitution? Is the house of lords to be voted useless?*"[66] Burke supplies a vinculum between the question of land and the constitution. The arbitrary abolition of the landmarks of the country based on a geometric logic is tantamount to throwing out the ancient constitution. If this leap of reasoning seems dubious, one need only return to the second half of the *Reflections*, where the creation of new cantons in France by the revolutionaries is part of the way the "conquerors" rename "the country of conquest." The contrast is between an old order that respected the natural division and organization of land and a new one that formulates this organization according to a mathematical rationalism disregarding local particularities and congealed loyalties. The new order of "geometry and arithmetic" for Burke is a product of unnatural or artificial reason, not unlike the idea of "instrumental reason" proposed by Theodor Adorno and Max Horkheimer, as a glance at the opening pages of the *Dialectic of Enlightenment* illustrates: "For the Enlightenment, whatever does not conform to the rule of computation and utility is suspect." The paragraph ends with their stark assertion "Enlightenment is totalitarian."[67]

In this regard one ought to compare Burke's critique of the philosophes, and of the Enlightenment more generally, with those that have emerged (for different reasons) in more recent critical discussions.[68] In particular, elements of Burke's critique seems to anticipate Adorno and Horkheimer's description of Enlightenment reason as instrumental reason. It is a manifest irony to make this claim knowing that Burke represents a political position possibly at the other end of the spectrum from the Hegelian Marxism of these members of the Frankfurt school. But it is worth comparing the similarity of the reading they make of

Francis Bacon and British thought more generally in the *Dialectic of Enlightenment* (1944) with Burke's understanding of the radical French philosophes (who were of course indebted to Bacon and other British thinkers).[69] As an instance of this circulation of ideas, and perhaps even terms passing from Bacon to Burke, consider their critique of the function of formal logic to Enlightenment thought:

> According to Bacon, too, degrees of universality provide an unequivocal logical connection between first principles and observational judgments.... Formal logic was the major school of unified science. It provided the Enlightenment thinkers with the schema of the *calculability of the world*. The mythologizing equation of Ideas with numbers in Plato's last writings expresses the longing of all demythologization: number became the canon of the Enlightenment. The same equations dominate bourgeois justice and commodity exchange.[70]

The emphasis on the dominance of number, and on calculability, is their focus, and they trace the expansion of these principles beyond their original spheres of application. They then cite lines from Bacon's *Advancement of Learning* that echo Burke's remarks, though Bacon meant these lines as a positive assertion, whereas for Burke this is a problem to be pondered: "Is not the rule, '*Si inaequalibus aequalia addas, omnia erunt inaequalia*,' an axiom of justice as well as of the mathematics? And is there not a true coincidence between commutative and distributive justice, and arithmetical and geometrical proportion?"[71] In Bacon's reference to arithmetical and geometrical proportion (moving from the domains of mathematics to the sphere of justice and ethics—perhaps politics?) we find introduced the same pair of terms that Burke will take aim against. However, Adorno and Horkheimer adduce these lines to illustrate the principle of equivalence that is made possible by this abstraction. It is this equivalence of all in bourgeois society that enables the rift between myth or "literature" and positivism or "science": "Bourgeois society is ruled by equivalence. It makes the dissimilar comparable by reducing it to abstract quantities. To the Enlightenment, that which does not reduce to number, and ultimately to the one, becomes illusion; modern positivism writes it off as literature."[72] With Burke, the "blame" for the rise of geometric reason lies with the abstraction immanent in French thought; for Adorno and Horkheimer, instrumental reason (while an internal element in Western rationality all along) becomes most visible in early English empiricist thought, in a trajectory that begins in this era and runs through to logical positivism in the twentieth century.[73] The possibility of this analysis has to do, in part, with the interchangeability in Frankfurt school usage of the terms *Enlightenment* with *civilization*, both of which implied the "domination of nature."[74]

There is reason, however, to see Burke as anticipating elements of a critique of Enlightenment thought that is more clearly articulated later on. The view of reason itself as bearing some relationship to a "colonizing" impulse, common to much postmodern thought (to a fault, perhaps), is akin to Burke's view of the philosophes. I discussed in the prologue the limitations of viewing all forms of knowledge collection as expressions of an inherently colonizing impulse, a consequence of the debates that were provoked by the appearance of Said's *Orientalism* in 1978. With particular reference to Napoleon's production and use of the *Description of Egypt* (published in 1810–26), Said convincingly argued, drawing on Foucault, for the link between such forms of knowledge and colonial power.[75] This encyclopedic impulse has often since been understood to be panoptical, necessarily linked with dominance in all such cases. Yet as I attempt to argue in my chapters on Diderot's contributions to Raynal's encyclopedic *Histoire des deux Indes*, the encyclopedic impulse can cut both ways in order to produce, in the latter case, a work that is (albeit inconsistently) an *anticolonial* encyclopedia.

In the case of Burke, the linkage between reason and a colonizing impulse has a different motive; it forms part of his defense of manners and custom. Previously the "mixed system of opinion and sentiment" that "had its origin in antient chivalry ... gave its character to modern Europe." It was this which "compelled stern authority to submit to elegance ... to be subdued by manners." The revolution alters this self-regulating system entirely, causing the disciplining function of manners to disappear: "But now all is to be changed. All the pleasing illusions, which made power gentle, and obedience liberal, which harmonized the different shades of life, and which, by a bland assimilation, incorporated into politics the sentiments which beautify and soften private society, are to be dissolved by *this new conquering empire of light and reason*. All the decent drapery of life is to be rudely torn off."[76] Mocking the language of light and illumination beloved of the philosophes and yoking it to the conquest of an empire that he described earlier, Burke brings out the violence latent in the otherwise cold forms of geometric rationality. In this passage, oft commented on, he conjures an image of manners as creating a utopic noncoercive state of hegemony (in Gramsci's sense) where "obedience" is gained without force.[77] Indeed other readers of Burke such as Pocock have found this concept of manners to be a central component of his social thought and have tried to elucidate it rather than limning its ideological contours in a manner that might limit it.⁷⁸

"Strangers to One Another"

It is significant that Burke should elaborate his critique of what I shall anachronistically call instrumental reason in the same passage where he identifies the revolutionaries as belonging to the "harsh race" of conquerors. With these examples pertaining to "arithmetic reason" from other parts of the text in mind,⁷⁹ I return to his description of the tactics used by the revolutionaries in their "colony" in order to introduce Burke's discussion of "population" and the "abstracted citizen." Having made the comparison between the revolutionaries as colonizers, Burke enumerates the means of subjugation:

> The policy of such barbarous victors, who contemn a subdued people, and insult their feelings, has ever been as much as in them lay, to destroy all vestiges of the antient country, in religion, in polity, in laws, and in manners; to confound all territorial limits; to produce a general poverty; to put up their properties to auction; to crush their princes, nobles, and pontiffs; to lay low every thing which had lifted its head above the level, or which could serve to combine or rally, in their distresses, the disbanded people, under the standard of old opinion.⁸⁰

Reading this passage, it would be easy to assume that Burke also has the East India Company's abuses in India in mind; indeed many of these charges repeat aspects of his characterization of the Company in the "Speech on Fox's East India Bill," written four years earlier.⁸¹ We begin to see already one answer to the question as to what set of beliefs might underlie his unusual position to defend the monarchy in France and to attack the merchants of the Company. However, Burke evokes a different basis for his observation, anchored in Roman history: "They [the revolutionaries] have made France free in the manner in which those sincere friends to the rights of mankind, the Romans, freed Greece, Macedon, and other nations. They destroyed the bonds of their union, under color of providing for the independence of each of their cities." What Burke hits upon are the contradictions implicit in the idea of a republic versus that of an empire. He attempts to unmask the claims made by the revolutionaries on the term *republic* by arguing that they operate in France like the latter: as an empire or imperial power. To render France "free" in this passage is an *ironic* description for its subjugation and reorganization with the interest of preserving power and quelling rebellion. What is produced is an alienated republic: "When the members who compose these new bodies of cantons . . . begin to act, they will find themselves, in a great measure, *strangers* to one another." They will lack the "civil habitudes or connexions, or any part of that natural discipline which is the soul of a true republic." Throughout these arguments, as Burke attempts to debunk the claim made on the term *republic*, what these entities become is spelled out: "Magistrates and collectors of revenue are now no longer acquainted with their districts, bishops with their dioceses, or curates with their parishes. These new *colonies of the rights of men* bear a strong resemblance to that sort of military colonies which Tacitus has observed upon in the declining policy of Rome." In a striking phrase, Burke endeavors to undo the link between the "rights of man" and freedom by associating it with the idea of a colony, more specifically a military colony. The domination of France by this regime of reason, by a *ratio* that relies more on geometric measuring and arithmetic calculation than on face-to-face interactions, forms part of the larger set of factors that contribute to the degradation of the human. The "legislators who framed the antient republics" were wise enough to avoid "metaphysics" and "mathematics" and to "study human nature." They heeded the operation of "habit" and understood this to operate as kind of "second nature" that supplemented the "first" nature, presumably human nature. By contrast, the methods of abstraction used by the philosophe-inspired revolutionaries reduce men as if they "were so many different species of animals."[82]

There are two apparently contradictory results of Burke's attack on the effects of geometric and arithmetic reasoning as they pertain to citizenship. Both results cause him to represent the subject produced as outside the category of the human. However, one way outside the human is to turn to the "animal," as above. This remains within the realm of nature in that it turns to the organic world for its analogy. The other rhetorical move is to shift beyond the realm of the organic and to describe the resulting subject as outside of nature. The contrast Burke makes is between the "ancient legislators," who understood the different classes of citizens and attempted to incorporate and account for these differences, and the "modern legislators," who "have attempted to confound all sorts of citizens, as well as they could, into one homogeneous mass." The ancient legislators, like the husbandman with his beasts, knew how to "assort" their various citizens, knew "not to abstract and equalize them all." Burke's language draws on an idea of "natural" difference and ideologically shifts this into an argument of natural inequality based on the particularity of each animal within the animal kingdom (itself a metaphor helpful to Burke's point). At the same time, this language also attacks the use of "abstraction" and "generality" as they are deployed to formulate a basis for the citizen in the abstract inasmuch as this underpins the idea of equality. Burke's critique, while operating on this ideological field, relies on the rejection of the possibility of a "social science": "They reduce men to loose counters merely for the sake of simple telling, and not to figures whose power is to arise from their place in the table."[83] There are multiple ways to read this passage. Its primary reference is to the language of banking as Burke puns upon the procedure of "telling coins"; hence the "place in the table" is also with reference to the bookkeeping made use of in finance, as people occupy a place analogous to digits in an accountant's columns. Yet the phrase gives rise to a secondary level of reference as Burke plays on the affinity between "telling" and "speaking" and the multiple valences of the word *figure* (as indicative of a number and some kind of being). The "reduction" of the human to a "loose counter" is only to extract a "simple telling." This limited and constrained incitement to speak used by the revolutionaries is contrasted with the ghostly "figure" who would have the power to arise from its "place in the table." It is this spectral element lost upon the arithmetic of the philosophes that Burke summons in his prophecy of despotic terror. (And it is the basis for some of the Gothic elements of this work.)[84] Burke's demons arise from the rationalist grid of the philosophes because they exceed its logic.[85]

In his mocking denunciation of the "colonies of the rights of men" Burke assails the creation of an abstract "population" by means of the new technologies of demography. He also attacks what he sees as a link between the production of the abstract population with the generation of abstract rights.[86] This component of his thought is clearer in his explicit discussion of the function of "population" in the self-justification given by the revolutionaries.[87] While Burke often uses the terms *arithmetic* and *geometric* interchangeably to designate what he condemns, their initial correspondence with a specific referent is much more exact: "The French builders, clearing away as mere rubbish whatever they found, and, like their ornamental gardeners, forming everything into an exact level, propose to rest the whole local and general legislature on three bases of three different kinds; one geometrical, one arithmetical, and the third financial; the first of which they call the *basis of territory*; the second, *the basis of population*; and the third, the *basis of contribution*." The geometric logic corresponds therefore to the basis of territory, while the arithmetic refers to the basis of population;

in addition there is a third element, a financial calculation which is tied to the basis of (monetary) contribution. As elsewhere, the disregard for the historically preexisting divisions of land and people is attacked as being unnatural in the manner of the strictly trimmed hedges of an "ornamental" garden. Yet whereas the "mensuration" of land on a geometric basis does not prove to be a difficult task, accomplishing the mensuration of population is another matter: "When they came to provide for population, they were not able to proceed quite so smoothly as they had done in the field of their geometry. Here their arithmetic came to bear upon their juridical metaphysics. Had they stuck to their metaphysic principles, the arithmetic process would be simple indeed. *Men, with them, are strictly equal, and are entitled to equal rights in their own government.*" Burke tries to point out the impossibility of instituting this principle at all political levels, that what is proclaimed at the abstract level cannot be carried out at the level of local government. Thus whereas existing "law, custom, usage, policy" had to yield to their "metaphysic principle," now this very principle must "yield itself to their pleasure." What follows is Burke's effort at demonstrating how the right to vote, which is purportedly given, must in fact be bought by a certain number of days of labor given to the state.[88] This, however, is of less interest to my argument than the earlier criticisms Burke proposes of the principle of equality.

Perhaps we can now see why for Burke the use of instrumental rationality is linked with the creation of the colonies of the rights of men. Through abstract techniques drawn on analogy with geometry and arithmetic, the revolutionaries have generated an alienated polity, which they however wish to endow with a disproportionate degree of power. That Burke sees the power endowed as disproportionate becomes clear when he confesses, "I readily admit . . . that in a republican government, which has a democratic basis, the rich do require additional security above what is necessary to them in monarchies. They are subject to envy, and through envy to oppression." If representation were based purely on population, a wealthy man would not have his interests fairly represented, even if he contributed a large portion of that district's wealth. Instead what is created is the possibility for many other democratic candidates "to cabal and intrigue, and to flatter the people at his expence and to his oppression."[89] (This reference to a cabal, famous in examinations of Burke's analysis of the French Revolution, is also part of his political vocabulary when he examines the operations of the East India Company.) There is an alternation, then, between his two criticisms of the revolutionaries. One rests on his understanding of the abstract rationality the revolutionaries employ in order to defend transformations made to state and society, and the other attacks the likely "cabal" against the propertied class that will ensue.

Burke's remarks return to us to the broader question of how to interpret the French Revolution as an event: Is it yet another episode in the battle between an old, vestigially feudal, landed class and a rising bourgeoisie? A. O. Hirschman cautions against the positing of such a bourgeois order, external to the older ethos, as a usurping power in the period and instead makes the case for endogenous elements within the old feudal honor code that were transformed. According to this argument, the "taming" of the passions and the use of "countervailing" passions go a long way in explaining how the seventeenth century provided new ideologies of personhood that account for the later transformations of the eighteenth century.[90] A second, different argument against the idea of a bourgeoisie with revolutionary potential is made by Pocock, who remarks that Burke nowhere employs the word *bourgeois* to describe the usurping class he sees at work in the French Revolution. Instead Burke borrows the term *burgher* from the Dutch. This may make all the difference in understanding his theory of the causes of the French Revolution. The burghers do indeed bear some similarity to the bourgeoisie: they are by their nature social and involved in trade, and these elements bring them in greater contact with one another, which is part of their strength. They are, however, not necessarily the same as the bourgeoisie; instead Burke refers to them as a "monied interest" (not employing the French term *bourgeoisie*). By "monied interest" he has in mind those who invested in the state and who financed the public debt.[91] Both Pocock's and Hirschman's interpretations are useful in understanding the difficulty that the classes of men who come to power in India pose for Burke. At times he sees this class in terms akin to the idea of a revolutionary bourgeoisie, at other times as petty despots.

Colonialism and the Cunning of History

I have argued that Burke sees the East India Company officials in India as akin to the revolutionaries in France. If this is so, and Burke sees the revolutionaries as burghers (this appears to be Pocock's point), then does he also see the "boys in India" as akin to burghers? (I refer to his description of the young men of the East India Company in India as no worse than "the boys whom we are whipping at school" but endowed with a premature authority that corrupts such youth.)[92] If Burke does not view them as burghers, what can be learned from his view? The difference itself would be revealing, both for developing his idea of the qualities of the class of the burghers in Europe and the characteristics of the class in India.

A second question is parallel to a point made often in criticisms of the application of historical and sociological terms drawn from European history to the Indian context:[93] Can one see Burke's reading of India as a mistranslation of terms like *feudal* and *bourgeois*? This would be to take cognizance of the difficulties that emerge from the very categories of analysis we use in setting the terms of our discussion. One must pose this question in order to address the multiple valences of the idea of modernity, whose often optimistic tinge appears quite false when applied to the colony precisely because *it arrives with colonialism* and moreover leads in some cases to an ironic effect: it causes a re-entrenchment of feudal classes rather than their obsolescence. (For example, for political reasons many petty kings in India established a newfound legitimacy based on alliances with various colonial companies or their states.)

In other words, in Europe, one reading of the French Revolution sees the rise of the bourgeoisie as showing the obsolescence of the feudal class. In many colonies this does not hold because the feudal class finds a new function as the mediators between the colonial power and the local population. Thus the feudal classes are, to draw on Marx's language, turned into a comprador class. It might be possible to argue that this was also the case in Europe and that thereby this "regression" is not unique to the colonial context. (I am less persuaded by that interpretation.) I would like to emphasize that in order to understand what is transformative about the modern era in the colony and in Europe we will need to accede to an insight that I believe Burke provides: the radical and ambivalent modernity characterizing a break with an older order emerges at the very same time in both colony and metropole, both India and France.

To this speculation I would add another concept: Hegel's cunning of reason,[94] extended and shifted to a broader cunning of history. Beyond the knowledge of any of the agents who undertake historical actions and decisions, there may be another logic at work that it is possible to detect only a posteriori. Those who participate in the great events of their day may believe that they are working precisely against a historical tendency, and yet in fact the larger maelstrom may make of them the gales that blow the winds of change. For Hegel this was the unfolding of a certain reason in history, the logic of freedom, in a teleological manner.[95] However, if we omit the teleological quality that Hegel ascribed to this movement, its usefulness is evident. Colonialism has been seen—even by its critics—as an instance of such a cunning of history: it performed a certain necessary world-historical transformation in spite of the intentions of its actors. As in Marx's writings on India, certain classes (the English merchants and bourgeoisie) perform a radical clearing away of thousands of years of obsolete work practices, modes of production, techniques of labor extraction. This certainly was Marx's presumption in some of his letters on India written for New York newspapers.[96] Without reference to the understudied *Ethnological Notebooks* of Marx, one may note the significance of certain categories—especially (oriental) despotism—as a description of one of the various modes that precede those of capitalist production and the forms of labor organization on which it depends. Oriental despotism is obviously not Marx's invention; it had broad currency already as a result of its significance in works such as Montesquieu's *L'Esprit des Lois*.[97] I would like to examine briefly the implications of oriental despotism (freedom's antithesis) as a representation of a flawed and even barbaric form of rule.

Despotism in France, Despotism in the Orient

If the circulation of the idea of oriental despotism in the eighteenth century is extremely widespread, its legacies also continue in political and popular thought well into the twentieth century. From the discussion of freedom in the oriental world in Hegel's *Philosophy of History* to the extensive debates among Marxist historians following Marx's description of the Asiatic mode of production, the specificity of an oriental form of despotism is often asserted and undermined.[98] Several recent discussions of Hegel have appeared with the aim of discussing the connection between the apparent abstractions of Hegelian thinking with particular historical events or potentially overlooked sources.[99] In the case of German idealism such a decoding of the abstract into the particular may be necessary and served as one influential manner in which the *Phenomenology* has been read.[100] However, with Burke one is dealing with a completely different kind of writing, one that involves an intimate engagement with the particular (what I referred to earlier as colonial knowledge). Because of Burke's role as a parliamentarian, he was from the outset more involved in issues of trade and commerce, which in his day brought him in touch with mercantile activities in the West Indies, North America, and Asia. It was only a consolidation of this fact when Burke actually involved himself in Indian affairs and in the impeachment trial of Warren Hastings before the House of Commons (1787–95). The concurrent events of the French Revolution, widely seen at the time by many in Britain as a response to an unjust despot, only focused the debate more sharply on the idea of freedom. In a chapter examining how the French Revolution appeared to many in England, Ronald Paulson notes that the first stage of the revolution (from 1788 to 1792) was seen by some with approval as celebrating the fall of despotism and the rise of constitutional monarchy. The rise of *parlement* Burke saw initially as an equivalent of the Whig aristocracy.[101] Typical of this first period of English responses to the revolution is that recorded in 1790 by Samuel Romilly:

> Who, indeed, that deserves the name of an Englishman, can have preserved a cold and deadly indifference, when he found a nation, which had been for ages enslaved, rousing on a sudden from their ignominious lethargy, breaking asunder their bonds, and, with an unanimity which has no example in history, demanding a free constitution: when he viewed all the fortresses of tyranny destroyed; when he saw the dungeons of state thrown open, and the prisons of superstition unlocked; when he beheld the Asiatic despotism of the king, and the feudal tyranny of his nobles at once abolished.[102]

In its reference to the overcoming of enslavement, lethargy, dungeons, and superstition, this remark is expressive of a classic understanding of the French Revolution and the philosophical energies of those who some saw as having inspired it. Paulson does not comment on the presence of the figure of the Asian despot in this passage, whose feudal tyranny refers to the French monarch and his noblemen, but the reference thereby illustrates how such terminology circulated in both directions: the paradigmatic image of tyranny was an Asian despot, who could be invoked to describe a tyranny within the French order. It was against such a preexisting set of discursive associations that Burke would direct his energies in his description of the East India Company officials (not native petty kings) as Asiatic despots, thereby doubling the irony (for the image came home in the body of the European Warren Hastings).[103] Much has been written about the fear of contagion from the colonies, which would find its way into Europe. Disease or monstrosity, what was at stake was the health of Europe put at risk by contact with the faraway, whose effect was to weaken one's character. In this case, we may see Romilly's reference as circumstantial, but it reminds us of the relatively persistent and sometimes overlooked contemporary juxtaposition of the near and the far. One need not turn to obscure texts to illuminate this presence.

Burke himself must address this common discursive association between the Orient and despotic governance in the *Reflections*. Because he is concerned to show the falsity of such an association (namely, that the French monarch is no such despot), his description of the stasis that reigns under an Asiatic despotism is in fact exaggerated. But in his exaggeration he helpfully limns in dark lines the figure of this despot:

> To hear some men speak of the late monarchy of France, you would imagine that they were talking of Persia bleeding under the ferocious sword of Taehmas Kouli Khân, or at least describing the barbarous anarchic despotism of Turkey, where the finest countries in the most genial climates in the world are wasted by peace more than any countries have been worried by war; where arts are unknown, where manufactures languish, where science is extinguished, where agriculture decays, where the human race itself melts away and perishes under the eye of the observer. Was this the case of France?[104]

Burke's answer is, not surprisingly, a resounding no, and he mocks the assertion that the abuses of the regime in France were anything like the oriental despotisms that reign in Persia and Turkey, where (stagnant) peace ruins the countries more than war. In these places the "arts are unknown . . . science is extinguished . . . the human race . . . perishes under the eye of the observer." He makes the feeble argument that in France, one had "a despotism rather in appearance than in reality." His motives for stating this are easier to understand when we keep in mind the location of this discussion within his argument, where the Turkish despot serves as the opening of a parenthetical digression in which Burke once again marshals a variety of evidence to rebut the comparison with the French monarch. I turn to an examination of that argument in order to substantiate the claims made in the preceding section and because it highlights Burke's relationship to the emerging technologies of the state.

"The Encrease of Mankind": Population and Despotism

Alfred Cobban's classic 1929 study of Burke asserts that he can be seen as the founder of the modern idea of the nation, partly as a way of resolving the tension between the absolute efficiency of the modern state versus the absolute freedom of the modern individual.[105] Burke saw absolute efficiency in the state being set up by the revolutionaries, in their geometric and arithmetic reasoning. He intended both to critique and to supplement this with something like history and accumulated experience, phrased in terms of the "organic" growth of society and often compared to a tree or to the natural geographic divisions of land—sinuous, curving rivers, and the like—which could not be reshaped to fit arbitrary *départements.* Yet in spite of his contribution to the modern use of the term, it appears to me that Burke relies quite heavily on sciences of the state, the study of population and political economy, to defend the French nation. Thus his rebuttal begins, "Among the standards upon which the effects of government on any country are to be estimated, I must consider the state of its population as not the least certain. No country in which population flourishes, and is in progressive improvement, can be under a *very* mischievous government."[106] Burke's discussion of despotism alternates with a discussion of population, where the latter is an index of the validity of ascribing the former as a description of a particular regime. For Burke in this passage the Enlightenment notion of progressive improvement is one way to evaluate the claims to rule of the *ancien régime*. The source of his data is a study by Jacques Necker, also cited by Richard Price.[107] Yet are the references to despotism in Burke necessarily linked to population in some conceptual manner, or are they perhaps coincidentally juxtaposed?

The answer to this question might be made clearer if we examine the structural set of terms within which despotism is located. First, one characteristic of despotic rule is its arbitrariness. Yet Burke demonstrates that this is in fact one quality of the revolutionaries' takeover of the French state, not the monarch's; recall that, for Burke, they neglect the local histories that defined regions in their application of a supposed geometric reason. By this and other means, Burke redefines the revolutionaries as despotic, and not the monarchy—which on the contrary was cognizant, by its very nature, of accumulated historical experience and thus structurally akin to the ancient constitution in Britain. It is therefore consistent with Burke's method to show by rational means why the monarchy was not arbitrary. Yet how does he justify this claim? He shows the monarchy, and not the revolutionary state, to be the bearer of progress. If we look at the definition of the word *revolution*, we see that it undergoes a transformation in this period, for which Burke's text is partially responsible. Its earlier usages, as its etymology suggests, imply a turning, a degree of circularity.[108] With Burke the idea of revolution takes on the sense of a profound upheaval. It is with Napoleon, according to Paulson, that the unidirectional sense of revolution (over its circular sense) is solidified. The idea of progress is obviously more naturally accommodated within this newer meaning. I would argue that the missing third term from Paulson's examination, however, is the one that helps define both of these other two terms, and that is *despotism*. For, as noted earlier, despotism is a kind of stasis. (Recall Burke's description of Turkey, where the arts wither, etc.) Each of these three spatial movements therefore implies a different political term: stasis implies despotism; circularity correlates with the older idea of revolution; and a unidirectional forward movement indicates progress (the new idea of revolution). The question or dispute is whether *progress* takes place under a monarchy or under a republic. Burke suggests that the French regime requires both reform and something resembling the British constitution, but before he can make this claim, he qualifies to a certain degree his defense of the regime:

> I do not attribute this population to the deposed government; because I do not like to compliment the contrivances of men, with what is due in a great degree to the bounty of Providence. But that decried government could not have obstructed, most probably it favored, the operation of those causes (whatever they were) whether of nature in the soil, or in habits of industry among the people, which has produced so large a number of the species throughout that whole kingdom, and exhibited in some particular places such prodigies of population. I never will suppose that fabrick of state to be the worst of all political institutions, which, by experience, is found to contain a principle favorable (however latent it may be) to the *encrease of mankind*.[109]

We see that Burke would like to have it both ways: to attribute to the French monarchy the successes of the land and yet also to claim that this outcome cannot be brought about by human reason and rationality alone. Something exceeds the limits of this; some elements are due to accident or gifts of nature or due to the "bounty of providence." The government presides over this success, whose causes ("whatever they were") and whose principle ("however latent it may be") Burke prefers to view as obscure, as both of his parenthetical remarks show. The basis for judgment is, famously, experience, which shows that state's ability to "encrease mankind."

If the discussion of population is one example of Burke's use of the technologies of the state, a second would be his shift to the discussion of wealth. Pocock has written an incisive and definitive interpretation of the *Reflections* with an emphasis on Burke's understanding of the revolution as one which concerned the circulation of paper money (referred to earlier). Here Burke discusses France's wealth because "the wealth of a country is another, and no contemptible standard, by which we may judge whether on the whole a government be protecting or destructive." This becomes the means by which he is able to adduce a lengthy list of France's achievements. In characteristic style, bordering on the overinflated, he inaugurates this list, but does so by positing a cause and then shrouding it: "*Some* adequate cause must have originally introduced all the money coined at its mint into that kingdom; and *some* cause as operative must have kept at home, or returned into its bosom such a vast flood of treasure as Mr Necker calculates to remain for domestic circulation." While he repeats the mixture of vagueness concerning the origin or certain cause of French splendor, the abstraction of origin is made up for by the concreteness of the countless items that follow. The procedure is panoptical in visual effect, as Burke surveys the land:

> When I bring before my view the number of her fortifications, constructed with so bold and masterly a skill . . . when I recollect how very small a part of that region is without cultivation . . . when I reflect on the excellence of her manufactures . . . when I contemplate the grand foundations of charity . . . when I survey the state of all the arts that beautify and polish life; when I reckon the men she has bred for extending her fame in war . . . I behold in all this something which awes and commands the imagination, which checks the mind on the brink of precipitate and indiscriminate censure.[110]

The evocation of awe and of that which "commands" the imagination recalls the operation of terror at work in Burke's description of the Sublime. As in that text, the object of the gaze is very clearly gendered female; beyond the obvious effect of the use of the feminine possessive adjective for the French nation ("her fortifications," etc.), he refers also to the "men she has bred," the act of reproduction serving as proof that the nation is not sterile, not infertile (as the land under Turkish despotism was precisely said to be). Whereas in Burke's early treatise on the Sublime a moment on the brink, a precipice, would be taken as an aesthetic analogue of the revolutionary moment, here such a moment is interrupted, and the eye that beheld the scene is "checked" from its "indiscriminate censure."[111] The effect of such a check on a runaway and otherwise unrestrained vision "demands that we should very seriously examine, what and how great are the latent vices that could authorise us at once to level so spacious a fabric with the ground. I do not recognize, in this view of things, the despotism of Turkey. Nor do I discern the character of a government, that has been, on the whole, so oppressive, or so corrupt, or so negligent, as to be utterly unfit *for all reformation*."[112] Finally we come to the conclusion of Burke's excursus on Turkish despotism as the differend to the French monarchy. In this passage are telescoped several components of his thought. The return of the discourse of the Sublime is here turned around so that the subject does not immerse himself into it but rather preserves the "spacious fabric" instead of leveling it with the ground (which is how Burke figures the revolutionary activity against the nation). The revolutionaries, by contrast, abrogate the Sublime and re-render its great heights in mundane proportions.

Despotism thus serves as a foil for Burke's defense of the French monarchy; it is more by contrast than resemblance with the despot that the French monarch is defined. It is perhaps another reason why Burke may be seen as a kind of cusp figure, witness to a period of historical transition. But this aspect of his position is revealed more by the variety of arguments he is willing to invoke: one that relies upon technologies of the state (this would be the more modern reason or defense) and one that asserts the primacy of historical continuity or inherited affections (the more classic conservative view with which he is identified). The conclusion he arrives at after his parenthetical comparison of Turkish despotism with the French is that "such a government well deserved to have its excellencies heightened; its faults corrected; and its capacities improved into a British constitution."[113] Burke makes use of a term, *improvement*, which circulates widely as a theme of politics and novels in the period, in order to advocate for reform and not revolution as the necessary transformation.

Symptoms of Modernity: The Role of Ireland

While my focus has been on how Burke's writings on France reveal the marks of his involvement in Indian affairs, several significant works in Irish studies elaborate the role of Ireland in his thought, as well as the profound impact his work had on Irish culture and literature.[114] Ireland's intimate colonial relationship to England as the "near other" is a common subject of reflection of these works, and because it bears some similarity to the Indian case it warrants the attention of those who wish to examine the status of Burke's writing as a kind of colonial discourse. Seamus Deane, for example, understands Burke's political prescriptions as a response to an emerging form of modernity, whose characteristics Burke was in the process of identifying. What I earlier referred to as instrumental rationality or geometric reason are examples of this, and both are attributed to the revolutionaries. But the *Reflections* also works by deploying the genre of travel writing crossed with that of the political pamphlet to create a "phantasmal France."[115] What should become evident here is the role France plays in Burke's imagination of England: France is England's other.

Burke attacks the despotism attributed by others to the king in France in part because he identifies many of these ills as more characteristic of the emerging new order of modernity. It is the revolutionaries who are identified with qualities characteristic of modernity both because of their relationship to the land and because of their relationship to their subjects. To their land they relate in the most impersonal of ways, treating it as a "territory of conquest." It is carved up based on external factors (as discussed earlier). However, the revolutionaries' relationship to their subjects is indicative of another, perhaps more fundamental aspect of a modern view: their different conception of the human. The French revolutionaries detach character from place. It is for this reason that the postrevolutionary French national character can be said to have produced the theory of cosmopolitan modernity.[116] Burke's idea of the English national character, as evinced by the discussion where he calls for reform, is premised on the idea of the rejection of revolution. His essay was revolutionary in its effect, but its aim was explicitly to preempt the further spread of the contagion of revolution elsewhere in Europe.

This assertion of how one may detect in Burke's discussion the symptoms of the fear of the emergence of modernity should be linked with two other elements of his thought. It is often said that the crowd serves as a key constellation in the *Reflections*, alongside the stock-jobbers, the men of letters, and the cabal. However, we should note the contradiction between Burke's uniformly negative view of the mob with the frequent invocation of population. In fact the mob is in a sense the flipside of population, but each emerges out of artificially separated discursive spaces. *Population* comes out of the technologies of the state, *crowd* from the language of alienated modernity that Burke perceives as emerging. The crowd, who famously strip the queen, are unable or unwilling to see humans as existing within a hierarchical structure. (This is connected with the "leveling vision" that Deane identifies as a new kind of "speculation" emerging in this period.) The crowd is also, I would add, inauthentic.[117] The question to be asked is, Which element does Burke see as characteristic of the modern: the population or the crowd? Can one hold both to be manifestations of it? Burke makes use of the former (population) in his defense of the French Crown, and of the latter (mob) to show its attack upon the Crown.

As becomes clear from some of his later writings, it is Rousseau (as Deane argues) who expresses the new relationship to modernity that Burke detects and rejects. Burke's obsession with and elevation of the royal family, which involves the elevation of the family in general, is part of his critique of a modernity that would demote the family's importance.

The demotion of its importance is shown in the lack of sympathy for the family by Jacobins, a sympathy that he posits as a kind of transhistorical, universal urge. The revolution, however, implicitly places national ties and loyalties above familial ones. One could call this the *ancien régime* view of human nature, which Burke is attempting to defend against the *tabula rasa*, Jacobin view of human nature.

Burke believed countries such as Ireland were at an even greater risk than England, precisely because they lacked the accretion of many centuries of experience stored up in various social institutions (whether manners—to speak of the realm of custom—or, more concretely, in the British form of Parliament). As a result, Ireland did not even know the virtues of that ancient civilization that had collapsed in France, let alone have the capacity to worry over the implications of their loss. On this view, Burke's attacks on the Protestant ascendancy in Ireland had to do with the inability of incorporating the mass of Catholics into civil society, and it was this civil society whose flawed state would be exacerbated by the conditions of a new emerging modernity.

There is a political parallel, then, in Burke's mind between three contexts (Ireland, India, France) and three groups (the Protestant ascendancy, Hastings and the East India Company, and the Jacobins). Each of these can be said to rule over its country "as a territory of conquest." Moreover each rules without the consent or the affection of those they dominate. Each also attempts to inaugurate a new social order based on a *tabula rasa* view of humanity. The detachment of local history from state policy in France, the similar denigration of old families and the altered rules of property in Bengal, and the Protestant ascendancy's willful neglect of the Catholic populace—all these enactments are counter to Burke's social vision. In his analysis of these three historical examples, the failings of a prevailing regime are made to reside in specific bodies or groups (a thought pursued in the following chapter): the revolutionaries and Rousseau in France; Hastings, or the East India Company, in India; the Protestant ascendancy in Ireland. As remarked earlier, Burke is not involved in a wholesale critique of imperialism but rather (in the case of India) in the reform of the East India Company. So, in the case of France, he prescribes the reform of the monarchy. He argues that the charges of oriental despotism that have been leveled against the French monarch do not hold. Instead these are the same sorts of charges he would level against Hastings: the newest oriental despot happened to be English. If it was Hastings whom Burke tried to make bear the blame for the evils of empire in India, in France the person he chose to attack was Rousseau. This, however, was in a 1791 text written after the *Reflections*, the *Letter to a Member of the National Assembly* (to which I will turn shortly).

Yet Hastings and Rousseau are two very different bearers of modernity, and one difficulty that arises in examining the analogies between these contexts is to understand the significance of this. Hastings, no philosopher, was willing to elaborate what Burke derisively called a "geographical morality":

> But he [Hastings] has told your Lordships in his defense, that actions in Asia do not bear the same moral qualities as the same actions would bear in Europe. . . . And having stated at large what he means by saying that the same actions have not the same qualities in Asia and in Europe, we are to let your Lordships know that these Gentlemen have formed a plan of *Geographical morality*, by which the duties of men . . . are not to be governed by their relation to the Great Governor of the Universe . . . but by climates, degrees of longitude . . . as if, when you have crossed the equinoctial line all the virtues die.[118]

Burke argued that Hastings made use of mere physical travel—movement across an equinoctial—to underpin an implicit relativism (the very language cited above mocks that as flaccid sophistry), one which held that a different moral code was needed in the tropics. With Rousseau, seen as an inspiration for Jacobinism *tout court*, Burke will note that he was already to be faulted for the abstract cosmopolitanism of his views. (One can be linked to the other.) In Rousseau it is the sovereignty of the individual judgment in isolation from a larger social order and from history with which Burke takes issue. It was for all these reasons that Burke found himself between India and France in 1790, the year of the publication of the *Reflections*. If this chapter has introduced some of the terms of Burke's analysis—custom, arithmetic reason, despotism, and conquest—that allowed him to shuttle between India and France (analytically, if not spatially), then the task of the following chapter as we cross our "degrees of longitude" will be to explore the full and robust articulation of these views in his later thought.

4 / Jacobinism in India, Indianism in English Parliament: Fearing the Enlightenment and Colonial Modernity

> *Our Government and our laws are beset by two different Enemies, which are sapping its foundation, Indianism and Jacobinism. In some cases they act separately, in some they act in conjunction: but of this I am sure; that the first is worst by far, and the hardest to deal with; and for this amongst other reasons, that it weakens[,] discredits, and ruins that force, which ought to be employed with the greatest Credit and Energy against the other; and that it furnishes Jacobinism with its strongest arms against all formal government.*
> —EDMUND BURKE, CORRESPONDENCE (1796)

Just what did Edmund Burke fear in the Jacobins of France, and what might that tell us about concurrent events taking place far off in colonial Bengal? Perhaps the question is better answered if we reverse it: Just what can colonial Bengal—or more broadly, events occurring at Britain's mercantile colonial frontier—tell us about Burke's fear of the emergence of modernity and revolutionary aspects of the Enlightenment that he saw in France? This chapter aims to raise questions of one field (eighteenth-century studies, studies of the Enlightenment) in tandem with another (postcolonial thought); the dialogue is implicit for the most part but follows a question raised by others on critical practices "in the wake of Eurocentrism."[1] The question will be not just how to read and interpret Edmund Burke but how to read the French Revolution though colonial India—provincializing Europe in this sense.[2] Burke is instructive for showing how the basis for this reading is already present (if latent) in central authors of the period; one does not even need to go to purportedly marginal texts to bring out this fact. Clarifying the subtitle to this chapter, what Burke feared is something overlooked by many who read his work on Europe or India in isolation: the coevality of the transformations taking place in many parts of the colonial world and metropolitan Europe which he captured in the couplet Indianism-Jacobinism. We can learn from this fear to challenge the frequent if implicit notion of a colonial lag time whereby a revolution occurs in Europe and then spreads elsewhere. These transformations were seen early on, by one who wished it were otherwise.

Conservative in some contexts and liberal in others, Burke's political views make much more sense in the context of a body of Enlightenment thought in which a passionate hatred of empire coexists alongside, indeed seems to depends on intellectual projects for which empire is a defining feature. My aim is to explore this by recuperating the global vision that Burke's notion of Jacobinism implied in tandem with Indianism (his own neologism). As discussed in the previous chapter, the concepts of custom and manners, which take on an ethnographic function in Burke's thought, explain to a degree the astonishing contradictions of his political writings: his profound sympathy with (if not explicit support of) the decision of American colonists to seek their independence in 1776,[3] his scathing attack on the Jacobin revolutionaries in 1790, and his even more passionate denunciation of Warren Hastings and the East India Company, which he undertook long before, during, and after the attacks on the revolution in France that seem to mark such a definitive break in his political thought. I would like to propose, however, that Burke's notion of Jacobinism was crucially shaped by his prior writings on India, where he saw a revolutionary form of modernity emerging in the upheavals caused by the East India Company—and this a decade before the events of 1789.

Travelogues, philology, ethnographies, vivid paintings and descriptions regarding Europe's colonies—in short, the kinds of knowledge practices associated with orientalism as Edward Said understood it—had been growing in number and flooding Europe for decades by this period.[4] For Burke the effect of this colonial knowledge on European thought prompted a curious mixture of imperious aspiration and critical self-reflection. In order to do justice to his thought and address the complexity of colonialism in the Enlightenment, I would like to explore Burke's critical views on empire but also consider a conceptual limit which he seems to reach in his critique of imperial sovereignty. Recent American conflicts between state interests, private companies, and domestic politics in a period of global interventions (I have the Iraq war in mind) only makes this eighteenth-century tale of mercantile empire—of companies effectively running what would only later become a state enterprise—more, not less, resonant.

This chapter focuses on two points of Burke's political triangle, France and India, leaving aside the third element, the Americas (considered in the following chapter). Parallel to this historical and political inquiry, I pose a theoretical question: By what means did Burke maintain his position as a staunch and early critic of British colonialism despite his deep suspicion of Enlightenment reason and its many impulses toward freedom and autonomy, which would seem to lend important support to such a critique through such notions as the universal rights of man? Understanding this may give us some insight into the persistent uses of universalist languages (whether in contemporary charters on human rights or in paeans to globalization), as well as their misappropriation for aims of dominance or subordination formerly accomplished by territorial empire.

This story regarding Burke and Hastings is significant because it represents one last moment of "scandal" in Britain's relations with its colonies before much of the politics of empire, as Nicholas Dirks has argued, became displaced from British officials to natives. (That is, scandalous officials such as Hastings gave way to the argument that certain types of natives were scandalous—and so began many nineteenth-century projects of reforming the native.)[5] The spectacle of a trial taking place in Parliament, of an impeachment that might stand as an epitome for the larger critique of empire, reveals how Burke made use of common discursive tropes (such as that of oriental despotism, discussed in chapter 3) for a different end. Emphasizing the effect of the Hastings trial on the historiography of India, Dirks disputes the remark cited earlier from J. R. Seeley that the British "seem, as it were, to have conquered and peopled half the world in a fit of absence of mind," and details how the view of an accidental acquisition of empire simply does not stand up to reason and evidence. Yet this, combined with the claim that Britain was almost inevitably filling a power vacuum created by a weakening Mughal state, was the argument made to Parliament. "The story that had been sold to Parliament throughout the eighteenth century, at least until Burke called Hastings to account, is transmuted here into an authoritative history of the origins of imperial rule in India."[6] Dirks's remark takes issue with prevailing understandings of the trial as discussed by many imperial historians, even the authoritative work of P. J. Marshall, who wrote in 2009, "Most historians, while recognizing Burke's absolute sincerity, now feel that Burke was attempting to pin the evils of a situation on one individual and that he had chosen the wrong one."[7] This thought is the starting point (albeit with a different political intention) for Sara Suleri's stimulating reading of the Hastings trial as one instance in a longer series of episodes expressing the symptom of colonial guilt or anxiety (where Hastings stands in as the wrong target of criticism). She reads Burke's "Speech on Fox's East India Bill" as a debate between state and merchant, as the theatrical staging of a conflict of discourses, whose eloquence exceeds the object; that is, Burke's rhetoric and even the length of the trial exceed the specific crimes with which Hastings is charged.[8] In her view the rapacity of empire itself is lost in this eloquence, and she therefore never goes so far as to consider Burke a critic of empire, as others readers have. The focus on Hastings as a narrative strategy was required, she argues, to give the failings of empire a scapegoat and thereby to allow the larger ideology of imperialism to remain intact. Her interest is more in the category of the Sublime as it is deployed in the trial (e.g., India is shrouded in obscurity and difficulty and thus lends itself to subsumption under the Sublime) and in the "colonizing" aspects of this category (beauty as a passive object of the spectator). She adduces the trial as an example of the inability to ascribe or account for colonial guilt and argues for the constant tendency of guilt to overflow its containment in one body (that of Warren Hastings) and to contaminate others.[9] Yet in her view, this is never allowed to reach the stage where it might prompt consideration of a more general responsibility or complicity.

I organize my questions regarding Burke's positions on Jacobinism in France and the East India Company in India around a reading of the *Reflections on the Revolution of France*, drawing additionally on his correspondence as I explore his understanding of Jacobinism and Indianism. Human vulnerability and fragility were central components of Burke's thought, and his critique of the Jacobin view of human nature as infinitely malleable was based on his belief that humans were, by contrast, embedded in a set of social relationships by means of an intergenerational contract or partnership (discussed in the previous chapter).[10] Burke argued that human nature was not as mutable as the revolutionary theory of the subject assumed; he saw this phenomenon at work both in the effects of the East India Company on Indian society and among the French Jacobins. Some of the affinities he perceived between these disparate contexts may be better understood if we elaborate his critique of Enlightenment reason (what he called "arithmetic" reason) and consider his response in both cases as shaped by fear of an emerging political modernity. By developing Burke's "theory of Jacobinism" (to borrow François Furet's phrase from another context), and by supplementing it with what he defines as a complementary element called Indianism, I explain how he identified through these two terms significant global phenomena particular to the modern period—so much so that he remarked, "Indianism and Jacobinism are the two great evils of our time."[11]

Unlike many existing discussions of Burke and India, this chapter therefore attempts to consider Burke's writings on France together with his writings on India rather than examining the latter in isolation.[12]

Perhaps because of the volume of Burke's output in relation to the Hastings trial, many who examine his interest in India do not connect this with his other writings on Europe.[13] A review of some central dates and certain aspects of the composition of the *Reflection on the Revolution in France* can make the case for considering the two together and provide us with a correlate for what Said notes in his reading of Jane Austen's *Mansfield Park* (1814): how to read the role of the passing yet persistent references to the West India planter, to Antigua, which sustain the material life of the Bertram estate in the novel.[14] Even in a work such as *Mansfield Park*, which is ostensibly set in a domestic space, there are signs of the imperium that give fundamental shape to the novel; so here with Burke: even in a work ostensibly about political turmoil in the heart of Europe, there are signs everywhere of the way the space of empire shapes the very terms of the description and the fear. Lorraine Daston argues, contrary to some prevalent views of Enlightenment thinkers, that they "did not scorn the imagination" but rather "paid it the respectful compliment of honest fear."[15] They feared the role of the imagination over sensation in making sense of the world. In this sense, they were less different from thinkers associated with Romanticism than is often asserted. Echoing this notion, we can certainly derive the same significance from Burke's respectful fear of the transformations taking place in colonial spaces of the Enlightenment.

Let us recall the circumstances of the composition of the *Reflections*, which Burke wrote relatively quickly in 1790 (perhaps in six to seven months) as a response to a letter from a young French gentlemen, Charles-Jean-François Depont, who was curious about Burke's views on the events in France.[16] Though this work now ranks as one of the more important—certainly notorious—documents of British eighteenth-century political thought, at the time Burke noted in his correspondence that he undertook the exercise partly as a respite from the Hastings impeachment trial, which by 1790 had already been dragging on for years. His interest in India had begun in the late 1770s, prompted in part by dealings that his kinsman William Burke had with the raja of Tanjore. (William had visited the raja in India on two separate journeys from Britain with a view to increasing his family fortune.) Edmund's views on the East India Company in this early period are not characterized by great criticism; this was to come later. By 1783 he is the author of the "Speech on Fox's East India Bill," which details a great number of Company abuses. His critical opinion of the Company has been established and was only to harden for the remainder of his life. By the time of the revolution in France in 1789, Burke knew more about Indian affairs than any other man involved in politics in Britain and counted many people with years of firsthand experience in India among his friends, such as Philip Francis. Orientalist scholars such as Nathaniel Halhed and William Jones were also among his correspondents.

In this regard, Burke's writings on France may actually have served as a means to escape the deep morass of the lengthy trial with which he had become inextricably involved.[17] In his mind India had been reduced primarily to the trial, and he expressed in his letters of 1789 a desire for "an honorable retreat from this Business."[18] Much later, in 1795, he would express this exhaustion in a much more graphic and visceral manner. "God knows what bitterness I feel in my Mouth," he opened his letter to William Windham that year, "in returning to my Indian Vomit."[19] Or again in 1796: "Mrs Burke has passed three very quiet Nights. . . . As for me this India Business has quite overwhelmed me."[20] Whereas the Hastings trial became an endless series of tasks to be accomplished, the events in France offered a new spectacle, a different event by which he might express his views on liberty, tradition, and reform.

The eventual demise of the *ancien régime* and the emergence of the cipher of the modern beginning in 1789—which was to so shock Burke—compelled him to intertwine his reflections on India and France (and America and Ireland) in such unusual ways in his later writings and correspondence, particularly from 1794–96. Several of the letters discussed below are among his final writings (1796); he was to die in July of the following year, occupied by his thoughts of Jacobinism and Indianism. Confirmed in his early prognostications on the former by the events of the Terror in France, and in his fear of the latter by the acquittal of Hastings alongside continuing abuses of power by the Company in its colonial outposts, the phenomena he named by these words were expressive of the evisceration of existing human character and the gutting of working structures of governance.

My aim is therefore to bring the debate on Burke's India writings back, as it were, to his writings on France in the wake of works by scholars such as Uday Mehta; the intermingling of these two issues in his late correspondence justifies such a move.[21] Marshall argues that the effects of this seven-year trial on the course of British imperial governance were minimal and may even have led to greater apathy and hostility on the part of the British public with regard to the issue.[22] As Philip Francis put it, "In proportion . . . as this great empire was extended, it seemed to excite less of the attention of either the House or the public."[23] Yet the effects of the trial on Burke's own thinking were, by contrast, extensive—decisive even. In the final pages of his study, Marshall remarks that "Burke later became convinced that the punishment of Hastings in India was necessary not only for its effect in India but also for its effect in Britain itself" and that the India-returned Nabobs were to be regarded as "the corrupters of the English political system, and later as potential recruits to Jacobinism."[24] It is with this concluding thought that I begin, for it illustrates perfectly well Burke's notion of Indianism.[25]

To clarify, by reattaching Burke's India writings with his other works, we may consider the unavoidable contradictions raised by the discussion of justice in the context of empire. It is not my intention to argue, as Marshall does, that Burke's writings on India are a "towering landmark in the debate about imperial responsibility in any context." Marshall overly limits the scope of Burke's criticisms as being directed specifically toward curbing the financial abuses of East India Company servants. As will become clear from the prophetic manner in which Burke wrote, the notion of Indianism loomed as a greater phenomenon than mere corruption. Burke's twinning of this term with Jacobinism possesses significance because it reveals a larger global political vision; for the purposes of this argument, this is more important than failing to find an empirical correlation between India-returned wealth and Jacobin political tendencies. Marshall rightly concludes that "what the impeachment did do was to enable Burke to enunciate a vision of what empire might be were it to be based on justice."[26] But it therefore also raises the question of whether this is possible at all, or whether empire and justice are exclusive terms, the one only possible at the expense of the other.[27]

It may strike some readers that Burke's view of the interventionist nature of the Hastings regime is at odds with some current historiography on India in this period. After all, why worry about Hastings's interference with the existing property and social order in India, when in fact later, during the Cornwallis administration, there is a more robust debate between the "Anglicists" and the "Orientalists" (i.e., those who wished to work with and preserve indigenous forms of property and the social order), between those who advocated the "permanent settlement" and the "ryotwari system," which brought the incipient proto-state of the East India Company into much greater contact with the people and peasantry?[28] Given this later history, was Burke not simply wrong in his perception of Hastings and the Company? I would argue that whether or not Burke's perception of the Company accords with later historical evaluations of Company, state, and society relations, it nonetheless is extremely revealing of his pattern of thinking. Some might put this down to the conspiratorial strain present in some of his writings (a cabal of company officials in India and a cabal of lawyers and theorists in

France), yet it testifies to the global scope of his political imagination in the period and to the centrality of empire even in his consideration of issues apparently limited to Europe itself.[29]

The Mingling of Classes: The Glorious Revolution, the French Revolution, and "Company" India

In the "Speech on Fox's East India Bill" (1783), of which Burke was the author in all but name, there occurs a concise description of the East India Company officials—who eventually constitute a formidably influential India-returned colonial class in Britain—which gathers together several of the key rhetorical and analytic elements that would later be named by the shorthand term *Indianism*. The speech illustrates a link between the India writings and the "men of talent"—intellectuals, writers, lawyers, and the like—Burke discusses in the *Reflections*, a group that he holds partially responsible for the excesses of Jacobinism: "There is nothing in the boys we send to India worse, than in the boys whom we are whipping at school, or that we see trailing a pike, or bending over a desk at home. But as English youth in India drink the intoxicating draught of authority and dominion before their heads are able to bear it, and as they are full grown in fortune long before they are ripe in principle, neither nature nor reason have any opportunity to exert themselves for remedy of the excesses of their premature power."[30] It might be said that Burke is merely dismissing the India-returned officials as an arriviste class, and indeed there is some truth to this remark. But his emphasis on the youth of the officials and his insistence on referring to them as boys grow out of a deeper sense of the corrosive effects of a "premature power." It is worth lingering on Burke's surprise: Why should he be so startled at the thought of boys running an empire? This requires that the youths, or children, be seen as a distinct category, that there exist a clear idea of what an adult is—the person who really should manage such an enterprise. As Philippe Ariès argues, the notion of childhood as a particular stage, and of children as a distinct group, itself has a history illustrated by his observation that mediaeval society, for example, made no great distinction between the adult and the child. We may wish to connect Burke's view of the "boys" of the East India Company as an arriviste class—a class that must pass through the *discipline* of a "necessary probation" (developed below)—with Ariès's argument that by 1720, in France at least, it became more common for the upper classes to both take note of and to criticize the excessive "coddling" of children in lower-class families. In the eighteenth century there emerged the idea of children as a distinct group viewed as fragile and needing to be "safeguarded and reformed." It is precisely this sentiment of reform to which Burke gives expression. What may be worrying Burke is that the youths are simply bypassing the necessary discipline of the school, one designed to reform as much as to educate,[31] and thus the reference to the "boys whom we are whipping at school" is not incidental but illustrative.

Burke's fear regarding the age of the "boys" in the East India Company reflects a larger crisis in Europe during a period when the categories of childhood and youth were in great flux. It is often remarked that the extremity of *Reflections* derives from Burke's being witness to a transition from a feudal to a bourgeois order, and so we see a similar shock in his view of the power granted to youth. "Generational tensions often characterize societies in the first stages of economic and political modernization," the historian John Gillis has written, "and Europe was no exception."[32] In referring to the petty punishments meted out to recalcitrant pupils, Burke is simply heir to an earlier view of the school that was shared by such figures as Hobbes and partially persisted. The school, in this case Oxford, was a place where boys were sent, Hobbes writes, "by their parents to save themselves the trouble of governing them at home, during that time wherein children are least governable."[33] Rendering "governable," one of the aims of the school, will come to play a significant role in the colonial context: the native will be viewed as similar to the (European) child, that is, not fully governable, an analogy that invests the parent-child relationship with other political stakes beyond that of dominance within the family. Implicit in these views of childhood is a teleological understanding of adulthood as the proper endpoint of development, which enables childhood to be seen as a necessarily imperfect stage. "This is the theory of progress applied to the individual life-cycle," Ashis Nandy writes. "Much of the pull of the ideology of colonialism and much of the power of modernity can be traced to the evolutionary implications of the concept of the child in the western worldview."[34] Certainly in the period in which Burke is writing this theory of progress is emergent rather than dominant, and the biological and evolutionary component would only be adjoined in the nineteenth century. Nonetheless compressed in Burke's statement are a host of anxieties that reveal a great deal regarding the links between the child/adult distinction, teleological notions of progress, and the colonial context.

It has been noted already that the passage cited earlier is in direct opposition to previous depictions of India: Burke inverts the figure of the oriental despot so that this position of absolute power is played by the East India Company official.[35] But if this observation is brought into proximate consideration with the passage in the *Reflections* in which Burke suggests that "men of talent" be allowed to enter the House of Commons only after a probation period, then the truth of this attack on an arriviste class could be acknowledged only after indicating some insurmountable contradictions. In Burke's analysis of the French Revolution, he referred favorably to the "miscibility" of the burghers as one reason England had avoided the bloodiness of the French Revolution.[36] This is a part of his understanding of the Glorious Revolution of 1688 and a view shared by many of his contemporaries. Yet when considering the India-returned colonials, he can only recoil in horror. Miscibility, or mixing, is not to be advocated here, though he already sees it happening in social, sexual, and financial settings:

> In India all the vices operate by which sudden fortune is acquired; in England are often displayed, by the same persons, the virtues which dispense hereditary wealth. Arrived in England, the destroyers of the nobility and gentry of a whole kingdom will find the best company in this nation, at a board of elegance and hospitality. Here the manufacturer and husbandman will bless the just and punctual hand, that in India has torn the cloth from the loom, or wrested the scanty portion of rice and salt from the peasant in Bengal, or wrung from him the very opium in which he forgot his oppression and his oppressors. They marry into your families; they enter into your senate; they ease your estates by loans. . . . There is scarcely an house in the kingdom that does not feel some concern and interest that makes all reform of our eastern government appear officious and disgusting; and, on the whole, a most discouraging attempt.[37]

Burke is obsessed with the vices produced by the acquisition of sudden fortune; in England the same impulse exists but is mitigated by the presence of "virtues" derived from hereditary wealth. What he seeks to effect here is a *break* in the identification of the newly wealthy colonial class as simply a new version of the self-made wealth of the merchant and manufacturer, that is, the burghers whom J. G. A. Pocock identifies in Burke's text when he cautions against an anachronistic reading that would see this class as synonymous with the bourgeoisie.[38] I would extend Pocock's influential reading of this passage in the *Reflections* to Burke's India writings, which Pocock does not consider. For Burke in these writings argues that there is a fundamental and qualitative difference between these new boys from India and the "manufacturers and husbandmen," even though both were examples of classes outside the gentry that attained great wealth. That he should assert this fundamental difference indicates how the "epochal" quality he saw at work in the French Revolution (which many critics have noted) equally distinguishes his understanding of the transformation of Indian society at the hands of the small numbers of Britons there.[39]

Indianism seeps in by various means: through intermarriage ("they marry into your families"), through political influence ("they enter into your senate"), and through money ("they ease your estates with loans").[40] That his list of warnings should begin with marriage alerts us to debates circulating in colonial frontiers regarding the dangers of mixtures and métissage; even though these were expatriate or settler Britons, the self-conception and racial identity of such a group are by no means clear, as Ann Laura Stoler shows in the context of French Indochina and the Netherlands Indies, and Linda Colley among the English in eighteenth-century India.[41] The great irony for Burke is that the "destroyers of the nobility and gentry" in India arrive in Britain to "find the best company in this nation." The "blessing" from an older class upon the very same hand "that has torn the cloth from the loom, or wrested the scanty portion of rice and salt from the peasant" is an image that is also meant to push the contradiction of this unreflective embrace to its extreme.[42] Usury and the buying of influence recur elsewhere in his writings, but they may simply be a pejorative set of names for phenomena he excuses in other contexts. In the "Speech on Fox's East India Bill," he criticizes the very mingling of classes which he implicitly praises in the *Reflections* when considering Britain's differences from France. In the following passage from the *Reflections* Burke makes use of the striking notion of a "miscible" relationship between landed and monied interests:

> By the vast debt of France a great monied interest had insensibly grown up, and with it a great power. By the ancient usages which prevailed in that kingdom, the general circulation of property, and in particular the mutual convertibility of land into money, and of money into land, had always been a matter of difficulty. . . . All these had kept the landed and monied interests more separated in France, *less miscible*, and the owners of the two distinct species of property not so well disposed to each other as they are in this country.[43]

One might deduce from this analysis that Burke thought that the intermarriage of an India-returned class with English women would actually be another way of defusing a potential threat created by exclusion; rather than enabling class *ressentiment*, intermarriage and mingling would do again for England what they had done a century earlier, in

1688. In France the monied interest was set in opposition to the landed interest, an unhealthy separation abetted by the difficulty of converting land into money and vice versa.[44] Though a legal reason is given for this, Burke is also aware of the role of cultural and symbolic "taints" in underpinning this class division. The landed interests in France, even when they "united themselves by marriage ... with the other description, the wealth which saved the family from ruin, was supposed to contaminate and degrade it."[45] In these few pages we have in miniature a theory of *ressentiment* as well as a recipe for its containment. From the idea of "miscible" orders in society to the "evil eye" which is cast by the people on monied property and the psychological observation of the "pride of wealthy [but not noble] men" who "felt with resentment an inferiority," Burke sketches a brittle, contingent, and fragile social order whose contradictions may erupt at any moment.[46] If intermarriage had enabled England to resolve its crises earlier, why respond so strongly against the India-returned boys? It would appear that in Burke's mind they were Jacobins of a more profound sort, themselves the destroyers of a class of gentry and the agents of "total revolution" and subversion. In fact they may have been the initial model whose activities allowed him to see almost a decade before the French Revolution what the sudden decimation of an old established order would mean.

The theory that class tension is at the core of the conflict of the French Revolution, as opposed to its more harmonious resolution in England's Glorious Revolution, is linked to what Burke sees as a penchant for novelty characteristic of a certain class. In understanding this, we find yet another example of the affinity Burke perceived in India and France. I have suggested that some of his suspicion of the operation of this new mercantile wealth in England can be attributed to his examination of the English East India Company officials (Indianism). In the *Reflections* this insight is visible in his description of the Jacobins, who seek an expression of power that takes its form through novelty:

> The monied interest is in its nature more ready for any adventure; and its possessors more disposed to new enterprizes of any kind. Being of a recent acquisition, it falls in more naturally with any novelties. It is therefore the kind of wealth which will be resorted to by all who wish for change.
>
> Along with the monied interest, a new description of men had grown up.... I mean the political Men of Letters. Men of Letters, fond of distinguishing themselves, are rarely averse to innovation.[47]

The first paragraph elaborates his earlier thesis that property, or the landed interest, is "sluggish" in contrast to the liquid rapidity of money; thus the landed interest needs to be "protected"—even by political over-representation—against the monied interest. He describes the monied interest as more inclined toward "adventure," attributing qualities of its possessors to its operation. The second paragraph moves from the naming of these qualities to a rather seamless reference to "Men of Letters." In a sense, the functions played by these two groups in France are unified in his earlier picture of the East India Company officials. The centrality of the figure of Rousseau in Burke's examination of Jacobinism echoes in the phrase "political architect" which he employed to describe the centrality of Warren Hastings in the upheavals caused by the East India Company.[48] The passage cited above already contains an outline of the vanity that Burke will ascribe to Rousseau in his emphatic observation that men of letters are "fond of distinguishing themselves."

Burke's attack on Rousseau in the *Letter to a Member of the National Assembly* of 1791 moves from a general diagnosis of the sickness of the French nation to a specific indictment of the figure of Rousseau.[49] Continuing pharmacological tropes of the illness of the French which he began to employ in the *Reflections*, he contends that "the state doctors" have made the nation "very sick . . . by their medicines." Having created this illness, "the charlatan tells them that what is past cannot be helped . . . that sickness is inevitable in all constitutional revolutions." Burke names the "modern philosophers" as the causes of the illness, and their policy regarding education. "Instead of forming their young minds to that docility, to that modesty, which are the grace and charm of youth, . . . they artificially foment these evil dispositions, and even form them into springs of action." Rather than instilling "docility" the Assembly recommends authors of "mixed or ambiguous morality," but are themselves caught in a cycle of false education: "The Assembly recommends to its youth a study of the bold experimenters in morality. Every body knows that there is a great dispute amongst their leaders, which of them is the best resemblance of Rousseau. In truth, they all resemble him. His blood they transfuse into their minds and into their manners. Him they study; him they meditate. . . . Rousseau is their canon of Holy writ." The corruption of youth is also part of Burke's charges against the boys of the East India Company, who return to Britain and contaminate the gentility of the existing class structure. The company officials return with wealth, but wealth gained in the lawless regime set in place by Hastings. Concerning Rousseau, Burke argues that the leaders of the French Revolution are engaged in a kind of childish mimicry. Within the psyche of Rousseau himself, Burke purports to find the same principle at work, which he views as the by-product of "vanity." "Their object," he writes, "is to merge all natural and social sentiment in inordinate vanity. In a small degree... vanity is of little moment. When full-grown, it is the worst of vices, and the occasional mimic of them all. It makes the whole man false. It leaves nothing sincere or trustworthy about him."[50] A figure of pure inauthenticity, a hollow man, the person struck with vanity becomes the "mimic" of various vices.

It is because in thought *and life* Rousseau dealt in abstractions that he was able to proclaim sympathy for a suffering being far away but was unable to shed a tear for the children he famously abandoned. As Burke sharply puts it, contrasting the abstract notion of benevolence with the fleshly encounter of the face-to-face, "Benevolence to the whole species, and want of feeling for every individual with whom the professors come in contact, form the character of the new philosophy."[51] There is a consonance here in his dismissive view of the generality of the "whole species" that takes precedence over the singularity of an ethical encounter, as Levinas understood it, staged between two particular individuals.[52] Rousseau, or rather the figure of Rousseau, represents a new kind of celebrity, one who can be known at large by a public persona, like a mask employed on the stage, but whose role within his "knowable community" may be a reprehensible one. Hence Burke writes, "Thousands admire the sentimental writer; the affectionate father is hardly known in his parish,"[53] identifying what is characteristically modern about the figure of Rousseau. This "ethics of vanity" takes the man "from his house and sets him on stage" to produce an "artificial creature, with painted, theatric sentiments... and *formed to be contemplated at a due distance.*"[54] Although Burke himself was keenly aware of the theatrical nature of politics—indeed, what was the trial of Warren Hastings if not an attempt to use the "spectacle" of a certain kind of publicly performed event for the sake of a political agenda?—here he levels the charge against Rousseau that his persona requires distance to operate.[55] In an intimate setting it falls away, or—to use Rousseau's own description, albeit to different effect—becomes "transparent."[56] And yet for Burke this transparency only lays bare what is reprehensible in Rousseau.

"The Two Great Evils of Our Time"

Rousseau becomes emblematic of something larger than himself; for Burke, he comes to represent the flaws and dangers of Jacobinism as such.[57] Similarly Warren Hastings comes to embody "Indianism." Together Burke named these forces the "two great evils of our time."[58]

Yet if these are the human representatives of two great evils, how did Burke specifically define the phenomena themselves? What common characteristics link Jacobinism and Indianism and allow Burke to move between France and India?

Earlier I wrote that *Reflections* can be read as a response to the emergence of a political modernity about which Burke is profoundly ambivalent. In its attempt to fundamentally reformulate human nature Jacobinism must ignore human finitude, human fragility and vulnerability. Burke takes no notice of Rousseau's transparency as exposing and foregrounding a certain personal vulnerability (through his confessional writings) and instead seizes upon Rousseau's "vanity," introducing a host of terms that a modern reader associates with psychoanalysis (mimicry, etc.).[59] This is of a piece with his suspicion of those who held an erroneous belief in personal inspiration, or "enthusiasm" in its etymological sense (to feel oneself infused by a god, derived ultimately from the Greek *en* + *theos*). In other words, what Rousseau took to be "transparency" became enthusiasm for Burke.[60] As Pocock argues, the movement of these terms from France to England is limited and defined by the manner in which the French events were necessarily inserted into a preexisting set of languages. Recall here how in the *Reflections* and elsewhere in British political discourse it was enthusiasm and the passions that had to be regulated. And yet Jacobinism would seem to be precisely the *cultivation* of this kind of enthusiasm.

There would appear to be even more fundamental components of Jacobinism disturbing to Burke: the seizure of church lands, the attack on organized religion, the circulation of paper money, and the threat to the idea of an ancient constitution. In identifying causes he named the unmoored intellectual class, who took pleasure in transgression. It is in a letter from late in Burke's life (1795) where we see the most explicit statement of a belief that was latent even in the earlier writings: "What is Jacobinism? It is an attempt ... to eradicate prejudice out of the minds of men."[61] Prejudice in modern language hardly sounds like a defensible practice, violating as it does the idea of a fair judgment. What Burke has in mind is an uneasy combination of these aspects of the term, upon which a positive valence is awkwardly placed. The recuperation of prejudice is of a piece with his defense of custom as a valid basis for action. He argues against those who would denigrate custom as having no rational basis within the formulation of a judgment—part of the *tabula rasa* vision of the human subject implied by Jacobinism. To put this in other terms, custom for Burke marks the necessary fore-conception at work in human judgment.[62]

Prejudice and the Definition of Jacobinism

The defense of prejudice may seem to be an argument for an irrational clinging to antiquated practices for their own sake; certainly this is how critics of Burke read (and often caricatured) his work.[63] However, for Burke prejudice is always connected with a more general critique of the primacy of individual reason. I cite a lengthy passage from the *Reflections* that brings together these concerns and binds them to Burke's financial critique of the revolutionary regime:

> In this enlightened age I am bold enough to confess, that we are generally men of untaught feelings; that instead of casting away all our old prejudices, we cherish them to a very considerable degree.... We are afraid to put men to live and trade each on his own private stock of reason; because we suspect that this stock in each man is small, and that the individuals would do better to avail themselves of the general bank and capital of nations, and of ages. Many of our men of speculation, instead of exploding general prejudices, employ their sagacity to discover the latent wisdom which prevails in them. If they find what they seek, and they seldom fail, they think it more wise to continue the prejudice, with the reason involved, than to cast away the coat of prejudice, and to leave nothing but the naked reason; because prejudice, with its reason, has a motive to give action to that reason, and an affection which will give it permanence. Prejudice is of ready application in the emergency; it previously engages the mind in a steady course of wisdom and virtue, and does not leave the man hesitating in the moment of decision, sceptical, puzzled, and unresolved. Prejudice renders a man's virtue his habit; and not a series of unconnected acts. Through just prejudice, his duty becomes a part of his nature.[64]

In contrast to the "enlightened" age, Burke valorizes "untaught feelings." But the emphasis of the latter phrase may rest more upon "untaught" rather than the language of feeling, for at the end of the paragraph he explains that prejudice "renders a man's virtue his habit." Burke implicitly draws upon Aristotle's discussion of habit in the *Nicomachean Ethics* as one way to ground his idea of prejudice.[65] But the registers on which Burke plays suddenly shift, seemingly in midsentence: "We are afraid to put men to live *and trade* each on his own private stock of reason" (emphasis mine). Turning the question of evaluative judgment during a life into the trading of private stock, Burke renders the use of reason into a kind of wager (or investment, at any rate). In introducing this financial language, he transmutes the idea of individual autonomy based upon the use of reason into the autonomy associated with the despised figure of the stock-jobber (assailed at length elsewhere). But thus far, to "trade" on "private stock" is only a partial development of the mercantile analogy; the next step presents a startling and fascinating union of two apparently disparate aspects of Burke's thought. The limits of individual reason are expressed as the smallness of the "stock in each man," and thus all men "would do better to avail themselves of the general bank and capital of nations, and of ages." This general bank is expressive of two kinds of collectives understood as transindividual: the first is that of the nation, and the second is the intergenerational relation between different "ages." Moreover the "general bank and capital" reveal how Burke perceives collective wisdom to be like collective capital; individual stock should in fact draw upon a larger pool of assets, so to speak. The "speculators" in France, by relying only on their private stocks—like the stock-jobbers and like the Jacobins who introduce valueless paper money—contrast with "our men of speculation" who, "instead of exploding general prejudices, employ their sagacity to discover the latent wisdom which prevails in them." Using speculation both in its financial and its philosophical sense, Burke suggests that the discovery of latent wisdom is a discovery of latent value, akin to the sounder economic policy that the English deploy. Jacobinism and the Jacobin "men of speculation"—philosophes and writers like Rousseau—"explode" the very prejudice that is the source of this value.

Burke argues not for the elimination of reason by feeling but "to continue the prejudice, *with the reason involved*" rather than "to cast away the coat of prejudice, and to leave nothing but the naked reason." Greater importance is placed upon the "coat" of prejudice; the language of clothing and of veiling has made its appearance before in the *Reflections* and always serves more than its apparently ornamental purpose. Thus Burke elsewhere speaks of the "decent drapery" of life.[66] By asserting that "naked" reason on its own will be unsuccessful in persuading and affecting, he is close to Hume's argument that reason alone fails to govern the human will; sentiment and affect go further.[67] "Naked reason" illustrates how that which is "transparent" and pellucid in the language of the French Enlightenment acquires for Burke the connotation of rawness, of something shorn from its context.[68] Since his definition of prejudice contains reason, it is clear that he did not advocate *ir*rationalism in politics; it was rather the priority of a certain kind of reason—"geometric" or "arithmetic" reason, as he calls it in the *Reflections*—against which he argued. In what way does this view of Jacobinism resemble or differ from the second "great evil," Indianism?

Indianism

The phenomenon that Indianism describes is already in Burke's field of vision during the composition of the *Reflections*, though one of its first uses is in 1794, in reference to the effort that occupied him for nearly two decades. He writes to Earl Fitzwilliam on June 21 that year, "Ten thousand thanks to you for having . . . recommended me to that seat which has given me an opportunity of shewing my good dispositions to the Country, and of combating, though with very feeble arms, and not much success, the two great evils of our time, Indianism and Jacobinism."[69] The seat for which Earl Fitzwilliam recommended him allowed him to make his long-promised departure from Parliament. The letter therefore has a valedictory quality, bidding farewell by naming those two causes that have preoccupied him the most. By this time the trial against Hastings was drawing to a close, and its result—the acquittal of Hastings in 1795—leads Burke to note the futility of his efforts. Yet the sense of partial failure in the trial is also extended to the inefficacy of his efforts to warn of the consequences of the French Revolution.

There is a related third area of concern about which Burke writes, and this is the Protestant ascendancy in Ireland. Certainly not a neglected issue in more recent scholarship of Burke, it is nonetheless not emphasized enough how he understood these three causes to relate to each other beyond their mere coincidence within the same historical period.[70] Burke's letter to Sir Hercules Langrishe on May 26, 1795, presents clearly the adjacency of these in his mind. Langrishe, an advocate of Catholic relief, spoke on the Catholic Question on May 2, 1795, and had written to Burke privately. It is to him that Burke responds with an expression of sympathy and defeat: "I must consign my feelings on that terrible disappointment [i.e., Catholic relief] to the same patience in which I have been obliged to bury the vexation I suffered on the defeat of the other great, just and honorable causes in which I have had some share; and which have given more of dignity than of peace and advantage to a long, laborious life." Burke has in mind the recent acquittal of Hastings and also the inefficacy of his writings against Jacobinism. He elaborates: "I can hardly overrate the malignity of the principles of Protestant ascendancy, as they affect Ireland; or of Indianism, as they affect these countries, and as they affect Asia, or of Jacobinism, as they affect all of Europe, and that of human society itself. The last is the greatest evil. But it readily combines with the others, and flows from them."[71] The principles of Indianism in this letter are malign "as they affect these countries, and as they affect Asia" because of the uprooting of Indian society caused by such entities as the East India Company. Elsewhere it is a phenomenon occurring in these countries that negatively impacts England as well. We are now in a position to understand the significance of the unexpected reference in the *Reflections* itself to the phenomenon that Indianism is supposed to identify, mentioned in passing in the previous chapter: "The power of the house of commons, direct or indirect, is indeed great; and long may it be able to preserve its greatness, and the spirit belonging to true greatness, at the full; and it will do so, as long as it can keep the breakers of the law in India from becoming the makers of law for England."[72] The response from Wollstonecraft, Paine, and others demonstrates that the *Reflections* is a text directed against English radicals as much as against the Jacobins in France. Its concerns are with England as much as with France, and consequently Burke later uses the term *Indianism* to describe the principle whereby men of talent but no property gain sudden wealth in the colonies, and then return home to England to subvert parliamentary representation and processes. This easy and rapid movement violates an argument that Burke outlines elsewhere in the *Reflections* regarding a period of "probation" necessary for those who would occupy positions of power: "You do not imagine that I wish to confine power, authority, and distinction to blood, and names, and titles. . . . Every thing ought to be open; but not indifferently to every man. . . . The road to eminence and power, from obscure condition, ought not to be made too easy. . . . If rare merit be the rarest of all rare things, it ought to pass through some sort of probation."[73] This idea of a *class on probation* catches Burke's own ambivalent relation to the elite order in Britain, as well as elucidating the ideological compromise he seeks to lay out between people of "ability" and people of "property" elsewhere in the work. It also brings us back to the economic argument proposed in the *Reflections* to explain the cause of revolution in France. The "miscibility" of burghers in the Glorious Revolution of 1688 led to a kind of compromise with the landed gentry. Rather than a conflict, as is now present in France, there was a partial melding of the two. But with the new opportunities created by the entry of the East India Company officials into India, there now is a re-creation of a circumstance in England which he sees in operation in France: a dynamic class of men detached from traditional impediments and filiations. Indianism in the English Parliament is the name for this pernicious circumstance.

Indianism seems to have two meanings in Burke's vocabulary: the one just described, which affects England, and a second that describes the set of principles "as they affect these countries, and as they affect Asia."[74] (Note that Burke may be using the plural "these countries" as a result of the expression "the Indies," still in use to refer to many places in addition to the Indian subcontinent.) Parallel to this force are the principles of "Jacobinism, as they affect *all* of Europe" (emphasis mine). In a kind of continental thinking, Burke identifies two nefarious political forces that spread over Asia and Europe. There is a trace of the paranoiac quality here seen elsewhere in his political thought (the cabal in France, etc.).

The letter to Langrishe, which considers the Protestant ascendancy in Ireland, also employs the category of "men of talent" that I have invoked from the *Reflections* and noted in the India writings. We return here to the hydraulic language of passion, enthusiasm, and most particularly talent—elements that need to be properly channeled by the state. Their improper use leads them to naturally flow toward a rebellious Jacobinism. Catholics, for Burke, ought in the Irish situation to be naturally contrary to a Jacobin impulse, since the latter represents a fundamentally antireligious tendency. Understanding his view of talent in the Irish situation goes some way to bringing out the strange and complex position he takes on Ireland's fate, steering a course between a muted anticolonialism and the defense of property under threat.[75] A fortnight earlier, in a letter to Earl Fitzwilliam in response to the same Irish debates, Burke writes, "I am very sorry to say, that the course they are pursuing in Ireland will Jacobinize all the Energies and all the active Talents of that Country. . . . Jacobinism is the Vice of men of Parts; and, in this age, it is the Channel in which all discontents will run. It is a vain conceit that property can stand against it, alone and unsupported."[76] Talents will be Jacobinized, and discontent will find its outlet in this channel. I would venture a speculation here that Jacobinism is thus similar to a kind of cathexis, but for Burke it is a false cathexis (recalling the false Sublime).[77] The full armory of his vocabulary appears even here in this letter on the Irish Question, with Jacobinism holding a central place.

Both Jacobinism and Indianism are therefore generalizable terms that emerge in one specific context but are used to name and describe events in another. To Langrishe, his Irish correspondent, Burke identifies Jacobinism "as the greatest evil. But it readily combines with the others, and flows from them." Yet a year later, writing to Loughborough in March 1796, he reverses the primary source of danger and writes (see this chapter's epigraph), "Our Government and our laws are beset by two different Enemies . . . Indianism and Jacobinism. In some cases they act separately, in some they act in conjunction: but of this I am sure; that the first is worst by far . . . and for this amongst other reasons, that it weakens[,] discredits, and ruins that force, which ought to be employed with the greatest Credit and Energy against the other; and

FIGURE 3. James Gillray, "The Impeachment, or 'The Father of the Gang Turned King's Evidence.'" Published May 1791 by S. W. Fores, No. 3 Piccadilly, London. Courtesy of the Library of Congress. Reflecting his later rift with Charles James Fox, Burke is shown holding Fox's head alongside Richard Sheridan (also involved in the impeachment trial against Hastings); the words Burke speaks refer to them as "abettors of Revolutions" and "plots and conspiracies" which aim at "the overthrow of the British Constitution."

that it furnishes Jacobinism with its strongest arms against all *formal* government."[78] By arguing that Indianism provides Jacobinism with arms against formal government, Burke has in mind the manner in which the East India Company structure informally became an empire; it has the power of a government without any of its formal structures. It is, as he once put it, "a State in disguise of a Merchant."[79] *Jacobinism* is a term that preexists Burke's use; *Indianism*, as I noted, is a word he invents, and we come closer to understanding what he meant to identify in coining it to name this informal power structure.[80] His primary motive in undertaking the impeachment trial against Hastings was to argue for a parliamentary oversight of the East India Company; consistent with his remark here, this was his way of reining in Indianism. His privileging of one over the other in different contexts probably has to do with his interlocutor: Irish links to revolutionary France were a more proximate and real threat, and so in speaking to Langrishe Jacobinism comes into the foreground.[81] However, his lengthy letter to Loughborough begins by decrying the pension awarded to Hastings, and so company abuses and Indianism loom larger.[82] Yet Indianism is the "hardest to deal with" because it appears to undermine from within the governmental use of force, which it weakens and discredits. The reason the use of force is weakened and discredited derives from the lack of a moral basis in its use. In other words, when state force is used to defend "a partnership agreement in a trade of pepper and coffee, callico or tobacco, or some other such low concern"[83]—to recall Burke's disparaging description in the *Reflections* of a state based on trade rather than more substantial principles—then this gradually delegitimizes the entity that presides over it.

The delegitimization of force is often in Burke's thoughts when he discusses Ireland, India, and France. The letter to Langrishe discussed earlier advocates the use of "wise lenient arts" which "ought to precede measures of vigour." That the "measures of vigour" refer to the use of force becomes clear in the following sentences; I would draw attention to their affinity with his earlier critique of contractarian theories of society:

> They [the measures of vigour; i.e., coercive measures] ought to be the *ultima*, not the *prima*, not the *tota* ratio of a wise government. God forbid, that on a worthy occasion authority should want the means of force, or the disposition to use it. But where a prudent and enlarged policy does not precede, and attend it too, where the hearts of the better sort of people do not go with the hands of the soldiery, you may call your constitution what you will, in effect it will consist of three parts, (orders, if you please,)—cavalry, infantry, and artillery, —and of nothing better.[84]

The loss of the American colonies, which Burke felt was due to the excessive use of force in place of reconciliation and lenient arts, may be the lingering sting underlying this passage. To rush to coercion, rather than finding ways to generate consent by winning over the hearts of the people, lays bare the institutions of force underlying the state. The constitution, which elsewhere Burke has understood as the product of different orders (or classes) of society, will appear to be little more than a militarized entity. The "nothing better" expressed here is a reduction of the constitution he identified earlier: the diminution of society to a mere contract or partnership agreement. In both cases what is lost is an element that is supposed to inspire "reverence" (for the state) or "respect" (for law).

It is the *absence* of this quality of reverence for the state which the term *Indianism* is meant to identify. The language of these letters comes back by many turns of phrase to the contrary relationship to law. "My Lord, My Lord," Burke exclaims to Loughborough, "I do not wonder, that your laws are *despised*, not only by the rich delinquents of India, but by whatever is most insignificant amongst the people." The despising of law, initiated by the delinquent behavior of Hastings and Company officials, leads to a more general disregard for law: "I do not wonder that the clearest and most manifest Treasons meet with an acquittal, when the first Tribunals in the Kingdom despise the Laws of which they are themselves at once the makers and the interpreters."[85] The acquittal of Hastings itself is then an instance of the despising of law characteristic of Indianism; we should also take Burke's emphasis here on the "makers of law" back to the line I reiterated from the *Reflections* on the breakers of law in India becoming the makers of law in England. Indianism is the expedient, but not moral, use of law and force.[86] We may now understand what Burke meant when writing that Indianism "weakens[,] discredits, and ruins that force" which ought to be employed against "the other [i.e., Jacobinism]." It is also clearer why he writes that "Our government *and our Laws*" are beset by the enemies of Indianism and Jacobinism.

The undermining of law is one aspect of the "internal" effects of Indianism, that is, as it acts upon England. Burke links this aspect with an analysis of men of "talent," and it proves to be another common element present in his examination of revolutionary France and the parts of India under Company rule. The "men of talent" in the French case are represented by several groups, but above all by the intellectual class, the men of letters. Perhaps surprisingly, the group Burke identifies in India as resembling this element are the East India Company officials—also men of talent unmoored from traditional class affiliations and restraints in England. The colony in India comes to represent an experiment in what it would look like to create a society shorn of its customary procedures and impediments to power. We may go further in clarifying the resemblance with France: in India, which Burke examines closely before turning his attention to France, he saw the preexisting set of social relationships and hierarchies intervened upon by an external force which, in turn, imposed a wholly new collection of laws—a *tabula rasa* before the more classical example associated with revolutionary France. Thus the characteristic modernity attributed so often to his vision of France is in a fundamental way shaped and given form by his examination of emerging colonial modernity in India. We may understand now why he insists on depicting the Jacobins as colonial conquerors when he writes that the "pretended citizens [i.e., the Jacobins] treat France exactly like a country of conquest" and hear a prophetic resonance of his future thoughts on France when he writes of India, "The country sustains, almost every year, the miseries of a revolution."[87] Telescoped in miniature here, in 1783, are the lineaments of an argument that would be replicated with surprising similarity in the *Reflections* of 1790.

The miseries of revolution in India caused by the upheavals instituted by Company officials—as they fundamentally altered rules of property,[88] customary law, and the social fabric—would recur to Burke as he surveyed the threat menacing the landscape of continental Europe. In more ways than one we can see that the emergence of a colonial modernity is not simply a peripheral element helpful in understanding the beginnings of modernity in Europe, but that it is constitutive of the very language used to describe and name that modernity.

5 / Atlantic Revolutions and Their Indian Echoes: The Place of the Americas in Burke's Asia Writings

(a) Reflections on the Revolution in St. Domingue/Haiti: The Treatise that Edmund Burke Almost Wrote

Were we to give them [the settlers of French descent in Quebec] the French Constitution—a constitution founded on principles dramatically opposed to ours, that could not assimilate with it on a single point: as different from it as wisdom from folly, as vice from virtue, as the most opposite extremes in nature—a constitution founded on what was called the rights of man? But let this constitution be examined by its practical effects in the French West India colonies. These, notwithstanding three disastrous wars, were most happy and flourishing till they heard of the rights of man. —EDMUND BURKE (MAY 6, 1791), WILLIAM COBBETT, PARLIAMENTARY HISTORY OF ENGLAND

Of the two Atlantic revolutions that occurred between 1770 and 1800 in the New World, one is granted a large place by historical memory and is hailed by many in the period and after as possessing a world-historical significance: the American Revolution. The other, in the French sugar colony of St. Domingue, has until recently been pushed aside or actively repressed, made into a sign for racialized violence rather than an expression for a more universal liberty. Burdened by the weight of liberators turned tyrants (Toussaint to Christophe), of blacks, *gens-de-couleur,* and whites in complex alliances, the purportedly mingled complicities for the practices of slavery and the bloody outbursts against it, the story of the Haitian Revolution is still one whose larger significance in the period and its legacies for the present are yet to receive the recognition they merit.

The events of the Haitian Revolution in the context of this study are crucial both for their apparent fulfillment of prophecy—of the famous episode in the *Histoire des deux Indes* calling for a "black Spartacus" in the New World to avenge the crime of slavery—and for the fear they inspired in a writer otherwise sympathetic to movements for justice in Europe's colonies; I have in mind Edmund Burke's horrified letters after a massacre of Europeans at Cap Français in French St. Domingue, which seem in tension with his passionate denunciations of fellow Briton Warren Hastings for the abuses he oversaw at the East India Company in Bengal. These letters gave me pause: Burke was indeed a strident defender of India in the period, but what would have happened if there had been violence there as in Haiti? Would he have been so certain of his desire to impeach Hastings in a seven-year trial in Parliament? My thoughts on Haiti began with these comparative historical speculations.

In this chapter I explore the circumstances and worries that underlay the formation of Indianism and Jacobinism as Burke used these terms. In order to explore what is particular about Burke's writings on India it is instructive to compare them with references and responses to events in St. Domingue in his letters and in a key speech delivered to Parliament. The historian P. J. Marshall has pursued in greater detail the possibilities of comparison between the making of one empire (India) and the unmaking of another (North America);[1] this chapter explores the resonances of this shift of imperial interests in Burke's thought and considers the logic of an implicit comparison (for St. Domingue and India are not, to my knowledge, explicitly compared although they are juxtaposed in one interesting late passage). The first part of this chapter explores the significance of Burke's comments on St. Domingue/Haiti in order to consider how the example of India is put under stress, while the second part returns to some of his earlier writings from the late 1770s and early 1780s to illustrate how the shifting imperial focus from the Americas to Asia is articulated at times as a "compensation."

The Absent Indian Jacobin: Haitian Insurgents and the Uses of Jacobinism

In an earlier chapter I addressed the acquisition of "sudden fortune" that is one component of Indianism and causes it to bear comparison with Jacobinism; here I examine one of the peculiarities of Burke's use of these terms. Because of his association of Jacobinism with thoughtless innovation, and for a variety of other reasons already considered, when Burke refers to Jacobins in India, he is referring to Warren Hastings and to East India Company officials, not to indigenous insurgent groups. This ought to surprise us, and yet it does not strike most readers of Burke as odd. What makes this unusual association discursively possible for Burke is the *absence* in his political purview of a native form of violent rebellion in the areas ruled over by the Company.[2] His descriptions of India are meant to evoke sympathy primarily by his descriptions of fallen nobility, great families laid low by the East India Company. There are, to be sure, also many references to the peasant made more miserable by Company reforms (these are crucial to his inversion of the imagery of oriental despotism), but his speeches during the Hastings trial focus more strongly on the concrete images of native gentry.[3] The touch of irony that is present in Burke's occasional use of the term *Jacobins* to describe company officials in India only comes into visible relief against the larger tableau of colonial events globally. Taking the case of St. Domingue (Haiti after its revolution) as a counterexample, it is possible to glimpse what Burke's views might have been had he detected a more organized and violent opposition in India in this period. I engage in this exercise of speculation based on historical counterfactual in order to bring out more sharply how fragile and contingent Burke's position on India may have been. As I noted earlier, he was not anticolonial so much as reformist of company abuses and anti-Company. Yet reading his fiery prose, one might be forgiven for overlooking this fact; indeed it seems an intentional effect of his writing to produce such a result. Hence he makes frequent remarks in his correspondence that he has been fighting for the liberation of the downtrodden. "I have spent the last 14 years of my existence," he wrote to Loughborough in the twilight of his life, on March 17, 1796, "in a labour hardly credible, in hopes of obtaining justice for an oppressed people."[4]

Justice is certainly a salient word in this sentence and certainly a good part of Burke's animus against the East India Company derived from the charges that its official had orchestrated the killing of Nandakumar.[5] In one of the many interesting exchanges of letters between Burke and Philip Francis (in Bengal), one can find further support for the assertion that Burke equates Company officials with the revolutionaries in France. He was not alone in seeing these two as kindred. In fact it became a cause of concern that many young Britons in the East India Company harbored sympathies with the Jacobins.[6] The letter also marks the decisive break in their friendship, since Burke is replying to Francis's criticism that the *Reflections on the Revolution in France* were loosely argued. "You are the only friend I have who will dare to give me advice," Burke writes as a valediction to a friendship he will no longer sustain, and he writes later in the letter of the affinities he sees between the Indian, French, and English contexts, "I should agree with you about the vileness of the controversy with such Miscreants as the Revolution society and the National assembly, and I know very well that they, as well as their allies the Indian delinquents, will darken the air with their arrows."[7] The "allies" of the French and British radicals in India—the Company officials—earn this lowly status for many reasons, to which I would also adjoin (to those others already explored) their trafficking in what Burke increasingly refers to as "murder." Burke asserts that one should always denounce such "approvers of murder,"[8] by which he certainly has Hastings in mind and probably also those who assaulted Marie-Antoinette (recalling the key episode from the *Reflections*). Had the violence not been visibly limited to the Company's actions in India, it is not clear that he would have been so steadfast in his support of the Indian downtrodden; it is with this thought in mind that I turn briefly to his discussion of Hispaniola in the following section.

The reference to justice in the letter to Loughborough certainly had precedents in earlier writings and correspondence. One use is of particular interest for the relation it has to the history of scholarship on Sanskrit and Oriental languages. As an illustration of the argument elsewhere regarding the possibility for orientalist scholarship to enable two conflicting possibilities—simply put, one in which such knowledge serves the aims of colonial dominance and another in which the reservoir of this knowledge serves to contest the legitimacy of such dominance—I refer to a fascinating line from a letter Burke sent to Sir William Jones on June 13, 1781, fifteen years before the letter to Loughborough. Burke had turned to Jones, a famed Sanskritist, in that year for advice and assistance regarding the Bengal Judiciary Bill.[9] This brief letter ends with a reference to a presumed similarity of disposition that he and Jones may share regarding Indian affairs. "I beg ... that you would be so kind as to breakfast with me," Burke writes, "and assist me with your opinion and advice on the conduct of the Bengal Bill. The natives of the East, to whose literature you have done so much justice, are particularly under your protection for their rights."[10] The sentence plays on the multiple idiomatic uses that involve the word *justice*; here the notion of "doing justice" to a literature allows Burke to shift to the idea of rights. The labor of Jones's various translations were indeed a central means by which an archive of Oriental literature was generated.[11] The generation of this archive, in turn, served the possibility of launching a defense against the imposition of radically new social and legal structures upon the land. The relationship of the generation of this Sanskritic archive to later nationalist aspirations, and their defenses of Indian tradition, is by now a well-documented (if no less complicated) phenomenon.[12] What is notable here is how the labor of literary translation enables Burke to extend the notion of "doing justice" to a language to "doing justice" to its people, and by a further extension to the "protection [of] their rights." It is not merely the protection of their rights, but that the natives of the East are presumed to be "under [Jones's] protection *for* their rights." Again, if I belabor the point in clinging to this sentence, it is to emphasize the affinity of the sentiment expressed here with my more general argument concerning what enables the possibility of speaking on behalf of another party.[13] Although it is important to keep in mind that in writing to Jones Burke had the particular achievements of his interlocutor in mind, nonetheless literature becomes the institution that enables an entitlement to protection or a right to rights. We may remark here that Burke's emphasis on concepts such as custom and tradition perhaps lent themselves more easily to the deployment of culture more generally as a basis for a limited anticolonial language (a practice that would reach its culmination in the languages of fully articulated anticolonial nationalism much later). His ability to speak on behalf of India or the peoples of the East in these examples (I mean his letters to Jones and Loughborough) contrast with his growing worries over violence in another colonial arena: the West Indies.

Hispaniola, or the Rights of Man in the Colonies

An insurrection of slaves in St. Domingue took place in August 1791; months before this, in April, Burke found an occasion in Parliament to make reference to events developing on the island of Hispaniola. However, his discussion of St. Domingue is made in the service of winning another argument. The events there provide the resonating knell for Burke's alarmist clanging against the spread of Jacobinism to Quebec. The issue to be discussed in the House on April 21, 1791, was the Quebec Bill, but it became entangled in a dispute that Burke was having with Charles James Fox, who disagreed with the position Burke had taken on the French Revolution in the *Reflections,* published only six months earlier. A week earlier, on April 15, Fox had praised the new constitution of France as "the most stupendous and glorious edifice of liberty, which had been erected on the foundation of human integrity in any time or country."[14] This constitution would itself be scrapped by the revolutionaries a year later, in 1792, but Fox maintained his approval of the revolution perhaps to provoke a rift with Burke in the Whig Party. When the opportunity arose to speak on the Quebec Bill, Burke used it as an occasion to return discussion to his position on the French Revolution "on the rather tenuous pretext that Quebec, being a French-speaking province, might conceivably be offered the new French Constitution."[15] Fox's admiration of the French constitution did not receive a proper reply from Burke until on May 6, 1791, when the House resumed consideration of the Quebec Bill. The passage below illustrates the confluence of several characteristics of Jacobinism in Burke's thought, distilled (if I may be permitted a pharmacological expression myself) to a symbolically rich alembic. I cite the passage at length because there is much I wish to comment upon within it:

> Were we to give them [the settlers of French descent in Quebec] the French Constitution—a constitution founded on principles dramatically opposed to ours, that could not assimilate with it on a single point: as different from it as wisdom from folly, as vice from virtue, as the most opposite extremes in nature—a constitution founded on what was called the rights of man? But let this constitution be examined by its practical effects in the French West India colonies. These, notwithstanding three disastrous wars, were most happy and flourishing till they heard of the rights of man. As soon as this system arrived among them, Pandora's box, replete with every mortal evil, seemed to fly open, hell itself to yawn, and every demon of mischief to overspread the face of the earth. Blacks rose against whites [in St. Domingue], whites against blacks, and each against one another in murderous hostility; subordination was destroyed, the bonds of society torn asunder, and every man seemed to thirst for the blood of his neighbour.
>
> "Black spirits and white
> Blue spirits and gray
> Mingle, mingle, mingle."[16]
>
> All was toil and trouble, discord and blood, from the moment that this doctrine was promulgated among them; and he [Burke] verily believed that wherever the rights of man were preached, such ever had been and ever would be the consequences.
>
> France, who had generously sent them the precious gift of the rights of man, did not like this image of herself reflected in her child, and sent out a body of troops, well seasoned too with the rights of man, to restore order and obedience. These troops, as

soon as they arrived, instructed as they are in the principle of government, felt themselves bound to become parties in the general rebellions and, like most of their brethren at home began asserting their rights by cutting off the head of their general.

Mr. Burke read the late accounts from St. Domingo, delivered to the national assembly, and added, that by way of equivalent for this information, M. Barnave announced the return of the members of the late colonial assembly to the true principles of the constitution. The members of an assembly no longer in existence had bequeathed their return to the principles of the constitution as their last act and deed as a body, and this was an equivalent for all the horrors occasioned by troops joining in a rebellion which they were sent to quell!

Ought this example to induce us to send to our colonies a cargo of the rights of man? As soon would he send them a bale of infected cotton from Marseilles.[17]

Burke returns to the opposition of an ancient constitution based on inheritance and custom and that of the French constitution of 1790–91, containing the rights of man. In his commentary on this episode, Conor Cruise O'Brien fails to appreciate the significance of the fact that the key rift between the two greatest speakers of their day was also over St. Domingue (indeed he removes Burke's remark that one ought to "let this constitution be examined by its practical effects in the French West India colonies"); he puts it down solely to the French constitution, but the real radicalism and threat of those principles is felt only by turning to its effects on the subversion of hierarchies in the colonies. Burke's position on slavery in the West Indies, as with much else, took on a gradualist approach. In other words, he was against the extension of slavery but argued for its gradual abolition.[18] It should be noted that Burke wrote this passage of May 1791 with a degree of prescience, several months before one of the main insurrections of slaves on the island in August. (There had, however, already been disturbances.) But where others see fit to once again praise Burke's prediction—indeed there is a continuous lineage in the criticism to the present day on Burke as a prophet[19]—I would place this remark within his own self-professed anti-Jacobin strategy; this diminishes to a degree the sharpness of the foresight by revealing the motives for his shrill cries. With reference to Burke's "Sketch of a Negro Code" (1792), Christopher Brown has argued that the reform of slavery (including its eventual abolition in some manner) was usually conceived of as part of a larger effort to extend the colonial project. The aim was to consider how "emancipation could sustain, and even advance, colonial enterprise."[20] Brown stresses that Burke's plan attempted to preserve some idea of the family, and to allow for property rights in the transition from slavery to freedom. Moreover, he argues, Burke made marriage a precondition to liberty less out of desire to acknowledge the slave's interests than because it was seen as a necessary training for liberty.[21] "Morality and manners" in this view were seen as a bridge to liberty.

"Black Spirits and White . . . Mingle, Mingle, Mingle"

In order to appreciate this passage on St. Domingue, I would like to connect it to another reference to it which Burke makes about two years later, in August 1793. The English press on August 23 had covered an attack by blacks on Cap Français in the French portion of Hispaniola; thousands of white inhabitants were killed.[22] In his letter to William Windham on the same day, Burke writes:

> What a dreadful affair is this of St Domingo. In horror with regard to the act, and as a cause of indignation against the actors, it exceeds the late massacre of Paris. The systematic plan of extermination the Jacobins have pursued in that fine island, and which they intended for every other island, seems to me to form the top of the climax of their wickedness. Their partisans here affect to shudder if twenty men are killed in a skirmish, and yet they are enthusiasts in favour of those who have reduced sedition, assassination, general robbery, general masacre [sic], and general combustion, into a sort of regular art, and a sort of morality. Every day we live will convince thinking men, that there are evils to which the calamities of war are blessings. Well! we have done very properly in a vigorous opposition to Jacobinism under the plausible disguise of peace. Had it gone on, in my opinion, the burning down of half of London, after the massacre of half its inhabitants, would have been a cheap composition for the whole kingdom. I do not flatter myself, that the English branch of the Jacobin family is a jot better than the French. If it were fifty per cent. better, I should still think it a most abominable thing. We must continue to be vigorous *alarmists*.[23]

Taking these two passages together, it is possible to make out two different explanations of Burke's opposition to Jacobinism. In the first passage, ostensibly concerning the Quebec Bill, Burke's animus is directed more precisely against the threat posed by "what was called the rights of man" in the colonies. His focus on the "practical effects" of the constitution in the French West India Colonies comes with the assertion that these were "happy and flourishing till they heard of the rights of man." Indeed they were economically flourishing (about happiness we cannot so easily speak); the significance of St. Domingue's sugar and coffee plantations in the world economy has been noted by many scholars. The prosperity of France, moreover, was also deeply mingled with the colony at the time.[24] The Pandora's box of the rights of man destroys subordination and the "bonds of society." (Surprisingly the multiple and ambivalent nuances of *bonds*—bondsman, bonded slave, etc.—in a slave society do not evoke a comment from Burke.)[25] What can be detected here is a moment of self-conscious crisis regarding the role of race in the colonies; if previously it was a rapid and unchecked class mobility enabled by opportunities there, in this passage the fear of class "miscibility" is replaced by a partially opaque reference to a kind of racial "mingling" in an incantation from the witches in *Macbeth*: "Black spirits and white / Blue spirits and grey / Mingle, mingle, mingle."[26]

In the first passage, on the Quebec Bill, Burke moves from an apocalyptic language (of hell yawning, demons of mischief, etc.) in the first half to the specific example of St. Domingue in the second, which is meant to prove how the rights of man lead to "discord and blood." His tone shifts now to a kind of bitter irony: France "generously" sends the "precious" gift of the rights of man, and in a permutation on the notion of vanity discussed earlier dislikes "the image of herself reflected in the child" and sends out troops.[27] The irony is sharpest in the next sentence, when he says to Parliament that the French troops, "instructed as they are in the principles of government, felt themselves bound to become parties in the general rebellions." The very principle of Jacobinism is a revolutionary tendency which for Burke is inherently unstable. His remarks become more extreme when he equates the claiming of these rights with the guillotine; the troops "like most of their brethren at home began asserting their rights by cutting off the head of their general." In fact Léger Félicité Sonthonax and Etienne Polverel, the commissioners sent by the National Assembly to Le Cap, St. Domingue, in September 1792, would have confirmed Burke's suspicions. Both were familiar with some of the antislavery thought of the Enlightenment; nonetheless it was a bold and unexpected step when, in part to win over the support of former slaves for the fledgling French republican regime, they delivered a "decree of General Liberty" on August 29, 1793, freeing the enslaved on the island. Freedom was to be short-lived, as the British, invading from Jamaica, would reestablish slavery during their occupation of the island. (Napoleon, moreover, reauthorized slavery in French colonies in 1802.) As part of their plan, Sonthonax and Polverel had the "Declaration of the Rights of Man and Citizen" translated into Creole and posted; copies were available to all men over eighteen.[28]

The reference by Burke to Antoine Pierre Barnave, chair of the French Committee on Colonies formed by the National Assembly in March 1790, recalls an episode when planter interests were reassured that the "constitution of France would not be applied to the colonies."[29] The primary concern was a fear that the metropole would interfere with the legality of slavery; to obviate this possibility, it was proposed that each colony create an "internal" regime (which would cover such issues as slavery), to be approved by Paris. It was only days after this speech from Burke in Parliament (May 6, 1791) that the National Assembly would hear complaints from Julien Raimond, a mulatto activist on racial discrimination (May 14, 1791) and vote—in principle—that free people of color born to two free parents would be granted political rights.[30] Though numerically this was a very small number of people, it was enough to send white planters away in anger from the French National Assembly, plotting either secession or an alliance with the British.

But it is in the final image that Burke fuses a metonym for colonial trade with the very mechanism (in his mind) for its subversion: "Ought this example [St. Domingue] induce us to send to our colonies a cargo of the rights of man? As soon would he [Burke] send them a bale of infected cotton from Marseilles." In comparing the rights of man to a shipment of infected cotton, Burke again evokes the "lower" colonial commodities (recall the mere partnership agreement of pepper, coffee, calico, and tobacco) and the language of contagion associated with the decimation of the peoples of the New World through the introduction of diseases such as small pox. However, in this case, the movement is in the opposite direction: from the imperium to the colony. Burke's fear is the union of these proclaimed rights from the imperium with the already present capacity for rebellion in the colonies.[31] As with Ireland, the risk was that one might "Jacobinize" the mass of the disaffected.[32]

The parliamentary speech discussed here, which is after all ostensibly concerned with the possibility of introducing a constitution modeled on either the French or the British one in Canada, makes one final and revealing return to St. Domingue. Burke rejects even the description of France as a republic, for it is (in his eyes) too monstrous to be called such. It is, rather, an "anomaly in government."[33] At a loss for words, Burke cites a passage from Milton:

". . . A shape,
If shape it might be called, that shape had none
Distinguishable in member, joint or limb;
or substance might be call'd that shadow seem'd
For each seem'd either; black it stood as night,
Fierce as ten furies, terrible as hell,
And shook a dreadful dart; what seemed his head
The likeness of a kingly crown had on."

. . . It was, he [Burke] added, "A shapeless monster, born of hell and chaos."[34]

It is striking that Burke returns to the images of furies, and of a dark miasma—both components of his image of St. Domingue earlier—in describing France. (These were also the very same lines from Milton he cited in his *Philosophical Enquiry* to illustrate the power of "obscurity" in inducing "terror").[35] It is perhaps the association of these images that causes him to turn from this description of France back to St. Domingue as he responds to a remark Fox had made earlier in the day in one of his speeches to Parliament. Fox had referred to an observation by Burke in his "Speech on Conciliation with America" (given in 1775, some sixteen years earlier) that "he could not draw a bill of indictment against a whole people" in arguing against Burke's intransigent position on France.[36] Was it not Burke who taught us, Fox asked, "that no revolt of a nation was caused without provocation"?[37] Burke's retort, which is at the core of his break with Fox, emphasizes the French colonial relation with St. Domingue as most revealing of its nature: "He knew not how to draw any such bill of indictment; but he would tell the House who could—the national assembly of France, who had drawn a bill of indictment against the people of St. Domingo. He could draw a bill of indictment against murder, against treason, against felony, or could draw such a bill against oppression; tyranny, and corruption, but not a bill of indictment against a whole people."[38] This is a fascinating remark that brings together many important concerns. When he refers to the National Assembly drawing a bill of indictment against the people of St. Domingue, what Burke appears to have in mind is the National Assembly's ruling on the status of free people of color, which undermined the planter class in St. Domingue.[39] Since these words were spoken in 1791, while the impeachment trial against Hastings was under way, his references to "oppression," "tyranny," and "corruption" would also certainly resonate with his uses of these terms there. The problem for Burke, as ever, is to explain to his opponents his "consistency."[40] In this complicated moment, Burke appears to side with the people of St. Domingue, by which he means the planters, against the metropole's undue interference—more than interference, their "indictment." Although in the Indian case, to which he may be indirectly gesturing, Burke is worried about Indianism (as I argued earlier), in the case of St. Domingue he seems to side with the West India planters against the French republican or revolutionary government. What the moment reveals are the pressures put on Burke's thought by the events in St. Domingue.

If we turn now to the second passage from August 1793, "the dreadful affair ... of St. Domingo" (cited earlier), the emphasis is no longer on the rights of man so much as on the routinization of violence that Burke sees as characteristic of Jacobinism. Again the movement of Burke's train of thought is instructive and illustrates the interwoven structure that underlies his conception of Jacobinism. "Their partisans here" (i.e., English Jacobins) claim to be disturbed when a small number of men are killed, and yet they are "enthusiasts" for the "general massacre," for the "systematic plan of extermination" turned "into a sort of regular art, and a sort of morality" in "that fine island."[41] Burke's emphasis on violence in the revolution, of the way it was rendered routine, banal, partly explains why he is read as a critic of totalitarianism. My earlier discussion of his attempt to link this "banality of evil" (to use Arendt's description of Eichmann's account of his actions during his trial) with a "geometric" rationality is consonant with his comment here.[42] But at the end of this passage, Burke's discussion of his strategy of "vigorous opposition to Jacobinism" shows the causal chain that he most fears: unrest in St. Domingue may find a confluence with French Jacobinism, and both of these will serve as a reminder of a threat to London. He writes, "Had it [English Jacobinism] gone on, the burning down of half of London, after the massacre of half its inhabitants, would have been cheap composition for the whole kingdom."[43]

In reading of the deaths of so many white inhabitants of St. Domingue, Burke could not have avoided the thought that abuses in India might have led to a similar outcome. But more explicitly on his mind is the vision of London set alight, and for this he had the Gordon Riots of 1780 to look back on as a warning.[44] (According to one account, the damage caused by these riots in London was greater than that caused by the initial disturbances in Paris during the French Revolution. Burke, it is said, was himself forced to defend his property with a sword.)[45] In noting this easy transition in the letter to Windham from "vigorous opposition" to "vigorous alarmism," I would suggest (to return to my earlier point) that the achievement of Burke's prophecy is diminished. In the end, what bearing does this discussion of the West Indies have on my earlier remarks on Burke's India writings? Burke cannot and will not refer to the white settlers in the West Indies as Jacobins. He cannot, first and foremost, because the planter class in St. Domingue was more conservative than many in the metropole in Paris. This is unsurprising given that it was the economic stakes of the planters that were most immediately threatened by the implications of the universal character of the Rights of Man. As is known, at the moment of the revolution in Paris, there were rumors in St. Domingue that the king had abolished slavery. Although in fact this was false—slavery was the one institution that was not abolished when noble titles, religious orders, and so on went by the wayside—nonetheless the planters themselves banned the "Declarations of the Rights of Man" within one month of its being published. Clearly they knew all too well what was at stake in the logical extension of the abolition of titles in France. As the historian Laurent DuBois puts it, in describing an earlier moment in March 1790 when the Colonial Committee (headed by Antoine Barnave) proposed a law that the constitution of France would *not* be applied to the colonies, "The colonies were safe from the dangers of universalism."[46] It is one example among many that could be adduced to illustrate what Partha Chatterjee calls the rule of colonial difference, whereby imperial prerogative is defined precisely by the right to declare "the colonial exception."[47]

Here a (French) Jacobin alliance with a (black) Jacobin uprising causes Burke to revert to horror and indignation: "We must be vigorous alarmists." Alarmism in St. Domingue, but speaking on "behalf of an oppressed people" in India: this contradiction can be understood only in terms of Burke's overlooking native resistance in India. It is evident that he would have been shocked at the violence committed by any native "Indian Jacobins," but he chose not to emphasize this. In their discursive absence, he could more strongly make the case for a vulnerable land whose riches and peoples had to be saved from the rapacious hand of the East India Company.

And yet we should not leave behind the question of Burke's understanding of St. Domingue without considering the way that it too appears in and shapes the text of the *Reflections on the Revolution in France*. (It is a further curiosity and entanglement that in 1795 Burke had actually recommended the French translator of the *Reflections*, Pierre-Gaëton Dupont, for employment in the Superior Council of St. Domingue.)[48] This moment occurs, interestingly, in a paragraph where Burke explains that the French revolutionary government must resort to force since that is all that is left to them after having "industriously destroyed" all "opinion" and "prejudice":

> The king is to call out troops to act against his people, when the world has been told . . . that troops ought not to fire on citizens. The colonies [Burke is referring to the French West Indies, and especially St. Domingue] assert to themselves an independent constitution and a free trade. They must be constrained by troops. In what chapter of your code of the rights of men are they able to read, that it is a part of the rights of men to have their commerce monopolized and restrained for the benefit of others. As the colonists rise on you, the negroes rise on them. Troops again—Massacre, torture, hanging! These are your rights of men! These are the fruits of the metaphysic declarations wantonly made, and shamefully retracted! . . . You lay down metaphysic propositions which infer universal consequences, and then you attempt to limit logic by despotism.[49]

Burke's remark that the rights are *shamefully* retracted ought to give pause, for it indicates a sympathy with those—in this case the white settlers—who have had their (commercial) rights betrayed by metropolitan France (in an echo of the situation of the North American colonies with respect to Britain; let us recall that Burke served as an agent for the Assembly of New York).[50] That this interpretation of Burke's ire is correct is indicated by the pejorative way in which he describes their "commerce" being "monopolized and restrained for the benefit of others." And yet it would appear that the solution to this is simply not to profess such unenforceable and ungrantable universal rights. A detailed note from the editor, L. G. Mitchell, indicates that this passage responds to the March 1790 decree by the National Assembly to allow all persons possessing property to vote, but neglects to mention the pivotal and decisive point that beneath these apparently neutral words was the debate around the granting of property rights to free people of color, which provoked white colonists to talk of secession.[51] The only way such a "metaphysic proposition" as the rights of man can be "limited" is through a reversion to "despotism," one that Burke appears to find not contingent but, as with the Pandora's box image, intrinsic to the abstract structure of the rights of man. Mitchell cites from Burke's revealing marginalia to his copy of Cormier's *Mémoire sur la Situation de Saint-Domingue* (Paris, 1792) in the possession of the Bodleian Library; it is a moment that illustrates the intimate linkage between the rights of man and violence for which Burke has been arguing, and it even goes so far as to imply that the cannibalism (with which the Caribbean—in its very name in fact—has been associated) has found its way back to France. Beside a passage in Cormier that reads "They have assassinated many whites without hatred.... Saying... this man was not cruel, we have killed him for the cause of the nation," Burke writes, "Crimes of the Right of Man," "Just the same thing done by the Virtuous Patriots in France," and "Cannibalism frequent in France also."[52] A clearer connection between the cool violence undertaken "without hatred" in both St. Domingue and France could not be adduced.

A "Transatlantic Morocco"

Late in Burke's life, in the "Fourth Letter on a Regicide Peace" (written in 1795, two years before his death, and published only posthumously in 1812), one finds a series of expressions both striking and disturbing for the extremity of their formulation. The immediate cause is a rivalry and war with the revolutionary regime in France being played out in Europe and in the colonies; nonetheless the expressions—some figures of speech, others geographic analogies—appear to bring to a crisis the conceptual armature of his thought and reveal an unseemly underside to the contrast that gradually has emerged in considering the role of the West Indies versus the East Indies (or India). The "Fourth Letter," which began as a reply to Lord Fitzwilliam, was written as a polemic against the British government's opening of discussions with France, and yet it is punctuated by a persistent series of colonial evocations. Consider the following, which is meant to bring out how abject the people of France have become: "France has no Public; it is the only nation I ever heard of, where the people are absolutely slaves, in the fullest sense, in all affairs public and private, great and small, even down to the mutest and most recondite parts of their household concerns. The Helots of Laconia, the Regardants to the Manor in Russia and in Poland, even the Negroes in the West Indies know nothing of so searching, so penetrating, so heart breaking a slavery."[53] These are not incidental examples, certainly not the last reference to the "Negroes in the West Indies," who will reappear momentarily in another guise (not as slaves but as insurgents). In his zeal to argue against any alliance with France, the nation and all it touches must be pushed out of the realm to nature (toward the monstrous, as we shall see). But perhaps Burke means to indicate that the reach of the space of politics extends into the most minute and capillary aspects of daily life (reaching the "most recondite parts of their household concerns") under the Jacobin order. What stands out is an abuse of the concept of slavery, which deforms Burke's thinking on this subject so much so that in his late writings, such as this, he is able to conflate the state of mind of those living under the Jacobins with the experience of the slave. He clarifies the odd remark of their suffering a "heart breaking" slavery (which would appear to call for sympathy) by following with the observation that "the servile wretches" would call for our "pity" had they not undertaken the "murder of the mildest of all Monarchs" and thereby deserve a greater punishment.

That the West Indies play a key role in imperial rivalry with France is clear, as is the manner in which Burke uses colonies such as St. Domingue to talk about France, and vice versa. He refers to a Franco-Spanish treaty of July 1795, in which Spain ceded to France the Spanish portion of St. Domingue/Santo Domingo, and is forced to reach beyond the physical world to describe the alliance: "In the Treaty . . . it was agreed, that Spain should not give any thing from her territory in the West Indies to France. . . . Here we have, formed, a new, unlooked-for, monstrous, heterogeneous alliance; a double-natured Monster; Republick above and Monarchy below. There is no Centaur of fiction, no poetic Satyr of the Woods . . . that can give an idea of it. None of these things can subsist in nature . . . ; but the moral world admits Monsters which the physical rejects."[54] This striking image of the monstrous expresses Burke's belief that the moral world enables "calamities" of this sort to be formed, which the natural world somehow disallows or obviates by being bound by natural laws. By encoding politics within the realm of nature, such an alliance must be figured as not merely contrary to nature, but beyond it. The turn to the mythological is rhetorically extended, though laced with a reflection on *realpolitik* and the balance of power:

> In this Metamorphosis, the first thing done by Spain, in the honeymoon of her new servitude, was . . . utterly to defy the most solemn Treaties with Great Britain. . . . She has yielded the largest and fairest part of one of the largest and fairest islands in the West Indies [Hispaniola], perhaps on the Globe, to the Usurped Powers of France. She compleats the title of those Powers to the whole of that important central island of Hispaniola. . . .
> The effect is no less than the total subversion of the Balance of Power in the West Indies, and indeed every where else.[55]

The dissemination of the forces of Jacobinism through the region are a component of Burke's fears in this passage, and they will also return to Britain—perhaps entering Parliament itself, much as Indianism threatened to do (discussed in chapter 5), as will be clear shortly.[56] There is a strategic importance placed on St. Domingue that makes unrest there all the more treacherous. Looking for a means to translate that importance—geographically and perhaps cartographically—Burke comes upon an arresting image: "It is sufficiently alarming, that she [France] is to have possession of this great Island [Hispaniola]. . . . But I go a great deal further, and on much consideration of the condition and circumstances of the West Indies, and of the genius of this new Republick . . . I say, that if a single Rock in the West Indies is in the hands of this *transatlantic Morocco*, we have not an hour's safety net there."[57] The "transatlantic Morocco" appears to refer to the fact that France would have control of a place like the "rock" of Gibraltar between Spain and Morocco, which controls access to the Mediterranean Sea. But more than this he means to evoke the menacing character of Morocco in the period: the Barbary Coast, pirates, and so on. The turn to this image is perhaps enabled by earlier remarks where Burke, in responding to the text of a pamphlet by Baron Auckland (one of the ostensible aims of the "Fourth Letter on a regicide peace"), remarks that "if *Piratical* France shall be established . . . in the West Indies" then Britain would be unable to pursue peace on any terms other than those dictated by France.[58] And again, referring to Auckland's text, Burke writes, "He does not indeed adopt a supposition, such as I make . . . that any thing, which can give them a single good port and opportune piratical station there, would lead to our ruin."[59] The proliferation of the language of piracy in the Caribbean contributes to the argument Burke wishes to make regarding France's interests in the region but is then also extended to a degree of racial scaremongering of the sort indicated earlier by the reference to the lines from the witches of Macbeth ("Black spirits and white . . . mingle, mingle, mingle").

A Man of Color in the Assembly

In arguing against an alliance with France and Spain, Burke rejects a suggestion made by Baron Auckland in his text that these two nations alongside England, the three powers in the region of the West Indies, should adopt "*analogy* in the interiour systems of Government in the several Islands, which we may respectively retain after the closing of the War."[60] The dangers in doing so are obvious to Burke, and he enumerates the implications: "If this Convention for analogous domestick Government is made, it immediately gives a right for the residence of a Consul (in all likelihood some Negroe or Man of Colour) in every one of your Islands; a Regicide Ambassador in London will be at all your meetings of West India Merchants and Planters, and, in effect, in all our Colonial Councils."[61] It would perhaps be unfair to call this scaremongering, since

Jean-Baptiste Belley, a black general born in Senegal who had fought alongside Toussaint Louverture in St. Domingue/Haiti, had in fact been sent as representative of the region to the National Assembly in Paris a year before this statement, in 1794. (His likeness is memorably captured for us in a painting done while he was still in Paris by Anne-Louis Girodet in 1797).[62] There was nothing to monger with such evidence in plain sight. It may have been with Belley in mind that the remark was made; if not, this is perhaps the obverse of Burke's prophecy regarding the French Revolution, though one that may appeal less than his examination of the Terror to come. In any case, his intention in this passage is to describe the likely infiltration of all the political institutions around colonial governance by such a figure, accompanied by a "Regicide Ambassador." In taking stock of this episode of Burke's view on the West Indies, it appears to me that one must supplement the more sympathetic readings of his fear on behalf of the vulnerable elements in a body politic with a troubled reflection upon what does not earn his sympathy.[63] This episode would appear to confirm that Burke may indeed worry about the vulnerable elements in a society, but he does not a priori care for those who are unrepresented. (Perhaps this is no surprise, given his critique of arithmetic rationality in the *Reflections,* discussed in chapter 4, directed against greater representation of the landless, etc., in the French Assembly.) For what we have in a figure such as General Belley is exactly the black Jacobin, a (black) *citoyen* who represents St. Domingue in the National Convention, which Burke indirectly holds out as a threat to England indicating what might happen should it make an alliance with France. After all, Burke was not the only one who had to speak on behalf of an oppressed people. Like his doppelgänger Burke, Belley too railed against a planter lobby ("West Indianism," Burke might have said), albeit in the French National Convention rather than in Parliament. It is worth contrapuntally putting their nearly contemporary words side by side. Speaking of the complex relation between predominantly white planters, *gens de couleur* (who could own property), and blacks (who could not), Belley asserts, "I attest that what the English and the Spanish possess of the French portion of Saint-Domingue was delivered to them by planters of all colors, owners of slaves. . . . I also attest that, if the English failed to take over all of Saint-Domingue, it is because the blacks who have become free and French have made a rampart with their bodies against this invasion and are bravely defending the rights of the republic."[64] With its reference to the "bodies" of blacks who have become "free and French," this serves as a fascinating example of Belley's attempt to speak of republican ideals beyond the category of race; it was to be short-lived

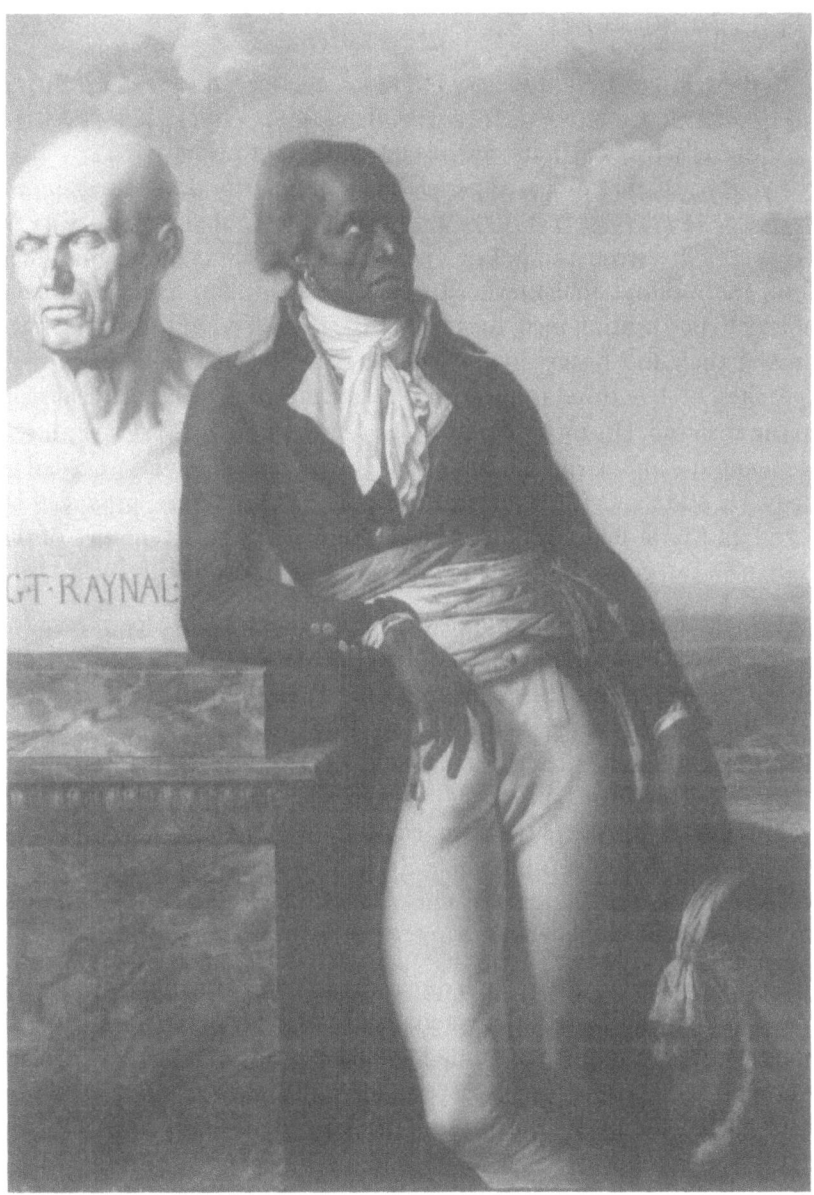

FIGURE 4. Anne-Louis Girodet, *Le Citoyen Jean-Baptiste Belley, Ex-Représentant de colonies*, 1798. Châteaux de Versailles et de Trianon, Versailles, France. Réunion des Musées Nationaux / Art Resource, New York. Belley, a general who fought alongside Toussaint Louverture, leans against a white marble bust of abbé Raynal for support; or perhaps his averted gaze suggests a looking beyond. One of many fascinating ambiguities around the painting, which pointedly depicts him wearing a tricolor (*tricolore*) sash with the colors of the Revolution.

with the reimposition of slavery in French colonies in 1802.[65] Exhorting his listeners to live up to their radical ideals (more radical, perhaps, than they initially realized?), he defends a key decree they have made: "They tell you, legislators of a free people, they dare write that your sublime decree of 16 Pluviôse [February 4, 1794, the decree abolishing slavery in France] is disastrous, impolitic and barbarous. The planters announce from the rooftops that they will have it recalled. You have given back liberty to two million men, torn from their homeland by greed; you have broken their too heavy chains." Belley's speech, like some of Burke's speeches, is structured to place into doubt the attribution of barbarism to the enslaved. His own presence at the convention, his very speech act, is meant to demonstrate a humanity that the planter "faction" needed to deny. He addresses the rhetorical construction, the figure, produced by a certain Marie-Benoît-Louis Gouly, a planter and representative of the Indian Ocean colony of Île de France (modern-day Mauritius):

> Which one of you was not filled with indignation and pity in reading the bizarre portrait that Gouli has made of the blacks? Is it, indeed, a man that this planter sought to paint? . . .
>
> Do you believe, citizen colleagues, that nature is unjust, that it has made some men to be the slaves of others, as the planters assert? Doesn't this unworthy claim show the principles of these horrible destroyers of the human species? I myself was born in Africa. Brought in childhood to the land of tyranny, through hard work and sweat I conquered a liberty that I have enjoyed honorably for thirty years, loving my country [i.e., France] all the while.

The brief testimony of a life that moves from Belley's birthplace in Africa to a slave-owning society, the gradual and self-made manner in which he obtains his freedom, are presented as evidence against the old (vaguely) Aristotelian idea of natural slavery and as proof of his republican patriotism. Unable to fully lift the image of the African out of the state of nature in his audience's eyes, Belley makes a Rousseauvian asset of this association. In an age when many philosophes—the Diderot of the *Supplément au voyage de Bougainville* or Rousseau in his "Discourse on Inequality"—sought to peel away the layers of artifice and convention that had encrusted themselves on civilized man, Belley deploys this proximity as part of the claim to humanity of enslaved Africans: "The torturers of the Blacks lie shamelessly when they dare assert that these oppressed men are brutes; if they do not have the vices of Europe, they have the virtues of nature; it is in their name, in the name of all my brothers . . . that I urge you to maintain your benevolent laws. These laws are, I know, the terror of slaves' tyrants."[66] Again like Burke, Belley is aware that he speaks on behalf of an absent mass of people; unlike Burke he establishes a clear kinship with them (his brothers; the parallel here would be Burke's concern with Ireland and the Protestant ascendancy). It is perhaps this intimacy and filiation with the party on behalf of which he speaks that makes it less necessary to establish the cosmopolitan sympathy invoked by Burke in moving beyond his "little platoon." Belley rhetorically plays upon an opposition between benevolence ("benevolent laws") and terror (itself a loaded and burdened word in the National Convention by 1795) and shifts the object of terror: not the terror of slavery that held St. Domingue's labor regime in place but the revolutionary emphasis on terror as "inflexible justice" (in Robespierre's famous words) administered or delivered, in this case, to the slave owner.[67]

And yet in spite of this example of horror (Burke had referred to his "horror with regard to the act" in his letter on St. Domingue), in the Indian case, as we have seen, Burke argues for the silent multitude whose case he has been representing—in fact at almost the same time as when this statement is made, in 1795, though the impeachment trial against Hastings would end that year in acquittal. In the Indian case, he felt strongly enough to make the following bold formulation, to which I will only briefly refer by way of comparison, when writing in a letter to Mary Palmer (niece of Joshua Reynolds) on January 19, 1786, regarding the dismay of many in London for the tenacity of his judgments against Hastings and other high-ranking figures associated with the East India Company: "In India affairs, I have not acted at all with any party from the beginning to the End.... I began this India Business in the administration of Lord North to which in all its periods [I was] in direct opposition.... I have no party in this Business, my dear Miss Palmer, but among a set of people, who have none of your Lilies and Roses in their faces; but who are the image of the great Pattern as well as you and I. I know what I am doing; whether the white people like it or not."[68] It is a remarkable line from a remarkable letter. I juxtapose these two statements in part because each is an explicit reflection on race in the period, on blackness (in the first case) and whiteness (in the second). Burke's tone—from nearly ten years earlier (1786), I should emphasize—in the letter to Mary Palmer signals a heroic independence from political parties, and indeed from a prevailing contempt which he implies exists for those without the "Lilies and Roses" in their faces. He invokes a humanitarian universalism, perhaps of a Christian variety, in the way that abolitionist discourse in the period employed it as well, when he sees the darker peoples mistreated by Hastings in equal possession of "the image of the great Pattern as you and I." His self-confidence and independence on this subject ("I know what I am doing") lead him to a peculiarly striking formulation indicating a break with the other group to which it is assumed he would keep his loyalties ("whether the white people like it or not"). By the time of the second statement in 1795, we can see the language of race serving the opposite function from the universalism just noted: to differentiate, to render other. The oscillation between these two functions is noticed elsewhere by Thomas Metcalf in his study of nineteenth-century British rule in India.[69] One striking illustration of the rendering other also reveals another function of Burke's language: by adjoining the racial other with a political antagonist (the Jacobins) he is able to bring out further his view that an alliance is unnatural. Consider the reference to Europe's traditional others, the figure of the Jew and the Moor familiar from at least the early modern period, in the following passage from 1795: "It is not peace with France, which secures that feeble Government [Spain's]; it is that peace, which ... decisively ruins Spain.... What things we have lived to see! The King of Spain in a group of Moors, Jews, and Renegadoes, and the Clergy taxed to pay for his conversion!"[70] This passage comes from the moment discussed earlier regarding Spain's alliance with revolutionary France. The unnatural affiliation between a monarch (the reference is to Charles IV) with such outcasts discloses the inverted world brought about by the Jacobins. (*Renegadoe* refers to a Christian convert to Islam, a figure common in captivity and piracy narratives, and also takes on an echo of the renegade slave or black insurrectionary that frames the context for the remark.) Burke's quip that the clergy is taxed for the king's "conversion" goes so far as to figure him as becoming Muslim (or, less fittingly with the image, a Jew).

To return to the remark regarding the "likelihood" of "some Negroe or Man of Colour" in residence as a consul, it is surprising that Burke plays upon the fear of such individuals and depicts their invasive presence in the meetings of colonial planters and merchants—two groups he has not been consistently kind to in his depiction of "Indianism" in the Indian case. The planters of the West Indies are therefore worth thinking about in relation to the concept of Indianism that he develops elsewhere: "Not one Order of Council can hereafter be made, or any one Act of Parliament relative to the West India Colonies even be agitated, which will not always afford reasons for protests and perpetual interference; the Regicide Republick will become an integral part of the Colonial Legislature; and so far as the Colonies are concerned, of the British too."[71] Once again Burke presents this as an example of Jacobin principles come home to haunt the British Parliament. It is therefore akin to Indianism, or perhaps more simply analogous to the Jacobinism component of that couplet. Note too the emphasis on the interference that the French colonies will give.

Burke was not so wrong in imagining this antagonism with England as one explicit aim of the French in their relations with peoples of African descent in the Caribbean. Consider the full context of the stirring words spoken by Georges Jacques Danton on February 6, 1794, from a convention called for the abolition of the slave trade: "Représentants du peuple français, jusqu'ici nous n'avions décrété la liberté qu'en égoïstes et pour nous seuls. Mais aujourd'hui nous proclamons à la face de l'univers, et les générations futures trouveront leur gloire dans ce décret, nous proclamons la liberté universelle. Hier, lorsque le président donna le baiser fraternel aux députés de couleur, je vis le moment où la Convention devait décréter la liberté de nos frères."[72] One of the three deputies embraced was in fact Belley himself; in any case, the contrast in sentiment with Burke regarding the function of the deputies of color in a political assembly could not be more striking. And yet the barb of this speech, so far as Britain is concerned, is yet to be spoken. Danton's words express the contradictory nature of much European anticolonial sentiment in the period in its mixture of a desire for a more genuine extension of the notion of liberty with a patronizing and fearful sense of the consequences for the formerly enslaved: "Mais après avoir accordé le bienfait de la liberté, il faut que nous en soyons pour ainsi dire les modérateurs. Renvoyons au comité de salut public et des colonies, pour combiner les moyens de rendre ce décret utile à l'humanité, sans aucun danger pour elle."[73] There is an echo here in the use of the term *modérateurs* with the language Diderot used to describe soft colonization (see chapter 1). The granting of liberty to the formerly enslaved is figured as imminent and is declared to the universe (the first citation), and then it must quickly be tempered with a degree of control, rendered useful, and removed from danger (the second). Finally we come to the contradictory crux of the speech, which promiscuously mingles nationalist imperial rivalry in alternation with high-minded altruism:

> Nous avions déshonoré notre gloire en tronquant nos travaux. Les grands principes développés par le vertueux Las Casas avaient été méconnus. Nous travaillons pour les générations futures, lançons la liberté dans les colonies, c'est aujourd'hui que l'Anglais est mort. (On applaudit.) En jetant la liberté dans le Nouveau Monde, elle y portera des fruits abondants, elle y poussera des racines profondes.

En vain Pitt et ses complices voudront par des considérations politiques écarter la jouissance de ce bienfait, ils vont être entraînés dans le néant, la France va reprendre le rang et l'influence que lui assurent son énergie, son sol et sa population.[74]

At the very moment where the universal claim of liberty is being made, Danton recalls the author of the *Destruction of the Indies* as model and forebear. Carrying forward what de Las Casas disputed with such antagonists as Sepulveda—whether the Indians of the New World were indeed "natural slaves" and merited the treatment they were receiving at the hands of the Spaniards—Danton makes the present moment regarding slavery in the Caribbean resonate with a larger historical significance. The image he deploys is that of a "seed" of liberty being thrown onto a fecund soil, in which it cannot help but put down roots and bear fruit. The imagined addressee of this speech is twice referred to as "future generations" ("générations futures"). A more contrasting vision of the future from Burke's bleak assessment—of the infiltration of representative assemblies by a republican regicide man of color (a triple threat, so to speak)—would be hard to find. And yet the motor or spring for this sentiment (as Montesquieu might say) is rivalry with the English. There is an alternation between the moral argument in favor of abolition alongside a self-interested realpolitik derived from this competing rivalry for predominance in the New World.

Cannibal Republics and Tropical Empires: The "Second Letter on a Regicide Peace"

Rather confusingly, Burke's "Second Letter on a Regicide Peace" was written the year after his fourth letter, in 1796, and published the year after that.[75] The letter was given an expressive subtitle, "On the Genius and Character of the French Revolution as It Regards Other Nations," which plays upon the two possible meanings of the phrase: with regard or respect to other nations, and as it regards or looks upon these other nations as sites for revolution. Burke's letter places the French Revolution in a global frame and even considers its significance in a deterritorialized sense. As he puts it, "The faction is not local or territorial. It is a general evil. Where it least appears in action, it is still full of life."[76] A kind of monster that feigns death in order to keep living, Jacobinism has lodged itself in the "center" of Europe by being "triumphant" in France.

Burke's aim is contradictory: on the one hand he describes the Jacobins as undertaking a civil war, as an element presumably immanent to a body politic; on the other he depicts France as taken over by something alien to it, in order to substantiate his larger argument in this letter that peace with such a nation is impossible and war necessary: "It is a dreadful truth ... in ability, in dexterity, in the distinctness of their views, the Jacobins are our superiors. They saw the thing right from the beginning. Whatever were the first motives to the war among politicians, they saw that in it's spirit, and for it's objects [sic], it was a *civil war*. . . . It is not France extending a foreign empire over other nations; it is a sect aiming at universal empire, and beginning with the conquest of France." This sentiment calls to mind his remark in the *Reflections* that the Jacobins treat France exactly like a country of conquest. Burke would clearly like to separate the authentic French nation which had been based on manners (as he had elaborated the term) to the new France which appears "not as a State, but as a Faction." Because he will turn shortly to discuss the West Indies and imperial compensation, we should be attentive to the discussion of the Jacobins in association with the idea of empire. "The conquest of France," he writes, "was a glorious acquisition. That once well laid as a basis of empire, opportunities never could be wanting to regain or replace what had been lost." Indeed the whole letter is a reflection of and on an imperial rivalry; here we have the first moment of an idea of imperial compensation, replacing what had been lost, with respect to the Jacobins. In the context of war with the Jacobins and as part of his argument against peace with them (a "regicide" peace, as the title of the letter names and prejudges it), Burke argues that England would be forced to negotiate and sacrifice some part of its possessions in a losing argument. It is in this context that the West Indies and the British conquests in the East are compared. Something, Burke fears, will have to be ceded to the Jacobins if a peace were reached: "I don't find it denied, that when a treaty is entered into for peace, a demand will be made on the Regicides to surrender a great part of their conquests on the Continent. Will they, in the present state of the war, make that surrender without an equivalent?" This equivalent is what causes Burke to discuss the West Indies and British interests there. Spain, in this theater of possession, is already too far gone: "She is a province of the Jacobin Empire." Britain, on the other hand, has more to lose since it has been more successful in its conquests: "Whence then can the compensation be demanded? Undoubtedly from that power which alone has made some conquests. That power is England. Will the allies then give away their antient patrimony, that England may keep Islands in the West Indies?" Burke's argument appears to be that Britain is being forced to choose either to give up all conquests in the West Indies in order to defend

158 / EDMUND BURKE

Europe from the Jacobins (including places such as Holland and Spain, which have been incorporated into the "Jacobin Empire") or to hold onto the West Indies at their expense. As he puts it, "Either we must give Europe, bound hand and foot to France; or we must quit the West Indies without any one object, great or small, towards indemnity and security."[77] It is striking how often one finds repeated permutations of the language of exchange in these pages: in addition to the image of Europe as hostage ("bound hand and foot"), Burke refers to the "funds of equivalents" and to a "ransom" paid to the Jacobins.

His gaze turns eastward in this survey of colonial possessions and prizes: "If we look to our stock in the Eastern world, our most valuable and systematick acquisitions are made in that quarter. Is it from France they are made? France has but one or two contemptible factories, subsisting by the offal of the private fortunes of English individuals to support them, in any part of India." The contemptuous manner in which the French possessions in India are discussed serves a variety of functions in Burke's argument. It underlies his point that British success in this area may indeed compensate for the losses in the West Indies, but it also points to the fact that the nations at whose expense success in the East is made is not France; in fact Britain will be undermining already weak European states. What the "Second Letter" makes clear is the manner in which Burke's desire to see Jacobin France defeated smothers any qualms about the imperial enterprise. The containment of Jacobinism (not unlike the logic of the cold war) legitimates a host of conquests and proxy wars that elsewhere a more cautious Burke would hesitate before: "I look on the taking of the Cape of Good Hope as the securing of a post of great moment. It does honour to those who planned, and to those who executed that enterprise." The securing of the Cape of Good Hope is one example Burke adduces to concede that such conquests are important (perhaps to prop up Holland), and yet his aim is to turn away from the colonial entanglements in order to make the case that France itself needs to be directly invaded; that these excursions to the West Indies and any expansion of activities in the East do not get to the cause of the current concern. They are merely a "roundabout road," as he calls it:

> So far as to the East Indies.
> As the West Indies, indeed as to either, if we look for matter of exchange in order to ransom Europe, it is easy to shew that we have taken a terrible roundabout road.[78]

First Europe as a hostage, and now the colonies as ransom: Burke casts each in these figurative roles in order to depict what is being given to the

Jacobins in the most dire manner—as a loss to Britain that will occur no matter what course is taken in the colonies. His point, reiterated by way of detour through the West and East Indies, is that Britain should not bother fighting with the Jacobin party outside of France; it is better to go to the heart of it: "When we come to balance our account . . . we shall reflect at leisure on one great truth, that it was ten times more easy totally to destroy the system itself, than when established, it would be to reduce it's [sic] power—and that this Republick, most formidable abroad, was, of all things, the weakest at home; that her frontier was terrible—her interior feeble." The "system" of Jacobinism, Burke argues, is "terrible" at the frontier or colonies, but feeble in its interior, which presumably refers to potential unrest within France itself that could be exploited. The aim of this strategy is to avoid the expense that has been "squandered away" on "tropical adventures" and to send an army directly into France. Motivated in part by this effort to dissuade his readers from the merits of a war with France in the West Indies, and referring to the large numbers of British soldiers who died from yellow fever at the time, Burke writes, "In these adventures it was not an enemy we had to vanquish, but a cemetery to conquer."[79] The very land was perilous to European soldiers, he argues, and relies for a contrast on one of his more racially formulated images of the black and mixed-race soldiers fighting for the French (in St. Domingue and elsewhere): "In a West India war, the Regicides have for their troops, a race of fierce barbarians, to whom the poisoned air, in which our youth inhale death, is salubrity and life. To them the climate is the surest and most faithful of allies."[80] Burke is repeating an argument made by others about the climatic harshness of life in the tropics for British soldiers, and that the black natives, mulattos, and *gens de couleur* are accustomed to it (presumably the groups that make up the "fierce barbarians"). Note too the evocation, as in some famous passages from the "Speech on Fox's East India Bill," of British youth, although here it is to drive home a contrasting point. In India the youth unnaturally lorded over vast expanses of land and people; in the West Indies they (equally unnaturally) meet an early death. The object of sympathy has very clearly shifted away from an oppressed native.

But more interesting and perhaps more revealing than this tally sheet of positive and negative racial reflections is the fantasy that then ensues as Burke imagines how it might have been different had Britain actually conquered France. It is a "what if," a lament for what was done wrongly by not invading France from Britain. "Had acquisitions in West Indies been our object, on success in France, every thing reasonable in those remote parts might be demanded with decorum, and justice, and sure effect."[81]

What follows is an image of Hispaniola that echoes a sentiment Diderot had analogously expressed for the South Pacific, of an island outpost for an empire—though in Diderot's case this was allegedly to serve first and foremost as a means of disseminating the Enlightenment.[82]

> The noblest island within the tropicks, worth all that we possess put together, is, by the vassal Spaniard, delivered into her [France's] hands. The island of Hispaniola, (of which we have but one poor corner, by a slippery hold) is perhaps equal to England in extent, and in fertility is far superior. The part possessed by Spain, of that great island, made for the seat and centre of a tropical empire, was not improved, to be sure, as the French division had been, before it was systematically destroyed by the cannibal Republick; but it is not only the far larger, but the far more salubrious, and more fertile part.[83]

The language of lost opportunity here is most salient: the noblest island, the most valuable, of superior fertility, and made to be the seat of a tropical empire; with the parallel made between its size and England's (which is in fact larger), one gets the sense of what was relinquished as a lush island akin to (and yet more precious than) a Britain in the Caribbean sea.

Burke frequently refers in these pages to the "cannibal republick"—by which he presumably means France—but one cannot help but wonder at the echo etymologically linking cannibal, Caliban, and Caribbean that is invoked. The "cannibal republick" is at once a figurative and a military association of France in league with its race of "fierce barbarians" in St. Domingue. Indeed having introduced the language of the barbarian to describe the native soldiers working for France, Burke metonymically shifts the term to include the Jacobins. Thus he is able to write in the next sentence of Hispaniola that "it was delivered into the hand of the barbarians without . . . any publick reclamation on our part . . . in defiance of the fundamental colonial policy of Spain herself."[84] The semantic floating of the idea of cannibalism continues, until it is conjoined with the other word Burke preeminently associates with Jacobinism, namely *terror*. That, at the least, appears to me the only way to explain an odd line such as the following, when Burke writes of Spain's violation of its treaty to Britain by ceding Hispaniola to France, "Whilst the Monarchies subsisted, this unprincipled cession was what the influence of the elder [French] branch of the House of Bourbon never dared attempt on the younger [the Spanish branch]: but *cannibal terrour* has been more powerful than family influence. The Bourbon Monarchy of Spain is united to the Republick of France, by what may be truly called the ties of blood."[85] As in the *Reflections,* but confirmed in 1796 with the turn of historical events, Burke's analysis of the decline of monarchy (part of the general decline of manners) is linked with the rise of terror (one causally enables the other). In this instance, cannibal terror is composed of French Jacobinism in league with the fierce barbarism of St. Domingue and exceeds the "family influence" of the house of Bourbon once common to both. When Burke ironically refers to the shared "blood," he plays upon the multiple meanings of the word and moves it from the figurative sense of "kinship" to its associations with violence, terror, and (of course) cannibalism. Both Spain and France have fused their halves of Hispaniola under its common reign. Before moving on to other matters in his "Second Letter," Burke's reflection on what he refers to at one point as the "West India War" closes with a fascinating and frenetic passage illustrating the formative role of imperial rivalry when he writes "that no power wholly baffled and defeated in Europe, can flatter itself with conquests in the West Indies. In that state of things, it can neither keep nor hold. No! It cannot even long make war, if the grand bank and deposit of it's [sic] force is at all in the West Indies."[86] The flattery of conquest hampered, Britain's bank broken in many ways, another form of compensation would have to be found. All that is left is the counterfactual lament for the invasion of France that did not occur: "Had we pursued the Idea ... we should have been the party invading, and not trembled ourselves from the terror of invasion. Then we should not have had to depend on the unforeseen accident of Imperial Victories for our instant preservation. We should ourselves have preserved the Empire; we should have preserved Europe.... Had we succeeded in such a plan, we might have enforced by power, and demanded with Justice, any rational compensation in the West Indies."[87] Britain's retreat from the new "cannibal republick" was in part the spur to its own eastern tropical empire, and there too the unforeseen accidents would be vital to its preservation. A rational compensation would be sought.

(b) Compensation in the East, or, From Virginia to Hindostan

These were the considerations, Gentlemen, which led me early to think, that, in the comprehensive dominion which the divine Providence had put into our hands, instead of troubling our understandings with speculations concerning the unity of empire, and the identity or distinction of legislative powers, and inflaming our passions with the heat and pride of controversy, it was our duty, in all soberness, to conform our Government to the character and circumstances of the several people who composed this mighty and strangely diversified mass. I never was wild enough to conceive, that one method would serve for the whole; I could never conceive that the natives of Hindostan *and those of* Virginia *could be ordered in the same manner, or that the* Cutchery *court and the grand jury of* Salem *could be regulated on a similar plan. I was persuaded that Government was a practical thing, made for the happiness of mankind, and not to furnish out a spectacle of uniformity, to gratify the schemes of visionary politicians. Our business was to rule, not to wrangle; and it would have been a poor compensation that we had triumphed in a dispute, whilst we lost an empire.* —EDMUND BURKE, "LETTER TO THE SHERIFFS OF BRISTOL, ON THE AFFAIRS OF AMERICA, APRIL 3, 1777"

The link between the colonies of the New World and India in Burke's mind which has thus far appeared indirectly need not be relegated to a minor role, for in some of his earlier writings, as this epigraph indicates, there is a much more explicit connection. Imperial historians are familiar with stories of military men and merchants moving from one part of the incipient British Empire to another, but it is instructive to recall the sometimes surprising causal chain of effects that were created in the period from the late 1770s to the 1790s and the general proximity of events otherwise understood as highly distinct. In a letter to Philip Francis, Burke's main source on Indian matters and his close friend, there is a quite striking example of this. Francis, appointed to the Bengal Council in 1773 and later one of Hastings's most resolved opponents in Bengal, was to receive a kinsman and friend of Edmund Burke named William Burke when the latter journeyed to Madras in 1780 to visit the raja of Tanjore.[88] William Burke, a truly fascinating secondary character, had spent time as secretary and register of Guadeloupe under the British (1760–61) and speculated on India stock futures on the Amsterdam exchange until their ruinous decline in 1769 prompted him to seek out a career and fortune in India. (William's shifting financial interests and geographic movements from the West Indies to the East obviously also illustrate a theme of this chapter. Unfortunately, he didn't fare much better by physically moving eastward. Upon his return to Britain from India in 1793, he was arrested for outstanding debts; Edmund Burke had him released on bond in 1796—very near the year of his own death—and had him smuggled to the Isle of Man, where he remained until his death in 1798.)[89] However, let me return to the fulcrum moment of the late 1770s and early 1780s. The war with the American colonists had already begun (with fighting breaking out in 1775), and the errors that Edmund Burke felt had led to this were much on his mind when thinking of India. After recommending William to Francis in a letter in 1778, he reflects upon the various European rivalries at play and reminds Francis of the importance of his position in India as it relates to the larger scene:

> You have, my dear Sir, a great Country to govern; and I have no doubt of the principles, on which you govern yourself in the management of it. I assure you that all your Wisdom, diligence and fortitude will be wanting to compensate to us in the East, what we have lost irrecoverably in the West, by the total absense of those qualities in those who ought most fully to have possessd them. We are still to all appearance proceeding exactly in the same Train; and of course our disasters are multiplied in proportion to the continuance of our Follies. A French War is added to the American; and there is all the reason in the World to expect a Spanish to be superadded to the French. The latter, though for years to be hourly apprehended, was no way provided for; and the former, though hanging over us, we know neither how to avert, nor to oppose when it shall come. It is thought that the rest of the Caribbee Islands will follow the fate of Dominica. We have no fleet in those Seas worth mentioning.[90]

The irrecoverable loss in the West, most immediately the North American colonies, are to be compensated for in the East—but by means of the cultivation of certain qualities absent in the management of the former.[91] This is a restatement of Burke's critical position on the intransigent response of the British to the American colonists. (Many commentators argue that Burke viewed the loss of the American colonies as the unnecessary and avoidable result of a simple policy error. Even a cursory reading of the "Speech on Conciliation with America" confirms this view.)[92] The continuation of those "follies" by proceeding "in the same Train" has left the settlements in the New World vulnerable to incursion from the Spanish and French. In this reference to Dominica it is primarily its falling into French hands (on September 8, 1778) that upsets Burke; its loss was balanced by the British capture of St. Lucia in December. The tabulations being made in this letter move from North America to the West Indies and from the New World to

FIGURE 5. [William Dent]: "Thunder, Lightning and Smoke, or the wind shifted from the North to the East." Published as the Act directs for the proprietor by W. Moore No. 48 near Bond Street & W. Dickie opposite Exeter change, London, April 22, 1788. Courtesy of The Lewis Walpole Library, Yale University. An apt illustration of shifting imperial interests from North America to South Asia. Warren Hastings wears a turban beneath a flag reading "India preserved." Beneath him are sacks of money; the open book reads "the curse of riches." Lord North lies hunched on the left with a fallen flag reading "America lost." The open book near him reads "the blessings of poverty." Edmund Burke's head (with spectacles), alongside Charles James Fox's, sits atop a weathervane on which is written "impeachment" and is supported by Philip Francis.

the Old in a manner that is quite revealing of the pivotal years of the late 1770s and early 1780s. These are the pluses and minuses of an imperial calculus whose sum would be known only in the following century.

Let's look more closely at the passage from the "Letter to the Sheriffs of Bristol" (1777) where Burke employs the striking phrase comparing the natives of Virginia and Hindostan as his eye surveys the imperial landscape stretching across a "mighty and strangely diversified mass." The manner in which Britain is figured, in an almost nonagential way, as having acquired possessions in America is attributed to a "Divine Providence" in an expression that calls to mind a moment in the later "Speech on Fox's East India Bill" (1783) where he states that the "Sovereign Disposer" had placed India in Britain's hands.⁹³ Leaving aside the other genuine question regarding the invocation of the divine, what these expressions have in common within his argument is that they serve to shift the focus away from a speculative deliberation upon the causes, etiology, and perhaps even the legitimacy of the acquisition of the conquest to the more "sober" question of how to govern over the "circumstances of several people" and craft laws suited to a place. In this regard one can detect the weighty presence of Montesquieu suffusing Burke's thoughts and words. Burke first mentions the "natives" of Hindostan and Virginia, conflating into one category (natives) what is elsewhere configured differently; in some of his writings on America, the (white) American settlers are understood as a species of true freedom-loving English people, Britain's kin, and the American Revolution is thereby understood as a kind of civil conflict.⁹⁴ Yet, to stay with this example, after the natives or peoples are mentioned, he then refers to the diverging legal systems crafted to fit them (the Cutchery court or the grand jury of Salem in Massachusetts).⁹⁵ This encounter with difference—how else to understand the "mighty and strangely diversified mass"?—is a central feature of the idea of the empire (a word he uses explicitly and frequently), and its management one of the greatest challenges. Burke eschews any plan to create one unified system for this entity (he is not "wild enough" to be attached to one method), and yet by yoking them together he clearly is thinking of them in a unified frame. The argument is precisely that one ought not to make use of an abstract universal principle to govern with. It is in contrast to the "wild" or mad rage for a "spectacle of uniformity"—which suits his later understanding of the universal empire of the French Revolution—that he proposes the idea of government as a "practical thing" concerned with happiness. What are the stakes of such a contrast between two models of governance, between the ideas of "visionary politicians" and the businesslike approach of those operating with practical reason? The undue concern for consistency or conformity to a single rule would allow for a "triumph in dispute," but this is "poor compensation" for the loss of an empire. So it is that the "poor compensation" of 1777 is transmuted into the "compensation in the East" in the 1778 letter to Francis, a compensatory structure of imperial investment that shadows the movement of many people across this diversified mass from Occident to Orient.

The implicit conceptual difficulties which in fact begin to arise have to do with the difference between America being a *settler* colony and British outposts in India being run by a small number of European residents. Nonetheless, following the logic of Burke's letter to Francis, what are "those qualities" that were "totally absent"? To find the answer to this one must look ahead and examine the following fascinating passage from his "Speech on Bengal Judicature Bill, 27 June 1781," where Burke notes, "We had suffered enough in attempting to enervate the system of a country, and we must now be guided as we ought to have been with respect to America, by studying the genius, the temper, and the manners of the people, and adapting to them the laws that we establish."[96] With its mixture of genuine understanding pressed into the service of a well-governed empire, the sentiment expressed here augurs the variety of practices which the British initiated in nineteenth-century India. In a circular way, this citation ties together many of the themes this reading of Burke began with: here one can see how the use of custom and manners became central to the formulation of law in the colonial state.[97] But more than how this became the case, with the North American experience in our purview we can now see why, for it was in America where Britain had suffered by enervating the system. This passage may also represent a kind of transition, since the Montesquieuian language of studying the spirit of the laws shades into the information-gathering system of empire now familiar in examinations of the culture of colonialism since Said's *Orientalism*. But I have cited this passage precisely to show how one may find a different set of causal connections that derive more from an imperial world system (which includes the Americas, the two Indies considered together) rather than an exclusive focus on one part of this system (the East, the Orient), which may be seen as a subset.

The "Speech on the Bengal Judicature Bill" (1781) and the "Speech on Restoring Lord Pigot" (1777) date from an earlier period in Burke's writing than the *Reflections* and thus require some clarification of context. In turning to these two speeches my intention is to illustrate my thesis concerning the intimate relation of the loss of the American colonies and of events in the West Indies with the policies formulated toward India. Burke's initial position on the East India Company was to protect it from undue interference from the government regulation. Indeed his views in the early 1770s on the East India Company expressed simple fascination with the wealth it generated. A decade before his attacks on it, he could write that the East India Company had become "a great, a glorious Company." Bringing out some of the psychology of imperial ambition, perhaps unintentionally, he remarked, "Europe will envy, the East will envy. I hope we shall remain an envied People."[98] The greatest irony, given his later disparaging descriptions of the "boys" who returned to England with amassed fortunes, was his admiration of the large estates and houses of the returning Nabobs: "Rising with unequal'd grandeur, I think there is something of a divine providence in it."[99] However, as evidence of abuses mounted, particularly in the example of the Company's supporting the claims of the nawab of Arcot over the raja of Tanjore, Burke became much more critical. The bulk of his writings from the mid-1780s onward, which has been the primary focus of the previous chapters, reflect this.

Rebels in Boston and Officers in Madras: The Case of Lord Pigot

The significance of the "Speech on Restoring Lord Pigot" (1777) is as an early example of the abuse of power (what Burke is fond of calling "delinquency") that led to the focus on East India Company corruption—a central element in Burke's late concept of Indianism. As I noted, the passage cited from the "Speech on the Bengal Judicature Bill" of 1781 ties together the fundamental importance Burke attached to custom and manners, visible in the *Reflections* almost a decade later, with a colonial experience just past (America) and another about to take on greater importance (India). But the earlier "Speech on Restoring Lord Pigot" had already given voice to Burke's fears as he ranged between disparate regions: "Some people are great Lovers of uniformity—They are not satisfied with a rebellion in the West. They must have one in the East: They are not satisfied with losing one Empire—they must lose another— Lord N[orth] will weep that he has not more worlds to lose."[100] These are only the closing lines of a speech permeated by comparative references to India and America.

Lord Pigot had been selected by the Company in 1775 to be governor of Madras for a second term and to establish a new counterbalance to the Company's old alliance with Muhammed Ali, nawab of Arcot (the nawab of the Carnatic). The raja of Tanjore, whose state had been conquered for the nawab in 1773, was to have his state restored. Led by Paul Benfield, a majority of the Madras Council (whose interests were threatened because of loans to the nawab of Arcot) overthrew Pigot on August 24, 1776, imprisoned him, and assumed control of the Madras government. Pigot was to die in the Madras jail two years later. This was an egregious early example of Company servants disobeying their Court of Directors in Leadenhall Street, London.[101]

At the time of the Company "coup," Benfield and his allies, along with the supporters of Pigot, both sent emissaries to Britain to defend their position publicly. Burke, for a variety of reasons having to do with party alliances, spoke on behalf of reinstating Pigot; in the end it was resolved that both sides in the dispute were to be recalled to England and replaced by a new governor and council.[102] The speech is famous for Burke's early expression that the East India Company should be "free from *Court influence* that it might always be under *publick Control*." This foreshadows the later arguments for parliamentary oversight of the Company that Burke would advocate in proposing reforms. The freedom from court influence is also a genuine concern, but it remains as a trace of Burke's earlier position regarding the freedom of the Company to trade. In this context the freedom from court influence is also a response to the judicial decision to recall both sides in the dispute, Pigot and his enemies. Burke was not in favor of recalling Pigot because he argued that this action would "confound the guilty and the innocent." Having Pigot return to London would be demoting someone who was unjustly imprisoned in the first place only to ask him why the event happened. As he put it, "The effect of this example of indiscriminate punishment will be to teach confederacy in wrong. To make in future a common cause against the Company and secure *plunder* there since they cannot secure *protection here*."[103] What Burke is beginning to propose, as he will articulate explicitly later in this document, is an argument for the legitimate basis of rule of law—a cornerstone of the liberal defense of the monopolization of power by the state. This monopolization can be justified by the open and public discussion of laws deriving from a written constitution or charter.[104] It is telling that the means by which he comes to this discussion is through further reference to British policy in America: "The Magistrates in Boston were supposed negligent; you changed them and the constitution of the whole province. They [the Madras Council] claim not only [to] justifye their act by necessity but assume to be the legal government of the Country."[105] Burke's point in referring to this incident is to note the severity of the response to the negligent British subordinates in America, while in India a similar insubordination is not rebuked.

There is a parallel I am implicitly considering between this moment, when Burke asks his audience in Parliament to be consistent in their considerations of America and India, and the similar moments in his writings on St. Domingue in relation to India. The example of St. Domingue and Burke's reflections upon it (in his letters from 1791–93) put his critical position on India under stress, and yet here the example of India puts his earlier stated positions on America under stress. In both cases race seems to play a key role: the race of the (subcontinental) Indian natives is not like the race of American colonists (and elicits a different response), and the "race war" represented by the uprising of St. Domingue's former slaves is not like the Indian example (and thereby demotes its significance).

This disparity leads Burke to state clearly why such a muddled and tepid response to the Madras Council is ruinous, and in touching on this we inadvertently come upon one of the central contradictions of political liberalism as it takes on the objective of imperialism. Burke writes:

1. The obedience of the governors is the freedom of the people.
2. Nothing can make a military Government tolerable, but the last degree of subordination and discipline.
3. We have not the happiness of being yet able to introduce any portion of *freedom* into that Country—let us not take away every thing which makes *arbitrary power tolerable.*
4. The checks of a free Government work upward and originating from the people go up to the supreme head. The checks of an arbitrary government work downwards—and whatever weakens the power of the Supreme head exposes the people to all manner of powers and oppression.[106]

Each of these sentences is written in a telescopic and pithy manner; indeed the textual editor of this speech remarks that it is a collation of notes Burke made to himself for use in intervening in the parliamentary debate. For clarity I have inserted numerals in brackets and will refer to them in my comments. In line 1, he couples the *obedience* of the governors to the *freedom* of the people. But this raises the unavoidable question as to which people are free. Presumably Burke refers to the subjects of the Company and its influence in Madras. Line 2 seems to rely on the contrast between a freely formed government and a military government, whose best hope is to be rendered only "tolerable" by a predictable and transparent chain of command. Line 3 contradicts line 1 in its use of freedom, for here it is acknowledged that "we have not the happiness of being yet able to introduce any portion of freedom into that country"; instead what line 3 presents is a constant deferral to the future ("not . . . yet"). It presents the necessary postponing of freedom. The use of the term *happiness* in line 3 is curious; it seems akin to the idea of "felicity": it is not yet felicitous for us to introduce freedom. This reduces the introduction of freedom to chance and fortune. The second part of line 3 implies that what makes arbitrary power tolerable is its adherence to rule of law. Line 4 reestablishes the opposition differently from line 2, where the opposition seemed to be between a free government and a military one. In line 4, however, it becomes the opposition between a free government and an *arbitrary* government. Because the latter, which more accurately describes the structure in place in Madras, works "downwards"—from the sovereign or supreme head down to the people—insubordination requires an immediate response. (The upward movement from the people to a supreme head, the counterexample that is implied, presumably describes England.)

A Just Rebellion

The references to America, often implicit, are meant to call forth from Parliament a consistent application of punitive measures. It is both a rhetorical strategy and an argument by political analogy: "If one were to judge by the Bills now before you, if there be any one *ruling* passion in Parliament it is the abhorrence of *Rebellion*." The bill to which Burke is referring pertains to captured American shipping, discussed for the third time on May 23, 1777.[107] It is perhaps not surprising that in this year the discussion of India in Parliament should be shot through with discussion of America. Nonetheless Burke's effort is to concatenate and bring together a series of events in North America with those in Madras. This becomes clearest in the final paragraphs of this document, where Burke also appears to be laying the ground for a sound comparison between Madras and Boston along with a basis for their distinction. The distinction, it turns out, will hinge upon the understanding of a just "rebellion": "But there is a great difference if the people rebel, it may be from a sense of *grievance* and all government is subordinate to them. Their rebellion *may* be right—but the rebellion of subordinate office against the superior never can be so for they derive no authority but from him. And if *they* rebel what *principle* or example of obedience is left for the people."[108] What we find here is Burke's careful way of allowing himself to support (in a limited manner) the decision of the American colonists to rebel, and yet to make use of Parliament's overwhelming lack of sympathy for the American cause to support his argument that the insubordination regarding Pigot be punished. Thus he argues that if a "*people* rebel," as in the American case, it may be from a just sense of grievance. Government is subordinate to them, and so in some cases their rebellion may be right. The Indian example, however, Burke reduces to the rebellion of subordinate *officers*, in which case it lacks any basis because their authority is derivative of their superior's. This complicated maneuver operates in rhetorical manner by its use of the word *subordinate* in two contrary ways: (1) the (American) people may rebel because government is *subordinate* to them; (2) the Company officers in Madras may not rebel because they occupy a *subordinate* office to their superior's. And yet in spite of Burke's own limited support for the decision of the American colonists to secede, he argues by political analogy that because rebellion is what aggrieves Parliament, it should particularly repress a rebellion among company officials, for theirs is even less warranted than the Americans'. What is already apparent from this passage is the complicated use of the word *people* as it relates to the word *settler* or *native*. When did the English colonists in America pass from the category of settlers to a people in their own right—a people, we might add, who are "of our own European blood and colour"?[109] He takes the English settlers or colonists in America to be justified in their rebellion. He finds the English Company servants in India to be merely insubordinate officers. Burke is able to imagine America as a place of white settlement more easily than India; historically this is not surprising given the process of English migration to Virginia and Massachusetts in (primarily) the seventeenth century. Nonetheless the juxtaposition of India with America, of the natives of Hindostan with those of Virginia, brings to a useful crisis the category of colonist (or settler) and with it the right of a people to rebel. India, in this figuration, can hope only for a well-run despotism (an efficient chain of command from top to bottom, as Burke explains) rather than a sovereignty of the people (from bottom to top) characteristic of a free people.

But the complicated status of the term *settler* or *native* in relation to the people also arises in his discussion of India, as I noted in his first proposition, "[1.] The obedience of the governors is the freedom of the people," where "the people" seems to refer to the natives of India. If in fact "the people" here refers to the people of Britain, whose freedoms are threatened by insubordination, then one has to remark upon the sudden shift in statements 2 and 3 to India, where military government and arbitrary power operate. This would make statement 4 expressive of a fundamental tension akin to that noted of John Stuart Mill: support of liberalism at home, despotism abroad.[110] When Burke writes that "whatever weakens the power of the Supreme head exposes the people to all manner of powers and oppression," there is a very evident uncertainty as to whether "the people" to which he refers are the people of Britain or of India. If what we find here, in one of his earliest writings on India, is a linkage of the two, then this is also a basis for his later concept of Indianism. Indeed in a different version of this paragraph (included in the notes to this speech), there is a much more explicit formulation of the effects of this event:

> If we may judge by the charges for which you are preparing tomorrow [i.e., regarding America] of all things in the world you detest a rebellion. This [Pigot's imprisonment in India] is Rebellion—the worst of Rebellions a rebellion of *subordinate Government*. A Rebellion of *a standing Army*. A *Rebellion* of a *standing army* of foreign

Troops. A *Rebellion* under the auspices of a *foreign Prince*. A Rebellion caused and abetted by *Bribery here*.

This Nabob aspires even to buy the Company and *to bribe the Parliament*.

If you refuse you shew that it is not rebellion but freedom that you hate—that if any infamous Cabal of interested Clerks shall rise in rebellion; if Troops shall mutiny—they are sure of protection here—a British Parliament will bear them out.[111]

In this stronger version, Burke makes a series of metonymic links (a rebellion of subordinate government/standing army/foreign troops/foreign prince), ending with bribery in Parliament. The restatement of the link between the nabob and Parliament renders the distant subversion more proximate. In its references to nabobs, cabal, bribery, the proximity of the colony to Parliament, and the specter of insubordination at home, this short paragraph anticipates many of the central elements of Burke's later definition of Indianism. This paragraph (the penultimate one) precedes the final lines already cited—"Some people are great Lovers of uniformity—They are not satisfied with a rebellion in the West. They must have one in the East"—but now the use of the word *rebellion* seems to have two potentially contradictory meanings. Rebellion in the West, in America, means a settler revolt (almost a civil war between kindred freedom-loving peoples); but what does rebellion in the East, in India, mean? A revolt of subordinate officers (not a native revolt).[112] The word *rebellion* is brought into crisis by these divergent uses and by these internal contradictions.

Experience from Remote Countries

I conclude my reading in this chapter with one final passage drawn from the closing pages of Burke's "Speech on Conciliation with America" (1775), which brings together yet again these colonies about to be lost in the West with those waxing dominions in the East, although in this case with regard to the fundamental question of extraction and revenue. Having already decried the fixed levels of revenue set for the various colonies of America as a form of "ransom" (a "ransom by auction" designed to break the union of the colonies), Burke protests against increasing and "compounding our demands" by drawing a colonial comparison meant to underline the difference between the sapling of liberty planted in America by English offspring and the vast Banyan of a money tree that is India:

But to clear up my ideas on this subject—a revenue from America transmitted hither—do not delude yourselves—you can never receive it—No, not a shilling. We have experience that from remote countries it is not to be expected. If, when you attempted to extract revenue from Bengal, you were obliged to return in loan what you had taken in imposition; what can you expect from North America? for certainly, *if ever there was a country qualified to produce wealth, it is India; or an institution fit for the transmission, it is the East-India company.* America has none of these aptitudes.[113]

This certainly does clear up many ideas; Burke's remark makes reference to a 1767 episode when Britain extracted revenue from the East India Company, precipitating a financial crisis in the Company that required a loan (or bailout, to give this a contemporary color) from Parliament in 1773.[114] Burke is underlining—at this early stage in his thinking with regard to India, I should emphasize—that America is a worthy extension of England and merits a soft touch; India is a counterexample illustrating that even a place offering such a potentially lucrative extraction, overseen (or subordinated) by an institution ideally designed for this task, was burdened by it. (There is a tension in Burke's remark between the neutral term *transmission* and the whiff of rapaciousness suggested by *extraction*.) America, lacking these "aptitudes," is instead naturally inclined toward the practices of freedom and will chafe at restrictions placed upon it for the manifold historical reasons that Burke explores throughout this speech. His description of what he desires from America can be understood in terms of Foucault's notion of "pastoral power," namely that desire which gradually emerges on the part of the ruled to be loved by those they govern, reinforced (I would add) by a settler colonial notion of "kindred blood."[115] What makes Britain unique for Burke among European powers is this willing and freely granted love rather than the coercion of slavery, which helps retain the "unity of empire."[116] As he puts it, compressing three key factors (pastoral power, a settler-colonial ideal, and the concept of population): "As long as you have the wisdom to keep the sovereign authority of this country as the sanctuary of liberty . . . wherever the chosen race and sons of England worship freedom, they will turn their faces towards you. The more they multiply, the more friends you will have. . . . Slavery they can have anywhere. It is a weed that grows in every soil. They may have it from Spain, they may have it from Prussia."[117] To keep with my initial remarks on the conjuncture of India and America in Burke's thought, Burke expresses a sentiment here that would find transmuted form in his India writings when he works to "contrive some method of governing India *well*, which will not of necessity become the means of governing Great Britain *ill*,"[118] words spoken to "preserve the British Constitution from its corruption." Empire, at this early stage in Burke's thinking, takes on a nearly religious character in its ability to suffuse all and provide the sentiments that mere laws and statutes fail to elicit. In an extraordinary passage that serves as a foil to the epigraph commencing the second part of this chapter, Burke describes this permeating and uniting force:

> Do not dream that your letters of office, and your instructions, and your suspending clauses, are the things that hold together the great contexture of this mysterious whole. These things do not make your government. Dead instruments, passive tools as they are, it is the spirit of the English communion that gives all their life and efficacy to them. It is the spirit of the English constitution, which, infused through the mighty mass, pervades, feeds, unites, invigorates, vivifies every part of the empire, even down to the minutest member.[119]

In its contrast between the "dead instruments" of government and the living spirit of English communion—quickly becoming the English constitution—that pervades empire like an ether, we see manifested a colonial "great chain of being" that reaches down in a capillary manner to the smallest unit. This cuts against the remarks he made only two years later (after the outbreak of the American Revolution), in his 1777 "Letter to the Sheriffs of Bristol," that he did not seek to reflect on the "unity of empire" joining the natives of Virginia and Hindostan; instead of a "mighty mass" joined by this ether, it became a "mighty and strangely *diversified* mass" fractured and irreconcilable.[120] From sameness to difference: even the very ether pervading the universe changed to accommodate this transformation.

From Political Analogy to Political Concatenation

The movement from the Americas to India, from India to France, and from thence to Ireland (and not necessarily in one direction) is what I would designate by the term *political concatenation*. Concatenation is defined as a "union in a series or chain, of which the things united form as it were links."[121] In line with one definition from social theory, the concept of concatenation describes the manner by which various divergent and disparate struggles may be joined together and thus demonstrates the persistently fragile nature of forms of hegemony that are in need of constant reassertion.[122] By invoking this term I mean to emphasize that concatenation is a more common feature of the operation of political speech generally; while I have culled the term from scholars associated with radical democratic politics, it is apparent that the technique may be used by both the right and the left.

Political concatenation, in this particular case, identifies the movement by which Burke shifts from Company abuses in colonial Bengal to the Jacobin order, and beyond. Whereas the concept of analogy describes how he places into consideration particular regions or nations, his aim is more focused and greater than the mere making of analogies; concatenation (to create a deeper set of relations and links) more precisely identifies the intention of his writing. To understand this one needs to reiterate the continuity between Burke's aesthetic and political works, his early and late writings. His treatise on aesthetics (from 1757) and on the fundamental role of the imagination prevent him from making the common error of overlooking the importance of affect and sympathy.[123] Sympathy, Burke acknowledges, is a fundamental element in the formulation of a political judgment, and his India writings are a constant attempt to remap the foreign onto the familiar.[124] It is thus by means of this aesthetic capacity that he can lay the ground for concatenation between different geographic spaces and political contexts. Political sympathy must make use of a prior aesthetic capacity, in a manner that is consonant with his argument (*pace* Hume) that it is primarily the latter that has sway over the individual.

This examination of the movement from one topic or geographical region to the next in Burke's thought has therefore not been chronological but rather aimed to locate a quality that appears to be merely incipient or peripheral to a text (such as Indianism in the British Parliament in the *Reflections*) and then to trace both its previous manifestations and later development. By situating Burke's concern over Indianism and Jacobinism within this continuum, the implications of other central components of his political thought—such as custom, manners, talent—are far more explicable.

As noted earlier, the critique of modernity that one finds in Burke's attack on the Jacobins and his notion of geometric rationality owe a great deal to his prior examination of East India Company activity in India. If this is so, then the movement he makes along a chain of political analogies that he sets up ought to be recognized as having woven together an ensemble of locations (India, France, Ireland, North America, St. Domingue/Haiti) which, in the nineteenth century, will be prized apart in most considerations. Burke inherits an established though often ignored discourse of anticolonialism from the Enlightenment, which he transmutes into a form of both external and internal critique. (Thus his tirades against the Jacobins may now be seen as intimately linked with his attacks on Company rule in India, while the latter are integral to his defense of Parliament from domestic cabal.) Burke is indeed, as many of his interpreters have asserted, a transitional figure, yet I would alter the form of the transition to which he is witness: not only a witness of the transition from an aristocratic to an emerging bourgeois ethos but also a witness to the shift from an early mercantile colonial empire to a formally regulated one. Understanding this movement explains the curious quality of his language, which replicates some of the anticolonial rhetoric of the Enlightenment but yokes it to a political position that consistently found a strong basis to critique this outlook. Whereas such figures as Diderot were led, as one important study would have it, from atheism to anticolonialism,[125] Burke is brought to his limited anticolonial position by a very contrary impulse, perhaps even from his own disposition toward piety (hence the importance of terms such as *reverence* and *respect*). These are two very different paths to anticolonial position, yet, having said this, one must also note that what one witnesses here is European anticolonialism at its aporetic limit. One would have to wait until the discourses of full sovereignty as they emerged in the period of decolonization long after this to find a complete and robust statement of the claim to freedom and autonomy. (And these, in turn, reach a limit moment in the failure of decolonization in the era of globalization.)

The movement along an analogical chain (an image at the etymological root of *concatenation*) allows one to see how and why Indianism and Jacobinism are central terms in Burke's vocabulary: they reveal how colonial and revolutionary political systems share many similar characteristics.[126] Both nurture the use of abstraction, partly as a result of the necessary estrangement of rulers from the ruled; both involve the confiscation of land, and that by "upstart" rulers. In both a faction takes power and produces a nation that becomes an inauthentic mimic of itself, a spectral and ghostly nation. For these various reasons, Burke aims to *break* the existing analogy circulating among his contemporaries between the American Revolution and the French Revolution; in place of the former, he attempts to insert the colonial model of domination as the proper way to understand the Jacobin order. His notion of Jacobinism is that of an emerging form of alienated modernity dependent on a particular view of human nature unmoored from all affiliations and eviscerated of all inherited qualities. Against this his entire project can be read as an effort to embed, in a highly contentious and interested manner, that subject back into a world of necessary constraints—which, however, also produce meaning.

Epilogue. Hating Empire Properly: European Anticolonialism at Its Limit

> *The blacks were taking their part in the destruction of European feudalism begun by the French Revolution, and liberty and equality, the slogans of the revolution, meant far more to them than to any Frenchman. That was why in the hour of danger Toussaint, uninstructed as he was, could find the language and accent of Diderot, Rousseau, and Raynal, of Mirabeau, Robespierre, and Danton.*
> —C. L. R. JAMES, *THE BLACK JACOBINS* (1938)

What might C. L. R. James have meant by this passage, which makes the case—following a Hegelian model of consciousness, where it is the slave whose ability to grasp the concept of freedom exceeds that of his master—that the slogans of the revolution meant far more to the insurgent blacks of St. Domingue than to any Frenchman?[1] If for Kant it was a motto (or slogan, *Wahlspruche*) of the Enlightenment to "dare to know" (*sapere aude*), what can be made of such daring which manifested itself in an anticolonialism whose significance was misread for centuries and culminated in a revolution excluded from the category of revolution?[2] It was certainly a different form of daring, and it was the proximate sense of danger (as James puts it) that enabled Toussaint to "find the language" of many of the Enlightenment figures I have been tracing in this book. The language he found, I would like to suggest, was able to cross a conceptual limit that both Diderot and Burke encountered in their critiques of empire.[3] And yet what I have tried to explore, in a manner that diminishes a looming Manichaeanism that would pose Toussaint's understanding against his European counterparts, are the persistent internal critiques of empire that one finds within the spectrum of European thought on the subject. In a partial sense, this has been a recuperative gesture, removing in the case of Diderot's writings for Raynal the dismissive pall that many influential interpretations of the work (from nineteenth-century readers such as John Morley to many twentieth-century critics) had put upon it, ignoring the request to correlate his work with exclusive referents from within Europe. Or, in the

TOUSSAINT READING THE ABBÉ RAYNAL'S WORK.

case of Burke, restoring his thought—even when motivated by the affect of fear rather than calling for the new—to the broader and more global ensemble of locations with which he occupied himself.

It is certain that what James found in Toussaint was in fact an early figure for the decolonization to come that he sought and that he was to see in his lifetime beginning with Ghana in 1957.[4] (His links with the young Nkrumah in the context of Pan-Africanism in New York and London are often noted in this context.) Toussaint was also, I should add, a figure who unabashedly drew inspiration from aspects of the "Radical Enlightenment" (in Jonathan Israel's sense) in his synthesis of political strategies and concepts from West Africa and Europe (a running debate and theme in the scholarship on the West Indies, one that finds a parallel in the South Asian context over the degree to which colonialism represented a fundamental rupture in the social fabric of Indian society or merely another layer).[5] This produced an outlook with a profound entanglement and imbrication with the revolutionary languages of Europe, and it was thereby an emblem for James of an anticolonialism that was not purely and *reductively oppositional* at its outset—hence the fascinating claims made at various points by Haitian insurgents on elements of French revolutionary culture, such as singing the "Marseillaise" while charging headlong toward an invading French force (altering and expanding its meaning through their iteration).[6] What is significant here is the appropriation of revolutionary culture and its symbols. James emphasized this aspect of Toussaint even in his imaginative reworking of the Haitian archive.[7] This understanding of Toussaint may also explain why James himself, similarly wishing to avoid a purely oppositional position to Europe, often frustrated his interlocutors in the 1960s with reference to himself as a "black European"—in other words, not disavowing a filiation (with Europe, with the West) that rendered more complex and

FIGURE 6 (opposite page): "Toussaint Reading the Abbé Raynal's work." From *J. R. Beard, 1800–1876. The Life of Toussaint L'Ouverture, the Negro Patriot of Hayti: Comprising an Account of the Struggle for Liberty in the Island, and a Sketch of Its History to the Present Period* (London: Ingram, Cooke, 1853). Courtesy of Documenting the American South, The University of North Carolina at Chapel Hill Libraries. A recurrent element in narratives of Toussaint's life: his reading of Raynal's work. "A courageous chief only is wanted." A domestic scene with emphasis on his repose; books are on the shelf behind, and a quill rests in an inkpot on the desk: the Haitian Revolution imbricated with the radical Enlightenment.

irreducible his stance as an anticolonial critic.[8] James's own perception of his intellectual formation, his education in colonial schools of the West Indies, even his explicit admiration of Burke—"Burke, begun as a school chore, had rapidly become for me the most exciting master of prose in English"—seems only to reinforce this.[9]

James was clearly attuned to the schisms within Europe, and one can read *The Black Jacobins* as a counterhistory of the Enlightenment; in fact its publication in 1938 already implies the plural of the noun that others (most recently J. G. A. Pocock) have called for in the past decade, and it furthermore undertakes the project of "reclaiming" the Enlightenment (in this pluralized form), which, rather periodically, is also argued for.[10] The book was also an iteration of the concept of Enlightenment that transformed and broadened its significance by focusing on (not evading, hiding, or apologizing for) its *contradictions*. We see this in the work when, in describing the causes of Toussaint's eventual demise in contrast to Dessalines, James writes, "Yet Toussaint's error sprang from the very qualities that made him what he was. . . . Toussaint's failure was the failure of enlightenment, not of darkness."[11] James meant to draw a contrast between (as he describes him) the "uneducated" Dessalines who could act without reflecting on the larger question of inclusion (of whites against a French invasion of the island) and Toussaint's desire to adhere to a more universal ideal; thus his "failure" was not caused by a turn to "darkness"—a cynical and short-sighted view. Needless to say, it was this method and perspective deployed by James which Edward Said understood as "contrapuntal,"[12] narrating a dominant element cross-cut and interrupted by an insurgent one.

Indeed it was one effect of this approach that James was thereby able to capture how a single event, or a single term, could contain multiple contradictory meanings. As if to reiterate his point regarding liberty and equality, he repeats his assertion in a different form a hundred pages later that these "slogans of the revolution" meant *more* to the blacks of St. Domingue. It is a passage that illustrates how, for James, there is something excessive in the colonial reception of a radical Enlightenment idea, something in addition and beyond its meaning in Europe. Of the invading French army sent in by Napoleon under Leclerc, James writes:

> None of the French rank-and-file in San Domingo guessed that they were fighting to restore slavery. The war was for them a revolutionary war.
>
> But Toussaint's soldiers and generals, illiterates and ex-slaves, had been moulded by the same revolution. . . . The liberty and

equality which these blacks acclaimed as they went into battle meant far more to them than the same words in the mouths of the French.[13]

The "same revolution," the same event, causes a certain misprision in significance, and it is here that James asserts that the meaning was greater for the blacks than for the French, and he emphasizes this by referring to (mere?) words in the "mouths of the French." (It is James's critique of a certain kind of nominalism; it appears again elsewhere in a rebuke of some of Robespierre's radical remarks).[14]

Drawing on elements of James's model, then, this book has attempted an estrangement that is premised on the productive possibilities of discursive schisms and evanescent moments of insurgency, an estrangement from the familiar images of Diderot and Burke that follows as far as it is possible to do so their critique of empire. In the case of Diderot, we can put it more sharply: his occasional hatred of empire. Moreover, with due apologies to Theodor Adorno, from whose work *Minima Moralia: Reflections from Damaged Life* I draw the expression, we can learn what it means to "hate" empire properly, namely to engage in a form of critique that explores its inconsistencies.[15]

Hating Empire Properly

I conclude with two propositions that reiterate some aims of this work. First, examining the ideologies of empire is vital if we are to have an understanding of the implications of the knowledge-power linkage described by Said (and drawn from the method and spirit, we might say, of Foucault). Second, following arguments against empire requires a comparative consideration, for example, India alongside St. Domingue or Haiti, *les indes orientales* and *les indes occidentales*. Moreover one needs to consider that arguments against empire often fulfill certain political fantasies in the period (and it is important to learn how to read or interpret these contradictory fantasies). New interpretations from the past decade have brought out sharply the rich possibilities for a critique of European hegemony that existed within the languages of political thought in the eighteenth century.[16] We also have contributions that trace the turn toward empire and the logic of liberal imperialism.[17] A radical like Diderot, I have argued in contrast to these emphases, comes upon the impasse of a colonialism by consent, a "consensual colonialism," partly as a product of his initial hatred of forms of dominance and conquest.

However, these works from political theorists need to be considered alongside an almost parallel set of questions from those in area studies or cultural history, alongside philologists (in the rich sense, as Nietzsche meant it when he referred to himself as such), and those who studied Oriental languages—orientalists in the old (honorable?) sense of the word.[18] It appears to me that from our vantage point nearly thirty years later, we can bracket the polemic and counterpolemic around Said's work and instead place at the center the kinds of scholarship and knowledge production that it did enable. In addition to the scholarship from political theorists mentioned earlier, I also have in mind earlier works such as Uday Mehta's *Liberalism and Empire* some of the work of subaltern studies and its associates, Partha Chatterjee and Dipesh Chakrabarty.[19] (I do not mean to imply that these authors were carrying out Said's project, but rather that their aims were consonant with the kind of project Said proposed, the kinds of questions he framed—as several of the homages to Said from these scholars have made explicit.)[20] In this list, I am no doubt collapsing many generations of scholars and scholarly projects, beginning with Ranajit Guha's early work, *Rule of Property for Bengal* (published in 1963), and the work of some of his younger colleagues and students.[21] What the work of all these scholars has in common is a consideration of how an object of knowledge is constituted (hence my invocation of Adorno, who similarly reflected on this problematic)[22]—how an object called the Orient was produced through several discourses: that of the novelist, the Jesuit, the administrator, the savant (to name a few examined by Said and by specialists such as Sylvia Murr). To make a distinction, if what an older generation of anticolonial scholars and intellectuals sought to examine was the British colonial state's complicity in the formation of certain types of knowledge, for a more recent generation formed in the postcolonial era in South Asia (and certainly not only there), the concerns were more explicitly about the failures of the emancipatory aims of the sovereign states, the complicity of some elites, and the marginalization of various groups (tribal, caste, etc.) by the discourse of dominant nationalism. James was certainly aware of both components of this critique with regard to the colonial state and power; unlike Adorno, his resolution was shaped by a commitment to a humanism inspired by Marx's thought. (Indeed he once quipped that the phrase *Marxist humanism* was redundant: to be one implied being the other.)

Adorno's Belated Positivist Savage

Thinking of (or rather thinking with) this unlikely pair, James and Adorno, we can nonetheless find an affinity: a commitment (perhaps derived from a mutually shared interest in Hegel and dialectics) to an immanent critique of the West.[23] This, after all, is what Adorno meant by his enigmatic yet provocative remark that "one must have tradition in oneself, to hate it properly."[24] But what, we might ask, constitutes the "proper"? Is it the *Eigentliche,* the ownmost, of which Heidegger spoke (certainly not a figure with whom Adorno expressed any sympathy)?[25] The German expression he uses shows that it is not this; his sentence concludes with the phrase "um sie *recht* zu hassen"—I will return to this momentarily.[26] At the very least, Adorno appears to suggest a rigorous engagement with tradition, an immersion ("in sich selber haben"), which would then authorize its "proper" hating. An improper hating would seem to be an example of that which is purely oppositional, a rejection from an external position—what James might have seen as the "temptation" to proclaim an African critique of the European Enlightenment; it would fall prey to another species of the blackmail of the Enlightenment, in this case choosing outright rejection.

Taking the examples of Diderot and Burke considered in this book, what might "hating" empire properly mean? I would like to propose this affectively troubling expression as a commitment to a certain intellectual and political consistency, thinking of India and Haiti as coeval spaces of the Enlightenment. By extending the frame of Enlightenment critique beyond that which Adorno imagined and considering the limitations of his framework, I do not mean to look upon previous generations with an arrogance from the present, accusing them of failing to consider a category we now hold to be central (such as race, gender, or religion). There is, nevertheless, a responsibility to engage with these valuations, to supplement these genealogies, to argue with these judgments.

Properly hating empire, in this autocritical spirit, thereby involves a two-step process: a critique of the ideology of the "classical" empires of the eighteenth and nineteenth centuries (and their effects on the formations of concepts and systems of thought) as well as a critique of postcolonial regimes, as Fanon foresaw, and their parallel abuses of terms and concepts.[27] Empire in this usage may itself be a sign for certain forms of dominance (a catachresis). Let us return to the aphorism or fragment that contains Adorno's remark, often cited but perhaps without due regard to its interesting and pertinent context, which is itself a reminder of the need to engage in a persistent critique of the terms of one's analysis. The title of this aphorism (*Minima Moralia*, part 1, number 32) is "Savages are not more noble" (*Die Wilden sind nicht bessere Menschen*) and is striking for its compression and illustration of several arguments made in earlier chapters of this book. This observation, composed during Adorno's stay (or exile, as he viewed it) in Los Angeles in 1944,[28] catches a key moment, on the cusp of what would be post–World War II decolonization—not to mention the greater public awareness of the concentration camps that would ensue and that so mark Adorno's thought. He writes, "There is to be found in African students of political economy, Siamese at Oxford, and more generally in diligent art-historians and musicologists of petty-bourgeois origins, a ready inclination to combine with the assimilation of new material, an inordinate respect for all that is established, accepted, acknowledged. An uncompromising mind is the very opposite of primitivism [*Wildheit*], neophytism, or the 'non-capitalist world.'"[29] What Adorno appears to detect in these foreign students (ironically, we assume, referred to as the *Wilden* or savages) as well as those from a petit bourgeois class background is "an inordinate respect" ("einen unmäßigen Respekt") for established knowledge; possessing, we might say, the zeal of a convert, their reaction to primitivism produces an "uncompromising mind." His fear, consonant with his remarks on American society at the time, was directed at this uncompromising commitment to positivism, which he and Max Horkheimer linked with the violence of abstraction in their joint work from the same year, *The Dialectic of Enlightenment*.[30] Adorno proceeds to describe the circumstances that allow for a more resolutely critical approach, presumably one that maintains a distance from both positivism and superstition or myth (again drawing on the terms used in *Dialectic of Enlightenment*); this disposition requires "experience, a historical memory [*historisches Gedächtnis*], a fastidious intellect and above all an ample measure of satiety." Lacking these elements, Adorno implies, these converts relapse: "It has been observed time and again how those recruited young and innocent to radical groups have defected once they felt the force of tradition."[31] The German expression now allows us to see what it is that one must have: the "Kraft der Tradition" or "power of tradition."[32] It is this which one must have in oneself, "um sie recht zu hassen."

This is (speaking figuratively) Adorno's Bandung moment—namely his encounter with the social phenomena that would give rise to the Bandung Conference just over ten years later (1955)—for, in this tableau that commences with an African political economist, a Siamese student at Oxford (presumably Adorno is recalling his own brief stay there),[33] he then presents his reader with another odd third-worldist intellectual formation: a Carnap worshipper in India. (He plays upon the variety of forms of "worship" in India, a passing familiarity demonstrated in scattered references to German Indology in his works from this period.)[34] What Adorno points to is a simpleminded return to positivism, an implied "catching-up" or (as I referred to it earlier) a colonial lag time: "Late-comers [*Spätkommer*] and newcomers [*Neukommer*] have an alarming affinity to positivism, from Carnap-worshippers in India [*den Carnapverehrern in Indien*] to the stalwart defenders of the German masters Matthias Grünewald and Heinrich Schütz." We are returned to a narrative of development and progress (or at the very least a necessary sequence) that has been critically examined by many. To be clear, Adorno does not attribute this quality solely to the Indian worshipper of one of the leading proponents of logical positivism (Rudolf Carnap), but his remark does imply a theory of affect, of desire, which can serve to explain his view of the colonized mind: "It would be poor psychology to assume that exclusion arouses only hate and resentment [*Haß und Ressentiment*]; it arouses too a possessive, intolerant kind of love, and those whom repressive culture has held at a distance can easily become its most diehard defenders."[35] A fascinating observation on the interrelation of hate and resentment with love—albeit a possessive, intolerant love ("*unduldsame Art von Liebe*"). Adorno tellingly uses the word borrowed from French, *ressentiment*, indelibly marked for him by Nietzsche's discussion (and perhaps Max Scheler's).[36] Moreover the German term translated as "diehard defender" is *Schutztruppe*, which has a greater military connotation, significant given the date of composition. In fact the *Schutztruppe* were originally the German military forces in colonial Africa, some of whom were drawn from native populations. Colonial soldiers defending European imperial interests: the zeal of our Carnap worshipper is strong indeed.

The danger, for Adorno, is that of socialism "lapsing theoretically into positivism,"[37] expressing once again his deep suspicion for a form of thought which (to him) was a dark undercurrent of the Enlightenment, now manifested in the violence (and violent "rationality") of Auschwitz. With an awareness, perhaps, of both Chinese and Indian Marxist movements, he declares, "It can happen easily enough that in the Far East Marx is put in the place vacated by Driesch and Rickert," which bespeaks his fear of the dominance of crude economism with regard to human capacities (a mere imitation of a flawed idea of progress) replacing the complexity of either a scientific critique of the mechanistic view of living organisms (Hans Driesch) or a Neo-Kantian argument against positivist epistemology (Heinrich Rickert). That, at least, is what the subsequent line explores: "There is some reason to fear that the involvement of non-Western peoples [*nichtokzidentalen Völker*] in the conflicts of industrial society, long overdue in itself, will be less to the benefit of the liberated peoples than to that of rationally improved production and communications, and a modestly raised standard of living."[38] The legacy of the Enlightenment, in other words, is reduced to a merely rationalized sphere of production. One ends up, however, as with the return of superstition in the Enlightenment (an argument made in *Dialectic of Enlightenment*), with a belated positivist savage through the involvement of these formerly excluded peoples. If one keeps two historical contexts in view—the European eighteenth century and the era of decolonization, which was also that of increased reflections on the violence of World War II (especially, for Adorno, the Holocaust)—it is striking to consider Adorno's pessimism regarding Enlightenment reason alongside his misrecognition (in *Minima Moralia*) of the significance of third-world intellectual formations. It was a misrecognition because he could see them only in terms of a pattern drawn from Europe; they were merely a bad repetition of an already known form of positivism. He could not recognize their peculiar formations as expressive of the manifold cultural and political contradictions of empire; that is, the subject formation of these intellectuals under imperialism intended their "love" of Europe. (Indeed, as an obverse to my discussion of hating empire properly, one could well write a reflection on the long history of loving empire.) Their response to this—at times against this—produced the moments of identity and difference, similarity and misprision.[39]

This reading of the context and use of Adorno's expression accounts for why I have modulated and altered his expression. Recalling his method and implying the same degree of responsibility to the object, the aim of this book has been not "hating tradition properly" but "hating empire properly"[40]—that is to say, entering into its terms and allowing the internal contradictions to be heightened rather than covered by a politic veil (to evoke Burke's image regarding the hazy origins of most states). Moreover, recalling the full phrase Adorno used, "One must have tradition in oneself to hate it properly," it is undeniable that even the analogous remark is also true: One must have empire in oneself to hate it properly. That is, the form of reflection we have produced here to critique empire is certainly also partly the intellectual result of the epistemological worlds it caused to collide (or accidentally enabled), and yet acknowledging this degree of complicity ought not to undercut the ability of the analytic gaze (*theoria*) or focused attention on phenomena or events whose sublated form is with us even today. (Here I myself have sensed the persistent shadow of American engagements in Afghanistan and Iraq that undeniably form and deform my conscious effort to reflect and examine the eighteenth-century material in this book.) If we must counter the pessimism of the intellect, this is accomplished by critiquing the space that we inhabit and transcribing the affects and passions (whether indignation or *ressentiment*, despair or hope) into history.

This moment in Adorno's work serves also a revealing analogue to the impression made on the thought of Diderot and Burke from the 1780s and 1790s; in both cases there was a reflection on those left outside of the global aims of the Enlightenment. I have tried to follow Foucault's remark on the epochal quality of Kant's thought—philosophy thinking of its present[41]—through a reading that reconstitutes some vital and often absent components of their world. Certainly the German-Jewish relationship to Europe offers a potential model, within limits, of the experience of the colonized, and it is this that makes Adorno's writing resonant: its liminal, insider/outsider status, its peculiar combination of an antagonistic relation to culture (hating tradition) with a commitment to (tragic?) immersion within it.[42]

Indeed it is this form of entanglement—a subtle form of inhabitation accompanied by a thoroughgoing critique or even antagonism—that very likely prompted Foucault to observe his own debt to the Frankfurt school: "I would like right away to note, in approaching this problem which makes us brothers with the Frankfurt School, that to make Aufklärung the central question at once means a number of things."[43] Elsewhere, in his brief but remarkable essay "Kant on Enlightenment and Revolution," he discusses the significance of Kant's actual reference to the event of the French Revolution. It is, for Kant, an example of a "prognostic sign" that confirms the idea of progress. And progress is, in turn, the key proof of the definition of Enlightenment. Now what Foucault discusses as a pivotal moment in Kant with regard to the French Revolution seems even more true of and pertinent to the Haitian Revolution: "So it is not the revolutionary process itself which is important. Never mind whether it succeed or fail, that is nothing to do with progress, or at least with the sign of progress which we are looking for. The success or failure of the revolution are not signs of progress or a sign that there is no progress."[44] This is an essential point: it is not success or failure that is important but rather (as he elaborates it) the disposition that is revealed; once revealed "it will never be possible to forget [it]."[45] I think it was this heritage, this *tradition*, that C. L. R. James sought to excavate. Foucault's point is more apt for the Haitian than the French Revolution, since the former has been actively forgotten (by some) precisely because it was judged a "failure," or the current state of Haiti has served for its critics as a post facto proof of the revolution's failure. The impossibility of forgetting a disposition once revealed is what underwrote the likelihood to repetition that Kant affirmed: "For this event is too important, too much interwoven, with the interests of humanity and of too widespread an influence on every part of the globe not to be recalled to memory by the peoples at the occasion of each favourable circumstance, so that they would then be aroused to a repetition of new attempts of this kind."[46] Strikingly, Arendt suggests a fascinating link in Kant's thought between this moment and an explicit argument he makes against colonial tutelage (though she does not use that phrase), namely deferring freedom until a people are "ripe" for it. Kant's words are resonant here, again with regard to the Haitian Revolution, and allow us to see that he was able to extend his own notion of *Unmündigkeit* (an "immaturity" proximate with "tutelage") from the oft-cited opening line of his "What Is Enlightenment?"[47] Arendt quotes from Kant's *Religion within the Limits of Reason Alone*: "I cannot admit the expression used even by intelligent men: A certain people ... is not yet ripe for freedom [*ist zur Freiheit nicht reif*]; the bondmen of a landed proprietor are not yet ripe for freedom. . . . According to such a presupposition freedom will never arrive; for we cannot *ripen* to this freedom unless we are already set free."[48] Although Arendt rather interestingly connects this passage on revolution with an Irish rebellion against English authority in 1798 upon which Kant also commented, its references to "bondmen" and proprietors find an echo in our discussion.[49]

It is by thinking with the authors who struggled to produce a genealogical account of the Enlightenment and its legacies—Adorno and Foucault, but also James—that we can best situate and revive the arguments for and against Enlightenment and revolution addressed in this book. We may close with a remark from Foucault that catches the spirit of this disposition, one that cleaves to the importance and significance of these authors and texts but solicits them to speak on the question, in our case, of empire and colonialism: "Let us leave to their piety those who wish us to preserve alive and intact the heritage of *Aufklärung*. Such piety is doubtless the most touching of treasons. It is not the legacy of *Aufklärung* which it is our business to conserve, but rather the very question of this event and its meaning, the question of the historicity of the thought of the universal, which ought to kept present and retained in mind as that which has to be thought."[50] It is the most "touching of treasons" ("la plus touchante des trahisons") because it betrays an Enlightenment principle (that of questioning) while claiming to conserve its legacy. It is an alleged fidelity that actually does harm; we could live well without it. His dismissive view of such piety, and the touch of mockery suggested by this language, is an echo of the spirit behind Adorno's remark: tradition is to be kept present, retained in mind, yet subject to critique. Moreover Foucault's insistence on placing at the center of his investigation "the very question of this event and its meaning" returns us to a mode of inquiry (he suggests calling it historico-philosophical) that finds an affinity in the style of history (which is not exactly history) Diderot composed for the *Histoire des deux Indes* or Burke in his deeper consideration of the significance of the French Revolution alongside revolutions in India. In neither case do we find an example of a level and flat narration of facts. Instead there is an acknowledgment of the urgency at hand (which elicits, I would emphasize again, an opposing diagnosis from Burke). In the epigraph from James, it is the "hour of danger" that prods Toussaint to "find" the language of the eminent philosophes and revolutionary orators. Why did he have to find this language when it was in plain sight? It was because he had to use it differently, to misuse or (better, if more elusive) "ab-use" the language of the Enlightenment. Similarly discarding the protective piety around the heritage of the Enlightenment, Gayatri Spivak notes (speaking in Cape Town) that it is imperative "to think of geopolitical rather than cosmopolitical answers to the question 'What is Enlightenment?' The post-colonial academy must learn to use the Enlightenment from below; strictly speaking, ab-use it. If there is one academic lesson to learn from the revolutionary political experiment in South Africa, it is this one. Not to abuse it, except in the eyes of those who still think it can only be used from above, those who must ignore the hyphen in order to protect themselves."[51] Ab-using the Enlightenment, recalling Nietzsche's invocation of the term and Spivak's iteration, is a way of marking the limit, of indicating how that limit was crossed.

In a recent discussion of the significance of Max Weber and modernization theory, the anthropologist and social theorist Arjun Appadurai has argued that what is "exported" from Europe in the eighteenth century intellectually is less a unified system than a fractured set of debates and unresolved contradictions which are played out in the colonies.[52] But what if this system—the various discourses associated with the Enlightenment, in this case—was fractured to begin with even in its point of origin (what I have referred to as an internal plurality)? Anticolonial thought within Europe—or enmeshed with the revolutionary languages of Europe, as in Haiti—can thereby provide resources for thinking, or thinking at the limit, and allow us to avoid the "blackmail" of the Enlightenment and to further avoid, by extending Foucault's remark, the "blackmail" of colonialism: that is, either acknowledge that it enabled some degree of progress, or else revert to an embrace of illiteracy, internal forms of oppression, barbarism, and so on. Instead a consideration of colonial spaces of the Enlightenment, such as Haiti and India, ought to enable us to reflect on the shortcomings of universalist discourses and to heed the creative appropriations of these discourses by figures such as Toussaint and Belley (some of which find resonance in the later era of twentieth-century decolonization, as James seems to suggest).[53] Moreover one consequence of this might be that the full "meaning" and significance of the fragmentary discourses of the Enlightenment are manifest only in the colonies, rendered legible only by means of the colonies—the Indies East and West.

Notes

Prologue

1. See Louis Sala-Molins, *Les misères des Lumières: Sous la raison, l'outrage* (Paris: R. Laffont, 1992), translated as *Dark Side of the Light: Slavery and the French Enlightenment*, trans. John Conteh-Morgan (Minneapolis: University of Minnesota Press, 2006). Similarly, with regard to the Renaissance, see Walter Mignolo, *The Darker Side of the Renaissance: Literacy, Territoriality, and Colonization* (Ann Arbor: University of Michigan Press, 1995).

2. Ranajit Guha, *History at the Limit of World-History*, Italian Academy Lectures (New York: Columbia University Press, 2002) opens with one such consideration of the need to examine, in particular, philosophy's "complicity" with colonialism; his focus is Hegel. By contrast, Sankar Muthu, *Enlightenment against Empire* (Princeton: Princeton University Press, 2003), tries to excavate and give form to an Enlightenment that stood against this alliance.

3. "Letter to a Member of the National Assembly," in Edmund Burke, *The Writings and Speeches of Edmund Burke*, ed. Paul Langford and William B Todd (Oxford: Oxford University Press, 1981–), 8:294–335.

4. See vol. 1 of J. G. A. Pocock, *Barbarism and Religion*, 4 vols. (New York: Cambridge University Press, 1999–), titled "The Enlightenments of Edward Gibbon." For an insightful collection of postmodern engagements with this question, see Daniel Gordon, *Postmodernism and the Enlightenment: New Perspectives in Eighteenth-Century French Intellectual History* (New York: Routledge, 2000). A different approach is taken by Richard Rorty, who attempts to distinguish between the political and the philosophical projects of the Enlightenment. See his contribution to Keith Michael Baker and Peter Hanns Reill, *What's Left of Enlightenment? A Postmodern Question* (Stanford: Stanford University Press, 2001).

5. An early question posed by Reinhart Koselleck, *Futures Past: On the Semantics of Historical Time*, Studies in Contemporary German Social Thought (Cambridge, Mass.: MIT Press, 1985). See in particular the chapter "Modernity and the Planes of History."

6. As with the term *Enlightenment*, there seem to be many who are eager to proclaim the death of postcolonial thought, or its end. The term may die with a whimper, but what it identified, its enabling tensions, certainly has not. I discuss this further in my contributions to Patricia Yaeger, "Editor's Column: The End of Postcolonial Theory? A Roundtable with Sunil Agnani, Fernando Coronil, Gaurav Desai, Mamadou Diouf, Simon Gikandi, Susie Tharu, and Jennifer Wenzel," *PMLA* 122 (2007).

7. David Scott, *Conscripts of Modernity: The Tragedy of Colonial Enlightenment* (Durham, N.C.: Duke University Press, 2004) has productively explored the intersection of Enlightenment and modernity, as has (in a very different manner) Aamir Mufti, *Enlightenment in the Colony: The Jewish Question and the Crisis of Postcolonial Culture* (Princeton: Princeton University Press, 2007). More broadly, this study shares the interpretive approach of such works as the chapters on the eighteenth century in Sanjay Krishnan, *Reading the Global: Troubling Perspectives on Britain's Empire in Asia* (New York: Columbia University Press, 2007); Betty Joseph, *Reading the East India Company, 1720–1840: Colonial Currencies of Gender*, Women in Culture and Society (Chicago: University of Chicago Press, 2004); Srinivas Aravamudan, *Tropicopolitans: Colonialism and Agency, 1688–1804*, Post-Contemporary Interventions (Durham, N.C.: Duke University Press, 1999); and the reflections on Kant's New Hollander in Gayatri Chakravorty Spivak, *A Critique of Postcolonial Reason: Toward a History of the Vanishing Present* (Cambridge: Harvard University Press, 1999).

8. "What Is Enlightenment?," in Michel Foucault, *The Foucault Reader*, ed. Paul Rabinow (New York: Pantheon Books, 1984); Michel Foucault, "What Is Critique?," trans. Kevin Paul Geiman, *What Is Enlightenment? Eighteenth-Century Answers and Twentieth-Century Questions*, ed. James Schmidt (Berkeley: University of California Press, 1996).

9. Foucault, *The Foucault Reader*, 42. "Cet éthos implique d'abord qu'on refuse ce que j'appellerai volontiers le 'chantage' à l'*Aufklärung*." Michel Foucault, "Qu'est-ce que les Lumières?," *Dits et écrits, 1954–1988*, ed. Daniel Defert, François Ewald, and Jacques Lagrange, Bibliothèque des sciences humaines (Paris: Gallimard, 1994), 4:571.

10. Foucault, "What Is Critique?," 383.

11. Ibid., 387. "Et je proposerais donc, comme toute première définition de la critique, cette caractérisation générale: l'art de n'être pas tellement gouverné." Michel Foucault, "Qu'est-ce que la critique? [Critique et Aufklärung], Compte rendu de la séance du 27 mai 1978," *Bulletin de la Société française de la Philosophie* 84.2 (1990): 38.

12. François Hartog, *Régimes d'historicité: Présentisme et expériences du temps*, La librairie du XXIe siècle (Paris: Seuil, 2003). See also the insightful remarks on Hartog's limitations with regard to questions of colonialism in Abdelmajid Hannoum, "Review: What Is an Order of Time?," *History and Theory* 47.3 (2008).

13. David Scott, "Colonial Governmentality," *Social Text* 43 (Autumn 1995): 192, revised and reprinted in David Scott, *Refashioning Futures: Criticism after Postcoloniality*, Princeton Studies in Culture/Power/History (Princeton: Princeton University Press, 1999).

14. Charles Baudelaire, *The Painter of Modern Life and Other Essays*, trans. Jonathan Mayne, Art and Letters, 2nd ed. (London: Phaidon, 1995), 36.

15. Foucault, *The Foucault Reader*, 41–42.

16. Talal Asad, "Conscripts of Western Civilization," *Dialectical Anthropology: Essays in Honor of Stanley Diamond*, ed. Christine Ward Gailey (Tallahassee: University Press of Florida, 1992); Scott, *Conscripts of Modernity*.

17. Scott, *Conscripts of Modernity*, 107.
18. Ibid., 163-64.
19. C. L. R. James, *The Black Jacobins: Toussaint L'Ouverture and the San Domingo Revolution*, 2nd ed. (New York: Vintage Books, 1989); Scott, *Conscripts of Modernity*, 111.
20. Scott, *Conscripts of Modernity*, 107.
21. See Sudipta Kaviraj, "An Outline of a Revisionist Theory of Modernity," *European Journal of Sociology* 46.3 (2005); Arjun Appadurai, *Modernity at Large: Cultural Dimensions of Globalization*, Public Worlds (Minneapolis: University of Minnesota Press, 1996); Partha Chatterjee, "Our Modernity," *Empire and Nation: Selected Essays* (New York: Columbia University Press, 2010); Sibylle Fischer, *Modernity Disavowed: Haiti and the Cultures of Slavery in the Age of Revolution* (Durham, N.C.: Duke University Press, 2004).
22. Kaviraj, "An Outline of a Revisionist Theory of Modernity," 497-98.
23. Dipesh Chakrabarty, *Provincializing Europe* (Princeton: Princeton University Press, 2000).
24. A topic discussed in Michel-Rolph Trouillot, *Silencing the Past: Power and the Production of History* (Boston: Beacon Press, 1995). Several of the important studies from the late 1980s and early 1990s, such as those by Simon Schama, *Citizens: A Chronicle of the French Revolution* (New York: Knopf, 1989); Keith Michael Baker, *Inventing the French Revolution: Essays on French Political Culture in the Eighteenth Century*, Ideas in Context (New York: Cambridge University Press, 1990); and François Furet and Mona Ozouf, eds., *A Critical Dictionary of the French Revolution* (Cambridge, Mass.: Belknap Press, 1989), pass over the question of Haiti and Toussaint Louverture. Noted by Nick Nesbitt, *Universal Emancipation: The Haitian Revolution and the Radical Enlightenment*, New World Studies (Charlottesville: University of Virginia Press, 2008), 214.
25. I have in mind the otherwise very insightful work by Conor Cruise O'Brien, *The Great Melody: A Thematic Biography and Commented Anthology of Edmund Burke* (Chicago: University of Chicago Press, 1993).
26. Fischer, *Modernity Disavowed*.
27. "We are far enough from the Revolution to experience only a pale version of the enthusiasms which disturbed the sight of those who led it, yet near enough to be able to empathize with the spirit which guided it and to understand it. Soon it will be difficult to do such a thing." Alexis de Tocqueville, *The Ancien Régime and the French Revolution*, trans. Gerald Bevan, Penguin Classics (New York: Penguin, 2008), 20.
28. "Ancien Régime," in Furet and Ozouf, *A Critical Dictionary of the French Revolution*, 604-5.
29. Gordon, *Postmodernism and the Enlightenment*, 1.
30. Ibid.
31. Ania Loomba discusses this move: "By pointing out how deeply its knowledge systems were imbricated in racial and colonialist perspectives, scholars such as [Martin] Bernal, Said or Spivak have contributed to, indeed extended, the discrediting of the project of the European Enlightenment by post-structuralists such as Foucault. The central figure of Western humanist and Enlightenment discourses, the humane, knowing subject, now stands revealed as a white male colonialist. Through its investigations, colonial discourse analysis adds this powerful new dimension to the post-structuralist understanding that meaning is always contextual, always shifting." Ania

Loomba, *Colonialism-Postcolonialism*, The New Critical Idiom (London: Routledge, 1998), 66. But already she asks in the following line, lending nuance to this assertion, "Is this going too far?"

32. See in particular Ranajit Guha, "A Conquest Foretold," *Social Text* 54 (Spring 1998), whose argument is developed in Guha, *History at the Limit of World-History*.

33. Guha, "A Conquest Foretold," 86.

34. Fischer, *Modernity Disavowed*, 22.

35. Jacques Derrida, *The Gift of Death*, Religion and Postmodernism (Chicago: University of Chicago Press, 1995). "Provincializing Europe cannot ever be a project of shunning European thought. For at the end of European imperialism, European thought is a gift to us. We can talk of provincializing it only in an anticolonial spirit of gratitude." Chakrabarty, *Provincializing Europe*, 255.

36. Richard Bourke, "Sovereignty, Opinion and Revolution in Edmund Burke," *History of European Ideas* 25 (1999): 118.

37. Jonathan Israel, *Radical Enlightenment: Philosophy and the Making of Modernity, 1650–1750* (Oxford: Oxford University Press, 2001); Muthu, *Enlightenment against Empire*.

Introduction

1. For a study that considers the East India Company, the Royal Africa Company, and the Hudson's Bay Company together, see D. K. Fieldhouse, *The Colonial Empires: A Comparative Survey from the Eighteenth Century*, 2nd ed. (London: Macmillan, 1982).

2. Edmund Burke and William Burke, *An Account of the European Settlements in America* (London: R. and J. Dodsley, 1757). This work is often ascribed to William Burke and is omitted by the authoritative modern edition of Edmund Burke by Paul Langford. This edition does, however, refer to "his participation in the *Account of the European Settlements*" as demonstrating "a formidable knowledge of the history of the ancient world, of colonial America, and of England and Ireland." Edmund Burke, *The Writings and Speeches of Edmund Burke*, ed. Paul Langford and William B Todd, 9 vols. (Oxford: Oxford University Press, 1981–), 1:3.

3. Sudipta Sen, "The State and Its Colonial Frontiers," *Distant Sovereignty: National Imperialism and the Origins of British India* (New York: Routledge, 2002).

4. Ibid., 6.

5. Thomas R Metcalf, *Ideologies of the Raj*, The New Cambridge History of India (New York: Cambridge University Press, 1997), 18, 21–24. Metcalf astutely explains the relationship between a Whig conception of society and the influence of the physiocrats, in relation to the "ancient institutions of the country [India]."

6. Burke, "Letter to a Member of the National Assembly," *Writings and Speeches*, 8:314. I discuss this remark in chapter 4, where Burke expatiates on Rousseau's "philosophy of vanity."

7. Uday Singh Mehta, *Liberalism and Empire: A Study in Nineteenth-Century British Liberal Thought* (Chicago: University of Chicago Press, 1999).

8. On the indissoluble links between the notion of revolution and the idea of the ancien régime, see François Furet, "Ancien Régime," *A Critical Dictionary of the French Revolution*, ed. François Furet and Mona Ozouf (Cambridge, Mass.: Belknap Press, 1989).

9. For the view that Burke should not be understood as an anti-Enlightenment thinker, see Richard Bourke, "Sovereignty, Opinion and Revolution in Edmund

Burke," *History of European Ideas* 25 (1999): 118. On the distinction between the moderate and radical Enlightenment, see Jonathan Israel, *Radical Enlightenment: Philosophy and the Making of Modernity, 1650–1750* (Oxford: Oxford University Press, 2001).

10. Fieldhouse, *The Colonial Empires*, 101; Ian K. Steele, "The Anointed, the Appointed, and the Elected: Governance of the British Empire, 1689–1784," *The Oxford History of the British Empire: The Eighteenth-Century*, ed. P. J. Marshall (New York: Oxford University Press, 1998), 119–26.

11. John William Kaye, *The Administration of the East India Company: A History of Indian Progress*, 2nd ed. (London: R. Bentley, 1853), contains a comprehensive discussion of the founding of the Company in part 1, chapter 4. Also see Ramkrishna Mukherjee, *The Rise and Fall of the East India Company* (New York: Monthly Review Press, 1974), 95.

12. Rajat Kanta Ray, "Indian Society and the Establishment of British Supremacy, 1765–1818," *The Oxford History of the British Empire: The Eighteenth-Century*, ed. P. J. Marshall (New York: Oxford University Press, 1998), 513.

13. Ibid., 514.

14. Kaye, *The Administration of the East India Company*, part 1, chapter 4; H. V. Bowen, "British India, 1765–1813: The Metropolitan Context," *The Oxford History of the British Empire: The Eighteenth-Century*, ed. P. J. Marshall (New York: Oxford University Press, 1998), 530–51.

15. Holden Furber, *John Company at Work: A Study of European Expansion in India in the Late Eighteenth Century*, Harvard Historical Studies (Cambridge: Harvard University Press, 1948), 309, cited in Ray, "Indian Society and the Establishment of British Supremacy," 514. Irfan Habib has revisited and recalculated these figures. See "Colonization of the Indian Economy, 1757–1900," *Essays in Indian History: Towards a Marxist Perception* (Delhi: Tulika, 1995), 296–306.

16. Sen, *Distant Sovereignty*, 3. This argument is one of the primary claims made in Sen's study.

17. Mukherjee, *The Rise and Fall of the East India Company*, 111–12. See in particular chapter 3, "[The East India] Company and Its European Rivals."

18. Ibid., 132.

19. Ibid., 109–32.

20. J. R. Seeley, *The Expansion of England* (London: Macmillan, 1909). This work was originally delivered as a lecture series in Cambridge in 1881. See the discussion in David Armitage, *The Ideological Origins of the British Empire*, Ideas in Context (New York: Cambridge University Press, 2000), 16–17. Armitage argues that Seeley's work may have had the opposite effect from what he intended: instead of unifying the study of the "first" British Empire in the Americas with the "second" British Empire in India and elsewhere, it created imperial history as a separate subfield, with a focus on the latter.

21. Guillaume Thomas Raynal, *Histoire philosophique et politique des établissemens et du commerce des Européens dans les deux Indes*, 10 vols. (Genève: Jean-Léonard Pellet, 1782), 1:2.

22. "To be attached to the subdivision, to love the little platoon we belong to in society, is the first principle (the germ as it were) of public affections" (Burke, "Reflections on the Revolution in France," *Writings and Speeches*, 8:97). See Raymond Williams, *The Country and the City* (New York: Oxford University Press, 1973).

23. Volumes 5, 6, and 7 of Burke's *Writings and Speeches* concern India.

24. In Diderot's case, this is due partly to the textual history of the *Histoire des deux Indes* discussed in chapter 1.

25. There are important exceptions to this: the chapters on Burke in Sara Suleri, *The Rhetoric of English India* (Chicago: University of Chicago Press, 1992), though she does not consider his French writings in detail alongside the India writings; Srinivas Aravamudan, *Tropicopolitans: Colonialism and Agency, 1688–1804*, Post-Contemporary Interventions (Durham, N.C.: Duke University Press, 1999), has distinct considerations of both Raynal and Burke.

26. Isaac Kramnick and David Bromwich, in their respective selections of texts from Burke, go some way in assisting readers to understand his writings on these disparate contexts together. John Hope Mason and Robert Wokler also include selections from the *Histoire des deux Indes* in their collection of political writings from Diderot, as has Laurent Versini in his volume of political writings. See Edmund Burke, *The Portable Edmund Burke*, ed. Isaac Kramnick (New York: Penguin Books, 1999); Edmund Burke, *On Empire, Liberty, and Reform: Speeches and Letters*, The Lewis Walpole Series in Eighteenth-Century Culture and History, ed. David Bromwich (New Haven: Yale University Press, 2000); Denis Diderot, *Political Writings*, Cambridge Texts in the History of Political Thought, ed. John Hope Mason and Robert Wokler (Cambridge: Cambridge University Press, 1992); Denis Diderot, *Oeuvres*, Bouquins, ed. Laurent Versini, 5 vols. (Paris: R. Laffont, 1994), vol. 3.

27. The questionnaire is mentioned by Gianluigi Goggi in his entry on the *Histoire des deux Indes* in Roland Mortier and Raymond Trousson, *Dictionnaire de Diderot* (Paris: Honoré Champion Editeur, 1999), 225. I discuss Burke's passing interaction with Raynal in the opening of chapter 3.

28. Gianluigi Goggi, "Angleterre," in ibid., 32.

29. Gita May, "Diderot and Burke: A Study in Aesthetic Affinity," *PMLA* 75.5 (1960): 528, note 5.

30. John Morley, *Burke*, English Men of Letters (London: Macmillan, 1879), 66.

31. Gianluigi Goggi, "Angleterre," in Mortier and Trousson, *Dictionnaire de Diderot*, 31. Translation mine.

32. Fieldhouse, *The Colonial Empires*, 57–60, details the pivotal nature of this year.

33. Robert Darnton, *The Forbidden Best-Sellers of Pre-Revolutionary France* (New York: Norton, 1995); Reinhart Koselleck, *Critique and Crisis: Enlightenment and the Pathogenesis of Modern Society* (Oxford: Berg, 1988). As I discuss in chapter 1, neither Darnton nor Koselleck (among other critics) takes an interest in the colonial content of the work.

34. Cited by Emma Rothschild, "Global Commerce and the Question of Sovereignty in the Eighteenth-Century Provinces," *Modern Intellectual History* 1.1 (2004): 10. See her fascinating discussion of this remark.

35. Edward W. Said, *Orientalism* (New York: Pantheon Books, 1978), 12. Within French studies, Yves Citton proposes to get around "the so-often repeated clichés about the threats and promises of 'Alterity'" by arguing that "the real challenge of modernity, as it emerged in the eighteenth-century is that of *multiplicity*: not simply the 'difference' presented by one absolutized 'Other,' which tends to keep us prisoners of binary oppositions (male/female, inside/outside, civilized/savage)—but the particular form of helplessness caused by the solicitations and possibilities which . . . force us to (fail to) look in all directions at the same time" (378). While his article is a helpful overview of the broad range of works that reflect this "multiplied" and global world

(and thereby make it less insular), he seems uninterested in the relations of power that enable the constitution of the colonial object in this period. Simply dismissing binary oppositions and replacing them with multiplicity ought not to obviate the need to address this question. The reference here to "the particular form of helplessness," for example, is to an eighteenth-century European reader faced with this broad range of knowledge and textual authority, but what were the conditions of possibility that enabled the production of this? I would like to explore how the texts I examine from Diderot and Burke were more *troubled* by this question of helplessness from the other side (indeed, it was their specter). Yves Citton, "Specters of Multiplicity: Eighteenth-Century Literature Revisited from the Outside In," *French Global: A New Approach to Literary History*, ed. Christie McDonald and Susan Rubin Suleiman (New York: Columbia University Press, 2010), 372–87.

36. Sankar Muthu, *Enlightenment against Empire* (Princeton: Princeton University Press, 2003). My focus, as will be clear, is on the contradictory impulses in Diderot's thought that culminate in a limit on his critique of empire.

1 / *Doux Commerce, Douce Colonisation*

1. "Arrêtons-nous ici et plaçons-nous au temps où l'Amérique et l'Inde étaient inconnues. Je m'adresse au plus cruel des Européens et je lui dis: Il existe des régions qui te fourniront de riches métaux, des vêtements agréables, des mets délicieux. Mais lis cette histoire et vois à quel prix la découverte t'en est promise. Veux-tu, ne veux-tu pas qu'elle se fasse? Croit-on qu'il y eût un être assez infernal pour dire: JE LE VEUX. Eh bien! il n'y aura pas dans l'avenir un seul instant où ma question n'ait la même force." From a chapter titled "Réflexion sur le bien & le mal que la découverte du Nouveau-Monde a fait à l'Europe." Guillaume Thomas Raynal, *Histoire philosophique et politique des établissemens et du commerce des Européens dans les deux Indes*, 10 vols. (Genève: Jean-Léonard Pellet, 1782), bk. 19, chap. 15, p. 298. References are to this edition, except where otherwise noted, cited in the following manner: *Histoire*, 19:15, 298. Translations of passages and chapter headings from this work are mine throughout.

"Qu'attestent ces forts dont vous avez hérissé toutes les plages? Votre terreur et la haine profonde de ceux qui vous entourent. Vous ne craindrez plus, quand vous ne serez plus haïs. Vous ne serez plus haïs, quand vous serez bienfaisants. Le barbare, ainsi que l'homme civilisé, veut être heureux." From a chapter titled "Principes que doivent suivre les Français dans l'Inde, s'ils parviennent à y rétablir leur considération et leur puissance," Denis Diderot, *Oeuvres*, Bouquins, ed. Laurent Versini, 5 vols. (Paris: R. Laffont, 1994), 3:699.

2. I have in mind several studies that have appeared on the South Pacific. See Jonathan Lamb, *Preserving the Self in the South Seas, 1680–1840* (Chicago: University of Chicago Press, 2001); Alex Calder, Jonathan Lamb and Bridget Orr, eds., *Voyages and Beaches: Pacific Encounters, 1769–1840* (Honolulu: University of Hawai'i Press, 1999). Roy Porter's focus on this topic was more on its relation to later anthropological writing and the manner in which this expresses the traveler's nostalgia. See "Circumnavigation: Bougainville and Cook" in *Haunted Journeys: Desire and Transgression in European Travel Writing* (Princeton: Princeton University Press, 1991), 86–122. For his other discussion of Cook and Bougainville, see "Enlightenment and Beyond" in *The Enlightenment* (London: Humanities Press International, 1990), 61–63.

3. Edward W. Said, *Orientalism* (New York: Pantheon Books, 1978).

4. From the famous entry "Encyclopedia" in Denis Diderot, *Rameau's Nephew and Other Works*, trans. Jacques Barzun and Ralph H. Bowen (Indianapolis: Bobbs-Merrill, 1964), 277. "En effet, le but d'une encyclopédie est de rassembler les connaissances éparses sur la surface de la terre." Diderot, *Oeuvres*, 1:363.

5. While an extended discussion of the French *philosophes* is not present in *Orientalism*, they do figure in Edward W. Said, *Culture and Imperialism* (New York: Vintage Books, 1994). See 240 and 246, where Raynal and Diderot are mentioned in relation to French anticolonialism.

6. Said, *Orientalism*, 12, emphasis mine.

7. I use the term *hegemony* as elaborated by Antonio Gramsci, *Selections from the Prison Notebooks of Antonio Gramsci* (New York: International Publishers, 1985), and developed by Ranajit Guha, *Dominance without Hegemony* (Cambridge: Harvard University Press, 1997).

8. See the critical edition, Louis-Antoine de Bougainville, *Voyage autour du monde*, Imago mundi, ed. Michel Bideaux and Sonia Faessel (Paris: Presses de l'université de Paris-Sorbonne, 2001). An English translation of Bougainville's text was published in 1772, a year after the French edition.

9. It appeared posthumously in 1798.

10. A literal translation of the title is *Philosophical and Political History of the Settlements and of the Commerce of Europeans in the Two Indies*. Note that *établissements* in French can mean both a settlement and a commercial enterprise, or *comptoir*.

11. Denis Diderot, *Political Writings*, Cambridge Texts in the History of Political Thought, ed. John Hope Mason and Robert Wokler (Cambridge: Cambridge University Press, 1992), 165–214. I will also refer to the selection in volume 3 of Diderot, *Oeuvres*, 581–759.

12. It is also said that he was not ashamed to confess being well paid for his contributions. Hans Wolpe reminds us that Diderot was not rich and that he conceived of his work as a kind of political alliance working as a "machine of war" against the *ancien régime*. Hans Wolpe, *Raynal et sa machine de guerre: L'Histoire des deux Indes et ses perfectionnements* (Stanford: Stanford University Press, 1957), 12.

13. French scholarship on the *Histoire* began in earnest in the 1970s after a proper catalogue of the documents in the Fonds Vandeul had been undertaken. Michèle Duchet, among the earliest of scholars to write on Diderot's relation to the *Histoire*, focuses primarily upon the New World, and more particularly upon the debates around slavery among the Physiocrats, the administrators, and the philosophes. Michèle Duchet, *Anthropologie et histoire au siècle des Lumières: Buffon, Voltaire, Rousseau, Helvétius, Diderot*, Bibliothèque d'anthropologie (Paris: François Maspero, 1971); Michèle Duchet, *Diderot et l'histoire des deux Indes ou, l'écriture fragmentaire* (Paris: A.-G. Nizet, 1978). Almost contemporary with her first work is Yves Benot, *Diderot, de l'athéisme à l'anticolonialisme* (Paris: François Maspero, 1970). One other comprehensive study (cited earlier) precedes these: Wolpe, *Raynal et sa machine de guerre*. Important articles from the past two decades include Anthony Pagden, "The Effacement of Difference: Colonialism and the Origins of Nationalism in Diderot and Herder," *After Colonialism: Imperial Histories and Postcolonial Displacements*, ed. Gyan Prakash (Princeton: Princeton University Press, 1995); Sankar Muthu, "Enlightenment Anti-Imperialism," *Social Research* 66.4 (1999), elaborated in Sankar Muthu, *Enlightenment against Empire* (Princeton: Princeton University Press, 2003). The series Studies on Voltaire and the Eighteenth Century has dedicated several volumes

to different aspects of the *Histoire*. These include Hans-Jürgen Lüsebrink and Manfred Tietz, eds., *Lectures de Raynal: L'Histoire des deux Indes en Europe et en Amérique au XVIIIe siècle* (Oxford: Voltaire Foundation, 1991); Hans-Jürgen Lüsebrink and Anthony Strugnell, *L'Histoire des deux Indes: Réécriture et polygraphie* (Oxford: Voltaire Foundation, 1995).

14. Cited by Arthur M. Wilson, *Diderot, sa vie et son oeuvre* (Paris: Laffont, Ramsay, 1985), 571. "No, No ... Do continue to do what I've asked of you. ... I know a bit better than you the taste of the public. It will be your lines which will save them from the boredom of my endless calculations."

15. Ibid., 584-85.

16. Ibid., 595.

17. One nineteenth-century British reader tellingly bound his English translation of the *Histoire*, by Justamond, with his own abbreviated translation of the title on the spine: "The History of *Both* the Indies." Guillaume Thomas Raynal, *A Philosophical and Political History of the Settlements and Trade of the Europeans in the East and West Indies*, trans. J. Justamond, 3rd ed. (London: T. Cadell, 1777), in the possession of the John Carter Brown Library.

18. Anthony Pagden, *Lords of all the World: Ideologies of Empire in Spain, Britain and France 1500-1800* (New Haven: Yale University Press, 1995). A similar distinction between the "first" British Empire focused on the Atlantic and the "second" British Empire focused on Asia has, however, been the subject of much dispute among imperial historians. See P. J. Marshall, "Britain without America—A Second Empire?," in P. J. Marshall, ed., *The Oxford History of the British Empire: The Eighteenth Century* (New York: Oxford University Press, 1998). For a comparative study of the Spanish, French, and British empires that effectively deploys this distinction, see D. K. Fieldhouse, *The Colonial Empires: A Comparative Survey from the Eighteenth Century*, 2nd ed. (London: Macmillan, 1982).

19. This is done with regard to the Levant in chapter 4 of Srinivas Aravamudan, *Tropicopolitans: Colonialism and Agency, 1688-1804*, Post-Contemporary Interventions (Durham, N.C.: Duke University Press, 1999). Chapter 7 of his work concerns Raynal. See also Srinivas Aravamudan, "Progress through Violence or Progress from Violence? Interpreting the Ambivalences of the *Histoire des deux Indes*," *Progrès et Violence au XVIIIe Siècle*, ed. Valerie Cossy and Deidre Dawson (Paris: Honore Champion Editeur, 2001).

20. Alexis de Tocqueville, *Democracy in America* (New York: Penguin, 1984), 132.

21. See Letters 1-4, "On the Quakers," in Voltaire, *Letters Concerning the English Nation*, Oxford World's Classics, ed. Nicholas Cronk (New York: Oxford University Press, 2009). More specifically, Voltaire praises the Quakers for winning *land* from the Indians by means of trade. By this and other inducements they were able to procure territory in a less violent manner than the Jesuits. Duchet, *Anthropologie et histoire au siècle des Lumières*, 211.

22. For a discussion of *doux commerce*, see "Money Making and Commerce as Innocent and *Doux*" in Albert O. Hirschman, *The Passions and the Interests: Political Arguments for Capitalism before Its Triumph* (Princeton: Princeton University Press, 1981). See also his discussion of Montesquieu, 70-80. The meaning of *doux* in French includes the quality of sweetness.

23. See Jenny Davidson, *Breeding: A Partial History of the Eighteenth Century* (New York: Columbia University Press, 2009).

24. On this, see the lucid discussion in James Tully, "Rediscovering America: The *Two Treatises* and Aboriginal Rights," *An Approach to Political Philosophy: Locke in Contexts* (Cambridge: Cambridge University Press, 1993). Tully notes, "The agricultural argument was only one of many justifications for dispossession and English settlement in North America" (169). Richard Tuck, *The Rights of War and Peace: Political Thought and the International Order from Grotius to Kant* (New York: Oxford University Press, 1999), pursues a similar line of thought in his chapter "From Locke to Vattel," especially 167–79.

25. Bartolomé de Las Casas, *A Short Account of the Destruction of the Indies*, trans. Nigel Griffin (New York: Penguin Books, 1999). De Las Casas is routinely invoked— with great esteem—in the pages of the *Histoire des Deux Indes* as a forerunner in his critique of the violence of conquest. His fascinating exchange with Sepulveda pivoted around the idea of "natural slavery" (drawn from Aristotle's idea of a "slave by nature" in the *Politics*) and its applicability to natives of the New World. The classic discussion of this debate, and more broadly of the school of Salamanca, is Anthony Pagden, *The Fall of Natural Man: The American Indian and the Origins of Comparative Ethnology*, Cambridge Iberian and Latin American Studies (Cambridge: Cambridge University Press, 1982). Pagden notes, however, that de Las Casas disputed the use of the term *conquest* as applied to such a "gentle" people as the Amerindians. Anthony Pagden, "*Ius et Factum*: Text and Experience in the Writings of Bartolomé de Las Casas," *New World Encounters*, ed. Stephen Greenblatt (Berkeley: University of California Press, 1993), 94.

26. See Duchet, *Anthropologie et histoire au siècle des Lumières*. The most comprehensive biography of Diderot, Arthur M. Wilson, *Diderot* (New York: Oxford University Press, 1972), 591, also describes him as a "populationist."

27. Michel Foucault, *The History of Sexuality* (New York: Vintage Books, 1980), 1:77. Foucault does not comment on the role of the foreign elements (a strange mix of Oriental and African motifs) in Diderot's libertine novel. Keeping in mind Diderot's later participation the *Histoire des deux Indes* might allow for a reading that does more than simply taking note of his use of exotic locales.

28. For one early feminist reading of the text, which considers the *Supplément* alongside "Sur les femmes" (1772) and emphasizes Diderot's critique of marriage and the disaggregation of sexuality from morality, see Blandine McLaughlin, "Diderot and Women," *French Women and the Age of Enlightenment*, ed. Samia I. Spencer (Bloomington: Indiana University Press, 1984). She is, however, careful to note Diderot's otherwise very conventional views of the capacities of women. She remarks too on the biographical irony of Diderot's choosing his own daughter's spouse and arranging this marriage the very month before he wrote the *Supplément* (303).

29. Anthony Strugnell, *Diderot's Politics: A Study of the Evolution of Diderot's Political Thought after the Encyclopédie*, International Archives of the History of Ideas (The Hague: Nijhoff, 1973), 115. In discussing Diderot's response to Dom Deschamps's *Lettres sur l'esprit du siècle*, Strugnell writes, "Dom Deschamps has succeeded in striking a hidden chord in Diderot. He had aroused in him an anarchic trait which three years later would find its full expression in the *Supplément au Voyage de Bougainville*." However, this may be an outdated view of his opinion, since Strugnell is involved in the critical edition of the *Histoire des deux Indes*, whose first volume (at the time of this writing) has appeared: Guillaume Thomas Raynal, *Histoire philosophique et politique des établissements et du commerce des Européens dans les deux Indes*, ed.

Anthony Strugnell (Ferney-Voltaire: Centre international d'étude du XVIIIe siècle, 2010). See also Anthony Strugnell, "La voix du sage dans l'Histoire des deux Indes," *Diderot, les dernières années, 1770-84: Colloque du bicentenaire, 2-5 septembre 1984 à Edimbourg*, ed. Peter France and Anthony Strugnell (Edinburgh: Edinburgh University Press, 1985). Strugnell has, finally, most recently taken issue with reading Diderot as a straightforward critic of colonialism (primarily Yves Benot's interpretation) in "Diderot's Anti-colonialism: A Problematic Notion," *New Essays on Diderot*, ed. J. E. Fowler (Cambridge: Cambridge University Press, 2011), 74–85.

30. The term *heterosexual matrix* is from Judith Butler, *Gender Trouble: Feminism and the Subversion of Identity* (New York: Routledge, 1990), chap. 2.

31. The incident is Diderot's reworking of Antoine de Bougainville's own description of the discovery of the "true" gender of Jean(ne) Baret by a crowd of animated Tahitians. One account of her fascinating life is John Dunmore, *Monsieur Baret: First Woman around the World, 1766-68* (Auckland, N.Z.: Heritage Press, 2002).

32. "Orou — . . . We have a circulation of men, women, and children . . . which is of far greater importance than the circulation of commodities, which are no more than the product of people's work." Diderot, *Political Writings*, 60.

33. His relationship to abbé Galiani needs to be addressed in order to develop and answer to this question.

34. Diderot, *Political Writings*, 64.

35. Although it belongs to an earlier moment in Diderot's thinking, Emma Rothschild points to a passage from 1765 in the *Salons* which is worth putting alongside this remark from the character of Orou regarding population and the peopling of "empty" land. Diderot compares the painter Joseph Vernet, with reference to his series *Les Ports de France* (not an incidental subject), to a colonial administrator who creates a country and has "men, women, children in reserve, with whom he populates his canvas as one populates a colony." Cited by Emma Rothschild, "A Horrible Tragedy in the French Atlantic," *Past and Present* 192.1 (2006), 90. This rich example—comparing a colony to a blank canvas—gives inklings of an aestheticism overlapping the political project of colonization, one that Diderot would elsewhere eschew. For the original passage, see Diderot, *Oeuvres*, 4:356.

36. Diderot's early translation of Shaftesbury introduced him to the ideas of sensualism, which influenced *Les bijoux indiscrets*. We see echoes of that view here, namely that the body and sensual experience are the basis for knowledge. Here the impediments to the progress of European society have to be overcome by transforming the sexual and social relationships that encompass the human body.

37. For the reference to "mine and thine," see Diderot, *Political Writings*, 42.

38. Ibid., 66.

39. Ibid., 46.

40. Ibid., 69.

41. The classic description of this notion remains its richest: Marcel Mauss, *The Gift: The Form and Reason for Exchange in Archaic Societies*, trans. W. D. Halls (New York: Norton, 1990).

42. Diderot, *Political Writings*, 64, emphasis mine.

43. Wilson, *Diderot*, 590.

44. Diderot, *Political Writings*, 70.

45. Ibid., 71.

46. Ibid., 65.

47. For an examination of this work, with brief reference to Diderot, see Kathleen Wellman, "Physicians and Philosophes: Physiology and Sexual Morality in the French Enlightenment," *Eighteenth-Century Studies* 35.2 (2002): 271. Diderot refers to Vandermonde often in the *Histoire*, as in his entry on "Créoles," *Oeuvres*, 3:706.

48. Guillaume Thomas Raynal, *Histoire philosophique et politique des établissemens et du commerce des Européens dans les deux Indes*, 10 vols. (Genève: Chez J.-L. Pellet, 1780), 10:134. "Le vœu de chasteté répugne à la nature et nuit à la population; le vœu de pauvreté n'est que d'un inepte ou d'un paresseux; le vœu d'obéissance à quelqu'autre puissance qu'à la dominante et à la loi, est d'un esclave ou d'un rebelle." Cited in Strugnell, *Diderot's Politics*, 225, in relation to Diderot's views on the church.

49. Diderot, *Political Writings*, 178.

50. Ibid., 178. "N'aurait-il pas été plus humain, plus utile et moins dispendieux, de faire passer dans chacune de ces régions lointaines quelques centaines de jeunes hommes, quelques centaines de jeunes femmes? Les hommes auraient épousé les femmes, les femmes auraient épousé les hommes de la contrée. La consanguinité, le plus prompt et le plus fort des liens, aurait bientôt fait des étrangers et des naturels du pays une seule et même famille." Diderot, *Oeuvres*, 3:693.

51. From the *Reflections on the Revolution in France*, Edmund Burke, *The Writings and Speeches of Edmund Burke*, ed. Paul Langford and William B Todd, 9 vols. (Oxford: Oxford University Press, 1981–), 8:102. Burke makes this remark with regard to heritable property as an institution and means to pass on virtue.

52. "Des étrangers et des naturels du pays" ; "une seule et même famille." Diderot, *Oeuvres*, 3:693.

53. "Le commerce s'établit sans trouble entre des hommes qui ont des besoins réciproques, et bientôt ils s'accoutument à regarder comme des amis, comme des frères, ceux que l'intérêt ou d'autres motifs conduisent dans leur contrée." Ibid., 3:693.

54. Diderot, *Political Writings*, 170.

55. The movement of goods is presented in the *Histoire* as reciprocal rather than in one direction. "Les productions des climats placés sous l'équateur, se consomment dans les climats voisins du pole; l'industrie du Nord est transportée au Sud; les étoffes de l'Orient sont devenue le luxe des Occidentaux." Raynal, *Histoire philosophique et politique des établissemens et du commerce des Européens dans les deux Indes*, 1:2. Marx's distinction between commercial capitalism and industrial capitalism is obviously absent from the *Histoire*; the absence enables the paean to commerce. Burke's view of colonial commerce in this period, as Part II explores, grows more ambivalent than this. As we see from these examples, Diderot's view of commerce remained more optimistic, provided one was able to rein in the destructiveness of missionaries evidenced in the South American example.

56. Strugnell, *Diderot's Politics*, 223.

57. As a further argument against the idea of Diderot as an "aestheticist" thinker, consider his fascinating speculations on the fate of philosophy, history writing, and great artistic achievements in an era of thriving commerce. Akin to Walter Benjamin in a later era, Diderot asserts the intimate links between these monuments of civilization and the "barbarism" of conquest: "Ce fut dans les temps où cette bête féroce, qu'on appelait le peuple romain, ou se dévorait elle-même ou s'occupait à dévorer les

nations, que les historiens écrivirent et que les poètes chantèrent." There is an ambivalence to this, certainly, but, as I will explore momentarily, he presents the Swiss model as one to be emulated and not avoided. He concedes the point (which Nietzsche will exactly invert in his aesthetic "justification" of a culture nearly a century later) that a merchant is probably not the best subject for an epic poem, but that this matters little for the question of happiness: "Un grand négociant est-il un personnage bien propre à devenir le héros d'un poème épique? Je ne le crois pas." The thirteen Swiss cantons, which probably do not contain a single beautiful statue between them, in fact show that one does not need the "luxury" of art to sustain the happiness of nations: "Heureusement toute cette espèce de luxe n'est pas fort essentielle au bonheur des nations. Peut-être ne trouverait-on pas une belle statue dans toute la Suisse, et je ne pense pas que les treize cantons en soient plus malheureux." All passages are from Diderot, Oeuvres, 3:594.

58. "Les Indiens auraient adopté le culte de l'Europe, par la raison qu'une religion devient commune à tous les citoyens d'un empire, lorsque le gouvernement l'abandonne à elle-même, et que l'intolérance et la folie des prêtres n'en font pas un instrument de discorde." Ibid., 3:693.

59. "Le dernier mot de Diderot dans le dialogue permanent entre l'homme sauvage et l'homme civilisé dont le XVIIIe siècle n'arrive pas à se tirer? On notera d'abord que Diderot compare les 'nations sauvages' et 'les nation civilisées' pour donner l'avantage aux premières en 1770, aux secondes en 1780." Ibid., 3:585–86.

60. Ibid..

61. Terry Jay Ellingson, *The Myth of the Noble Savage* (Berkeley: University of California Press, 2001) argues that the phrase, in fact, is nowhere used by Rousseau, and traces its origin to other sources: "Like some other anthropological folklore, this particular invented tradition is not only wrong but long since known to be wrong; and its continuing vitality in the face of its demonstrated falsity confronts us with a particularly problematic current in the history of anthropology" (3). A. O. Lovejoy too had been careful to comment on Rousseau's "supposed primitivism" in "The Supposed Primitivism of Rousseau's Discourse on Inequality," *Modern Philology* 21 (1923).

62. "This Strange Institution Called Literature" in Jacques Derrida, *Acts of Literature*, ed. Derek Attridge (New York: Routledge, 1992), 36.

63. Strugnell, *Diderot's Politics*, 216.

64. John Hope Mason, *The Irresistible Diderot* (London: Quartet Books, 1982), 343. Bernard Papin, *Sens et fonction de l'utopie tahitienne dans l'oeuvre politique de Diderot* (Oxford: Voltaire Foundation, 1988), also seems surprisingly dismissive of Diderot as a political thinker (see the preface). Although the work promisingly reviews the idea of utopia as an alternative to a present political order, it is striking that such an in-depth discussion regarding politics and political ideas makes little effort to understand the colonial frame of the book; for instance, why take up Tahiti as an example? Why not also consider Bougainville's original voyage and why Diderot chose to discuss and parody this?

65. Robert Darnton, *The Forbidden Best-Sellers of Pre-Revolutionary France* (New York: Norton, 1995). Darnton discusses the *Histoire des deux Indes* as a crucial text in reconsidering the Enlightenment based on the disparity between texts routinely considered canonical and those which in reality were the most widely read and circulated. It is a vital argument in this regard, though Darnton seems uninterested in the content of the work—by which I mean its references to the two Indies.

66. The omitted paragraph would be the final one to a section given the title "National Character at Home and Overseas" Diderot, *Political Writings*, 177–79.

67. Diderot, *Oeuvres*, 693, emphasis mine: "Tels seraient les heureux effets que produirait, dans une colonie naissante, l'attrait du plus impérieux des sens. Point d'armes, point de soldats: mais beaucoup de jeunes femmes pour les hommes, beaucoup de jeunes hommes pour les femmes."

68. "L'Europe a fondé par-tout des colonies; mais connoît-elle les principes sur lesquels on doit les fonder? . . . Ne peut-on découvrir par quels moyens & dans quelles circonstances?" Raynal, *Histoire philosophique et politique des établissemens et du commerce des Européens dans les deux Indes*, 1:2.

69. Diderot, *Political Writings*, 86, translation modified based on the original. "L'empire de Russie occupe une étendue de 32 degrés en latitude et de 165 en longitude. Civiliser à la fois une aussi énorme contrée me semble un projet au-dessus des forces humaines, surtout lorsque je me promène sur la lisière et que je trouve ici des déserts, là des glaces, ailleurs des barbares de toute espèce." Diderot, *Oeuvres*, 3:511.

70. "If in the whole reign, the Empress were to civilize only this district, she would have achieved a great deal." Diderot, *Political Writings*, 96.

71. Ibid., 86. "La troisième, ce serait d'accepter une colonie de Suisses; de la placer convenablement; de lui assurer ses privilèges et la liberté; d'accorder les mêmes privilèges et la même liberté à tous ceux de ses sujets qui entreraient dans la même colonie. Les Suisses sont agriculteurs et soldats; ils sont fidèles. Je sais par cœur toutes les objections qu'on peut opposer à ces moyens; elles sont si frivoles que je ne me donne pas la peine d'y répondre." Diderot, *Oeuvres*, 3:512.

72. "Si j'avais à civiliser des sauvages, que ferais-je? Je ferais des choses utiles en leur présence, sans leur rien ni dire, ni prescrire. J'aurais l'air de travailler pour ma seule famille et pour moi. Si j'avais à créer une nation à la liberté, que ferais-je? Je planterais au milieu d'elle une colonie d'hommes libres, très libres, tels, par exemple, que les Suisses, à qui je conserverais bien strictement ses privilèges, et j'abandonnerais le reste au temps et à l'exemple." Diderot, "Idée systématique sur la manière d'amener un people au sentiment de la liberté et à l'état policé," *Oeuvres*, 3:326.

73. "I remember seeing a monkey perform the same maneuver that it is denied [by a traveler's account] a pongo can do. It is true that my ideas not then being directed to this problem, I myself committed the error for which I reproach our travelers, and I neglected to examine whether the monkey's intention was in fact to sustain the fire, or simply, as I believe, *to imitate the action of a man*. Whatever the case, it is well demonstrated that the monkey is not a variety of man." *Discourse on Inequality*, footnote J, collected in Jean-Jacques Rousseau, *The First and Second Discourses* (New York: St. Martin's Press, 1964), 208, emphasis mine. For the original French passage, see Jean-Jacques Rousseau, *Oeuvres complètes*, Bibliothèque de la Pléiade (Paris: Gallimard, 1964), 3:211. The question of originality and imitation arises again later, in postcolonial thought, when reflecting on the formation and education of the colonial subject; this theme implicitly underlies the tension in the subtitle of Partha Chatterjee, *Nationalist Thought and the Colonial World: A Derivative Discourse?*, Third World Books (London: Zed Books, 1986). A more ambivalent, pessimistic view of the derivative nature of the colonial subject (and colonial society) is explored in narrative form by V. S. Naipaul, *The Mimic Men* (London: Penguin, 1969). The role of mimicry in "post-Enlightenment English colonialism" is also the topic of Homi K. Bhabha, "Of Mimicry and Man: The Ambivalence of Colonial Discourse," *The Location of Culture* (London: Routledge, 1994).

74. Diderot, *Oeuvres*, 3:693.

75. "L'avantage physique de croiser les races entre les hommes comme entre les animaux, pour empêcher l'espèce de s'abâtardir, est le fruit d'une expérience tardive, postérieure à l'utilité reconnue d'unir les familles pour cimenter la paix des sociétés." Ibid., 3:705.

76. "Les créoles sont en général bien faits. À peine en voit-on un seul affligé des difformités si communes dans les autres climats. . . . L'histoire ne leur reproche aucune de ces lâchetés, de ces trahisons, des ces bassesses, qui souillent les annales de tous les peuples. À peine citerait-on un crime honteux qu'ait commis un créole." Ibid., 3:706. These curious and fascinating pages also suggest that Diderot conceived of America as a "creole nation," in which he included various peoples of European descent. (He appears to be thinking by association with the many meanings of *creole*, from a biological crossing to cultural mixture.) He discusses, in a manner that recalls by contrast Burke's reflections on the southern colonies of America, the effect that owning and ordering slaves has on the dominant: it will lead to a form of laziness that enables the emergence of tyranny. But, he continues, "s'ils cessaient un jour d'avoir des nègres pour esclaves et des rois éloignés pour maîtres, ce serait peut-être le peuple le plus étonnant qu'on eût vu briller sur la terre." Certainly akin with the many remarkable passages on America that made the *Histoire des deux Indes* popular there. His high praise evokes the racial mixture of America: "Tous ces ressorts feraient peut-être d'une race equivoque et melangée la nation la plus florissante que la philosophie et l'humanité puissent désirer pour le bonheur de la terre." Then, in a style that recalls the manner of his address to the reader one finds elsewhere, he writes, "Jeunes créoles, venez vous exercer en Europe, y pratiquer ce que nous enseignons. . . . Laissez en Amérique vos nègres, dont la condition afflige nos regards." It is ambiguous, certainly, but this particular exhortation to the "creole" seems to be to all inhabitants of America. Citations from ibid., 3:708-9.

77. Wolpe, *Raynal et sa machine de guerre*, 8, notes that Napoleon considered himself a "zélé disciple de Raynal" ("zealous disciple of Raynal"). It is important to note that this inconsistency is far more evident in the ensemble gathered by Raynal from many authors. (I examine Diderot's own conceptual limit shortly.)

78. Uday Singh Mehta, *Liberalism and Empire: A Study in Nineteenth-Century British Liberal Thought* (Chicago: University of Chicago Press, 1999).

79. Duchet, *Anthropologie et histoire au siècle des Lumières*, 215.

80. Guillaume Thomas Raynal, *Histoire philosophique et politique des établissemens et du commerce des Européens dans les deux Indes* (Paris: A. Costes, 1820), 1:25: "fait honneur à la religion chrétienne de l'abolition de l'esclavage. Nous oserons n'être pas de son avis. C'est quand il y eut de l'industrie et des richesses dans le peuple que les princes le comptèrent pour quelque chose. C'est quand les richesses du peuple purent être utiles aux rois contre les barons que les lois rendirent meilleure la condition du peuple."

81. "Dans ces sociétés mercantiles, la découverte d'une île, l'importation d'une nouvelle denrée, l'invention d'une machine, l'établissement d'un comptoir . . . la construction d'un port, deviendront les transactions les plus importantes; et les annales des peuples demanderont à être écrites par des *commerçants philosophes*, comme elles l'étaient autrefois par des historiens orateurs." Diderot, *Oeuvres*, 3:689, emphasis mine.

82. "Il s'établit en Europe un esprit de trocs et d'échanges." Ibid., 3:689. Adam Smith's reflection upon Greek and Roman colonies in relation to those of modern European merits closer attention. See Donald Winch, *Classical Political Economy and Colonies* (Cambridge: Harvard University Press, 1965). Emma Rothschild, *Economic*

Sentiments: Adam Smith, Condorcet, and the Enlightenment (Cambridge: Harvard University Press, 2001), proposes a more interesting context for some of Smith's thought, such as the much cited (if rarely used) image in his work of the invisible hand.

83. Smith refers to a 1773 edition of the *Histoire des deux Indes* in book 4, chapter 7, "Of Colonies," in *An Inquiry into the Nature and Causes of the Wealth of Nations*, ed. Edwin Cannan (Chicago: University of Chicago Press, 1976). For a consideration of Smith and Raynal in relation to larger questions of commerce, see Emma Rothschild, "Global Commerce and the Question of Sovereignty in the Eighteenth-Century Provinces," *Modern Intellectual History* 1.1 (2004).

84. "La découverte d'un nouveau monde pouvait seule fournir des aliments à notre curiosité. Une vaste terre en friche, l'humanité réduite à la condition animale, des campagnes sans récoltes, des trésors sans possesseurs, des sociétés sans police, des hommes sans mœurs: combien un pareil spectacle n'eût-il pas été plein d'intérêt et d'instruction pour un Locke, un Buffon, un Montesquieu! Quelle lecture eût été aussi surprenante, aussi pathétique que le récit de leur voyage! Mais l'image de la nature brute et sauvage est déjà défigurée. Il faut se hâter d'en ressembler les traits à demi effacés, après avoir peint et livré à l'exécration les avides et féroces chrétiens qu'un malheureux hasard conduisit d'abord dans cet autre hémisphère." Diderot, *Oeuvres*, 3:689–90.

85. The future anterior became a theme of Derrida's later thought, but was present in early work, as the following citation illustrates: "The future [the à-venir] can only be anticipated in the form of an absolute danger. It is that which breaks absolutely with constituted normality and can only be proclaimed, presented, as a sort of monstrosity. For that future world and for that within it which will have put into question the values of sign, word, and writing, for that which guides our future anterior, there is as yet no exergue." Jacques Derrida, *Of Grammatology*, trans. Gayatri Chakravorty Spivak (Baltimore: Johns Hopkins University Press, 1976), 5.

86. Rousseau, *The First and Second Discourses*, 210. "Depuis trois ou quatre cens ans que les habitans de l'Europe inondent les autres parties du monde et publient sans cesse de nouveaux recueils de voyages et de rélations, je suis persuadé que nous ne connoissons d'hommes que les seuls Européens; encore paroît-il aux préjugés ridicules qui ne sont pas éteints, même parmi les Gens de Lettres, que chacun ne fait guéres sous le nom pompeux d'étude de l'homme, que celle des hommes de son pays. Les particuliers ont beau aller et venir, il semble que la Philosophie ne voyage point." Rousseau, *Oeuvres complètes*, 212. This footnote from Rousseau also contains a prolonged consideration of the orangutan in the Congo, whose place in the later history of evolutionary arguments and scientific racism requires more consideration than I can give it here. Rousseau refers to several observers who point to similar social characteristics shared by blacks (les Nègres) and the orangutan. His remark also serves to qualify the assertion that much eighteenth-century thought is free from the racial views more prevalent in the nineteenth century. And yet it is not clear from note 10 whether Rousseau agrees with this observation; in effect he cites it primarily to note that its reliability cannot be verified given the current impoverished state of knowledge on these places. See *Oeuvres complétes* 208–11, and the conclusion on 214.

87. Rousseau, *The First and Second Discourses*, 212. "Non toûjours des pierres et des plantes, mais une fois les hommes et les mœurs." Rousseau, *Oeuvres complètes*, 213.

88. Rousseau, *The First and Second Discourses*, 210.

89. "Il n'y a guéres que quatre sortes d'hommes qui fassent des voyages de long cours; les Marins, les Marchands, les Soldats, et les Missionnaires; Or on ne doit guéres

s'attendre que les trois premiéres Classes fournissent de bons Observateurs... et quant à ceux de la quatriéme, occupés de la vocation sublime qui les appelle... on doit croire qu'ils ne se livreroient pas volontiers à des recherches qui paroissent de pure curiosité." Rousseau, *Oeuvres complètes*, 212.

90. Rousseau, *The First and Second Discourses*, 212, translation modified. "Les Académiciens qui ont parcouru les parties Septentrionales de l'Europe et Méridionales de l'Amérique avoient plus pour objet de les visiter en Géometres qu'en Philosophes... nous ne connoissons point les Peuples des Indes Orientales, fréquentées uniquement par des Européens plus curieux de remplir leurs bourses que leurs têtes.... Supposons un Montesquieu, un Buffon, un Diderot, un Duclos, un d'Alembert, un Condillac, ou des hommes de cette trempe voyageant pour instruire leurs compatriotes, observant et décrivant comme ils savent faire, La Turquie, l'Egipte, la Barbarie... les Malabares, le Mogol, les rives du Gange... puis dans l'autre Hemisphére, le Méxique, le Perou.... Supposons que ces nouveaux Hercules, de retour de ces courses mémorables, fissent ensuite à loisir l'Histoire naturelle Morale et Politique de ce qu'ils auroient vu, nous verrions nous mêmes sortir un monde nouveau de dessous leur plume, et nous apprendrions ainsi à connoître le nôtre." Rousseau, *Oeuvres complètes*, 213–14.

91. Walter Benjamin, *Illuminations* (New York: Schocken Books, 1986), 83–110.

92. "Où est-il, ce grand homme, que la nature doit peut-être à l'honneur de l'espèce humaine? Où est-il, ce Spartacus nouveau, qui ne trouvera point de Crassus? Alors disparaîtra le Code Noir." Guillaume Thomas Raynal, *Histoire philosophique et politique des établissemens et du commerce des Européens dans les deux Indes* (Maestricht: Chez Jean-Edme Dufour, 1774), tome 3 of the quarto, 204. Crassus was the Roman general who put down the uprising led by Spartacus (73–71 bce); the *Code Noir* was Louis XIV's edict from 1685 which established a legal definition of slavery and (allegedly) regulated the treatment of slaves. (It also contained provisions requiring conversion to Catholicism and exiling all Jews from French colonies.) In practice even its minimal limitations on harsh treatment were often ignored. See Laurent Dubois and John D. Garrigus, *Slave Revolution in the Caribbean, 1789–1804: A Brief History with Documents* (New York: Palgrave Macmillan, 2006), 49–54, for the original decree. This passage from the *Histoire* is altered in the later edition; see Raynal, *Histoire philosophique et politique des établissemens et du commerce des Européens dans les deux Indes*, 11:24, 139. The phrase calling for an "avenger of the New World" is itself a reworking of an episode from the 1771 novel by Louis Sébastian Mercier, *L'An deux mille quatre cent quarante* (Geneva: Slatkine Reprints, 1979), chap. 22, p. 178.

93. The notion that Toussaint had read Raynal's histoire, suggested by C. L. R. James, *The Black Jacobins: Toussaint L'Ouverture and the San Domingo Revolution*, 2nd ed. (New York: Vintage Books, 1989), 24–25, and by Aimé Césaire, *Toussaint Louverture: La Révolution française et le problème colonial* (Paris: Présence Africaine, 1981), 197, is vividly conveyed in the painting of the Haitian general Jean-Baptiste Belley, painted by Anne-Louis Girodet in 1797, which portrays him leaning against a bust of Raynal. Belley (to whom I return in chapter 5) had fought alongside Toussaint before joining the French revolutionary army. For a discussion of this painting, see Viktoria Schmidt-Linsenhoff, "Male Alterity in the French Revolution—Two Paintings by Anne-Louis Girodet at the Salon of 1798," *Gendered Nations: Nationalisms and Gender Order in the Long Nineteenth Century*, ed. Ida Blom, Karen Hagemann, and Catherine Hall (New York: Berg, 2000); Darcy Grimaldo Grigsby,

Extremities: Painting Empire in Post-Revolutionary France (London: Yale University Press, 2002).

94. See Jennifer Pitts, *A Turn to Empire: The Rise of Liberal Imperialism in Britain and France* (Princeton: Princeton University Press, 2005), and the chapter on "The Crisis of Liberal Imperialism" in Karuna Mantena, *Alibis of Empire: Social Theory and the Ideologies of Late Imperial Rule* (Princeton: Princeton University Press, 2009).

2 / On the Use and Abuse of Anger for Life

1. The first epigraph: "The spectacle of vast countries pillaged, ravaged and reduced to the cruelest servitude will reappear. The earth covers the cadavers of thousands of peoples that you have let or made perish. But they will be exhumed, they will demand vengeance to the skies and to the earth, and they will obtain it." From the chapter "Ought the Company Privilege Be Renewed?" in Guillaume Thomas Raynal, *Histoire philosophique et politique des établissemens et du commerce des Européens dans les deux Indes*, 10 vols. (Genève: Jean-Léonard Pellet, 1782), bk. 3, chap. 41, p. 171. Henceforward cited in this chapter as *Histoire*, 3:41, 171, or 3:171 when the chapter is omitted. The company to which Diderot refers is the British East India Company and the official charter granting it a right to monopoly trade in India, expiring in 1780. The decision on this was postponed until 1784.

English translations throughout this chapter, unless otherwise noted, are my own. Original eighteenth-century French spelling conventions have for the most part been maintained. I have drawn from the full collection of writings in the edition of the *Histoire des deux Indes* cited earlier. However, I have greatly benefited from Yves Benot's judicious selection from the work collected in Guillaume Thomas Raynal, *Histoire philosophique et politique des deux Indes*, Découverte, ed. Yves Benot (Paris: François Maspero, 1981).

The second epigraph: "You are proud of your enlightenment [*lumières*], but what good is it to you? What utility would there be in it for the Hottentot!" *Histoire*, 2:18, 258.

2. J. G. A. Pocock, *Virtue, Commerce, and History: Essays on Political Thought and History, Chiefly in the Eighteenth Century*, Ideas in Context (Cambridge: Cambridge University Press, 1985).

3. This idea of affect finds an echo in Pocock's description of enthusiasm in Burke and his discussion of Voltaire's negative view of religion as opinion. J. G. A. Pocock, *Barbarism and Religion*, 4 vols. (New York: Cambridge University Press, 1999–), 1:102. See also Lynn M. Festa, *Sentimental Figures of Empire in Eighteenth-Century Britain and France* (Baltimore: Johns Hopkins University Press, 2006), chap. 5. Festa reads the work in relation to sentimentalism and stresses the role of tears and the figure of the man of feeling (219–20). Her interesting reading, however, underplays the function of indignation and anger in the text which this chapter explores.

4. I return to Nietzsche's influential essay from 1874, "On the Use and Abuse of History for Life" ("Vom Nutzen und Nachteil der Historie für das Leben"), at the end of this chapter. Unsurprisingly, the title has been variously translated. For example, Friedrich Wilhelm Nietzsche, *On the Advantage and Disadvantage of History for Life*, trans. Peter Preuss (Indianapolis: Hackett, 1980).

5. I have in mind Spivak's reading of the Algerian novelist and essayist Assia Djebar. See Gayatri Chakravorty Spivak, "Ghostwriting," *Diacritics* 25.2 (1995). She connects these with Derrida's later readings of similar metaphors in the writings of Marx.

Jacques Derrida, *Specters of Marx: The State of the Debt, the Work of Mourning, and the New International*, trans. Peggy Kamuf (New York: Routledge, 1994).

Given his previous engagements with postcolonial thought, an important exception to this is the stimulating chapter on "The Imaginary Resentment of the Dead" in Ian Baucom, *Specters of the Atlantic: Finance Capital, Slavery, and the Philosophy of History* (Durham, N.C.: Duke University Press, 2005).

6. "It is necessary that, sooner or later, there be justice." *Histoire*, 3: 41, 171. This idea of futural justice, a justice deferred, recalls Derrida's reflection on justice, *à-venir*. See Jacques Derrida, "Force of Law: 'The Mystical Foundation of Authority,'" *Deconstruction and the Possibility of Justice*, ed. David Carlson, Drucilla Cornell, and Michel Rosenfeld (New York: Routledge, 1992). The idea of the future perfect is briefly discussed in chapter 1.

7. "Settlements of the Dutch at the Cape of Good Hope."

8. "If my speech [*discours*] offends you, it is because you are not more human than your predecessors, it is because you see in the hatred which I have ascribed to them that which I have for you." *Histoire*, 2 :18, 259. The history of the word Khoikhoin contains a short sketch of misrecognition analogous to many of the larger themes of this chapter. The word Hottentot, according to the OED, appears in Jan Van Riebeck's journal of 1652. In 1670 its meaning was explained as "stutterer" or "stammerer," due to the palatal clicks that are characteristic of the Khoikhoin languages. "Hottentot," *Oxford English Dictionary*, 2nd edition, 1989. Riebeck (1619–77), a Dutchman, established Cape Town in the same year of the journal cited earlier (1652).

9. Denis Diderot, *Oeuvres*, Bouquins, ed. Laurent Versini, 5 vols. (Paris: R. Laffont, 1994), 3:699.

10. It would be a worthy enterprise to explore the concept of colonial *ressentiment* more broadly. Here I remain closer to the specific uses of the term and concept as it appears in the *Histoire des deux Indes*. I retain the French term, *ressentiment*, since the valences of the French are distinct from the English *resentment*.

11. A short glimpse at the table of contents of each of the ten volumes in the octavo edition of the *Histoire* reveals this movement. The ten volumes are composed of nineteen books (in effect two books per volume in the octavo edition, save for the tenth volume, which contains a single book, book 19). Consider the organization of books 1–5 as an example. These concern European colonization and settlement in Asia (*les Indes orientales*, in the language of the work) and proceed chronologically based on the arrival of each national group in Asia. This order is therefore Portugal, Holland, Spain, England, France, and then "minor colonizers." The minor colonizers discussed include Denmark, Sweden, and Prussia.

12. This also recalls the thesis of the classic work by the scholar and Trinidadian nationalist Eric Williams, *Capitalism and Slavery* (London: Andre Deutsch, 1987).

13. Emphasis mine. The original passage is more comprehensive: "Pour les physiocrates en effet, l'ordre moral et l'ordre physique dérivent l'un de l'autre, et tous deux des lois qui règlent la production et la répartition des richesses. Humanitarisme et économie politique ne sont donc qu'une seule et même chose: de la condition faite à l'homme dépend nécessairement la quantité et la qualité travail fourni. Tels sont les principes que les physiocrates appliquèrent à l'analyse du travail coloniale, dont il démontrèrent qu'il constituait un frein pour le mise en valeur des Îles de la Louisiane, de la Guyana. Plus qu'un crime, l'esclavage était une faute, et l'erreur économique était double: la main d'œuvre servile n'était pas en elle-même rentable, et de plus la

manière de traiter les esclaves constituait un véritable gaspillage du capital initialement investi." Michèle Duchet, *Anthropologie et histoire au siècle des Lumières: Buffon, Voltaire, Rousseau, Helvétius, Diderot*, Bibliothèque d'anthropologie (Paris: François Maspero, 1971), 164.

14. "You are proud of your enlightenment [*lumières*], but what good is it to you? What utility would there be in it for the Hottentot! Is it therefore so important to know how to speak of virtue without practicing it! What obligation would you have to the savage, when you will have brought him arts without which he is satisfied, manufactures which would do nothing but multiply his needs and labors, and laws for which he would no longer be promised any more security than you have?" *Histoire*, 2:18, 258.

15. "Vous riez avec mépris des superstitions de l'Hottentot. Mais vos prêtres ne vous empoisonnent-ils pas en naissent de préjugés qui font le supplice de votre vie, qui sèment la division dans vos familles, qui arment votre contrées les unes contre les autres?" *Histoire*, 2:18, 257.

16. "Crush the infamy!" Used several times by Voltaire in closing his letters to d'Alembert and interpreted (with accompanying disputes) to refer to Christianity, the Church, or superstition.

17. "Mais il est très vrai que les Hottentots n'ont qu'un testicule. On l'a souvent remarqué." *Histoire*, 2: 18, 255.

18. See the chapter on Raynal (and Diderot) in John Morley, *Diderot and the Encyclopaedists*, 2 vols. (London: Macmillan, 1905).

19. Emphasis mine. "C'est ainsi que, dans les révolutions, les factieux ont des signes à l'aide desquels ils se reconnaissent, malgré le tumulte et au milieu de la mêlée ... c'est le son d'un instrument qui réveille ceux auxquels il s'adresse; tandis qu'il laisse dans l'assoupissement du sommeil ou dans la sécurité ceux qui n'en ont pas la clef." *Histoire*, 2:18, 255.

20. Without writing at length on this remark, I would note that for Montaigne the cannibal functions as an expression of irony, or so the closing line of his celebrated essay seems to indicate: "All this is not too bad—but what's the use? They don't wear breeches" (i.e., they are naked). But for Diderot, the cannibal is not merely a figure but also an empirical referent. This is perhaps one impact of colonial knowledge as it developed in the eighteenth century. However, for a fascinating discussion (in a new historicist vein) of the three Brazilian natives to whom Montaigne refers, see George Hoffman, "Anatomy of the Mass: Montaigne's 'Cannibals,'" *PMLA* 117.2 (2002).

21. "Telle fut, selon toute apparence, la première origine de la plupart de ces usages singuliers que nous retrouvons chez les Sauvages, & même dans les sociétés policées." *Histoire*, 2:18, 256.

22. "Fuyez, Malheureux Hottentots, fuyez! Enfoncez-vous dans vos forêts. Les Bêtes féroces qui les habitent sont moins redoutables que les monstres sous l'empire desquels vous allez tomber." *Histoire*, 2:18, 258.

23. "Il en est temps, Riebeck approche.... Ni le Hottentot ni l'habitant des contrées qui vous restent à dévaster ne l'entendront." *Histoire*, 2:18, 259.

24. "Hâtez-vous donc, embusquez-vous; & lorsqu'ils se courberont d'une manière suppliante & perfide, percez-leur la poitrine." *Histoire*, 2:18, 259. "Therefore make haste, and wait in ambush. And when they bow down in a suppliant and perfidious manner, pierce them in the chest."

25. See the discussion (and deployment within the article itself) of affect in Ranajit Guha, "A Conquest Foretold," *Social Text* 54 (Spring 1998), to which I referred in the

prologue. Diderot's tone is a striking contrast with the apologists of conquest whom Guha examines.

26. Emphasis mine. "Croyez-vous donc que la corruption dans laquelle vous êtes plongés, vos haines, vos perfidies, votre duplicité ne révoltent pas plus ma raison que la mal propreté de l'Hottentot ne révolte mes sens?" *Histoire*, 2:18, 257.

27. "Si vous vous en sentez le courage, prenez vos haches, tendez vos arcs, faites pleuvoir sur ces étrangers vos flèches empoisonnées. Puisse-t-il n'en rester aucun pour porter à leurs citoyens la nouvelle de leur désastre!" *Histoire*, 2:18, 258.

28. "Corruption des Portugais dans l'Inde." *Histoire*, 1:24.

29. "La fanatisme de religion"; "le brigandage dans les finances"; "une foule de ces chanteuses & de ces danseuses, dont l'Inde est remplie." *Histoire*, 1:24, 172.

30. Pocock's masterful study of Edward Gibbon begins by acknowledging and then placing outside the purview of the work Raynal's *Histoire des deux Indes*. "The peoples of the Atlantic coastlands," he writes, "'Europe' in its narrowly Latin sense—had embarked on a conquest of the global ocean, leading to commercial empires in Asia, the colonisation of the Americas and the massive forced diaspora of enslaved Africans. The great Enlightened histories of these processes in world history—Raynal's *Histoire des deux Indes,* Robertson's histories of America and India—lie beyond the scope of the present volume; the processes they describe were already transforming the history of Enlightened Europe, by enlarging the controlled rivalry of France and Britain into a contest for maritime empire, and their presence is to be felt even in Gibbon's *Decline and Fall*." Pocock, *Barbarism and Religion*, 2:3. He addresses the significance of Raynal in J. G. A. Pocock, "Commerce, Settlement and History: A Reading of the *Histoire des Deux Indes*," *Articulating America: Fashioning a National Political Culture in Early America*, ed. Rebecca Starr (Lanham, Md.: Rowman & Littlefield, 2000).

31. "Il seroit triste d'arrêter les yeux sur le déclin d'une nation ... qui auroit éclairé le monde, ... sans être le fléau de ses voisins ou des régions éloignées." *Histoire*, 1:24, 174.

32. "Il est doux d'entrevoir la chûte de cette tyrannie." *Histoire*, 1:24, 175.

33. "Entraîné par l'habitude." *Histoire*, 1:24, 175.

34. "Barbarous Europeans! The splendor of your undertakings does not impress me. Their success has not removed the garb of injustice from them. I have often embarked in my thoughts upon the vessels which lead you to these faraway countries. But, descending to the earth with you, and becoming witness to your infamy, I have separated myself from you, I plunged myself into the ranks of your enemies, *I have taken up arms against you, I have bathed my hands in your blood*. I make here the solemn profession of this. And if, for one moment, I cease to view you as a thick storm cloud of ravenous and cruel vultures—with as little morality and conscience as these birds of prey—then let my work, let my memory (if I may be permitted the hope of leaving one behind) fall into the ultimate contempt and become an object of execration!" *Histoire*, 1:24, 175, emphasis mine.

35. There is also the suggestion, it appears to me, of the philosophe as *parasite* to and on these journeys.

36. The question of Diderot's atheism is an old debate. For one early consideration, see Aram Vartanian, "From Deist to Atheist: Diderot's Philosophical Orientation 1746–1749," *Diderot Studies* 1 (1949): 46–63.

37. Morley, it should be remarked, did *not* view Diderot's thought in this way and remarked on the foolishness of seeing a link between his writings and the Terror. Morley, *Diderot and the Encyclopaedists*, 2:255–56.

38. "Dangers qui menacent la Jamaïque dans son propre sein." *Histoire*, 14:26.

39. *Ressentiment*, if used in Nietzsche's sense, invokes a Christian context. As such, it is associated not directly with an expressed form of hatred (which is the case in the Jamaican example) but rather with its opposite. The Christian revolution is successful precisely because it advocates a love that for Nietzsche is born of hatred of the strong. Friedrich Wilhelm Nietzsche, *Genealogy of Morals*, ed. Walter Kaufmann (New York: Vintage Press, 1996).

40. "Sauver dans les montagnes une liberté que semblait leur offrir la fuite de leurs tyrans vaincus." *Histoire*, 14:26, 281.

41. Consider, in this context, Burke's response to the massacre of European settlers at Cap-Francois in St. Domingue/Haiti (examined in chapter 5).

42. "Le ressentiment de la nature violée par une police barbare mit tant de fureur dans l'âme des Noirs achetés par les Blancs que ceux-ci, pour couper, disaient-ils, la racine du mal, résolurent, en 1735, d'employer toutes les féroces de la colonie à détruire un ennemi justement implacable." *Histoire*, 14:26, 282–83.

43. Emphasis mine. "Aussitôt les lois militaires prennent la place de toute administration civile." *Histoire*, 14:26, 283.

44. *On Montesquieu's springs*. Because it will recur later in this book with reference to Robespierre, let me say a word regarding Charles de Secondat's fascinating use of the mechanical image of the spring in explaining the three principles he detects behind democratic, monarchic, and despotic governments in *The Spirit of the Laws*. Each form of government has a particular spring which is responsible for "movement" under that regime. His first use is in the famous paragraph that opens the chapter titled "On the Principle of Democracy" (part 1, book 3, chapter 3): "There need not be much integrity for a monarchical or despotic government to main or sustain itself. The force of the laws in the one and the prince's ever-raised arms in the other can rule or contain the whole. But in a popular state there must be an additional spring which is VIRTUE [Mais, dans état populaire, il faut un ressort de plus, qui est la VERTUE]" (22). Montesquieu is certainly prompted to bring this metaphor into his philosophy by the language he employs in introducing a distinction three paragraphs before the one cited (part 1, book 3, chapter 1). "There is this difference," he writes, "between the nature of the government and its principle: its nature is that which makes it what it is, and its principle, that which makes it act. The one is its particular structure, and the other is the human passions that set it in motion" (21). The English unavoidably mutes the many references to mechanical motion in the original: "Il y a différence entre la nature du gouvernement et son principe que sa nature est ce qui le fait être tel, et son principe *ce qui le fait agir*. L'une est sa structure particulière, et l'autre les passions humaines *qui le font mouvoir*." If virtue is the first, rather well-known spring that Montesquieu identifies, the second is honor. "I hasten and I lengthen my steps," he clarifies, "so that none will believe I satirize monarchical government. No; if one spring is missing, monarchy has another. HONOR [Non; s'il manque d'un ressort, il en a d'un autre: L'HONNEUR]" (26). Yet if virtue and honor are springs for democracy and monarchy, respectively, that affect which predominates in a despotism is a spring that cannot be relaxed (and is therefore more fixed component than effective spring). This is made clear by Montesquieu's careful initial *avoidance* of the term in his definition of its principle: "Just as there must be *virtue* in a republic and *honour* in a monarchy, there must be FEAR in a despotic government" (pt. 1, bk. 3, chap. 9, p. 28). When his spring does once again make its appearance only several sentences after

this, it is partially by way of contrast, since it is more obviously affixed to the other two forms of government. "A moderate government can," he observes, "as much as it wants and without peril, relax its springs. It maintains itself by its laws and even by its force. But when in a despotic government the prince ceases for a moment to raise his arm . . . all is lost, for when the spring of the government, which is *fear*, no longer exists, the people no longer have a protector" (28). Fear, *la crainte*, is an inhibitive affect, a spring that must be permanently coiled. For Montesquieu, therefore, a spring that can be relaxed indicates an autonomous principle (virtue or honor) as opposed to incessant tension required of a heteronomous principle imposed from without (fear). *Ressentiment*, to conclude, is the result of an inhibitive affect; it is a counterspring created against and as a result of the state of slavery. References are to Charles de Secondat Montesquieu, *The Spirit of the Laws*, Cambridge Texts in the History of Political Thought (Cambridge: Cambridge University Press, 1989).

45. I have in mind Burke's many descriptions of Hastings as an oriental despot.

46. Emphasis mine. "S'ils [the rebellious slaves] sont vaincus, ce n'est pas sans vengeance. Leur sang est au moins confondu avec celui de leurs barbares maîtres." *Histoire*, 14:26, 283.

47. See Foucault's remarkable observations on the distinction between the savage and the barbarian in *Society Must Be Defended: Lectures at the Collège de France, 1975–76*, trans. David Macey, ed. Mauro Bertani, Alessandro Fontana, and François Ewald (New York: Picador, 2002), 194–97. As he remarks there, the barbarian is *not* a "vector for exchange." The savage, however, is such a vector since in the legal narratives by jurists it is he who renounces savagery to enter civil society. The barbarian, by contrast, is the "vector for domination."

48. "Qu'il cède la plaine à la multitude des troupes, à l'attirail des armes, . . . des munitions et des hôpitaux, et . . . se retire au cœur des montagnes, sans bagage, sans toit, sans provisions; la nature saura bien l'y nourrir et l'y défendre." *Histoire*, 14:26, 283–84.

49. Duchet, *Anthropologie et histoire au siècle des Lumières*, 138.

50. The term is spelled variably, also as *marronnage*, depending on whether one consults English or French scholarship.

51. "Il brave enfin les noms injurieux de brigand et d'assassin que lui prodiguera sans honte une grande nation assez lâche pour s'armer tout entière contre une poignée d'hommes chasseurs et assez faible pour ne pouvoir les vaincre." *Histoire*, 14:26, 284.

52. "Ce gouverneur sage." *Histoire*, 14:26, 284.

53. "Les nègres esclaves résolurent d'être libres aussi." *Histoire*, 14:26, 285.

54. "Mais l'impatience de la liberté déconcerta l'unanimité du complot." *Histoire*, 14:26, 285.

55. "Cependant, leur tyrans savouraient avec avidité les tourments de ces misérables, dont le seul crime était d'avoir voulu recouvrer par la vengeance des droits que l'avarice et inhumanité leur avaient ravis." *Histoire*, 14:26, 286.

56. Emphasis mine. "C'est ainsi que les Anglais, ce peuple si jaloux de sa liberté, se jouent de celles des autres hommes." *Histoire*, 14:26, 287.

57. Emphasis mine. "C'est à cet excès de barbarie que le commerce et l'esclavage des nègres ont dû conduire des usurpateurs. Tels sont les progrès de l'injustice et de la violence. Pour conquérir le Nouveau Monde, il a fallu sans doute en égorger les habitants. Pour les remplacer, il fallait acheter des nègres, seuls propres au climat, aux travaux de l'Amérique." *Histoire*, 14:26, 287.

58. *Histoire*, 14:26, 287.

59. See chapter 4 of this book for a discussion of Indianism as the "despising" of law.

60. "Mais enfin la cruauté même a son terme dans sa nature destructive. Un moment suffit; une descente heureuse à la Jamaïque y peut faire passer des armes à des hommes qui ont l'âme ulcérée et le bras levé contre leurs oppresseurs." *Histoire*, 14:26, 287.

61. "Le Français qui ne songera qu'à nuire à son ennemi sans prévoir que la révolte des nègres dans une colonie les peut soulever dans toutes ira hâter une révolution pendant la guerre." *Histoire*, 14:26, 287.

62. Benot, "Avertissement," in Raynal, *Histoire philosophique et politique des deux Indes*.

63. "L'Anglais placé entre deux feux perdra sa force, son courage, et lassera la Jamaïque en proie à des esclaves et à des conquérants qui se la disputeront par de nouvelles horreurs. Voilà l'enchaînement de l'injustice." *Histoire*, 14:26, 287–88.

64. "Elle s'attache à l'homme par des nœuds qui ne se rompent qu'avec le fer. Le crime engendre le crime; le sang attire le sang, et la terre demeure un théâtre éternel de désolation, de larmes, de misère et de deuil, où les générations viennent successivement se baigner dans le carnage, s'arracher les entrailles et se renverser dans la poussière." *Histoire*, 14:26, 288.

65. I discuss Burke's notion of an "intergenerational contract" in the following chapter.

66. *Histoire*, 1:24, 175.

67. "Description des isles Marianes. Singularités qu'on y a observées." *Histoire*, 6:22.

68. "Les îles Mariannes furent découvertes en 1521 par Magellan. Ce célèbre navigateur les nomma îles des Larrons parce que leurs sauvages habitants, qui n'avaient pas la moindre notion du droit de propriété, inconnu dans l'état de nature, enlevèrent de ses vaisseaux quelques bagatelles qui tentèrent leur curiosité." *Histoire*, 6:22, 323.

69. "Qui y relâchaient de temps en temps en allant du Mexique aux Indes orientales y déposèrent quelques missionnaires." *Histoire*, 6:22, 324.

70. "Livre Sixième: Découverte de l'Amérique. Conquête du Mexique. Etablissemens espagnols dans cette partie du Nouveau-Monde." *Histoire*, 6:9, 203.

71. Chapter 21, "Liaisons du Mexique avec les Philippines." *Histoire*, 6:21, 315.

72. "Dix ans après, la Cour de Madrid jugea que les voies de la persuasion ne lui donnaient pas assez de sujets, et elle appuya par des soldats les prédication de ses apôtres." *Histoire*, 6:22, 324.

73. "La plupart d'entre eux se firent massacrer plutôt que de se soumettre." *Histoire*, 6:22, 324.

74. "Pour ne pas laisser après eux des enfants esclaves." *Histoire*, 6:22, 324.

75. "Restes infortunés d'un peuple autrefois nombreux." *Histoire*, 6:22, 325.

76. "Un homme actif, humain, éclairé"; "il ne réussît à rendre son île agricole." *Histoire*, 6:22, 325.

77. "Cette idée élevée l'a fait cultivateur lui-même. A son exemple, les naturels du pays ont défriché les terres dont il leur avait assuré la propriété." *Histoire*, 6:22, 325.

78. "Leurs champs se sont couverts de riz, de cacao, de maïs, de sucre, d'indigo ... dont depuis un siècle ou deux, on leur laissait ignorer l'usage. Le succès a augmenté leur docilité." *Histoire*, 6:22, 325. There is a typographical error in the 1782

Pellet edition; I have therefore relied here on Benot's modern edition. Raynal, *Histoire philosophique et politique des deux Indes*, 104.

79. "Le succès a augmenté leur docilité. Ces enfants d'une nature brute dans qui la tyrannie et la superstition avaient achevé de dégrader l'homme ont exercé, dans des ateliers, quelques arts de nécessité première et fréquenté. ... Leurs jouissances se sont multipliées avec leurs occupations, et ils ont été enfin heureux dans un des meilleurs pays du monde, tant il est vrai qu'il n'y a rien dont on ne vienne à bout avec la douceur et par la bienfaisance, puisque ces vertus peuvent éteindre le ressentiment dans l'âme même du sauvage." *Histoire*, 6:22, 325.

80. "Principes que doivent suivre les Français dans l'Inde, s'ils parviennent à y rétablir leur considération et leur puissance." Diderot, *Oeuvres*, 3:699.

81. "I have taken up arms against you. I have bathed my hands in your blood."

82. "La consolation de voir diminuer la passion de ses enfans chéris pour le vin de cocotier, & de voir augmenter leur goût pour le travail!"

83. Emphasis mine. "Si, dès l'origine, les espagnoles avoient eu les vues raisonnables du sage Tobias, les Marianes auroient été civilisées & cultivées. Ce double avantage auroit procuré à cet archipel une sureté qu'il ne sauroit se promettre d'une garnison de cent cinquante hommes concentrée dans Guam." *Histoire*, 6:22, 326.

84. "Tranquilles pour leur possessions, les conquérans se seroient livrés à l'amour des découvertes qui étoient alors le génie dominant de la nation." *Histoire*, 6:22, 326.

85. After a lengthy discussion of *rima,* or breadfruit, this chapter discusses three singular or remarkable qualities of the Mariana Island's inhabitants (to which the chapter's title makes reference). These are the absence of the knowledge of fire, the dominance of women in their social structure, and their uniquely simple yet rapid canoes, capable of journeying long distances. *Histoire*, 6:22, 320–23.

86. "Secondés par le talent de leurs nouveaux sujets pour la navigation, leur activité auroit porté les arts utiles & l'esprit de société dans les nombreuses isles qui couvrent l'océan Pacifique & plus loin encore. L'univers eût été, pour ainsi dire, agrandi par de si glorieux travaux." *Histoire*, 6:22, 326.

87. "Sans doute que toutes les nations commerçantes auroient tiré, avec le temps, quelque utilité des relations formées avec ces régions, jusqu'alors inconnues, puisqu'il est impossible qu'un peuple s'enrichisse sans que les autres participent à ses prospérités." *Histoire*, 6:22, 326.

88. "Si nous ne nous trompons, cet ordre de choses valoit mieux pour l'Espagne qu'une combinaison qui réduit les Marianes à fournir des refraîchissemens aux galions qui retournent du Mexique aux Philippines." *Histoire*, 6:22, 326.

89. Nietzsche, *On the Advantage and Disadvantage of History for Life,* 7. "'Übrigens ist mir alles verhaßt, was mich bloß belehrt, ohne meine Tätigkeit zu vermehren oder unmittelbar zu beleben.' Dies sind Worte Goethes, mit denen, als mit einem herzhaft ausgedrückten *Ceterum censeo*, unsere Betrachtung über den Wert und den Unwert der Historie beginnen mag. In derselben soll nämlich dargestellt werden, warum Belehrung ohne Belebung, warum Wissen, bei dem die Tätigkeit erschlafft, warum Historie als kostbarer Erkenntnis-Überfluß und Luxus uns ernstlich, nach Goethes Wort, verhaßt sein muß." Friedrich Wilhelm Nietzsche, "Vom Nutzen und Nachteil der Historie für das Leben," *Werke in drei Bänden,* ed. Rolf Toman, vol. 1 (Köln: Könemann, 1994), 154.

90. Nietzsche's essay famously distinguishes between monumental, antiquarian (*antiquarische*), and critical history, each with its distinct limitations. In the case of

antiquarian history, at a certain point "the historical sense no longer preserves life but mummifies it," and "it merely understands how to *preserve* life, not how to generate it. Therefore it always underestimates what is in process of becoming." Nietzsche, *On the Advantage and Disadvantage of History for Life*, 21.

91. Ibid., 7. "Gewiß, wir brauchen die Historie, aber wir brauchen sie anders, als sie der verwöhnte Müßiggänger im Garten des Wissens braucht, mag derselbe auch vornehm auf unsere derben und anmutlosen Bedürfnisse und Nöte herabsehen. Das heißt, wir brauchen sie zum Leben und zur Tat, nicht zur bequemen Abkehr vom Leben und von der Tat." Nietzsche, "Vom Nutzen und Nachteil der Historie für das Leben," 154.

3 / Between France and India in 1790

1. G. Goggi, "Histoire des deux Indes," in Roland Mortier and Raymond Trousson, *Dictionnaire de Diderot* (Paris: Honoré Champion Editeur, 1999), 225. Also see the entry on "Angleterre" by R. Niklaus in the same volume for a brief but helpful overview of Diderot's interest in England and his interactions with many of its literary and philosophical figures.

2. "Abbe Raynal has been here; he will probably take Bristol in his way from the North to Portsmouth.... I have wrote by him to you, and some others of our friends." Edmund Burke, *The Correspondence of Edmund Burke*, ed. Thomas Copeland, 10 vols. (Chicago: University of Chicago Press, 1958–78), 3:363. To Richard Champion, dated July 9, 1777.

3. Ibid., 3:353. To Richard Champion, dated June 13, 1777.

4. Ibid., 3:364, note 1.

5. Ibid., 6:267–68. To Claude-François de Rival, dated June 1, 1791.

6. Condorcet's work is another worthy component of the edifice of anticolonial and antislavery thought from the eighteenth century, though it is beyond the scope of the present work to consider it.

7. Page references to "Reflections on the Revolution in France" make use of Leslie Mitchell's edition in Edmund Burke, *The Writings and Speeches of Edmund Burke*, eds. Paul Langford and William B Todd, 9 vols. (Oxford: Oxford University Press, 1981–), vol. 8. I have also benefited from other editions, notably Edmund Burke, *Reflections on the Revolution in France and on the Proceedings in Certain Societies in London Relative to that Event*, Pelican Classics, ed. Conor Cruise O'Brien (Baltimore: Penguin Books, 1969).

8. Sudipta Sen, *Distant Sovereignty: National Imperialism and the Origins of British India* (New York: Routledge, 2002), xv, makes the observation that "Burke had thus made a remarkable case for the natural and common source of rights and obligations for a possible constitutional arrangement of British India, which would, of course, never come to fruition." Sen examines the relation of British authority in Bengal to the prior authorization bestowed to the East India Company by the Mughal emperor.

9. "Es sind viele antirevolutionäre Bücher für die Revolution geschrieben worden. Burke hat aber ein revolutionäres Buch gegen die Revolution geschrieben." Novalis, *Shriften* (Darmstadt: Wissenschaftliche Buchgesellschaft, 1965), 2:464.

10. See Isaac Kramnick, *The Rage of Edmund Burke: Portrait of an Ambivalent Conservative* (New York: Basic Books, 1977), who claims that Burke experienced the conflict of an "aristocratic personality" with a "bourgeois personality." Tom Furniss, *Edmund Burke's Aesthetic Ideology: Language, Gender, and Political Economy in*

Revolution, Cambridge Studies in Romanticism (Cambridge: Cambridge University Press, 1993), develops this thesis in a less exclusively psychological manner and draws very different conclusions from the same observation.

11. Burke, *Writings and Speeches*, 8:146–47.

12. The geographic associations of coffee would probably include the Dutch East India Company's cultivation of it in Java, but by the later eighteenth century St. Domingue in the West Indies was a major producer. Each of these commodities undoubtedly has a mobile history, as cultivation and production in one domain was attempted in another.

13. Frederick Whelan, *Edmund Burke and India: The Political Morality of Empire* (Pittsburgh: University of Pittsburgh Press, 1996), emphasizes this.

14. Burke, *Writings and Speeches*, 8:147.

15. See her discussion of rank in Mary Wollstonecraft, *A Vindication of the Rights of Men in a Letter to the Right Honourable Edmund Burke: Occasioned by his Reflections on the Revolution in France; and, A Vindication of the Rights of Woman: With Strictures on Political and Moral Subjects*, ed. David Lorne Macdonald and Kathleen Dorothy Scherf (Orchard Park, N.Y.: Broadview Press, 1997), 82.

16. For an elaboration of the role of inheritance in Burke's political thought, see "Burke and the Ancient Constitution" in J. G. A. Pocock, *Politics, Language, and Time: Essays on Political Thought and History* (Chicago: University of Chicago Press, 1989).

17. Cf. his discussion of time in Burke, *Writings and Speeches*, 8:216–17, where he writes, "It is one of the excellencies of a method in which time is amongst the assistants, that its operation is slow, and in some cases imperceptible."

18. Ibid., 8:96.

19. The *Histoire des deux Indes* certainly contributed to setting in place the figure of the Company official as a despot. Additionally, William Mackintosh's *Travels in Europe, Asia, and Africa* (1782) contained long descriptions of the indolence and extravagance of the British in Calcutta. See the discussion of anti-Company writings in Kate Teltscher, *India Inscribed: European and British Writing on India 1600–1800* (Delhi: Oxford University Press, 1995), chaps. 4–5.

20. Burke, *Writings and Speeches*, 8:95.

21. The term *miscible* is Burke's own. See J. G. A. Pocock, *Virtue, Commerce, and History: Essays on Political Thought and History, Chiefly in the Eighteenth Century*, Ideas in Context (Cambridge: Cambridge University Press, 1985), 211.

22. Does Burke's fear of miscibility in the colonial case relate to a fear of mixture, of hybrid class forms? Is there some link between miscibility and miscegenation, as Robert Young, *Colonial Desire: Hybridity in Theory, Culture, and Race* (New York: Routledge, 1995), considers in another context? In support of this view, there is frequent discussion of the marrying off of these India-returned men to the daughters of the English noble families.

23. Burke, *Writings and Speeches*, 8:99.

24. Ibid., 8:100. The sentence continues, "They [the levellers] load the edifice of society, by setting up in the air what the solidity of the structure requires to be on the ground." Marx would famously make use of the same image to discuss the language of "bourgeois" political economy's analysis of value. In relation to the metaphors of inversion, air, and flight, I return to Burke's comments on the "aëronauts" of France later in this chapter.

25. Ibid., 8:100–101.

26. Marilyn Butler, *Burke, Paine, Godwin, and the Revolution Controversy*, Cambridge English Prose Texts (New York: Cambridge University Press, 1984). Don Herzog, *Poisoning the Minds of the Lower Orders* (Princeton: Princeton University Press, 1998), makes a strong case for the links of this contempt with a broader conservative action against democracy. See especially chapter 11, "The Trouble with Hairdressers."

27. For a study of the Sublime interpreted as a "republican" aesthetic, see part 1 of Furniss, *Edmund Burke's Aesthetic Ideology*. One should also connect this debate, and its underlying use of social categories of gender, with the association of luxury with effeminacy (a debate in which Mandeville and Adam Smith participated). See G. J. Barker-Benfield, *The Culture of Sensibility: Sex and Society in Eighteenth-Century Britain* (Chicago: University of Chicago Press, 1992).

28. Burke, *Writings and Speeches*, 8:101.

29. Ibid., 8:102.

30. Benjamin Disraeli, *Tancred, or the New Crusade* (London: Longmans, Green, 1907), 141. This phrase plays a significant role in Edward Said's definition of orientalism. Edward W. Said, *Orientalism* (New York: Pantheon Books, 1978), 5.

31. Burke, *Writings and Speeches*, 8:159.

32. This topic is addressed by Pocock, *Virtue, Commerce, and History* and by Istvan Hont and Michael Ignatieff, *Wealth and Virtue: The Shaping of Political Economy in the Scottish Enlightenment* (Cambridge: Cambridge University Press, 1983).

33. Burke, *Writings and Speeches*, 8:102.

34. Emma Rothschild, *Economic Sentiments: Adam Smith, Condorcet, and the Enlightenment* (Cambridge: Harvard University Press, 2001).

35. "The Political Economy of Burke's Analysis of the French Revolution" in Pocock, *Virtue, Commerce, and History*, 194.

36. Pocock's primary emphasis in this essay concerns Burke's attention to public debt and the printing of paper money as a part of his critique of the revolutionaries in France. Ibid., 195.

37. On the significance of this concept, see Istvan Hont, "The Language of Sociability and Commerce: Samuel Pufendorf and the Theoretical Foundations of the 'Four-Stages' Theory," *The Languages of Political Theory in Early-Modern Europe*, ed. Anthony Pagden (New York: Cambridge University Press, 1987).

38. Pocock, *Virtue, Commerce, and History*, 198. What significance can be made of the fact that manners are gendered for the dominant male subject? Wollstonecraft will go some way in answering this question in her response to Burke.

39. Burke, *Writings and Speeches*, 8:130, cited in Pocock, *Virtue, Commerce, and History*, 199. See Pocock's introduction to Edmund Burke, *Reflections on the Revolution in France*, ed. J. G. A. Pocock (Indianapolis: Hackett, 1987), xxxiii, for the significance of Burke's reference to the "oeconomical politicians."

40. "Letters on a Regicide Peace," Burke, *Writings and Speeches*, 9:242, cited in Pocock, *Virtue, Commerce, and History*, 209.

41. Pocock, *Virtue, Commerce, and History*, 210.

42. Furniss, *Edmund Burke's Aesthetic Ideology*, 11.

43. Ibid., 11–12.

44. "Speech on Mr. Fox's East India Bill," Burke, *Writings and Speeches*, 5:402–3.

45. I have in mind Derrida's use of singularity in relation to literary language in his discussion of Paul Celan. See "Shibboleth" in Jacques Derrida, *Acts of Literature*, ed. Derek Attridge (New York: Routledge, 1992).

46. "Speech on Fox's East India Bill" in Burke, *Writings and Speeches*, 5:389.

47. *On Michelet's Barbary and Europe's Barbarians*: it is undoubtedly a mark of the successful dissemination of colonial knowledge in the short period that divides Burke's remark (1783) from Jules Michelet, *Introduction à l'histoire universelle* (Paris: L. Hachette, 1843), that allows this most garrulous of French historians to invert the sympathy that Burke's statement perhaps helped to establish in the eighteenth-century European mind. Recall how Burke concludes the passage above: "If I were to take the whole aggregate of our possessions there, I should compare it, as the nearest parallel I can find, with the empire of Germany." Coming full circle, Michelet writes:

> *Indeed, Germany is a kind of India in Europe, huge, vague, drifting and fecund, like its God, the Proteus of pantheism.* As long as Germany has not been pressed in upon and sealed off by the powerful barriers of the monarchies surrounding it, the Indo-Germanic tribe [*la tribu indo-germanique*] has overflowed, streamed across Europe, and changed it while changing itself. Yielded up, then, to its natural mobility, it knew neither walls nor city. "Each family," says Tacitus, "stops where its whim detains it, at a wood, a meadow, a spring." But while, behind Germany, mounted the tide of another Barbary—Slavs, Avars, and Hungarians—while, in the west, France was sealed off, it became necessary to live more densely in order not to lose land and to build forts, to *invent* cities. . . . Cast into the center of Europe as battlefield in every war, Germany attached itself, willy-nilly, to feudal organization, *and remained barbarian in order not to perish*. This is what explains the wonderful spectacle of still young and virgin race that we see committed as though by a magic spell to a transparent civilization, the way a suddenly sealed-off liquid remains fluid in the center of an imperfect crystal." (Emphasis added)

The centrality of Tacitus to both Burke (who also cites him later in this chapter) and Michelet, and indeed more generally the importance of the figure of the simple European barbarian (in this case the rustic Germanic tribes who are the subject of Tacitus's *Germania*, written ca. ad 98), cannot be overemphasized. The Roman view of Europe as barbarous is invoked in texts ranging from Edward Gibbon's *Decline and Fall of the Roman Empire* to the famous opening of Joseph Conrad's *Heart of Darkness*. In the passage above from Michelet, it is worth pondering what made it discursively possible for Germany to become a miasmic and hazy "India in Europe." It may, contrariwise, also be the very liminal state that India continued to occupy on the frontier of Europe's colonial knowledge in 1831 that led Michelet to reach for it as a figure of how to *estrange* the false familiarity by which Germany had been understood. It is certain that the category, in philology and comparative linguistics, of *indogermanisch* (in English this becomes— more inclusively?— Indo-European) also played a role in leading Michelet to this comparison. On the strategic uses of the categories of Indo-Aryan and Indo-European (to draw together as well as to push apart), see the chapter on William Jones in Thomas R. Trautmann, *Aryans and British India* (Berkeley: University of California Press, 1997).

48. Burke, *Writings and Speeches*, 9:102.

49. Michel Foucault, *The Foucault Effect: Studies in Governmentality* (London: Harvester Wheatsheaf, 1991), 93.

50. Burke, *Writings and Speeches*, 8:53. The gentleman was Charles-François Depont. One modern study of him is Robert Foster, *Merchants, Landlords, Magistrates:*

The Depont Family in Eighteenth-Century France (Baltimore: John Hopkins University Press, 1980).

51. Burke, *Writings and Speeches*, 8:53.

52. Ibid., 8:53, 293.

53. One anthology of Burke's writings emphasizes this aspect of his thought. Edmund Burke, *On Empire, Liberty, and Reform: Speeches and Letters*, The Lewis Walpole Series in Eighteenth-Century Culture and History, ed. David Bromwich (New Haven: Yale University Press, 2000).

54. The idea of a "vessel of the commonwealth" circulates in different permutations in this work; at another moment he figures the British constitution (which steers or guides the state) as a "ship" that "proceeds in her course." Burke, *Writings and Speeches*, 8:220.

55. Ibid., 8:293.

56. See Pocock's discussion of the importance of paper money in his essay "The Political Economy of Burke's Analysis of the French Revolution" in Pocock, *Virtue, Commerce, and History*.

57. Burke, *Writings and Speeches*, 8:230.

58. One example of this expectation is expressed by Wollstonecraft, *The Vindications*, 78.

59. Ibid., 44.

60. Burke, *Correspondence*, 6:71, 73.

61. Burke, *Writings and Speeches*, 8:293.

62. For one discussion of the way the loss of the colonies in the New World shapes the form that European colonization takes in later places (such as India), see Anthony Pagden, *European Encounters with the New World: From Renaissance to Romanticism* (New Haven: Yale University Press, 1993). He proposes a useful distinction between the "first colonies" of the Spaniards and others in the New World, and the "second" colonies in Asia. This is a reprise of Seeley's distinction between the First and Second British Empire.

63. Burke, *Writings and Speeches*, 8:103.

64. Ibid., 8:130. A variety of parodic rebuttals to Burke made use of this porcine reference. "If the poor were swine, the rich were merely 'HOGS OF QUALITY'"; so wrote J. Parkinson in *An Address to Edmund Burke from the Swinish Multitude* (1793), cited in Leslie Mitchell in ibid., 8:130, note 1.

65. See the anthropological reflection on this by Paul Connerton, *How Societies Remember*, Themes in the Social Sciences (Cambridge: Cambridge University Press, 1989). A similar reflection on place and memory very evidently forms part of Pierre Nora, *Les Lieux de Mémoire*, Bibliothèque illustrée des histoires (Paris: Gallimard, 1984).

66. Burke, *Writings and Speeches*, 8:105, emphasis mine

67. Max Horkheimer and Theodor W. Adorno, *Dialectic of Enlightenment*, trans. John Cumming (New York: Continuum, 1994), 6. For a meticulous overview of the authorship of this collaborative work and debates around its significance for critical theory, see Anson Rabinbach, "The Cunning of Unreason: Mimesis and the Construction of Anti-Semitism in Horkheimer and Adorno's *Dialectic of Enlightenment*," *In the Shadow of Catastrophe: German Intellectuals between Apocalypse and Enlightenment* (Berkeley: University of California Press, 1997).

68. The affinities of Burke's critique of rationalism with the title essay of Michael Oakeshott, *Rationalism in Politics and Other Essays* (Indianapolis: Liberty Fund, 1991), is more obvious.

69. The examination of Francis Bacon is part of the first chapter, "The Concept of Enlightenment," in Horkheimer and Adorno, *Dialectic of Enlightenment*, 3–42.

70. Ibid., 7, emphasis mine.

71. Bacon, *Works*, 2:126, cited in ibid..

72. Ibid., 7.

73. I return briefly in the epilogue to a reference by Adorno to Rudolph Carnap and logical positivism. But their view of the damage caused to critical thinking by the dominance of formalism and number is clear: "The task of cognition does not consist in mere apprehension, classification, and calculation, but in the determinate negation of each im-mediacy. Mathematical formalism, however, whose medium is number, the most abstract form of the immediate, instead holds thinking firmly to mere immediacy. Factuality wins the day; cognition is restricted to its repetition; and thought becomes mere tautology." Ibid., 27.

74. On this latter point, see Martin Jay, "The Jews and the Frankfurt School: Critical Theory's Analysis of Anti-Semitism," in Anson Rabinbach and Jack David Zipes, *Germans and Jews Since the Holocaust* (New York: Holmes & Meier, 1986), 294.

75. Said, *Orientalism*, 83–86.

76. Burke, *Writings and Speeches*, 8:127, 128, emphasis mine.

77. See Antonio Gramsci, *Prison Notebooks*, European Perspectives (New York: Columbia University Press, 1992). The essays in E. P. Thompson, *Customs in Common: Studies in Traditional Popular Culture* (New York: New Press, 1991), also demonstrate that such a state of undisturbed hegemony never existed.

78. "Political Economy" in Pocock, *Virtue, Commerce, and History*.

79. See David Simpson, *Romanticism, Nationalism, and the Revolt against Theory* (Chicago: University of Chicago Press, 1993), 56. Simpson notes that Burke's jab against the arithmetical aspects of the revolutionaries fits with the establishment press's characterization of the British radicals—Paine, Godwin, Price, Priestley—as "bloodless arithmeticians." While Simpson focuses on the rhetorical effects of Burke's description and its role in debates in the public sphere, in this reading I attempt to extend its theoretical implications.

80. Burke, *Writings and Speeches*, 8:230.

81. This passage also has resonances with Nietzsche's later view of the hampering of noble individuals by the multitude or herd; this "hatred of the weak for the strong" is one component of his understanding of *ressentiment* in the *Genealogy of Morals*. I discuss *ressentiment* with regard to Diderot's thought in chapter 2.

82. Burke, *Writings and Speeches*, 8:230, 231, 232, emphasis mine.

83. Ibid., 8:232.

84. Among the Gothic elements in this text, I would include the discussions of the monstrous and cannibalism. Again Wollstonecraft frequently and very astutely refers to Burke's use of these images: "I perceive, from the whole tenor of your reflections, that you have a moral antipathy to reason; but, if there is anything like argument, or first principles, in your wild declamation, behold the result;—that we are to reverence the rust of antiquity, and term the unnatural customs, which ignorance and mistaken self-interest have consolidated, the sage fruit of experience.... These are *gothic notions* of beauty—the ivy is beautiful, but, when it insidiously destroys the trunk from which it receives support, who would not grub it up?" Wollstonecraft, *The Vindications*, 38, emphasis mine.

85. This observation, however, raises some consequent questions. Do the gothic elements arise as a way of exceeding the rationalism of the philosophes? And how does

one interpret Burke's attempts to impute to the philosophes the very metaphysics with which such ghosts and the like are associated?

86. On the technologies of population, see "Governmentality," in Foucault, *The Foucault Effect*. The following citation from Foucault's essay illustrates one way to locate the *Reflection*'s deployment of the concept of population within the larger sweep of European political thought, through a distinction of three forms of the state: "And maybe we could even ... reconstruct in this manner the great forms and economies of power in the West. First of all, the state of justice, born in the feudal type of territorial regime which corresponds to a society of laws—either customs or written laws—involving a whole reciprocal play of obligations and litigation; second, the administrative state, born in the territoriality of national boundaries in the fifteenth and sixteenth centuries and corresponding to a society of regulation and discipline; and finally a governmental state, essentially defined no longer in terms of its territoriality, of its surface area, but in terms of the *mass of its population* with its volume and density, and indeed also with the territory over which it is distributed.... This state of government which bears essentially on population and both refers itself to and makes use of the instrumentalization of economic *savoir* could be seen as corresponding to a type of society controlled by the apparatuses of security" (104). Foucault's description of the third variety of state, the governmental, describes that form which mobilizes the concept of population. See the discussion of population I made in chapters 1 and 2 with regard to Diderot's notion of wealth in the *Supplément* and the *Histoire des deux Indes*.

87. It is also part of Burke's argument for reform rather than revolution that France has a large and growing population. Like others in the period, Burke argues that a thriving and numerically large population is an index of good governance. Michèle Duchet notes that this view was the motive for many of the attacks on Spanish colonialism in the New World, which destroyed precisely what was an asset: an indigenous population necessary to cultivate the land. See *Anthropologie et histoire au siècle des Lumières: Buffon, Voltaire, Rousseau, Helvétius, Diderot*, Bibliothèque d'anthropologie (Paris: François Maspero, 1971).

88. Burke, *Writings and Speeches*, 8:220–21, 222, 223, emphasis mine.

89. Ibid., 8:225, 226.

90. "The Idea of Glory and Its Downfall" in Albert O. Hirschman, *The Passions and the Interests: Political Arguments for Capitalism before Its Triumph* (Princeton: Princeton University Press, 1981), 9.

91. Pocock, "Edmund Burke and the Redefinition of Enthusiasm," in Keith Michael Baker, *The French Revolution and the Creation of Modern Political Culture* (Oxford: Pergamon Press, 1987), 28.

92. "Speech on Fox's India Bill (1 December 1783)," in Burke, *Writings and Speeches*, 5:402–3. This passage is discussed in the following chapter.

93. On this question, see "Marx after Marxism" in Dipesh Chakrabarty, *Provincializing Europe* (Princeton: Princeton University Press, 2000); Ranajit Guha, *History at the Limit of World-History*, Italian Academy Lectures (New York: Columbia University Press, 2002).

94. See Hirschman, *The Passions and the Interests*, and Partha Chatterjee, *Nationalist Thought and the Colonial World: A Derivative Discourse?*, Third World Books (London: Zed Books, 1986), for interesting deployments of this Hegelian notion. Chatterjee also makes use of this idea in part 1 of *The Politics of the Governed: Reflections on Popular Politics in Most of the World* (New York: Columbia University Press, 2004).

95. This is most pronounced in Georg Wilhelm Friedrich Hegel, *Lectures on the Philosophy of World History: Introduction, Reason in History*, trans. H. B. Nisbet, Cambridge Studies in the History and Theory of Politics (New York: Cambridge University Press, 1980), composed in the 1830s.

96. A selection of the relevant letters is in Robert C. Tucker, *The Marx-Engels Reader* (New York: Norton, 1972). For a defense of Marx's writings on India, see "Marx on India: A Clarification" in Aijaz Ahmad, *In Theory: Classes, Nations, Literatures* (London: Verso, 1994).

97. Charles de Secondat Montesquieu, *The Spirit of the Laws*, Cambridge Texts in the History of Political Thought (Cambridge: Cambridge University Press, 1989). For other predecessors, also see Ann Thomson, "L'Empire ottoman, symbole du despotisme oriental?" in Marie-Elise Palmier-Chatelain and Isabelle Gadoin, *Rêver d'orient, connaître l'orient: Visions de l'orient dans l'art et la littérature britanniques* (Lyon: ENS, 2008).

98. See the comprehensive collection of writings on this subject in Anne Baiey and Josep Llobera, eds., *The Asiatic Mode of Production* (London: Routledge & Kegan Paul, 1981).

99. See Susan Buck-Morss, "Hegel and Haiti," *Critical Inquiry* 26.4 (2000), for an example of the former. She asks what the contemporary political source might have been that prompted Hegel to make the master and slave dialectic the central metaphor, and model of the psyche, employed in the *Phenomenology of Mind*. The essay has been reprinted in Susan Buck-Morss, *Hegel, Haiti, and Universal History* (Pittsburgh: University of Pittsburgh Press, 2009). Guha, *History at the Limit of World-History*, also asks what historical factors went into Hegel's denial of the possibility of a claim to world-historical relevance. For Guha, this was linked with the requirement that the nation possess the modern state form. Historiography thus becomes possible only when such a state form has been achieved.

100. For example, C. L. R. James, *Notes on Dialectics* (London: Allison & Busby, 1980), reads the *Science of Logic* as an allegory of the labor movement.

101. Ronald Paulson, *Representations of Revolution, 1789-1820* (New Haven: Yale University Press, 1983), 37.

102. Samuel Romilly, *Thoughts on the Probable Influence of the French Revolution on Great-Britain* (London: J. Debrett, 1790), cited in ibid., 43.

103. For a lengthier discussion of these images see Teltscher, *India Inscribed*, chap. 5.

104. Burke, *Writings and Speeches*, 8:176.

105. "Burke and the Origins of the Theory of Nationality" in Alfred Cobban, *Edmund Burke and the Revolt against the Eighteenth Century: A Study of the Political and Social Thinking of Burke, Wordsworth, Coleridge, and Southey* (London: G. Allen & Unwin, 1929).

106. Burke, *Writings and Speeches*, 8:177.

107. See the chapter on Necker in vol. 1 of Franco Venturi, *The End of the Old Regime in Europe, 1776-1789*, 2 vols. (Princeton: Princeton University Press, 1991).

108. Paulson, *Representations of Revolution*, 52.

109. Burke, *Writings and Speeches*, 8:178, emphasis mine.

110. Ibid., 8:178, 179, 179-80, emphasis mine.

111. Furniss provides a detailed and convincing reading of Burke's *Reflections* as a conservative rewriting of the aesthetic ideology implicit in the earlier treatise on the Sublime. Furniss, *Edmund Burke's Aesthetic Ideology*.

112. Burke, *Writings and Speeches*, 8:180.

113. Ibid.

114. Two seminal texts in Irish studies begin with readings of Burke, and particularly of the *Reflections*: Declan Kiberd, *Inventing Ireland* (Cambridge: Harvard University Press, 1996), and Seamus Deane, *Strange Country: Modernity and Nationhood in Irish Writing Since 1790* (New York: Oxford University Press, 1997). Kiberd's discussion of Burke, while it opens his work, remains brief. See also Luke Gibbons, *Edmund Burke and Ireland: Aesthetics, Politics and the Colonial Sublime* (New York: Cambridge University Press, 2003). Gibbons examines the comparison Burke makes in the *Reflections* between the march that led the royal family from Versailles on October 6, 1789, to a "procession of American savages, entering into Onondaga." Burke, *Writings and Speeches*, 8:117. Onondaga, in contemporary New York State, refers to the significance of the Iroquois Confederacy of Six Nations, which is explored in Luke Gibbons, "'Subtilized into Savages': Edmund Burke, Progress, and Primitivism," *South Atlantic Quarterly* 100.1 (2001), and forms part of chapter 7 of his book on Burke.

115. See "Phantasmal France, Unreal Ireland: Sobering Reflections," the first chapter of Deane, *Strange Country*. Many of these arguments are developed further in Seamus Deane, *Foreign Affections: Essays on Edmund Burke* (Cork, Ireland: Cork University Press / Field Day, 2005).

116. Deane, *Strange Country*, chap. 1.

117. I use the term *inauthentic* in Heidegger's sense, in his analysis of "Das Man," the "they." For Heidegger this reflects an inauthentic mode of being. See Martin Heidegger, *Being and Time* (New York: Harper, 1962), sections 25–27.

118. From "Opening of Impeachment, 16 February 1788," Burke, *Writings and Speeches*, 6:346. Compare on this point Diderot's biting remark that the mask of the civilized falls off at the frontier: "The greater the distance from the capital, the looser the mask becomes. At the frontier, it falls off." Denis Diderot, *Political Writings*, Cambridge Texts in the History of Political Thought, ed. John Hope Mason and Robert Wokler (Cambridge: Cambridge University Press, 1992), 178.

4 / Jacobinism in India, Indianism in English Parliament

1. John Mowitt, "In the Wake of Eurocentrism: An Introduction," *Cultural Critique* 47 (2001).

2. Dipesh Chakrabarty, *Provincializing Europe* (Princeton: Princeton University Press, 2000).

3. I discuss Burke's sympathy with American colonists in chapter 5 with reference to his "Speech on Conciliation with America" (1775).

4. Edward W. Said, *Orientalism* (New York: Pantheon Books, 1978).

5. See Nicholas B. Dirks, *The Scandal of Empire: India and the Creation of Imperial Britain* (Cambridge: Harvard University Press, 2006). His argument is suggested in an earlier work, Nicholas B. Dirks, *Castes of Mind: Colonialism and the Making of Modern India* (Princeton: Princeton University Press, 2001), 63. There has been surprisingly little written from a comparative perspective regarding another great trial that put the governance of empire at center-stage; I refer to the fascinating controversy surrounding Governor Eyre's responses to the uprisings in Jamaica in 1865, in which J. S. Mill, Carlyle, Ruskin, Charles Kingsley, and many others took part. On this see Bernard Semmel, *Democracy versus Empire: The Jamaica Riots of 1865 and the Governor Eyre Controversy* (New York: Doubleday, 1969), and more recently Catherine

Hall, *Civilising Subjects: Metropole and Colony in the English Imagination, 1830–1867* (Oxford: Polity, 2002), and Tim Watson, *Caribbean Culture and British Fiction in the Atlantic World, 1780–1870* (New York: Cambridge University Press, 2008), chap. 4.

6. Dirks, *Castes of Mind*, 305.

7. P. J. Marshall, "Hastings, Warren," *Encyclopædia Britannica* (2009). Also see P. J. Marshall, *The Impeachment of Warren Hastings* (London: Oxford University Press, 1965).

8. Sara Suleri, *The Rhetoric of English India* (Chicago: University of Chicago Press, 1992), chaps. 2–3.

9. Ibid., chap. 3.

10. Edmund Burke, *The Writings and Speeches of Edmund Burke*, ed. Paul Langford and William B. Todd, 9 vols. (Oxford: Oxford University Press, 1981–), 8:147.

11. "Augustin Cochin: The Theory of Jacobinism" in François Furet, *Interpreting the French Revolution* (Cambridge: Cambridge University Press, 1981), chap. 3; Edmund Burke, *The Correspondence of Edmund Burke*, ed. Thomas Copeland, 10 vols. (Chicago: University of Chicago Press, 1958–78), 7:22.

12. Marshall, *The Impeachment of Warren Hastings*, for example, limits its focus to Burke's writings on India.

13. One important study that addresses Burke's writings on Europe and India together is Conor Cruise O'Brien, *The Great Melody: A Thematic Biography and Commented Anthology of Edmund Burke* (Chicago: University of Chicago Press, 1993). See the chapters titled "India 1767–1791" and "France, Ireland, India 1791–1797." While O'Brien brings out some of the significant affinities between these two contexts (Europe and Asia), his argument hinges on the idea that Burke became taken up with India in part to atone for the guilt of a late awakening to the Irish cause—and even to atone for his father's conversion from Catholicism to Protestantism (271–72, 468). In my opinion this reduces the significance of Burke's India writings to that of compensation by an overemphasis on a psychological explanation.

14. Edward W. Said, *Culture and Imperialism* (New York: Vintage Books, 1994), 85–87. Said notes there that "Austen's imagination works with a steel-like rigor that we might call geographic and spatial clarification," which is also particularly apt in considering Burke's geographic associations for Indianism and Jacobinism.

15. Lorraine Daston, "Enlightenment Fears, Fears of Enlightenment," *What's Left of Enlightenment? A Postmodern Question*, ed. Keith Michael Baker and Peter Hanns Reill (Stanford: Stanford University Press, 2001), 122.

16. O'Brien, *The Great Melody*, 400–401.

17. Regina Janes, "Edmund Burke's Flyting Leap from India to France," *History of European Ideas* 7.5 (1986).

18. Letter to Philip Francis, December 11, 1789, in Burke, *Correspondence*, 6:55, cited in ibid. It is worth noting that this letter, primarily concerned with financial reforms in France, comes only weeks after Burke's letter to Charles-Jean-François Depont (the addressee of the *Reflections*), which contains his first views on the French Revolution. See *Correspondence*, 6:39–50.

19. Letter to William Windham, January 8, 1795, in Burke, *Correspondence*, 8:113.

20. Letter to French Laurence, March 11, 1796, in Burke, *Correspondence*, 8:413.

21. Uday Singh Mehta, *Liberalism and Empire: A Study in Nineteenth-Century British Liberal Thought* (Chicago: University of Chicago Press, 1999).

22. Marshall, *The Impeachment of Warren Hastings*, 184, 187–88.

23. Quoted in ibid., 189.
24. Ibid., 190–91. Also see P. J. Marshall, "Introduction," Burke, *Writings and Speeches*, vol. 5, *India: Madras and Bengal, 1774–1785* and "Introduction," vol. 7, *India: The Hastings Trial 1789–1794*.
25. For a brief consideration of the relationship between Indianism and Jacobinism see David Bromwich, "The Context of Burke's *Reflections*," *Social Research* 58.2 (1991). Janes, "Edmund Burke's Flyting Leap from India to France" makes the argument that the rapidity of Burke's diagnosis of the events in France was due to his observations on India but does not examine how these developed in his final years and correspondence. Frederick Whelan, *Edmund Burke and India: The Political Morality of Empire* (Pittsburgh: University of Pittsburgh Press, 1996), presents an interesting analysis specifically of Burke's and Hastings's writings on India in terms of the contrast between a "political moralist" and a "successful practitioner of *raison d'état*" (2).
26. Marshall, "Introduction," Burke, *Writings and Speeches*, 7:2, 5:25, 7:17, 23.
27. A question raised by Mehta, *Liberalism and Empire*.
28. On this matter, see Thomas R. Metcalf, *Ideologies of the Raj*, The New Cambridge History of India (New York: Cambridge University Press, 1997), chaps. 1 and 2; Eric Stokes, *The English Utilitarians and India* (Oxford: Clarendon Press, 1959), pt. 1, "The Doctrine and Its Setting." For an account of the establishment of the ryotwari system and the permanent settlement, see, respectively, Burton Stein, *Thomas Munro: The Origins of the Colonial State and His Vision of Empire* (Delhi: Oxford University Press, 1989); Ranajit Guha, *A Rule of Property for Bengal: An Essay on the Idea of Permanent Settlement*, 2nd ed. (New Delhi: Orient Longman, 1982). Sudipta Sen, *Distant Sovereignty: National Imperialism and the Origins of British India* (New York: Routledge, 2002), argues that within the structure of the Company "a certain species of statehood was being formed" (3).
29. In contrast to the cosmopolitanism of Kant, if Burke were to accede to such an idea it would most certainly be based on the idea of practical reason, a phronetic idea of skill or *techné* (to draw terms from Aristotle's *Nicomachean Ethics*). So here the global scope of his imagination results in part from the need to speak on such matters in Parliament. As he wrote early on, "It is, I own, not uncommon to be wrong in theory, and right in practice; and we are happy that it is so. Men often act right from their feelings, who afterwards reason but ill on them from principle: but as it is impossible to avoid an attempt at such reasoning, and equally impossible to prevent its having some influence on our practice, surely it is worth taking some pains to have it just, and founded on the basis of sure experience." "Enquiry into the Sublime and the Beautiful" in Burke, *Writings and Speeches*, 1:228.
30. "Speech on Fox's India Bill (1 December 1783)," in ibid., 5:402–3.
31. Philippe Ariès, *Centuries of Childhood* (London: Pimlico, 1996), 125, 128, 129, 130.
32. John R. Gillis, *Youth and History: Tradition and Change in European Age Relations, 1770–Present*, Studies in Social Discontinuity (New York: Academic Press, 1981), 37.
33. Cited in ibid., 9.
34. Ashis Nandy, *Traditions, Tyranny, and Utopias: Essays in the Politics of Awareness* (Delhi: Oxford University Press, 1987), 57.
35. Mehta, *Liberalism and Empire*. However, Kate Teltscher, *India Inscribed: European and British Writing on India 1600–1800* (Delhi: Oxford University Press, 1995),

reviews the large body of anti-Company literature that circulated in this period and on which Burke draws.

36. Burke, *Writings and Speeches*, 8:159.

37. "Speech on Fox's East India Bill," in ibid., 5:403.

38. Pocock wishes to prevent the easy subsumption of Burke's analysis within a Marxist language. "Editor's Introduction," Edmund Burke, *Reflections on the Revolution in France*, ed. J. G. A. Pocock (Indianapolis: Hackett, 1987), xxx.

39. Burke's view of the epochal quality of the French Revolution is proposed by Stephen White, *Edmund Burke: Modernity, Politics, and Aesthetics* (Thousand Oaks, Calif.: Sage Publications, 1994), and Seamus Deane, *The French Revolution and Enlightenment in England, 1789–1832* (Cambridge: Harvard University Press, 1988).

Thus the thesis on contagion in some studies of colonial discourse may be unnecessarily reductive or too exclusive in focus. If we understand the variety of Burke's interests and find the same logic at work in each (contagion, conspiracy, cabal), then the specificity of this to a *colonial* context seems undermined. Here Indianism is a force not unlike Jacobinism. When Burke speaks of Jacobinizing those in Ireland who might be a great dyke against this force, he describes something akin to the "Indianizing" (to extend the term on analogy with Burke's use of the other term) of the British elites discussed in the passage cited earlier. There is a language of contagion here, but it is as relevant to England's relationship to France as it is to England's relationship to India.

40. Compare the similarity of some of these remarks to Burke's description of Rousseau and the Jacobin men of letters as "vitiat[ing] their female pupils" in "Letter to a Member of the National Assembly," Burke, *Writings and Speeches*, 8:316.

41. Ann Laura Stoler, "Sexual Affronts and Racial Frontiers," 198–237, in Frederick Cooper and Ann Laura Stoler, eds., *Tensions of Empire: Colonial Cultures in a Bourgeois World* (Berkeley: University of California Press, 1997). In this context, she makes the important point that "métissage was first a name and then made a thing. It was so heavily politicized because it threatened both to destabilize national identity and the Manichean categories of ruler and ruled" (226). We see this at work in the fears on which Burke is playing in the passage cited. Linda Colley argues that many Britons who came to India in the eighteenth century experienced less culture shock because their small numbers required a greater degree of assimilation within Indian society. See Linda Colley, *Captives: Britain, Empire and the World, 1600–1850* (London: Jonathan Cape, 2002), 253.

42. I would connect this image of a meek peasant whose "scanty portion" of rice is being taken with the absence of a (native) Indian Jacobin in Burke's thought, discussed in chapter 5.

43. Burke, *Writings and Speeches*, 8:159, emphasis mine.

44. See J. G. A. Pocock, *Virtue, Commerce, and History: Essays on Political Thought and History, Chiefly in the Eighteenth Century*, Ideas in Context (Cambridge: Cambridge University Press, 1985), 211, for a discussion of Burke's use of the term *miscible*.

45. Burke, *Writings and Speeches*, 8:159.

46. Ibid.

47. Ibid., 8:159–60.

48. Noted in White, *Edmund Burke*, 53. Burke uses the term "political architect" contemptuously in the opening paragraph of a speech on the "state of the Representation of the Commons in Parliament" on May 7, 1782: "Our political architects have

taken a survey of the fabrick of the British Constitution. It is singular, that they report nothing against the Crown, nothing against the Lords; but in the House of Commons every thing is unsound; it is ruinous in every part." The editors note that the speech was never delivered. Burke argues against bold experiments with an ancient institution such as the British constitution and mocks the report's suggestions. I have cited from another edition since this does not yet appear in the collected works (one volume remains to be published). Edmund Burke, *Miscellaneous Writings*, ed. E. J. Payne, Library of Economics and Liberty, 1990, http://www.econlib.org/library/LFBooks/Burke/brkSWv4c2.html.

49. Burke, *Writings and Speeches*, 8:294–335.

50. Ibid., 8:300, 312, 313.

51. Ibid., 8:314.

52. This notion, an essential component of Levinas's thought, is discussed in "Ethics as First Philosophy" in Emmanuel Levinas, *The Levinas Reader*, ed. Seán Hand (New York: Blackwell, 1989), and developed at length in "Ethics and the Face" in Emmanuel Levinas, *Totality and Infinity: An Essay on Exteriority*, Martinus Nijhoff Philosophy Texts (The Hague: M. Nijhoff, 1979), 194–219.

53. Burke, *Writings and Speeches*, 8:315. The vanity Burke discusses here is picked up by Carl Schmitt in his attempt to define more strictly "political romanticism" in relation to romanticism in general. In discussing Hippolyte Taine's explanation of Jacobinism in terms of an *esprit classique*, Schmitt writes, "Narcissistic dogmatists, rendered incapable of any matter-of-fact experience as a result of their *raison raisonnante*, try to form the world according to the axioms of the political geometry. Rousseau moves essentially within the space of this *moule classique*." Carl Schmitt, *Political Romanticism*, trans. Guy Oakes (Cambridge, Mass.: MIT Press, 1986), 28.

54. Burke, *Writings and Speeches*, 8:315, emphasis mine.

55. For a reading of Burke and theater, see Paul Hindson and Tim Gray, *Burke's Dramatic Theory of Politics*, Avebury Series in Philosophy (Aldershot, England: Avebury, 1988).

56. Rousseau himself endlessly reiterated his transparency as a sign of his honesty and inability to dissemble. See "The Transparency of Crystal" in Jean Starobinski, *Jean-Jacques Rousseau, Transparency and Obstruction*, trans. Arthur Goldhammer (Chicago: University of Chicago Press, 1988), 254–70, for a subtle reading of this.

57. That Rousseau was Swiss from Geneva does not stop Burke from taking him as emblematic of the follies of French thought. On the significance of the composition of Rousseau's *Discourse on the Origin of Inequality* in a village *outside of* Geneva but nonetheless "dedicated to the citizens of Geneva," see ibid., 287.

58. Burke, *Correspondence*, 8:553.

59. So far from seeing the confessional mode as a vulnerable exposition of the self, Burke views it as another testament to Rousseau's vanity. "It is from this same deranged, eccentric vanity," Burke writes, "that this, the insane Socrates of the National Assembly, was impelled to publish a mad confession of his mad faults." Burke, *Writings and Speeches*, 8:314.

60. J. G. A. Pocock, "Edmund Burke and the Redefinition of Enthusiasm" in vol. 3 of Keith Michael Baker, *The French Revolution and the Creation of Modern Political Culture* (Oxford: Pergamon Press, 1987). See also the collection of essays, Lawrence Eliot Klein and Anthony J. LaVopa, *Enthusiasm and Enlightenment in Europe, 1650–1850* (San Marino, Calif.: Huntington Library, 1998).

61. Burke, *Correspondence*, 8:129.

62. I take the term from the discussion of fore-conception (*Vorgriffe*) in Martin Heidegger, *Sein und Zeit*, 8th ed. (Tübingen: M. Niemeyer, 1957), ¶32, 150. The term *fore-conception* is elaborated in relation to *fore-sight* and *fore-having* as they operate in interpretation. Gadamer develops these observations in a manner that makes their relevance for an understanding of Burke much more obvious when he discusses "prejudices as conditions of understanding" (245): "Thus 'prejudice' certainly does not mean a false judgment, but it is part of the idea that it can have a positive and a negative value.... There are such things as *préjugé légitimes*. This seems a long way from our current use of the word. The German *Vorurteil*, like English 'prejudice' and even more than the French '*préjugé*,' seems to have become limited in its meaning, through the enlightenment and its critique of religion, and have the sense simply of an 'unfounded judgment.'" Hans Georg Gadamer, *Truth and Method* (New York: Crossroad, 1984), 240.

63. For a comprehensive collection of responses, see Gregory Claeys, ed., *The Political Writings of the 1790s: The French Revolution Debate in Britain* (London: Pickering & Chatto, 1995). Marilyn Butler, *Burke, Paine, Godwin, and the Revolution Controversy*, Cambridge English Prose Texts (New York: Cambridge University Press, 1984), has concise selection of responses. For a discussion of the many visual caricatures of Burke, which spanned the extent of his career, see Nicholas K. Robinson, *Edmund Burke: A Life in Caricature* (New Haven: Yale University Press, 1997).

64. Burke, *Writings and Speeches*, 8:138.

65. In the *Nicomachean Ethics*, 2:1, Aristotle connects moral virtue (*ethiké*) with habit (*ethos*). Burke's words resonate with two phrases in particular. "This is confirmed by what happens in states," Aristotle writes, "for legislators make the citizens good by forming habits in them, and this is the wish of every legislator" (1103a). "Thus, in one word, states of character (*hexeis*) arise out of like activities. This is why the activities we exhibit must be of a certain kind; it is because the states of character correspond to the differences between these. It makes no small difference, then, whether we form habits of one kind or of another from our very youth; it makes a very great difference, or rather *all* the difference" (1103b). Aristotle, *The Nicomachean Ethics*, trans. David Ross (New York: Oxford University Press, 1998). In a sense, Burke's view is at variance with the emphasis on the legislator's role in forming habit through a change in law in the first remark. The second observation supports Burke's assertion that "prejudice renders a man's virtue his habit." Burke even attempts to recuperate the notion of "just prejudice" in a manner akin to Gadamer's observation regarding *préjugé légitimes* cited earlier.

66. Burke, *Writings and Speeches*, 8:127.

67. "But though reason ... be sufficient to instruct us in the pernicious or useful tendency of qualities and actions; it is not alone sufficient to produce any moral blame or approbation.... It is requisite a *sentiment* should here display itself." David Hume, *An Enquiry Concerning the Principles of Morals* (Indianapolis: Hackett, 1983), 83. The argument is similar to Hume's consideration of reason and taste: "Reason, being cool and disengaged, is no motive to actions.... Taste, as it gives pleasure or pain ... becomes a motive to action, and is the first spring or impulse to desire and volition" (88).

68. See James Chandler's reading of this passage in "Political Liberties: Burke's France and the 'adequate representation' of the English," vol. 3, p. 47 of Baker, *The French Revolution and the Creation of Modern Political Culture*.

69. Burke, *Correspondence*, 7:552.

70. "The Seven Sages," Yeats's poem published in 1933, names this trio of concerns, but adds to them a fourth: the American colonies. O'Brien, *The Great Melody*, draws its title from this poem, which is written as a dialogue among seven speakers:

> *The Sixth.* Whether they knew or not,
> Goldsmith and Burke, Swift and the Bishop of Cloyne
> All hated Whiggery; but what is Whiggery?
> A levelling, rancorous, rational sort of mind
> That never looked out of the eye of a saint
> Or out of drunkard's eye.
> *The Seventh.* All's Whiggery now,
> But we old men are massed against the world.
> *The First.* American colonies, Ireland, France and India
> Harried, and Burke's great melody against it.
> . . .
> *The Sixth.* What schooling had these four?
> *The Seventh.* They walked the roads
> Mimicking what they heard, as children mimic;
> They understood that wisdom comes of beggary.

W. B. Yeats, *The Collected Poems of W. B. Yeats*, ed. Richard J. Finneran (New York: Collier Books, 1989), 241.

71. Burke, *Correspondence*, 8:254.

72. Burke, *Writings and Speeches*, 8:96.

73. Ibid., 8:101.

74. Burke, *Correspondence*, 8:254.

75. See ibid., 8:256, where he explains, "Next to religion, *property* is the great point of the Jacobin attack."

76. Ibid., 8:243.

77. The basis for the idea of the "false Sublime" is to be found in an anonymous letter that J. T. Boulton, editor of the authoritative edition of *Sublime and Beautiful*, attributes to Burke. See his "Editor's Introduction" in Edmund Burke, *A Philosophical Enquiry into the Origin of Our Ideas of the Sublime and Beautiful*, ed. James Boulton (Notre Dame, Ind.: University of Notre Dame Press, 1968). Ronald Paulson, in describing the link between a speech read in the House of Commons on April 11, 1794, and the *Sublime and Beautiful*, writes, "This passage, with its reference to the 'terrible' and to painting, recalls Burke's own *Philosophical Enquiry into the Sublime and the Beautiful*, in terms of which he is now saying that the *true sublime* in government is a mixture of fear and awe or admiration, whereas the *false sublime*, a perversion of this . . . , generates only fear and a grotesque energy." Ronald Paulson, *Representations of Revolution, 1789–1820* (New Haven: Yale University Press, 1983), 66, emphasis mine.

78. Burke, *Correspondence*, 8:432.

79. "Opening of Impeachment, 15 February 1788," Burke, *Writings and Speeches*, 6:283.

80. The *Oxford English Dictionary*, as late as 1989, included the term *Indianism* but nowhere cited Burke's (idiomatic and personal) use. The definition of 1989 is "Action or policy devoted to the interests of Indians; advocacy of (North American) Indians," and the first usage is from 1651. The second usage listed skips over the eighteenth

century entirely and is from 1871. By 2009 there is an additional entry for the word, which lists a 1692 English translation of Bernier first; the second usage given from 1795 is Burke's own. See "Indianism, n.," *Oxford English Dictionary*, 2nd ed. (New York: Oxford University Press, 1989) and "Indianism, n.," *Oxford English Dictionary*, 3rd ed. (New York: Oxford University Press, 2009). It is clear that Burke sought to coin a word on analogy with *Jacobinism* and found it in this term. That the Jacobins were originally a club fit well with the hint of conspiracy he wished to emphasize in the structure of the East India Company.

81. Arthur O'Conner spoke on the Catholic Question in the Irish House of Commons, describing the political abuses the Irish were suffering, on the day when Burke responded by letter to both Langrishe and Earl Fitzwilliam. O'Conner later became a primary figure in the United Irishmen, fled to France, and married Condorcet's daughter. Burke, *Correspondence*, 8:242, note 6.

82. "I have spent the last fourteen years of my existence in a Labour hardly credible, in hopes of obtaining Justice for an oppressed people. Tell me, my Lord, is it very soothing to find, the whole of that Labour end in a vast remuneratory Pension to the person, whom you and I have uniformly thought the principle oppressor of that people?" Burke, *Correspondence*, 8:425.

83. Burke, *Writings and Speeches*, 8:147.

84. Burke, *Correspondence*, 8:255.

85. Ibid., 8:431–32, emphasis mine.

86. What Burke means by the "moral" use of law as it relates to the Indian colony is a crucial aspect of the contradictory rhetorical positions he takes: critic of England's empire, but also a proponent for its reform (not its abolition). In the "Speech on Fox's East India Bill" he argued that governing India well was not only compatible with British interests but vital for the preservation of their integrity: "I must beg leave to observe, that if we are not able to contrive some method of governing India *well*, which will not of necessity become the means of governing Great Britain *ill*, a ground is laid for their eternal separation; but none for sacrificing the people of that country to our constitution. I am however far from being persuaded that any such incompatibility of interest does at all exist. On the contrary I am certain that every means, effectual to preserve India from oppression, is a guard to preserve the British constitution from its worst corruption." Burke, *Writings and Speeches*, 5:383.

87. Ibid., 8:230; "Speech on Fox's India Bill," 5:427. The number of times Burke uses the phrase *total revolution* and permutations of it in this speech is utterly striking. To take just the following pages (427–29): "In the year 1781, a total revolution took place in that establishment [the administration of justice]"; "the whole criminal jurisdiction of these courts . . . was in one day, without notice . . . totally subverted"; "This revolution may well be rated for a most daring act, even among the extraordinary things that have been doing [*sic*] in Bengal since our unhappy acquisition of the means of so much mischief"; "It was in this very situation, that one man had the hardiness to conceive, and the temerity to execute, a total revolution in the form and the persons composing the government of a great kingdom"; and finally, in a conclusion to this passage, Burke remarks, "By this means the ancient plan of the company's administration was destroyed."

88. See Guha, *A Rule of Property for Bengal*, for an incisive study of the effects of Physiocratic thought on new forms of property law and revenue in India. Philip Francis (one of the main architects of the law that established the permanent settlement)

and Burke were very close friends; Francis even served as an advisor to Burke during the impeachment trial of Hastings. This friendship came to an end with Francis's severe criticisms of Burke's proof sheets for the *Reflections* (82–83).

5 / Atlantic Revolutions and Their Indian Echoes

1. P. J. Marshall, *The Making and Unmaking of Empires: Britain, India, and America c.1750–1783* (New York: Oxford University Press, 2005).

2. This is in spite of the active resistance presented by figures such as Tipu Sultan, who in fact made efforts to league with the revolutionary French regime, going so far as to send envoys to France. He had good reason to mistrust France given his previous experience of betrayal. See "Tipu and the French: 1784–1788" in Mohibbul Hasan Khan, *History of Tipu Sultan* (Calcutta: Bibliophile, 1951), 122–131. See also Kate Brittlebank, *Tipu Sultan's Search for Legitimacy: Islam and Kingship in a Hindu Domain* (Delhi: Oxford University Press, 1997).

3. That the two most famous episodes in Burke's writings and speeches from this period pertain to the violation of a vulnerable female body—Marie-Antoinette in the *Reflections* and native princesses in the Hastings trial—shows another affinity in the argumentative strategy Burke employs, and a gendered one at that. Regina Janes argues, in fact, that Burke got the idea of emphasizing the episode with Marie-Antoinette in the *Reflections* from observing the success of Richard Sheridan's speech in Parliament during the trial. (It was considered the most spectacular of the speeches, with one listener fainting during its delivery.) See Regina Janes, "Edmund Burke's Flyting Leap from India to France," *History of European Ideas* 7.5 (1986).

4. Edmund Burke, *The Correspondence of Edmund Burke*, ed. Thomas Copeland, 10 vols. (Chicago: University of Chicago Press, 1958–78), 8:425.

5. Nandakumar, a high-level administrator in Bengal under the nawabs and the East India Company, had publicly accused Hastings of taking bribes in 1775. Soon after, charges were in turn brought against him for forgery. (Burke's own estimation of Nandakumar's character was ambivalent.) Elijah Impey, presiding judge and a friend of Hastings, delivered summary judgment and had him put to death. The quick and overwhelming response was generally thought to have silenced Hastings's potential critics in Bengal. An effort in 1788 in the House of Commons to impeach Impey for this had failed, and so this charge of "judicial murder" did not figure largely in Burke's legal case against Hastings (though it was invoked to imply guilt). See Frederick Whelan, *Edmund Burke and India: The Political Morality of Empire* (Pittsburgh: University of Pittsburgh Press, 1996), 145–49. For a defense of Impey that is also significant for what it reveals of Victorian disputes over empire, see James Fitzjames Stephen, *The Story of Nuncomar and the Impeachment of Sir Elijah Impey*, 2 vols. (London: Macmillan, 1885). Stephen's rather authoritarian defense of force is discussed with great insight by Eric Stokes for its relation to Stephen's dispute with John Stuart Mill. Stephen saw himself as upholding a "liberalism of the intellect" rather than a "liberalism of sentiment" to which Mill had fallen prey. See "Utilitarianism and Late-Nineteenth-Century Imperialism" in Eric Stokes, *The English Utilitarians and India* (Oxford: Clarendon Press, 1959), especially 287–95. There are a number of Victorian defenses of Hastings from prominent figures, including Alfred Comyn Lyall, *Warren Hastings* (London, New York: Macmillan, 1902), and John Strachey, *Hastings and the Rohilla War* (Oxford: Clarendon Press, 1892). Also to be considered among these is Thomas Babington Macaulay, *Warren Hastings*, ed. Joseph Villiers Denney (Boston: Allyn and Bacon, 1907).

6. See Sisir Kumar Das, *Sahibs and Munshis: An Account of the College of Fort William* (New Delhi: Orion Publications, 1978), 1–5. As Das notes, citing an interesting passage from Richard Wellesley (1760–1842), governor-general of Bengal from 1797 to 1805 and later the person to face down Tipu Sultan, "Wellesley had some apprehension against the doctrines of the French Revolution which found their way among a section of officers in the Company. He observed: 'during the convulsions with which the doctrines of the French Revolution have agitated the continent of Europe, erroneous principles of the same dangerous tendencies had reached the minds of some individuals in the civil and military service of the Company in India ... The progress of this mischief would at all times be aided by the defective and irregular education of the writers and cadets; an Institution tending to fix and establish sound and correct principles of religion and government in their minds at an early period of life, is the best security which can be provided for the stability of the British power in India.'" Ironically, and against Burke's remarks elsewhere, Wellesley wished to counteract these tendencies by getting young European boys to come to India for training at the college of Fort William in Indian languages in order to better preserve and govern "British power in India," but also to correct the "irregular education" that abetted their Jacobin sympathies. For a more recent discussion of Wellesley, with some consideration of Burke's influence upon him, see Kapil Raj, *Relocating Modern Science: Circulation and the Construction of Knowledge in South Asia and Europe, 1650–1900* (New York: Palgrave Macmillan, 2007), 146.

7. Burke, *Correspondence*, February 20, 1790, 6:88, 91. In Francis's letter to Burke on the manuscript copy of the *Reflections* he received, he writes that Burke's response in the Marie-Antoinette episode was "downright foppery" (6:91), especially when Burke describes how reading of it "did draw Tears from me and wetted my Paper" (6:91). Dismissing the relevance of whether Marie-Antoinette's virtues merited such a response, Burke invokes an episode from *Hamlet* (II, ii, 564–65) that is significant for what it reveals of the role of sentiment. "What, are not high Rank ... ingredients of moment in forming the interest we take in the Misfortunes of Men? The minds of those who do not feel thus are not even Dramatically right. 'What's Hecuba to him or he to Hecuba that he should weep for her?' Why because she was Hecuba, the Queen of Troy, the Wife of Priam, and sufferd in the close of Life a thousand Calamities. I felt too for Hecuba when I read the fine Tragedy of Euripides upon her Story: and I never enquired into the Anecdotes of the Court or City of Troy before I gave way to the Sentiments which the author wished to inspire; nor do I remember that he ever said one word of her Virtues" (6:90). In other words, a sentimental response has no relation to the degree of virtue of the object, which Burke in effect grafts onto an Aristotelian idea (from the *Poetics*) that the subjects of a tragedy ought to be "high" characters who fall low. The consonance of his logic here with his early view on aesthetics—inasmuch as it places great weight on sentiment over reason—cannot be underestimated.

8. Ibid., 6:92. See also the editor's note to another letter to Francis, dated March 10, 1790, 6:99.

9. For more on Burke's relationship to Jones, see Garland H. Cannon, "Sir William Jones and Edmund Burke," *Modern Philology* 54.3 (1957).

10. Burke, *Correspondence*, 4:352.

11. See Nicholas B. Dirks, *Castes of Mind: Colonialism and the Making of Modern India* (Princeton: Princeton University Press, 2001), which discusses the relationship between colonial governmentality and the imperial archive, and the legacy of this

nexus for postcolonial politics in India. Dirks demonstrates how the colonial archive established an evidentiary status as a transparent bearer of insights regarding the past.

12. See Sudipta Kaviraj, "On the Construction of Colonial Power: Structure, Discourse, Hegemony," *Contesting Colonial Hegemony: State and Society in Africa and India*, eds. Dagmar Engels and Shula Marks (London: British Academic Press, 1994), 45.

13. Though I have not taken up the specific theoretical arguments made by Gayatri Chakravorty Spivak's "Can the Subaltern Speak?," *Marxism and the Interpretation of Culture*, ed. Cary Nelson and Lawrence Grossberg (Urbana: University of Illinois Press, 1988), my remarks on this question are indebted to that essay and the controversies it has continued to provoke. A revised version forms part of Gayatri Chakravorty Spivak, *A Critique of Postcolonial Reason: Toward a History of the Vanishing Present* (Cambridge: Harvard University Press, 1999), chap. 3.

14. William Cobbett, *Cobbett's Parliamentary History of England* (London: T. C. Hansard, 1806), 29:249, cited in Conor Cruise O'Brien, *The Great Melody: A Thematic Biography and Commented Anthology of Edmund Burke* (Chicago: University of Chicago Press, 1993), 415, in a section that examines "the quarrel with Fox," on which I rely for material in this paragraph.

15. O'Brien, *The Great Melody*, 416.

16. Lines introduced as a song for the witches in *Macbeth* (IV, i, 46–48). But also from Thomas Middleton, *The Witch* (V, ii). For the variants on these lines, see the editor's note in William Shakespeare, *The Tragedy of Macbeth*, The Oxford Shakespeare, ed. Nicholas Brooke (Oxford: Clarendon Press, 1990), 170.

17. Cobbett, *Parliamentary History of England*, 29:366–67, dated May 6, 1791. This passage is cited selectively by O'Brien, *The Great Melody*, 418–19, with most of the crucial references to the West Indies omitted; I have therefore restored key lines from the original. Note that *Cobbett's Parliamentary History of England* is based on minutes taken during parliamentary sessions; it is for this reason that the passage makes frequent use of the third person to report the words spoken.

18. See his "Sketch of a Negro Code" (1792) in Edmund Burke, *The Writings and Speeches of Edmund Burke*, ed. Paul Langford and William B. Todd, 9 vols. (Oxford: Oxford University Press, 1981–), 3:131. A key letter on this is to Henry Dundas, April 9, 1792, in Burke, *Correspondence*, 7:122–25. This fascinating letter makes specific reference to the West Indies and argues against this topic being "disconnected" from the "African trade." He remarks astutely that "the true origin of the trade was not in the place it was begun at [i.e., the West African coasts], but at the place of its final destination [i.e., the West Indies]." One finds his suspicion of abstract reasoning present even in discussions of abolition: "A gradual abolition of slavery in the West Indies ought to go hand in hand with anything which should be done with regard to its supply from the coast of Africa. I could not trust a cessation of the demand for this supply to the mere operation of any abstract principle . . . knowing that nothing can be more uncertain than the operation of general principles" (123). Trapped by the discourse of civilization, he seems to place hope in the idea that "commerce" will "civilize the coast of Africa."

19. For example: "These utterances are all distinguished by Burke's extraordinary and sustained capacity to pierce through the superficial tranquility and look into the seething core of the Revolution in France. . . . It constitutes what I shall call the *clairvoyant* stage of Burke's statements on the French Revolution" (O'Brien, *The Great Melody*, 457). O'Brien means to pun upon the French meaning of the word, which literally means "clear-sighted," as well as the parapsychological sense in English.

Keeping in mind the Terror and wars of territorial conquest undertaken by France after the revolution, it is important not to unduly diminish the significance of Burke's gloomy forecast. For a liberal critic such as O'Brien, had France heeded such advice it might have avoided the excesses of the postrevolutionary regime. While the image of Burke as a prophet misunderstood or before his time is appealing, it does not seem to further an understanding of his views. Is post facto validation to be the basis for evaluating the success or failure of the French Revolution? Kant's discussion of the French Revolution as a "prognostic sign" of progress, raised in the epilogue, addresses this question.

20. Christopher Brown, "From Slaves to Subjects: Envisioning an Empire without Slavery, 1772–1834," in Philip D. Morgan and Sean Hawkins, *Black Experience and the Empire*, Oxford History of the British Empire Companion Series (Oxford: Oxford University Press, 2004), 122.

21. Brown does not cite it, but there is sober confirmation of his remarks if one turns to Burke's remarks on slavery in the American South that occur in the "Speech on Conciliation with America" (1775). There Burke writes, stretching credulity, "Slaves are often much attached to their masters. A general wild offer of liberty, would not always be accepted. History furnishes few instances of it. It is sometimes as hard to persuade slaves to be free, as it is to compel freemen to be slaves." Burke, *Writings and Speeches*, 3:131.

22. The events took place in June 1793. My thanks to David Geggus for discussing this reference with me. Jeremy Popkin, *Facing Racial Revolution: Eyewitness Accounts of the Haitian Insurrection* (Chicago: University of Chicago Press, 2007), 180–232, collects several vivid accounts of this event.

23. Burke, *Correspondence*, August 23, 1793, 7:415.

24. Laurent Dubois notes, citing the historian David Geggus, "By the eve of the revolution Saint-Domingue was 'the world's leading producer of both sugar and coffee.' It exported 'as much sugar as Jamaica, Cuba, and Brazil combined' and half the world's coffee." As for the entanglement of France's wealth with St. Domingue, as many as one million of France's 25 million inhabitants depended on the colonial trade, and approximately 15 percent of the members of the National Assembly owned colonial property. Laurent Dubois, *Avengers of the New World: The Story of the Haitian Revolution* (Cambridge, Mass.: Belknap Press, 2004), 21.

25. In a striking testament to the power of this rhetorical image, made to encapsulate the "meaning" of events in this period, there is a similar reference to Pandora's box to describe the decree of April 4, 1792, which serves as an interesting planter echo of Burke's use in his parliamentary speech. See Popkin, *Facing Racial Revolution*, "The Destruction of Cap Français in June 1793," 204. The decree of April 4, 1792, by the French National Convention granted full citizenship and political equality to free *gens de couleur* and free blacks (though it did not emancipate the enslaved).

26. These lines from *Macbeth* are also discussed by Samuel Johnson in his study of Shakespeare, who defends them against the charge of introducing "too much levity for the solemnity of enchantment." Interestingly, he invokes a description from Camden's *Account of Ireland* (from *Britannia*, published 1586) to show that such practices are in fact prevalent among the "uncivilised natives of that country." Johnson quotes Camden: "'When any one gets a fall,' says the informer of Camden, 'he starts up, and turning three times to the right digs a whole in the earth, for they imagine that there is a spirit in the ground, and if he falls sick in two or three days,

they send one of their women that is skilled in that way to the place, where she says, I call thee ... from the groves, the woods, the rivers, and the fens, from the Fairies red, black, white.' There was likewise a book written before the time of Shakespeare describing ... the 'colours' of spirits." Samuel Johnson, *The Works of Samuel Johnson* (London: W. Baynes and Son, 1824), 10:104–5. Thus the witches' lines, which are not racial in their origin, are given this valence by Burke's prefatory remark to the citation that in the French West India colonies "blacks rose against whites, whites against blacks." And yet even earlier in the song from *Macbeth* itself, the witches add to the cauldron such exotica as "liver of blaspheming Jew ... Nose of Turk, and Tartar's lips" (IV, ii, 26–29).

27. The parent-child relationship as a model for the metropole-colony relationship is something Burke very clearly presumes.

28. See Dubois, *Avengers of the New World*, 142–65; Popkin, *Facing Racial Revolution*, 184. For the text of Sonthonax's decree, see Laurent Dubois and John D. Garrigus, *Slave Revolution in the Caribbean, 1789–1804: A Brief History with Documents* (New York: Palgrave Macmillan, 2006), 120–25.

29. Dubois, *Avengers of the New World*, 47–48. Also see the section titled "Jurisdiction in the French Revolution" in David Brion Davis, *The Problem of Slavery in the Age of Revolution, 1770–1823* (New York: Oxford University Press, 1999), 137–48.

30. Davis, *The Problem of Slavery in the Age of Revolution*, 143; Dubois, *Avengers of the New World*, 89. For a consideration of the relationship of the Rights of Man to dominated or marginalized elements within French society, see Shanti Marie Singham, "Betwixt Cattle and Men: Jews, Blacks, and Women, and the Declaration of the Rights of Man," *The French Idea of Freedom: The Old Regime and the Declaration of Rights of 1789*, ed. Dale Van Kley (Stanford: Stanford University Press, 1994).

31. He was certainly justified in this fear; consider the symbolically rich and ironic episode noted by C. L. R. James, when French soldiers sent by Napoleon to quell rebellion on the island of St. Domingue wonder if they are fighting on the wrong side as they face insurgent former slaves singing the "Marseillaise." C. L. R. James, *The Black Jacobins: Toussaint L'Ouverture and the San Domingo Revolution*, 2nd ed. (New York: Vintage Books, 1989), 318. This is also commented upon by Susan Buck-Morss, "Hegel and Haiti," *Critical Inquiry* 26.4 (2000): 865.

32. Burke uses this term in a letter to Earl Fitzwilliam; the letter is cited in chapter 4.

33. Cobbett, *Parliamentary History of England*, 29:418.

34. Ibid., 29:418–19. The passage from Milton is from *Paradise Lost*, bk. 2, ll. 666–73.

35. Burke, *Writings and Speeches*, 1:231–32.

36. Cobbett, *Parliamentary History of England*, 29:379. The original phrase is slightly different: "I do not know the method of drawing up an indictment against an whole people." Burke, *Writings and Speeches*, 3:132.

37. Cobbett, *Parliamentary History of England*, 29:380.

38. Ibid., 29:419.

39. Abbé Grégoire and other deputies had raised the issue of race and citizenship on May 9, 1791, in the National Assembly. The ambiguous decree regarding *gens de couleur* occurred on May 15, 1791. Dubois and Garrigus, *Slave Revolution in the Caribbean*, 84. Burke's speech on May 11, 1791, takes place in this context and after the execution of the free-colored leader Vincent Ogé in February 1791, who had been agitating for a March 1790 decree granting citizenship right to free people of color to be implemented. Dubois, *Avengers of the New World*, 86–89; Carolyn Fick, *The Making of*

Haiti: The Saint Domingue Revolution from Below (Knoxville: University of Tennessee Press, 1990), 83.

40. Indeed he defends himself on the question of consistency even in this speech, by remarking that in the American case invoked by Fox, "he [Burke] was favourable to the Americans, because he supposed they were fighting, not to acquire absolute speculative liberty, but to keep what they had under the English constitution." Cobbett, *Parliamentary History of England*, 29:395. He refers again to Fox's attribution to him of a "shameless inconsistency" after the publication of his opinions on France (29:418).

41. For a discussion of the much overlooked "war within a war," which took place during the Haitian Revolution, see the subtle reflection on the making of history in Michel-Rolph Trouillot, *Silencing the Past: Power and the Production of History* (Boston: Beacon Press, 1995). The chapter titled "The Three Faces of *Sans Souci*: Glory and Silences in the Haitian Revolution" examines the erasure of consideration of the Haitian Revolution alongside the American and French Revolutions of the same period. Another fascinating work on St. Domingue before its transformation into Haiti is James E. McClellan, *Colonialism and Science: Saint Domingue in the Old Regime* (Baltimore: Johns Hopkins University Press, 1992). His introduction traces some of the implications of the neglect of the case of Haiti in otherwise very thorough studies of the region, such as Nicholas P. Canny and Anthony Pagden, *Colonial Identity in the Atlantic World, 1500–1800* (Princeton: Princeton University Press, 1987). See McClellan, 18–20.

42. Hannah Arendt, *Eichmann in Jerusalem: A Report on the Banality of Evil* (New York: Penguin Books, 1994), 252. Arendt's own horror at Frantz Fanon's apparent defense of violence in an anticolonial movement provides an interesting modern parallel to consider alongside Burke's view of St. Domingue. See Hannah Arendt, *On Violence* (New York: Harcourt Brace, 1970), 65, where she asserts that Fanon glorifies "violence for its own sake." As David Macey has noted in his exhaustive biography of Fanon, Arendt focuses exclusively on Fanon's use by black radical movements in the United States during the 1960s and nowhere mentions Algeria. David Macey, *Frantz Fanon: A Biography* (New York: Picador, 2000).

As a critic, Burke has been compared to George Orwell by some; in the discussion of massacre becoming a "regular art" among the Jacobins there is some affinity with Orwell's descriptions of Engsoc. See O'Brien's exchange with Isaiah Berlin, appended to O'Brien, *The Great Melody*, 609. In one of his most pronounced attempts to understand Burke in this manner, O'Brien writes, "The French Revolution was abundantly productive of liberal documents and liberal speeches, but its transactions were not in accord with those documents and speeches. The *Déclarations des Droits de l'Homme et du Citoyen* is no better a guide to the realities of the French Revolution than Stalin's Constitution of 1936 was a guide to the realities of life in the Soviet Union. Similarly Burke, in attacking the French Revolution and its would-be imitators in Britain, was no more reactionary than was George Orwell when he attacked the Russian Revolution and *its* would-be imitators in Britain" (608–9). O'Brien classes Burke as an Enlightenment thinker who is both a "pluralist" and concerned with what a "later age would call the totalitarian tendencies in the French Revolution" (609).

43. Burke, *Correspondence*, 7:415.

44. Burke mentions this explicitly in the parliamentary discussion: "He [Burke] recurred to the events of the year 1780, and mentioned the dreadful consequences of the riots occasioned by Lord George Gordon." From "Debate in the commons on the Quebec government bill," Cobbett, *Parliamentary History of England*, 29:386.

45. Burke was a discreet supporter of the Catholic Relief Act. Nonetheless when Lord Gordon led a group of 60,000 Protestant supporters who were angry at the bill's passage through the House of Commons, Burke's participation became known. His support for these measures, perceived as Irish issues, may have been partly responsible for his later loss of support in Bristol (the Gordon riots were in June 1780, and Burke withdrew from the September 1780 Bristol elections). Burke refers to this support as one of the "charges" against him in his "Speech at Bristol, in the Guildhall, Previous to the Election." See O'Brien, *The Great Melody*, 77–86. The more recent and far more comprehensive biography of Burke by F. P. Lock omits the colorful reference to a sword, but details how Burke dismissed soldiers sent to his house for protection and plunged into the crowd to engage in argument and discussion: "He preferred an aggressive defiance to skulking behind the barricades." F. P. Lock, *Edmund Burke*, 2 vols. (Oxford: Clarendon Press, 1998–2006), 1:468.

46. Dubois, *Avengers of the New World*, 84–85.

47. Partha Chatterjee, *Lineages of Political Society: Studies in Postcolonial Democracy*, Cultures of History (New York: Columbia University Press, 2011), 250.

48. Burke carried on a substantive correspondence with Pierre-Gaëton Dupont regarding the translation of the *Reflections* in 1790 (see Burke, *Correspondence*, 6:144). Several years later, in 1794, Burke refers to him as his "worthy and unfortunate friend" (10:29). In a letter to John King, undersecretary of state to the Duke of Portland in the Home Department, dated February 8, 1795, Burke writes, "I find, that De Curt, of whom the D[uke] of Portland spoke to me, is named agent to the superior Council, that is the supreme Court of Justice in Martinico [Martinique]. Dupont told me, you were so good as to suggest an employment of the same kind for him with regard to St Domingo. I think the employment of the utmost necessity on account of the appeals. I dont [sic] know so fit a man for it as Dupont who is a Lawyer that knows their language and ours and their Law, with a very tolerable notion of the English Law. Your opinion of his Talents and integrity agrees with mine; and you know how much I wish every thing he wishes" (9:442–43).

49. Burke, *Writings and Speeches*, 8:268–69.

50. On this matter, see Ross John Swartz Hoffman, *Edmund Burke, New York Agent*, Memoirs of the American Philosophical Society, vol. 41 (Philadelphia: American Philosophical Society, 1956).

51. Burke, *Writings and Speeches*, 8:268, note 1.

52. Translation mine. The Cormier passage reads, "Ils ont assassiné des Blancs sans haine... disant.... Cet homme n'étoit pas méchant, nous l'avons tué à cause de la nation." Ibid., 8:268, note 1.

53. Ibid., 9:87.

54. Ibid., 9:96.

55. Ibid., 9:96–97.

56. Note too that (masculine) France is figured as a rival suitor to Britain in pursuit of a feminized Spain; the yielding of the "fairest" part of that colony (St. Domingue) during her (Spain's) "honeymoon" is a sexual violation of the "solemn treaty."

57. Burke, *Writings and Speeches*, 9:98–99.

58. Ibid., 9:98, emphasis mine. Auckland's pamphlet was titled *Some Remarks on the Apparent Circumstances of War in the Fourth Week of October 1795*. See the editor's prefatory note, 9:44.

59. Ibid., 9:99. The word *piratical* is in fact used more than once in this passage to refer to France in the West Indies.

60. This is a citation from Auckland's text; the emphasis is Burke's own. Ibid., 9:99. For the original, see William Eden Auckland, *Some Remarks on the Apparent Circumstances of the War in the Fourth Week of October 1795* (London: Printed for J. Walter, 1795), 60.

61. Burke, *Writings and Speeches*, 9:99.

62. For an interpretation of this work, see Darcy Grimaldo Grigsby, *Extremities: Painting Empire in Post-Revolutionary France* (London: Yale University Press, 2002). For a description of Belley's journey from St. Domingue to Paris via Philadelphia (where he was forced to hide from angry white émigrés from St. Domingue), see Dubois, *Avengers of the New World*, 168–70.

63. See the thoughtful chapter on Burke in Jennifer Pitts, *A Turn to Empire: The Rise of Liberal Imperialism in Britain and France* (Princeton: Princeton University Press, 2005), which highlights Burke's sympathetic concern for a Jewish community on the island of St. Eustache. The idea of Burke's defense of the vulnerable element in a body politic is one that David Bromwich has also forcefully made.

64. From Belley's speech of 1795, "The True Colors of the Planters, or the System of the Hotel Massiac, Exposed by Gouli," in Dubois and Garrigus, *Slave Revolution in the Caribbean*, 147. Emphasizing their status as needlessly ignored "patriots," Belley continues, "It is certain that if these brave patriots had arms and ammunition, the undeserving blood of the English and the planter traitor would water this land that has been dirtied by their presence for too long" (147).

65. See Yves Benot and Marcel Dorigny, *Rétablissement de l'esclavage dans les colonies françaises, 1802* (Paris: Maisonneuve et Larose, 2003).

66. Jean-Baptiste Belley, "The True Colors of the Planters, of the System of the Hotel Massiac, Exposed by Gouli (1795)" in Dubois and Garrigus, *Slave Revolution in the Caribbean*, 144–47.

67. From his speech, "On the Moral and Political Principles of Domestic Policy," given on February 5, 1794. The full passage clearly invokes the language of Montesquieu with its reference to motivating springs (discussed in chapter 2): "Si le ressort du gouvernement populaire dans la paix est la vertu, le ressort du gouvernement populaire en révolution est à la fois *la vertu et la terreur*: la vertu, sans laquelle la terreur est funeste; la terreur, sans laquelle la vertu est impuissante. La terreur n'est autre chose que la justice prompte, sévère, inflexible; elle est donc une émanation de la vertu; elle est moins un principe particulier, qu'une conséquence du principe général de la démocratie, appliqué aux plus pressans besoins de la patrie." From "Sur les principes de morale politique," Maximilien Robespierre, *Œuvres complètes de Maximilien Robespierre*, ed. V. Barbier and Charles Vellay (Paris: Aux bureaux de la Revue historiques de la révolution française, 1910), 10:357.

68. Burke, *Correspondence*, 5:255.

69. Thomas R Metcalf, *Ideologies of the Raj*, The New Cambridge History of India (New York: Cambridge University Press, 1997).

70. Burke, *Writings and Speeches*, 9:97.

71. Ibid., 9:99.

72. "Representatives of the French people, until now we have only decreed liberty in a selfish manner and for ourselves alone. But today we make a proclamation directed to the universe—and future generations will find their glory in this decree—we decree universal liberty. Yesterday, when the president gave a fraternal kiss to the deputies of color, I saw the moment when the Convention would have to decree the liberty of our

brothers." Georges Jacques Danton, *Oeuvres de Danton, recueillies et annotées par A. Vermorel*, 2nd ed. (Paris: A. Faure, 1867), 247.

73. "But after having accorded the favor of liberty, it is necessary for us to be, so to speak, its 'moderators.' Let us return to the Committee of Public Safety and Colonies in order to arrange the means of rendering this decree useful to humanity, without any danger to it." Ibid., 247.

74. "We have dishonored our glory in cutting short our labor. The grand principles developed by [Bartolome de] Las Casas have been ignored. We labor for future generations—let us launch liberty in the colonies; it is today that the English are dead! [Applause.] In throwing liberty to the New World, it will carry very abundant fruits there, and will put down deep roots. In vain would [William] Pitt and his accomplices postpone by political consideration the pleasure of this favor. They will be pushed [*être entraînés*] into an abyss. France will regain the level and influence which will secure its power, its territory, and its population." Ibid., 247–48.

75. Burke, *Writings and Speeches*, 9:264.

76. Ibid., 9:265.

77. Ibid., 9:266–67, 264, 267, 270, 271.

78. Ibid., 9:271, 273, 272.

79. Ibid., 9:272–73. The editor notes that as many as 25,000 British army men died from yellow fever.

80. Ibid., 9:273.

81. Ibid., 9:274.

82. This is discussed in part 1.

83. Burke, *Writings and Speeches*, 9:274.

84. Ibid. Similarly, as noted earlier in this chapter, Burke writes "Cannibalism frequent in France also" in the margin of his volume of Cormier's *Mémoire sur la Situation de Saint-Domingue*.

85. Ibid., 9:275, emphasis mine.

86. Ibid.

87. See the footnote for the fragment from which this is taken, ibid., 9:276.

88. See the chapter on Philip Francis titled "A Young Alcibiades" in Ranajit Guha, *A Rule of Property for Bengal: An Essay on the Idea of Permanent Settlement*, 2nd ed. (New Delhi: Orient Longman, 1982). For a far more detailed study of Francis (and his rivalry with Hastings) written in a period still very invested in the British Empire in India, see Sophia Weitzman, *Warren Hastings and Philip Francis* (Manchester: University of Manchester Press, 1929). Weitzman makes the case that "Francis, as the source and inspiration of Burke's India policy, must be recognised as the moving spirit in Hastings' Impeachment" and was the "author, producer and stage manager of the whole performance" (171). Her deployment of the theatrical metaphor is explicit and apt.

89. George C McElroy, "Burke, William (1728–1798)," *Oxford Dictionary of National Biography*, ed. H. C. G. Matthew and Brian Harrison (Oxford: Oxford University Press, 2004). For an older but more detailed account, see Dixon Wecter, "Edmund Burke and His Kinsmen: A Study of the Statesman's Financial Integrity and Private Relationships," *University of Colorado Studies* 1.1 (1939).

90. Letter to Philip Francis, December 24, 1778, in Burke, *Correspondence*, 4:33.

91. See the interesting consideration of Burke's formulation of "doctrine of imperial sovereignty" in Richard Bourke, "Liberty, Authority, and Trust in Burke's idea of Empire," *Journal of the History of Ideas* 61.3 (2000).

92. This speech is from 1775. Burke, *Writings and Speeches*, 3:105–68.

93. "All these circumstances are not, I confess, very favorable to the idea of our attempting to govern India at all. But there we are; there we are placed by the Sovereign Disposer: and we must do the best we can in our situation. The situation of man is the preceptor of his duty." Ibid., 5:404.

94. "In this Character of the Americans, a love of Freedom is the predominating feature.... This fierce spirit of Liberty is stronger in the English Colonies probably than in any other people of the Earth.... The people of the Colonies are descendents of Englishmen. The Colonists emigrated from you, when this part of your character was most predominant.... They are therefore not only devoted to Liberty, but to Liberty according to English ideas, and on English principles. Abstract liberty is not to be found." From "Speech on Conciliation with America," ibid., 3:120.

95. The Oxford English Dictionary defines *cutchery* (from the Hindi term *kachahri*) as an office of administration or courthouse. A more detailed and entertaining discussion of the term is available in Henry Yule, A. C. Burnell, and William Crooke, *Hobson-Jobson; A Glossary of Colloquial Anglo-Indian Words and Phrases, and of Kindred Terms, Etymological, Historical, Geographical and Discursive* (London: J. Murray, 1903).

96. "Speech on Bengal Judicature Bill, 27 June 1781," in Burke, *Writings and Speeches*, 5:141. This passage is discussed by O'Brien, *The Great Melody*, 310–11.

97. The word *enervate*, which Burke uses here, also arises frequently in early eighteenth-century discussions of luxury and social progress.

98. See the discussion of envy and *ressentiment* with regard to Diderot in chapter 3. But Burke too argues that the success of the Glorious Revolution in England allowed it precisely to defuse an acute sense of class envy, unlike the case in France.

99. Cited in P. J. Marshall, "Introduction," Burke, *Writings and Speeches*, 5:2.

100. Ibid., 5:40.

101. O'Brien, *The Great Melody*, 305.

102. Marshall, introductory notes, "Restoring Lord Pigot," in Burke, *Writings and Speeches*, 5:35.

103. Ibid., 5:36, 37.

104. The revival of interest in Carl Schmitt raises many of these questions. Famous for his critique of liberal constitutionalism, Schmitt held the public nature of Parliament to be central to the idea of liberalism. In this very obvious sense, Burke's later attacks on secrecy and cabal and his very intimate and lifelong association with Parliament as an institution are at odds with this kind of conservatism (or reactionary radicalism, as some have called it). Burke attacked the closed and secret meetings that the East India Company made use of in his "Speech on the Secret Committee, 30 April 1781," ibid., 5:134–39 (written at about the same time as his "Speech on the Bengal Judicature Bill"). Schmitt's own rejection of Romanticism as a component of the conservative tradition makes him different from the manner in which Burke has often been read. Nonetheless this does not stop Schmitt from making frequent use of Burke for his agenda. Consider the following: "The aversion that Burke, de Maistre, and Bonald have for 'artifice' in political affairs, artificial constitutions based on the calculations of a clever individual, and the fabricators of constitutions and political geometricians arises from the feeling that the basis of all historical-political events lies in a superindividual power—where *basis* in their work signifies both causal explanation and normative justification or legitimation." Carl Schmitt, *Political Romanticism,*

trans. Guy Oakes (Cambridge, Mass.: MIT Press, 1986), 81. But Schmitt also sees the *public* nature of Burke's writing as central to its form: "When Burke discourses on duration or the national community and rises to a grandiose rhetoric, he always remains the statesmen with a great responsibility: He wants to make a case to a public of normal human beings and defend it before them" (130).

105. Burke, *Writings and Speeches*, 5:37.
106. Ibid., 5:39.
107. Ibid., 5:39, note 2.
108. Ibid., 5:40.
109. As with his arguments regarding France, Burke does not hesitate to make use of statistics regarding population when it aids his argument. So, in the opening of his discussion in the "Speech on Conciliation with America" on March 22, 1775, he writes, "The first thing that we have to consider with regard to the nature of the object is—the number of people in the Colonies [i.e., America]. I have taken for some years a good deal of pains on that point. I can by no calculation justify myself in placing the number below Two Millions of inhabitants of our own European blood and colour." Ibid., 3:111. This paragraph grounds the idea of the emergence of a "nation" out of a rapidly growing population: "Such is the strength with which population shoots in that part of the world. . . . Your children do not grow faster from infancy to manhood, then they spread from families to communities, and from villages to nations."
110. The expression is from Gayatri Spivak. For an early article on this, see Bhikhu Parekh, "Liberalism and Colonialism: A Critique of Locke and Mill," *The Decolonization of Imagination: Culture, Knowledge and Power*, ed. Jan Nederveen Pieterse and Bhikhu Parekh (London: Zed Books, 1995). For a more recent study of Mill, see chapter 5 of Pitts, *A Turn to Empire*.
111. Burke, *Writings and Speeches*, 5:40, note 2.
112. The deeper political question behind this is the just basis for a rebellion. This should be connected with the debate elsewhere in the *Reflections* concerning the right of the people to cashier kings, which speakers such as Dr. Price asserted in the revolution controversy. Price's assertion implied that the people are the basis of the sovereign's power, which Burke directly disputes in his work.
113. Burke, *Writings and Speeches*, 3:161–162, 164. My thanks to David Jakalski for drawing my attention to this passage.
114. Ibid., 3:164, editor's note 1.
115. Burke uses this phrase on ibid., 3:164. For this notion of pastoral power, see Michel Foucault, *The Foucault Effect: Studies in Governmentality* (London: Harvester Wheatsheaf, 1991).
116. Burke, *Writings and Speeches*, 3:165.
117. Ibid., 3:164–65.
118. "Speech on Fox's East India Bill," ibid., 5:383.
119. Ibid., 3:165.
120. Ibid., 3:316–17.
121. "Concatenation, *n.*," *Oxford English Dictionary*, 2nd ed. (New York: Oxford University Press, 1989), definition 2.
122. Ernesto Laclau and Chantal Mouffe, *Hegemony and Socialist Strategy: Towards a Radical Democratic Politics* (London: Verso, 1985), make use of the term in their Gramscian description of the structure of contemporary social movements.

123. "A Philosophical Enquiry into the Origin of Our Ideas of the Sublime and Beautiful" in Burke, *Writings and Speeches*, vol. 1.

124. See the persuasive chapter comparing the notions of sympathy within the thought of Adam Smith and Edmund Burke in Luke Gibbons, *Edmund Burke and Ireland: Aesthetics, Politics and the Colonial Sublime* (New York: Cambridge University Press, 2003).

125. Yves Benot, *Diderot, de l'athéisme à l'anticolonialisme* (Paris: François Maspero, 1970).

126. Seamus Deane, *Foreign Affections: Essays on Edmund Burke* (Cork: Cork University Press / Field Day, 2005), chap. 6, elaborates this with regard to Ireland.

Epilogue

1. C. L. R. James, *The Black Jacobins: Toussaint L'Ouverture and the San Domingo Revolution*, 2nd ed. (New York: Vintage Books, 1989), 198, emphasis mine. See the discussion of this moment in David Scott, *Conscripts of Modernity: The Tragedy of Colonial Enlightenment* (Durham, N.C.: Duke University Press, 2004), 219. Making reference to James, David Brion Davis, *The Problem of Slavery in the Age of Revolution, 1770–1823* (New York: Oxford University Press, 1999), also discusses the significance of Toussaint in relation to the thought of Hegel in the epilogue to his work, "Toussaint L'Ouverture and the Phenomenology of Mind," 557–64. However, his emphasis is on Hegel's "naive" acclaiming of Napoleon.

2. "An Answer to the Question: What Is Enlightenment?," in Immanuel Kant, *Kant: Political Writings*, Cambridge Texts in the History of Political Thought, ed. Hans Siegbert Reiss (Cambridge: Cambridge University Press, 1991), 54.

3. James makes a similar point regarding Robespierre's radicalism in comparison to Toussaint: "Robespierre, however, revolutionary as he was, remained bourgeois and had reached the extreme limit of the bourgeois revolution." James, *The Black Jacobins*, 177.

4. The closing pages of James's work make this clear: "The blacks of Africa are more advanced, nearer ready than were the slaves of San Domingo." Ibid., 375–77.

5. Jonathan Israel, *Radical Enlightenment: Philosophy and the Making of Modernity, 1650–1750* (Oxford: Oxford University Press, 2001).

6. James, *The Black Jacobins*, 317–18. For an interesting consideration of the limits of pure oppositionality within anticolonial thought, see Leela Gandhi, *Affective Communities: Anticolonial Thought, Fin-de-Siècle Radicalism, and the Politics of Friendship*, Politics, History, and Culture (Durham, N.C.: Duke University Press, 2006), chap. 2. There are many lines from *The Black Jacobins* to support this interpretation; let the following serve us here: "It is Toussaint's supreme merit that while he saw European civilisation as a valuable and necessary thing, and strove to lay its foundations among his people, he never has the illusion that it conferred any moral superiority." James, *The Black Jacobins*, 271. It is a passage that James adduces to remind readers that Toussaint did not possess a naïve understanding of Europe and European civilization.

7. "I can't sleep. There is something frightening in the air. And I have just opened my Raynal to read an even more frightening thing.... The Abbe is saying: 'A courageous chief only is wanted.' I have read it a thousand times before, but it is as if I had seen it for the first time." Spoken by the character of Toussaint in the play James wrote in 1938, also titled *The Black Jacobins*. C. L. R. James, *The C. L. R. James Reader*, ed. Anna Grimshaw (Oxford: Blackwell, 1992), 71.

8. "I can recall a discussion where several comrades and I were railing against Europe and its evils. C. L. R. intervened with 'But my dear Bracey, I am a Black European, that is my training and my outlook.' C. L. R. said this without apology." From a conversation with John Bracey in Chicago, reproduced in Paul Buhle, *C. L. R. James: His Life and Work* (London: Alison & Busby, 1986).

9. This passage, all the more appealing for coming from his autobiographical book on cricket, continues, "I already knew long passages of him [Burke] by heart. There in the very centre of all this was William Beldham [an eighteenth-century cricket player whose description James cites] and his cut. I passed over the fact which I noted instantly that the phrase, 'He hit the House just between wind and water,' had been used by Burke himself, about Charles Townsend in the speech on American Taxation." C. L. R. James, *Beyond a Boundary* (Durham, N.C.: Duke University Press, 1993), 6. In the opening pages of "How I Wrote the Black Jacobins (14 June 1971)," James links his early education in literary classics with a kind of instinct that led him to write on Toussaint Louverture. C. L. R. James, "Lectures on the Black Jacobins," *Small Axe* 8 (2000).

10. J. G. A. Pocock, *Barbarism and Religion*, 4 vols. (New York: Cambridge University Press, 1999–), 1:138. See Stephen Eric Bronner, *Reclaiming the Enlightenment: Toward a Politics of Radical Engagement* (New York: Columbia University Press, 2004). Bronner is, however, more interested in defending critical theory from a perceived nemesis in culturalism, deconstruction, and the like (162–63). The origin of such a defense of the Enlightenment in contemporary critical thought may be found in the dialogue Habermas conducted with several French thinkers, including Foucault. See chapters 9 and 10 of Jürgen Habermas, *The Philosophical Discourse of Modernity: Twelve Lectures*, trans. Frederick G. Lawrence, Studies in Contemporary German Social Thought. (Cambridge, Mass.: MIT Press, 1987).

11. James, *The Black Jacobins*, 288.

12. "The Voyage in and the Emergence of Opposition," in Edward W. Said, *Culture and Imperialism* (New York: Vintage Books, 1994).

13. James, *The Black Jacobins*, 306.

14. Speaking of Robespierre's radical comments on the "colonial question" and slavery, James writes, "It was magnificent but it was not abolition. It was only the word slavery Robespierre was objecting to—not the thing." Ibid., 77.

15. Theodor W. Adorno, *Minima Moralia: Reflections from Damaged Life*, trans. E. F. N. Jephcott (London: Verso, 1978), 52.

16. Sankar Muthu, *Enlightenment against Empire* (Princeton: Princeton University Press, 2003).

17. Jennifer Pitts, *A Turn to Empire: The Rise of Liberal Imperialism in Britain and France* (Princeton: Princeton University Press, 2005).

18. One overlooked but interesting example from the French context, which brings together a philological and historical approach, is Sylvia Murr, "Les conditions d'émergence du discours sur l'Inde au Siècle des Lumières," *Inde et littératures*, ed. Marie-Claude Porcher, vol. 7, Collection Purushartha (Paris: Editions de l'Ecole des hautes études en sciences sociales, 1983). Nietzsche's telling remark regarding philology makes clear his broader understanding of it as a species of critique: "I do not know what meaning classical philology would have for our age if not to have an untimely effect within it, that is, to act against the age and so have an effect on the age to the advantage, it is to be hoped, of a coming age." Friedrich Wilhelm Nietzsche, *On the*

Advantage and Disadvantage of History for Life, trans. Peter Preuss (Indianapolis: Hackett, 1980), 8. On this topic, see James I. Porter, *Nietzsche and the Philology of the Future* (Stanford: Stanford University Press, 2000).

19. Although Mehta's book does not put it this way, it is exemplary for showing the manner in which empire forms and deforms certain concepts deployed by liberalism. Uday Singh Mehta, *Liberalism and Empire: A Study in Nineteenth-Century British Liberal Thought* (Chicago: University of Chicago Press, 1999).

20. "I will long remember the day I first read *Orientalism*. . . . [It] was a book which talked of things I felt I had known all along but had never found the language to formulate with clarity. . . . The chain of thought that began with my reading of *Orientalism* led some five years later to a book on the construction of the political discourse of Indian nationalism." Partha Chatterjee, "Their Own Words? An Essay for Edward Said," *Edward Said: A Critical Reader*, ed. Michael Sprinker (Oxford: Blackwell, 1992), 194–95.

21. Ranajit Guha, *A Rule of Property for Bengal: An Essay on the Idea of Permanent Settlement*. Le Monde d'outre-mer, passé et présent (Paris: Mouton, 1963). On the question of intellectual generations, I have in mind David Scott, "Thinking through Intellectual Generations: Tradition, Memory, Criticism," unpublished lecture delivered at the University of Illinois at Chicago, April 27, 2011.

22. Theodor W. Adorno, "On Subject and Object," trans. Henry W. Pickford, *Critical Models: Interventions and Catchwords* (New York: Columbia University Press, 2005).

23. The contrasts between these two, however, were very stark on particular topics, such as popular or mass culture in America and the significance of jazz, both of which James expressed great interest in. See particularly his letter dated June 1953 in "Letters to Literary Critics," James, *The C. L. R. James Reader*, 220–31.

24. Adorno, *Minima Moralia: Reflections from Damaged Life*, 52. Neil Lazarus argues that the significance of this phrase for Adorno relates to the failure of tradition in delivering a "universalistically conceived notion of social freedom." Neil Lazarus, "Introduction: Hating Tradition Properly," *Nationalism and Cultural Practice in the Postcolonial World* (New York: Cambridge University Press, 1999), 3. His reading of this aphorism notes that it reveals Adorno as both "condescending" and "Eurocentric" while also remaining "radical" and "anti-capitalist"; Lazarus's focus is more on the ideological contradictions of "postcolonial studies" as an academically constituted field.

25. See Theodor W. Adorno, *The Jargon of Authenticity*, trans. Knut Tarnowski and Frederic Will (Evanston, Ill.: Northwestern University Press, 1973).

26. Theodor W. Adorno, *Minima moralia: Reflexionen aus dem beschädigten Leben*, Bibliothek Suhrkamp (Frankfurt am Main: Suhrkamp, 1982), 60, emphasis mine.

27. This seems to be the clear message of "Pitfalls of National Consciousness" in Frantz Fanon, *Wretched of the Earth* (New York: Grove Press, 1961). James himself notes the limitations of Toussaint, though he is reflectively ambivalent as to whether this failing lies with the European Enlightenment or with Toussaint himself. James, *The Black Jacobins*, 288–90. Nonetheless the shift from Toussaint to Dessalines in James's text is emplotted as a similar failing of certain principles, one that deforms the emancipatory language the former deployed.

28. Adorno, *Minima Moralia: Reflections from Damaged Life*, xvii, notes the year and place (as if to mark the displacement?). Detlev Claussen, *Theodor W. Adorno: One*

Last Genius, trans. Rodney Livingstone (Cambridge, Mass.: Belknap Press, 2008), 142, comments on the significance of this, and of the form of *Minima Moralia* deriving from fragments composed for Horkheimer's fiftieth birthday.

29. Adorno, *Minima Moralia: Reflections from Damaged Life*, 52.

30. Max Horkheimer and Theodor W. Adorno, *Dialectic of Enlightenment*, trans. John Cumming (New York: Continuum, 1994). For an interesting discussion of their views of America and of the links between *Minima Moralia* and *Dialectic of Enlightenment*, see Peter Uwe Hohendahl, *Prismatic Thought: Theodor W. Adorno, Modern German Culture and Literature* (Lincoln: University of Nebraska Press, 1995), 21-44.

31. Adorno, *Minima Moralia: Reflections from Damaged Life*, 52.

32. Adorno, *Minima moralia: Reflexionen aus dem beschädigten Leben*, 60.

33. See Stefan Müller-Doohm, *Adorno: A Biography*, trans. Rodney Livingstone (Cambridge: Polity Press, 2005), 193-95, for a compelling discussion of his letters written during his few years at Merton College, Oxford (1934-37).

34. Horkheimer and Adorno, *Dialectic of Enlightenment*, "The Transformation of Ideas into Domination," 211-14, makes a moral tale out of Brahmanical domination—"a gild of priests"—over India. There are other, brief references to the Vedas, mostly comparative in nature with Greek and Christian thought (13).

35. Adorno, *Minima Moralia: Reflections from Damaged Life*, 52, 52-53.

36. Max Scheler, *Ressentiment*, trans. Lewis Coser and William Holdheim, ed. Manfred S. Frings (Milwaukee, Wisc.: Marquette University Press, 1994).

37. Adorno, *Minima Moralia: Reflections from Damaged Life*, 53.

38. The philosopher and biologist Hans Driesch defended a notion of vitalism, implying a component of life beyond physical and chemical processes. Hans Driesch, *The History and Theory of Vitalism*, trans. C. K. Ogden (London: Macmillan, 1914). The meaning of Adorno's reference to Rickert is clear from the preoccupations of one of his most well-known works, Heinrich Rickert, *Science and History: A Critique of Positivist Epistemology*, The William Volker Fund Series in the Humane Studies (Princeton, N.J.: Van Nostrand, 1962).

39. This alternative is what Partha Chatterjee explores in his fascinating chapter, "Five Hundred Years of Fear and Love," in *Lineages of Political Society: Studies in Postcolonial Democracy*, Cultures of History (New York: Columbia University Press, 2011). He also, however, considers the paramount role of "pastoral power" in the context of the British rule of India, namely the desire to be loved by one's subjects: "What is new about the English rulers of India, as distinct from earlier indigenous regimes, is their need, already apparent from the later eighteenth century, to be loved by their alien Indian subjects" (40).

40. Adorno, *Minima Moralia: Reflections from Damaged Life*, 52.

41. Michel Foucault, "Kant on Enlightenment and Revolution," *Economy and Society* 15.1 (1986): 89. "Bref, il me semble qu'on voit apparaître dans le texte de Kant la question du présent comme événement philosophique auquel appartient le philosophe qui en parle." Michel Foucault, "Qu'est-ce que les Lumières (Extrait du cours du 5 janvier 1983)," *Dits et écrits, 1954-1988*, ed. Daniel Defert, François Ewald, and Jacques Lagrange, Bibliothèque des sciences humaines (Paris: Gallimard, 1994), 4:680.

42. Michael Rothberg, *Multidirectional Memory: Remembering the Holocaust in the Age of Decolonization* (Stanford: Stanford University Press, 2009) explores productively the intersection of these events.

43. Michel Foucault, "What Is Critique?," trans. Kevin Paul Geiman, *What Is Enlightenment? Eighteenth-Century Answers and Twentieth-Century Questions*, ed.

James Schmidt (Berkeley: University of California Press, 1996), 391. "Je voudrais tout de suite, en abordant ce problème qui nous rend fraternels par rapport à l'École de Francfort, noter que de toutes façons, faire de l'Aufklärung la question centrale, cela veut dire à coup sûr un certain nombre de choses." Michel Foucault, "Qu'est-ce que la critique? [Critique et Aufklärung], Compte rendu de la séance du 27 mai 1978," *Bulletin de la Société française de la Philosophie* 84.2 (1990): 45. See also Foucault's concluding remark to this essay: "C'est cette forme de philosophie qui, de Hegel à l'école de Francfort en passant par Nietzsche et Max Weber, a fondé une forme de réflexion dans laquelle j'ai essayé de travailler." Foucault, "Qu'est-ce que les Lumières (Extrait du cours du 5 janvier 1983)."

44. Foucault, "Kant on Enlightenment and Revolution," 93; Foucault, "Qu'est-ce que les Lumières (Extrait du cours du 5 janvier 1983)", 684.

45. Foucault, "Kant on Enlightenment and Revolution," 94.

46. Ibid. Foucault cites from Kant's *Conflict of the Faculties*, part 2, sections 6 and 7. See Immanuel Kant, *The Conflict of the Faculties (Der Streit der Fakultäten)*, trans. Mary J. Gregor (Lincoln: University of Nebraska Press, 1992), 153–61.

47. "Aufklärung ist der Ausgang des Menschen aus seiner selbstverschuldeten Unmündigkeit." "Enlightenment is man's emergence from his self-incurred immaturity." From "An Answer to the Question: What Is Enlightenment?" in Kant, *Kant: Political Writings*, 54.

48. Hannah Arendt, *Lectures on Kant's Political Philosophy* (Chicago: University of Chicago Press, 1989), 48. For the context of the passage, drawn from one of Kant's footnotes, see Immanuel Kant, *Religion within the Bounds of Bare Reason*, trans. Werner S. Pluhar (Indianapolis: Hackett, 2009), 209.

49. Arendt, *Lectures on Kant's Political Philosophy*, 46–48. (I have supplied Kant's original German phrase.) Arendt argues, nonetheless, that in spite of Kant's support for the outcome, he deems this rebellion itself is never "legitimate" or legal.

50. Foucault, "Kant on Enlightenment and Revolution," 95; Foucault, "Qu'est-ce que les Lumières (Extrait du cours du 5 janvier 1983)," 686–87.

51. *Abuse* is a rhetorical term for the "improper use of words" (OED, 2b), deployed first by George Puttenham, among others, and defined as catachresis. For this particular use, see Gayatri Chakravorty Spivak, "Thinking Academic Freedom in Gendered Postcoloniality," *The Anthropology of Politics: A Reader in Ethnography, Theory, and Critique*, ed. Joan Vincent (Malden, Mass.: Blackwell Publishers, 2002). She suggests that "Marx was perhaps the first European to attempt an ab-use of the Enlightenment, the public use of reason where the public was proletarian" (453). And more recently, "We who are interested in alternative Development propose an ab-use (not abuse) of the Enlightenment (understood in shorthand as 'the public use of reason'), a use from below." Gayatri Chakravorty Spivak, *Other Asias* (Malden, Mass.: Blackwell, 2008), 133.

52. Arjun Appadurai, "The Empire of Discipline: Telos, Power and Inquiry in Euro-Modernity," *Forum on Contemporary Theory: Transcending Disciplinary Decadence*, ed. Lewis Gordon and Prafulla Kar, unpublished conference paper, Jaipur, India, December 18–21, 2011.

53. Achille Mbembe has sharply examined the ongoing tension between French universalism and the persistence of racial difference. See his discussion of what ties "French colonial humanism" with the "principle of asymmetrical fraternity"; this leads, consequently, to the "disavowal of anticolonialism." Achille Mbembe, "Provincializing France?," *Public Culture* 23.1 (2011).

Bibliography

Adorno, Theodor W. *The Jargon of Authenticity*. Trans. Knut Tarnowski and Frederic Will. Evanston, Ill.: Northwestern University Press, 1973.
———. *Minima Moralia: Reflections from Damaged Life*. Trans. E. F. N. Jephcott. London: Verso, 1978.
———. *Minima moralia: Reflexionen aus dem beschädigten Leben*. 1951. Bibliothek Suhrkamp. Frankfurt am Main: Suhrkamp, 1982.
———. "On Subject and Object." Trans. Henry W. Pickford. *Critical Models: Interventions and Catchwords*. New York: Columbia University Press, 2005.
Ahmad, Aijaz. *In Theory: Classes, Nations, Literatures*. London: Verso, 1994.
Appadurai, Arjun. "The Empire of Discipline: Telos, Power and Inquiry in Euro-Modernity." *Forum on Contemporary Theory: Transcending Disciplinary Decadence*, ed. Lewis Gordon and Prafulla Kar. Unpublished conference paper, Jaipur, India, December 18–21, 2011.
———. *Modernity at Large: Cultural Dimensions of Globalization*. Public Worlds. Minneapolis: University of Minnesota Press, 1996.
Aravamudan, Srinivas. "Progress through Violence or Progress from Violence? Interpreting the Ambivalences of the *Histoire des deux Indes*." *Progrès et Violence au XVIIIe Siècle*, ed. Valerie Cossy and Deidre Dawson. Paris: Honore Champion Editeur, 2001.
———. *Tropicopolitans: Colonialism and Agency, 1688–1804*. Post-Contemporary Interventions. Durham, N.C.: Duke University Press, 1999.
Arendt, Hannah. *Eichmann in Jerusalem: A Report on the Banality of Evil*. New York: Penguin Books, 1994.
———. *Lectures on Kant's Political Philosophy*. Chicago: University of Chicago Press, 1989.
———. *On Violence*. New York: Harcourt Brace, 1970.

Ariès, Philippe. *Centuries of Childhood.* London: Pimlico, 1996.
Aristotle. *The Nicomachean Ethics.* Trans. David Ross. New York: Oxford University Press, 1998.
Armitage, David. *The Ideological Origins of the British Empire.* Ideas in Context. New York: Cambridge University Press, 2000.
Asad, Talal. "Conscripts of Western Civilization." *Dialectical Anthropology: Essays in Honor of Stanley Diamond,* ed. Christine Ward Gailey. Tallahassee: University Press of Florida, 1992.
Auckland, William Eden. *Some Remarks on the Apparent Circumstances of the War in the Fourth Week of October 1795.* London: Printed for J. Walter, 1795.
Baiey, Anne, and Josep Llobera, eds. *The Asiatic Mode of Production.* London: Routledge & Kegan Paul, 1981.
Baker, Keith Michael. *The French Revolution and the Creation of Modern Political Culture.* Oxford: Pergamon Press, 1987.
———. *Inventing the French Revolution: Essays on French Political Culture in the Eighteenth Century.* Ideas in Context. New York: Cambridge University Press, 1990.
Baker, Keith Michael, and Peter Hanns Reill. *What's Left of Enlightenment? A Postmodern Question.* Stanford: Stanford University Press, 2001.
Barker-Benfield, G. J. *The Culture of Sensibility: Sex and Society in Eighteenth-Century Britain.* Chicago: University of Chicago Press, 1992.
Baucom, Ian. *Specters of the Atlantic: Finance Capital, Slavery, and the Philosophy of History.* Durham, N.C.: Duke University Press, 2005.
Baudelaire, Charles. *The Painter of Modern Life and Other Essays.* Trans. Jonathan Mayne. Art and Letters. 2nd ed. London: Phaidon, 1995.
Benjamin, Walter. *Illuminations.* New York: Schocken Books, 1986.
Benot, Yves. *Diderot, de l'athéisme à l'anticolonialisme.* Paris: François Maspero, 1970.
Benot, Yves, and Marcel Dorigny. *Rétablissement de l'esclavage dans les colonies françaises, 1802.* Paris: Maisonneuve et Larose, 2003.
Bhabha, Homi K. "Of Mimicry and Man: The Ambivalence of Colonial Discourse." *The Location of Culture.* London: Routledge, 1994.
Blom, Ida, Karen Hagemann, and Catherine Hall. *Gendered Nations: Nationalisms and Gender Order in the Long Nineteenth Century.* New York: Berg, 2000.
Bougainville, Louis-Antoine de. *Voyage autour du monde.* 1771. Imago mundi. Ed. Michel Bideaux et Sonia Faessel. Paris: Presses de l'université de Paris-Sorbonne, 2001.
Bourke, Richard. "Liberty, Authority, and Trust in Burke's idea of Empire." *Journal of the History of Ideas* 61.3 (2000): 99–120.
———. "Sovereignty, Opinion and Revolution in Edmund Burke." *History of European Ideas* 25 (1999): 99–120.
Bowen, H. V. "British India, 1765–1813: The Metropolitan Context." *The Oxford History of the British Empire: The Eighteenth-Century,* ed. P. J. Marshall. New York: Oxford University Press, 1998.

Bracey, John. "Nello." *Urgent Tasks*, no. 12 (Summer 1981), http://www.sojourner truth.net/nello.html.
Brittlebank, Kate. *Tipu Sultan's Search for Legitimacy: Islam and Kingship in a Hindu Domain*. Delhi: Oxford University Press, 1997.
Bromwich, David. "The Context of Burke's *Reflections*." *Social Research* 58.2 (1991): 313–54.
Bronner, Stephen Eric. *Reclaiming the Enlightenment: Toward a Politics of Radical Engagement*. New York: Columbia University Press, 2004.
Buck-Morss, Susan. "Hegel and Haiti." *Critical Inquiry* 26.4 (2000): 821–65.
———. *Hegel, Haiti, and Universal History*. Pittsburgh: University of Pittsburgh Press, 2009.
Buhle, Paul. *C. L. R. James: His Life and Work*. London: Alison & Busby, 1986.
Burke, Edmund. *The Correspondence of Edmund Burke*. Ed. Thomas Copeland. 10 vols. Chicago: University of Chicago Press, 1958–78.
———. *Miscellaneous Writings*. Ed. E. J. Payne. Library of Economics and Liberty, 1990, http://www.econlib.org/library/LFBooks/Burke/brkSWv4c2.html.
———. *On Empire, Liberty, and Reform: Speeches and Letters*. Lewis Walpole Series in Eighteenth-Century Culture and History. Ed. David Bromwich. New Haven: Yale University Press, 2000.
———. *A Philosophical Enquiry into the Origin of Our Ideas of the Sublime and Beautiful*. Ed. James Boulton. Notre Dame, Ind.: University of Notre Dame Press, 1968.
———. *The Portable Edmund Burke*. Ed. Isaac Kramnick. New York: Penguin Books, 1999.
———. *Reflections on the Revolution in France*. Ed. J. G. A. Pocock. Indianapolis: Hackett, 1987.
———. *Reflections on the Revolution in France and on the Proceedings in Certain Societies in London Relative to That Event*. Pelican Classics. Ed. Conor Cruise O'Brien. Baltimore: Penguin Books, 1969.
———. *The Writings and Speeches of Edmund Burke*. Ed. Paul Langford and William B. Todd. 9 vols. Oxford: Oxford University Press, 1981–.
Burke, Edmund, and William Burke. *An Account of the European Settlements in America*. London: R. and J. Dodsley, 1757.
Butler, Judith. *Gender Trouble: Feminism and the Subversion of Identity*. New York: Routledge, 1990.
Butler, Marilyn. *Burke, Paine, Godwin, and the Revolution Controversy*. Cambridge English Prose Texts. New York: Cambridge University Press, 1984.
Calder, Alex, Jonathan Lamb, and Bridget Orr, eds. *Voyages and Beaches: Pacific Encounters, 1769–1840*. Honolulu: University of Hawai'i Press, 1999.
Cannon, Garland H. "Sir William Jones and Edmund Burke." *Modern Philology* 54.3 (1957): 165–86.
Canny, Nicholas P., and Anthony Pagden. *Colonial Identity in the Atlantic World, 1500–1800*. Princeton: Princeton University Press, 1987.

Casas, Bartolomé de Las. *A Short Account of the Destruction of the Indies.* 1542. Trans. Nigel Griffin. New York: Penguin Books, 1999.

Césaire, Aimé. *Toussaint Louverture: La Révolution française et le problème colonial.* Paris: Présence Africaine, 1981.

Chakrabarty, Dipesh. *Provincializing Europe.* Princeton: Princeton University Press, 2000.

Chatterjee, Partha. *Lineages of Political Society: Studies in Postcolonial Democracy.* Cultures of History. New York: Columbia University Press, 2011.

———. *Nationalist Thought and the Colonial World: A Derivative Discourse?* Third World Books. London: Zed Books, 1986.

———. "Our Modernity." *Empire and Nation: Selected Essays.* New York: Columbia University Press, 2010.

———. *The Politics of the Governed: Reflections on Popular Politics in Most of the World.* New York: Columbia University Press, 2004.

———. "Their Own Words? An Essay for Edward Said." *Edward Said: A Critical Reader,* ed. Michael Sprinker. Oxford: Blackwell, 1992.

Citton, Yves. "Specters of Multiplicity: Eighteenth-Century Literature Revisited from the Outside In." *French Global: A New Approach to Literary History,* ed. Christie McDonald and Susan Rubin Suleiman. New York: Columbia University Press, 2010.

Claeys, Gregory, ed. *The Political Writings of the 1790s: The French Revolution Debate in Britain.* London: Pickering & Chatto, 1995.

Claussen, Detlev. *Theodor W. Adorno: One Last Genius.* Trans. Rodney Livingstone. Cambridge, Mass.: Belknap Press, 2008.

Cobban, Alfred. *Edmund Burke and the Revolt against the Eighteenth Century: A Study of the Political and Social Thinking of Burke, Wordsworth, Coleridge, and Southey.* London: G. Allen & Unwin, 1929.

Cobbett, William. *Cobbett's Parliamentary History of England.* London: T. C. Hansard, 1806.

Colley, Linda. *Captives: Britain, Empire and the World, 1600–1850.* London: Jonathan Cape, 2002.

Connerton, Paul. *How Societies Remember.* Themes in the Social Sciences. Cambridge: Cambridge University Press, 1989.

Cooper, Frederick, and Ann Laura Stoler, eds. *Tensions of Empire: Colonial Cultures in a Bourgeois World.* Berkeley: University of California Press, 1997.

Danton, Georges Jacques. *Oeuvres de Danton, recueillies et annotées par A. Vermorel.* 2nd ed. Paris: A. Faure, 1867.

Darnton, Robert. *The Forbidden Best-Sellers of Pre-Revolutionary France.* New York: Norton, 1995.

Das, Sisir Kumar. *Sahibs and Munshis: An Account of the College of Fort William.* New Delhi: Orion Publications, 1978.

Daston, Lorraine. "Enlightenment Fears, Fears of Enlightenment." *What's Left of Enlightenment? A Postmodern Question,* ed. Keith Michael Baker and Peter Hanns Reill. Stanford: Stanford University Press, 2001.

Davidson, Jenny. *Breeding: A Partial History of the Eighteenth Century.* New York: Columbia University Press, 2009.
Davis, David Brion. *The Problem of Slavery in the Age of Revolution, 1770–1823.* 1975. New York: Oxford University Press, 1999.
Deane, Seamus. *Foreign Affections: Essays on Edmund Burke.* Cork, Ireland: Cork University Press / Field Day, 2005.
———. *The French Revolution and Enlightenment in England, 1789–1832.* Cambridge: Harvard University Press, 1988.
———. *Strange Country: Modernity and Nationhood in Irish Writing Since 1790.* New York: Oxford University Press, 1997.
Derrida, Jacques. *Acts of Literature.* Ed. Derek Attridge. New York: Routledge, 1992.
———. "Force of Law: 'The Mystical Foundation of Authority.'" *Deconstruction and the Possibility of Justice*, ed. David Carlson, Drucilla Cornell, and Michel Rosenfeld. New York: Routledge, 1992.
———. *The Gift of Death.* Religion and Postmodernism. Chicago: University of Chicago Press, 1995.
———. *Of Grammatology.* Trans. Gayatri Chakravorty Spivak. Baltimore: Johns Hopkins University Press, 1976.
———. *Specters of Marx: The State of the Debt, the Work of Mourning, and the New International.* Trans. Peggy Kamuf. New York: Routledge, 1994.
Diderot, Denis. *Oeuvres.* Bouquins. Ed. Laurent Versini. 5 vols. Paris: R. Laffont, 1994.
———. *Political Writings.* Cambridge Texts in the History of Political Thought. Ed. John Hope Mason and Robert Wokler. Cambridge: Cambridge University Press, 1992.
———. *Rameau's Nephew and Other Works.* Trans. Jacques Barzun and Ralph H. Bowen. Indianapolis: Bobbs-Merrill, 1964.
Dirks, Nicholas B. *Castes of Mind: Colonialism and the Making of Modern India.* Princeton: Princeton University Press, 2001.
———. *The Scandal of Empire: India and the Creation of Imperial Britain.* Cambridge: Harvard University Press, 2006.
Disraeli, Benjamin. *Tancred, or the New Crusade.* London: Longmans, Green, 1907.
Driesch, Hans. *The History and Theory of Vitalism.* Trans. C. K. Ogden. London: Macmillan, 1914.
Dubois, Laurent. *Avengers of the New World: The Story of the Haitian Revolution.* Cambridge, Mass.: Belknap Press, 2004.
Dubois, Laurent, and John D. Garrigus. *Slave Revolution in the Caribbean, 1789–1804: A Brief History with Documents.* New York: Palgrave Macmillan, 2006.
Duchet, Michèle. *Anthropologie et histoire au siècle des Lumières: Buffon, Voltaire, Rousseau, Helvétius, Diderot.* Bibliothèque d'anthropologie. Paris: François Maspero, 1971.

———. *Diderot et l'histoire des deux Indes ou, l'écriture fragmentaire.* Paris: A.-G. Nizet, 1978.
Dunmore, John. *Monsieur Baret: First Woman around the World, 1766–68.* Auckland, N.Z.: Heritage Press, 2002.
Ellingson, Terry Jay. *The Myth of the Noble Savage.* Berkeley: University of California Press, 2001.
Fanon, Frantz. *Wretched of the Earth.* New York: Grove Press, 1961.
Festa, Lynn M. *Sentimental Figures of Empire in Eighteenth-Century Britain and France.* Baltimore: Johns Hopkins University Press, 2006.
Fick, Carolyn. *The Making of Haiti: The Saint Domingue Revolution from Below.* Knoxville: University of Tennessee Press, 1990.
Fieldhouse, D. K. *The Colonial Empires: A Comparative Survey from the Eighteenth Century.* 2nd ed. London: Macmillan, 1982.
Fischer, Sibylle. *Modernity Disavowed: Haiti and the Cultures of Slavery in the Age of Revolution.* Durham, N.C.: Duke University Press, 2004.
Foote, Samuel. *The Works of Samuel Foote, Esq. In two volumes.* London: Vernor & Hood, 1799.
Foster, Robert. *Merchants, Landlords, Magistrates: The Depont Family in Eighteenth-Century France.* Baltimore: Johns Hopkins University Press, 1980.
Foucault, Michel. *The Foucault Effect: Studies in Governmentality.* London: Harvester Wheatsheaf, 1991.
———. *The Foucault Reader.* Ed. Paul Rabinow. New York: Pantheon Books, 1984.
———. *The History of Sexuality.* New York: Vintage Books, 1980.
———. "Kant on Enlightenment and Revolution." *Economy and Society* 15.1 (1986): 88–96.
———. "Qu'est-ce que la critique? [Critique et Aufklärung], Compte rendu de la séance du 27 mai 1978." *Bulletin de la Société française de la Philosophie* 84.2 (1990): 35–63.
———. "Qu'est-ce que les Lumières?" *Dits et écrits, 1954–1988,* ed. Daniel Defert, François Ewald, and Jacques Lagrange. Vol. 4. Bibliothèque des sciences humaines. Paris: Gallimard, 1994.
———. "Qu'est-ce que les Lumières (Extrait du cours du 5 janvier 1983)." *Dits et écrits, 1954–1988,* ed. Daniel Defert, François Ewald, and Jacques Lagrange. Vol. 4. Bibliothèque des sciences humaines. Paris: Gallimard, 1994.
———. *Society Must Be Defended: Lectures at the Collège de France, 1975–76.* Trans. David Macey. Ed. Mauro Bertani, Alessandro Fontana, and François Ewald. New York: Picador, 2002.
———. "What Is Critique?" Trans. Kevin Paul Geiman. *What Is Enlightenment? Eighteenth-Century Answers and Twentieth-Century Questions,* ed. James Schmidt. Berkeley: University of California Press, 1996.
Furber, Holden. *John Company at Work: A Study of European Expansion in India in the Late Eighteenth Century.* Harvard Historical Studies. Cambridge: Harvard University Press, 1948.

Furet, François. "Ancien Régime." *A Critical Dictionary of the French Revolution*, ed. François Furet and Mona Ozouf. Cambridge, Mass.: Belknap Press, 1989.

———. *Interpreting the French Revolution*. Cambridge: Cambridge University Press, 1981.

Furet, François, and Mona Ozouf, eds. *A Critical Dictionary of the French Revolution*. Cambridge, Mass.: Belknap Press, 1989.

Furniss, Tom. *Edmund Burke's Aesthetic Ideology: Language, Gender, and Political Economy in Revolution*. Cambridge Studies in Romanticism. Cambridge: Cambridge University Press, 1993.

Gadamer, Hans Georg. *Truth and Method*. New York: Crossroad, 1984.

Gandhi, Leela. *Affective Communities: Anticolonial Thought, Fin-de-Siècle Radicalism, and the Politics of Friendship*. Politics, History, and Culture. Durham, N.C.: Duke University Press, 2006.

Gibbons, Luke. *Edmund Burke and Ireland: Aesthetics, Politics and the Colonial Sublime*. New York: Cambridge University Press, 2003.

———. "'Subtilized into Savages': Edmund Burke, Progress, and Primitivism." *South Atlantic Quarterly* 100.1 (2001): 83–109.

Gillis, John R. *Youth and History: Tradition and Change in European Age Relations, 1770–Present*. Studies in Social Discontinuity. New York: Academic Press, 1981.

Gordon, Daniel. *Postmodernism and the Enlightenment: New Perspectives in Eighteenth-Century French Intellectual History*. New York: Routledge, 2000.

Gramsci, Antonio. *Prison Notebooks*. European Perspectives. New York: Columbia University Press, 1992.

———. *Selections from the Prison Notebooks of Antonio Gramsci*. New York: International Publishers, 1985.

Grigsby, Darcy Grimaldo. *Extremities: Painting Empire in Post-Revolutionary France*. London: Yale University Press, 2002.

Guha, Ranajit. "A Conquest Foretold." *Social Text* 54 (Spring 1998): 85–99.

———. *Dominance without Hegemony*. Cambridge: Harvard University Press, 1997.

———. *History at the Limit of World-History*. Italian Academy Lectures. New York: Columbia University Press, 2002.

———. *A Rule of Property for Bengal: An Essay on the Idea of Permanent Settlement*. Le Monde d'outre-mer, passé et présent. Paris: Mouton, 1963.

———. *A Rule of Property for Bengal: An Essay on the Idea of Permanent Settlement*. 2nd ed. New Delhi: Orient Longman, 1982.

Habermas, Jürgen. *The Philosophical Discourse of Modernity: Twelve Lectures*. Trans. Frederick G. Lawrence. Studies in Contemporary German Social Thought. Cambridge, Mass.: MIT Press, 1987.

Habib, Irfan. *Essays in Indian History: Towards a Marxist Perception*. Delhi: Tulika, 1995.

Hall, Catherine. *Civilising Subjects: Metropole and Colony in the English Imagination, 1830–1867.* Oxford: Polity, 2002.
Hannoum, Abdelmajid. "Review: What Is an Order of Time?" *History and Theory* 47.3 (2008): 458–71.
Hartog, François. *Régimes d'historicité: Présentisme et expériences du temps.* La librairie du XXIe siècle. Paris: Seuil, 2003.
Hegel, Georg Wilhelm Friedrich. *Lectures on the Philosophy of World History: Introduction, Reason in History.* Trans. H. B. Nisbet. Cambridge Studies in the History and Theory of Politics. New York: Cambridge University Press, 1980.
———. *Science of Logic.* Trans. A. V. Miller. London: George Allen & Unwin, 1969.
Heidegger, Martin. *Being and Time.* New York: Harper, 1962.
———. *Sein und Zeit.* 8th ed. Tübingen: M. Niemeyer, 1957.
Herzog, Don. *Poisoning the Minds of the Lower Orders.* Princeton: Princeton University Press, 1998.
Hindson, Paul, and Tim Gray. *Burke's Dramatic Theory of Politics.* Avebury Series in Philosophy. Aldershot, England: Avebury, 1988.
Hirschman, Albert O. *The Passions and the Interests: Political Arguments for Capitalism before Its Triumph.* Princeton: Princeton University Press, 1981.
Hoffman, George. "Anatomy of the Mass: Montaigne's 'Cannibals.'" *PMLA* 117.2 (2002): 207–21.
Hoffman, Ross John Swartz. *Edmund Burke, New York Agent.* Memoirs of the American Philosophical Society. Vol. 41. Philadelphia: American Philosophical Society, 1956.
Hohendahl, Peter Uwe. *Prismatic Thought: Theodor W. Adorno.* Modern German Culture and Literature. Lincoln: University of Nebraska Press, 1995.
Hont, Istvan. "The Language of Sociability and Commerce: Samuel Pufendorf and the Theoretical Foundations of the 'Four-Stages' Theory." *The Languages of Political Theory in Early-Modern Europe,* ed. Anthony Pagden. New York: Cambridge University Press, 1987.
Hont, Istvan, and Michael Ignatieff. *Wealth and Virtue: The Shaping of Political Economy in the Scottish Enlightenment.* Cambridge: Cambridge University Press, 1983.
Horkheimer, Max, and Theodor W. Adorno. *Dialectic of Enlightenment.* 1944. Trans. John Cumming. New York: Continuum, 1994.
Hume, David. *An Enquiry Concerning the Principles of Morals.* Indianapolis: Hackett, 1983.
Israel, Jonathan. *Radical Enlightenment: Philosophy and the Making of Modernity, 1650–1750.* Oxford: Oxford University Press, 2001.
James, C. L. R. *Beyond a Boundary.* 1963. Durham, N.C.: Duke University Press, 1993.
———. *The Black Jacobins: Toussaint L'Ouverture and the San Domingo Revolution.* 1938. 2nd ed. New York: Vintage Books, 1989.

———. *The C. L. R. James Reader.* Ed. Anna Grimshaw. Oxford: Blackwell, 1992.
———. "Lectures on the Black Jacobins." *Small Axe* 8 (2000): 65–112.
———. *Notes on Dialectics.* London: Allison & Busby, 1980.
Janes, Regina. "Edmund Burke's Flyting Leap from India to France." *History of European Ideas* 7.5 (1986): 509–27.
Johnson, Samuel. *The Works of Samuel Johnson.* Vol. 10. London: W. Baynes and Son, 1824.
Joseph, Betty. *Reading the East India Company, 1720–1840: Colonial Currencies of Gender.* Women in Culture and Society. Chicago: University of Chicago Press, 2004.
Kant, Immanuel. *The Conflict of the Faculties (Der Streit der Fakultäten).* Trans. Mary J. Gregor. Lincoln: University of Nebraska Press, 1992.
———. *Kant: Political Writings.* Cambridge Texts in the History of Political Thought. Ed. Hans Siegbert Reiss. Cambridge: Cambridge University Press, 1991.
———. *Religion within the Bounds of Bare Reason.* Trans. Werner S. Pluhar. Indianapolis: Hackett, 2009.
Kaviraj, Sudipta. "On the Construction of Colonial Power: Structure, Discourse, Hegemony." *Contesting Colonial Hegemony: State and Society in Africa and India,* ed. Dagmar Engels and Shula Marks. London: British Academic Press, 1994.
———. "An Outline of a Revisionist Theory of Modernity." *European Journal of Sociology* 46.3 (2005): 497–526.
Kaye, John William. *The Administration of the East India Company: A History of Indian Progress.* 2nd ed. London: R. Bentley, 1853.
Khan, Mohibbul Hasan. *History of Tipu Sultan.* Calcutta: Bibliophile, 1951.
Kiberd, Declan. *Inventing Ireland.* Cambridge: Harvard University Press, 1996.
Klein, Lawrence Eliot, and Anthony J. LaVopa. *Enthusiasm and Enlightenment in Europe, 1650–1850.* San Marino, Calif.: Huntington Library, 1998.
Koselleck, Reinhart. *Critique and Crisis: Enlightenment and the Pathogenesis of Modern Society.* Oxford: Berg, 1988.
———. *Futures Past: On the Semantics of Historical Time.* Studies in Contemporary German Social Thought. Cambridge, Mass.: MIT Press, 1985.
Kramnick, Isaac. *The Rage of Edmund Burke: Portrait of an Ambivalent Conservative.* New York: Basic Books, 1977.
Krishnan, Sanjay. *Reading the Global: Troubling Perspectives on Britain's Empire in Asia.* New York: Columbia University Press, 2007.
Laclau, Ernesto, and Chantal Mouffe. *Hegemony and Socialist Strategy: Towards a Radical Democratic Politics.* London: Verso, 1985.
Lamb, Jonathan. *Preserving the Self in the South Seas, 1680–1840.* Chicago: University of Chicago Press, 2001.
Lazarus, Neil. "Introduction: Hating Tradition Properly." *Nationalism and Cultural Practice in the Postcolonial World.* New York: Cambridge University Press, 1999.

Levinas, Emmanuel. *The Levinas Reader*. Ed. Seán Hand. New York: Blackwell, 1989.

———. *Totality and Infinity: An Essay on Exteriority*. Martinus Nijhoff Philosophy Texts. The Hague: M. Nijhoff, 1979.

Lock, F. P. *Edmund Burke*. 2 vols. Oxford: Clarendon Press, 1998–2006.

Loomba, Ania. *Colonialism-Postcolonialism*. The New Critical Idiom. London: Routledge, 1998.

Lovejoy, A. O. "The Supposed Primitivism of Rousseau's Discourse on Inequality." *Modern Philology* 21 (1923): 165–86.

Lüsebrink, Hans-Jürgen, and Anthony Strugnell. *L'Histoire des deux Indes: Réécriture et polygraphie*. Studies on Voltaire and the Eighteenth Century 333. Oxford: Voltaire Foundation, 1995.

Lüsebrink, Hans-Jürgen, and Manfred Tietz, eds. *Lectures de Raynal: L'Histoire des deux Indes en Europe et en Amérique au XVIIIe siècle*. Oxford: Voltaire Foundation, 1991.

Lyall, Alfred Comyn. *Warren Hastings*. London: Macmillan, 1902.

Macaulay, Thomas Babington. *Warren Hastings*. Ed. Joseph Villiers Denney. Boston: Allyn and Bacon, 1907.

Macey, David. *Frantz Fanon: A Biography*. New York: Picador, 2000.

Mantena, Karuna. *Alibis of Empire: Social Theory and the Ideologies of Late Imperial Rule*. Princeton: Princeton University Press, 2009.

Marshall, P. J. "Hastings, Warren." *Encyclopædia Britannica*. 2009.

———. *The Impeachment of Warren Hastings*. London: Oxford University Press, 1965.

———. *The Making and Unmaking of Empires: Britain, India, and America c. 1750–1783*. New York: Oxford University Press, 2005.

———, ed. *The Oxford History of the British Empire: The Eighteenth Century*. New York: Oxford University Press, 1998.

Mason, John Hope. *The Irresistible Diderot*. London: Quartet Books, 1982.

Mauss, Marcel. *The Gift: The Form and Reason for Exchange in Archaic Societies*. 1923. Trans. W. D. Halls. New York: Norton, 1990.

May, Gita. "Diderot and Burke: A Study in Aesthetic Affinity." *PMLA* 75.5 (1960): 527–39.

Mbembe, Achille. "Provincializing France?" *Public Culture* 23.1 (2011): 85–119.

McClellan, James E. *Colonialism and Science: Saint Domingue in the Old Regime*. Baltimore: Johns Hopkins University Press, 1992.

McElroy, George C. "Burke, William (1728–1798)." *Oxford Dictionary of National Biography*, ed. H. C. G. Matthew and Brian Harrison. Oxford: Oxford University Press, 2004.

McLaughlin, Blandine. "Diderot and Women." *French Women and the Age of Enlightenment*, ed. Samia I. Spencer. Bloomington: Indiana University Press, 1984.

Mehta, Uday Singh. *Liberalism and Empire: A Study in Nineteenth-Century British Liberal Thought*. Chicago: University of Chicago Press, 1999.

Mercier, Louis Sébastian. *L'An deux mille quatre cent quarante*. 1771. Geneva: Slatkine Reprints, 1979.
Metcalf, Thomas R. *Ideologies of the Raj*. The New Cambridge History of India. New York: Cambridge University Press, 1997.
Michelet, Jules. *Introduction à l'histoire universelle*. Paris: L. Hachette, 1843.
Mignolo, Walter. *The Darker Side of the Renaissance: Literacy, Territoriality, and Colonization*. Ann Arbor: University of Michigan Press, 1995.
Mill, John Stuart. *Collected Works of John Stuart Mill*. Toronto: University of Toronto Press, 1963.
Montesquieu, Charles de Secondat. *The Spirit of the Laws*. Cambridge Texts in the History of Political Thought. Cambridge: Cambridge University Press, 1989.
Morgan, Philip D., and Sean Hawkins. *Black Experience and the Empire*. Oxford History of the British Empire Companion Series. Oxford: Oxford University Press, 2004.
Morley, John. *Burke*. English Men of Letters. London: Macmillan, 1879.
———. *Diderot and the Encyclopaedists*. 1878. 2 vols. London: Macmillan, 1905.
Mortier, Roland, and Raymond Trousson. *Dictionnaire de Diderot*. Paris: Honoré Champion Editeur, 1999.
Mowitt, John. "In the Wake of Eurocentrism: An Introduction." *Cultural Critique* 47 (2001): 3.
Mufti, Aamir. *Enlightenment in the Colony: The Jewish Question and the Crisis of Postcolonial Culture*. Princeton: Princeton University Press, 2007.
Mukherjee, Ramkrishna. *The Rise and Fall of the East India Company*. New York: Monthly Review Press, 1974.
Müller-Doohm, Stefan. *Adorno: A Biography*. Trans. Rodney Livingstone. Cambridge: Polity Press, 2005.
Murr, Sylvia. "Les conditions d'émergence du discours sur l'Inde au Siècle des Lumières." *Inde et littératures*, ed. Marie-Claude Porcher. Vol. 7. Collection Purushartha. Paris: Editions de l'Ecole des hautes études en sciences sociales, 1983.
Muthu, Sankar. *Enlightenment against Empire*. Princeton: Princeton University Press, 2003.
———. "Enlightenment Anti-Imperialism." *Social Research* 66.4 (1999): 959–1007.
Naipaul, V. S. *The Mimic Men*. London: Penguin, 1969.
Nandy, Ashis. *Traditions, Tyranny, and Utopias: Essays in the Politics of Awareness*. Delhi: Oxford University Press, 1987.
Nesbitt, Nick. *Universal Emancipation: The Haitian Revolution and the Radical Enlightenment*. New World Studies. Charlottesville: University of Virginia Press, 2008.
Nietzsche, Friedrich Wilhelm. *Genealogy of Morals*. 1887. Ed. Walter Kaufmann. New York: Vintage Press, 1996.
———. *On the Advantage and Disadvantage of History for Life*. Trans. Peter Preuss. Indianapolis: Hackett, 1980.

———. "Vom Nutzen und Nachteil der Historie für das Leben." *Werke in drei Bänden*, ed. Rolf Toman. Vol. 1. Köln: Könemann, 1994.
Nora, Pierre. *Les Lieux de Mémoire*. Bibliothèque illustrée des histoires. Paris: Gallimard, 1984.
Novalis. *Shriften*. Vol. 2. Darmstadt: Wissenschaftliche Buchgesellschaft, 1965.
Oakeshott, Michael. *Rationalism in Politics and Other Essays*. 1962. New and expanded ed. Indianapolis: Liberty Fund, 1991.
O'Brien, Conor Cruise. *The Great Melody: A Thematic Biography and Commented Anthology of Edmund Burke*. Chicago: University of Chicago Press, 1993.
Pagden, Anthony. "The Effacement of Difference: Colonialism and the Origins of Nationalism in Diderot and Herder." *After Colonialism: Imperial Histories and Postcolonial Displacements*, ed. Gyan Prakash. Princeton: Princeton University Press, 1995.
———. *European Encounters with the New World: From Renaissance to Romanticism*. New Haven: Yale University Press, 1993.
———. *The Fall of Natural Man: The American Indian and the Origins of Comparative Ethnology*. Cambridge Iberian and Latin American Studies. Cambridge: Cambridge University Press, 1982.
———. "*Ius et Factum*: Text and Experience in the Writings of Bartolomé de Las Casas." *New World Encounters*, ed. Stephen Greenblatt. Berkeley: University of California Press, 1993.
———. *Lords of all the World: Ideologies of Empire in Spain, Britain and France 1500–1800*. New Haven: Yale University Press, 1995.
Palmier-Chatelain, Marie-Elise, and Isabelle Gadoin. *Rêver d'orient, connaître l'orient: Visions de l'orient dans l'art et la littérature britanniques*. Lyon: ENS, 2008.
Papin, Bernard. *Sens et fonction de l'utopie tahitienne dans l'oeuvre politique de Diderot*. Oxford: Voltaire Foundation, 1988.
Parekh, Bhikhu. "Liberalism and Colonialism: A Critique of Locke and Mill." *The Decolonization of Imagination: Culture, Knowledge and Power*, ed. Jan Nederveen Pieterse and Bhikhu Parekh. London: Zed Books, 1995.
Paulson, Ronald. *Representations of Revolution, 1789–1820*. New Haven: Yale University Press, 1983.
Pitts, Jennifer. *A Turn to Empire: The Rise of Liberal Imperialism in Britain and France*. Princeton: Princeton University Press, 2005.
Pocock, J. G. A. *Barbarism and Religion*. 4 vols. New York: Cambridge University Press, 1999–.
———. "Commerce, Settlement and History: A Reading of the *Histoire des Deux Indes*." *Articulating America: Fashioning a National Political Culture in Early America*, ed. Rebecca Starr. Lanham, Md.: Rowman & Littlefield, 2000.
———. *Politics, Language, and Time: Essays on Political Thought and History*. Chicago: University of Chicago Press, 1989.

———. *Virtue, Commerce, and History: Essays on Political Thought and History, Chiefly in the Eighteenth Century.* Ideas in Context. Cambridge: Cambridge University Press, 1985.
Popkin, Jeremy. *Facing Racial Revolution: Eyewitness Accounts of the Haitian Insurrection.* Chicago: University of Chicago Press, 2007.
Porter, James I. *Nietzsche and the Philology of the Future.* Stanford: Stanford University Press, 2000.
Porter, Roy. *The Enlightenment.* London: Humanities Press International, 1990.
———. *Haunted Journeys: Desire and Transgression in European Travel Writing.* Princeton: Princeton University Press, 1991.
Rabinbach, Anson. "The Cunning of Unreason: Mimesis and the Construction of Anti-Semitism in Horkheimer and Adorno's *Dialectic of Enlightenment.*" In *The Shadow of Catastrophe: German Intellectuals between Apocalypse and Enlightenment.* Berkeley: University of California Press, 1997.
Rabinbach, Anson, and Jack David Zipes. *Germans and Jews Since the Holocaust.* New York: Holmes & Meier, 1986.
Raj, Kapil. *Relocating Modern Science: Circulation and the Construction of Knowledge in South Asia and Europe, 1650–1900.* New York: Palgrave Macmillan, 2007.
Ray, Rajat Kanta. "Indian Society and the Establishment of British Supremacy, 1765–1818." *The Oxford History of the British Empire: The Eighteenth-Century,* ed. P. J. Marshall. New York: Oxford University Press, 1998.
Raynal, Guillaume Thomas. *Histoire philosophique et politique des deux Indes. Découverte.* Ed. Yves Benot. Paris: François Maspero, 1981.
———. *Histoire philosophique et politique des établissemens et du commerce des Européens dans les deux Indes.* Maestricht: Chez Jean-Edme Dufour, 1774.
———. *Histoire philosophique et politique des établissemens et du commerce des Européens dans les deux Indes.* 10 vols. Genève: Chez J.-L. Pellet, 1780.
———. *Histoire philosophique et politique des établissemens et du commerce des Européens dans les deux Indes.* 10 vols. Genève: Jean-Léonard Pellet, 1782.
———. *Histoire philosophique et politique des établissemens et du commerce des Européens dans les deux Indes.* Paris: A. Costes, 1820.
———. *Histoire philosophique et politique des établissements et du commerce des Européens dans les deux Indes.* Ed. Anthony Strugnell. Vol. 1. Ferney-Voltaire: Centre international d'étude du XVIIIe siècle, 2010.
———. *A Philosophical and Political History of the Settlements and Trade of the Europeans in the East and West Indies.* Trans. J Justamond. 3rd ed. London: T. Cadell, 1777.
Rickert, Heinrich. *Science and History: A Critique of Positivist Epistemology.* The William Volker Fund Series in the Humane Studies. Princeton, N.J.: Van Nostrand, 1962.
Robespierre, Maximilien. *Œuvres complètes de Maximilien Robespierre.* Ed. V. Barbier and Charles Vellay. Paris: Aux bureaux de la Revue historiques de la révolution française, 1910.

Robinson, Nicholas K. *Edmund Burke: A Life in Caricature.* New Haven: Yale University Press, 1997.
Romilly, Samuel. *Thoughts on the Probable Influence of the French Revolution on Great-Britain.* London: J. Debrett, 1790.
Rothberg, Michael. *Multidirectional Memory: Remembering the Holocaust in the Age of Decolonization.* Stanford: Stanford University Press, 2009.
Rothschild, Emma. *Economic Sentiments: Adam Smith, Condorcet, and the Enlightenment.* Cambridge: Harvard University Press, 2001.
———. "Global Commerce and the Question of Sovereignty in the Eighteenth-Century Provinces." *Modern Intellectual History* 1.1 (2004): 3–25.
———. "A Horrible Tragedy in the French Atlantic." *Past and Present* 192.1 (2006): 67–108.
Rousseau, Jean-Jacques. *The First and Second Discourses.* New York: St. Martin's Press, 1964.
———. *Oeuvres complètes.* Bibliothèque de la Pléiade. Vol. 3. Paris: Gallimard, 1964.
Said, Edward W. *Culture and Imperialism.* New York: Vintage Books, 1994.
———. *Orientalism.* New York: Pantheon Books, 1978.
Sala-Molins, Louis. *Dark Side of the Light: Slavery and the French Enlightenment.* Trans. John Conteh-Morgan. Minneapolis: University of Minnesota Press, 2006.
———. *Les misères des Lumières: Sous la raison, l'outrage.* Paris: R. Laffont, 1992.
Schama, Simon. *Citizens: A Chronicle of the French Revolution.* New York: Knopf, 1989.
Scheler, Max. *Ressentiment.* 1915. Trans. Lewis Coser and William Holdheim. Ed. Manfred S. Frings. Milwaukee, Wisc.: Marquette University Press, 1994.
Schmitt, Carl. *Political Romanticism.* 1919. Trans. Guy Oakes. Cambridge, Mass.: MIT Press, 1986.
Scott, David. "Colonial Governmentality." *Social Text* 43 (Autumn 1995): 191–220.
———. *Conscripts of Modernity: The Tragedy of Colonial Enlightenment.* Durham, N.C.: Duke University Press, 2004.
———. *Refashioning Futures: Criticism after Postcoloniality.* Princeton Studies in Culture/Power/History. Princeton: Princeton University Press, 1999.
Seeley, J. R. *The Expansion of England.* London: Macmillan, 1909.
Semmel, Bernard. *Democracy versus Empire: The Jamaica Riots of 1865 and the Governor Eyre Controversy.* New York: Doubleday, 1969.
Sen, Sudipta. *Distant Sovereignty: National Imperialism and the Origins of British India.* New York: Routledge, 2002.
Shakespeare, William. *The Tragedy of Macbeth.* The Oxford Shakespeare. Ed. Nicholas Brooke. Oxford: Clarendon Press, 1990.
Simpson, David. *Romanticism, Nationalism, and the Revolt against Theory.* Chicago: University of Chicago Press, 1993.
Singham, Shanti Marie. "Betwixt Cattle and Men: Jews, Blacks, and Women, and the Declaration of the Rights of Man." *The French Idea of Freedom: The*

Old Regime and the Declaration of Rights of 1789, ed. Dale Van Kley. Stanford: Stanford University Press, 1994.
Smith, Adam. *An Inquiry into the Nature and Causes of the Wealth of Nations.* 1776. Ed. Edwin Cannan. Chicago: University of Chicago Press, 1976.
Spivak, Gayatri Chakravorty. "Can the Subaltern Speak?" *Marxism and the Interpretation of Culture*, ed. Cary Nelson and Lawrence Grossberg. Urbana: University of Illinois Press, 1988.
———. *A Critique of Postcolonial Reason: Toward a History of the Vanishing Present.* Cambridge: Harvard University Press, 1999.
———. "Ghostwriting." *Diacritics* 25.2 (1995): 64–84.
———. *Other Asias.* Malden, Mass.: Blackwell, 2008.
———. "Thinking Academic Freedom in Gendered Post-coloniality." *The Anthropology of Politics: A Reader in Ethnography, Theory, and Critique*, ed. Joan Vincent. Malden, Mass.: Blackwell, 2002.
Starobinski, Jean. *Jean-Jacques Rousseau, Transparency and Obstruction.* Trans. Arthur Goldhammer. Chicago: University of Chicago Press, 1988.
Steele, Ian K. "The Anointed, the Appointed, and the Elected: Governance of the British Empire, 1689–1784." *The Oxford History of the British Empire: The Eighteenth-Century*, ed. P. J. Marshall. New York: Oxford University Press, 1998.
Stein, Burton. *Thomas Munro: The Origins of the Colonial State and His Vision of Empire.* Delhi: Oxford University Press, 1989.
Stephen, James Fitzjames. *The Story of Nuncomar and the Impeachment of Sir Elijah Impey.* 2 vols. London: Macmillan, 1885.
Stokes, Eric. *The English Utilitarians and India.* Oxford: Clarendon Press, 1959.
Strachey, John. *Hastings and the Rohilla War.* Oxford: Clarendon Press, 1892.
Strugnell, Anthony. "Diderot's Anti-colonialism: A Problematic Notion." *New Essays on Diderot*, ed. J. E. Fowler. Cambridge: Cambridge University Press, 2011.
———. *Diderot's Politics: A Study of the Evolution of Diderot's Political Thought after the Encyclopédie.* International Archives of the History of Ideas. The Hague: Nijhoff, 1973.
———. "La voix du sage dans l'Histoire des deux Indes." *Diderot, les dernières années, 1770–84: Colloque du bicentenaire, 2–5 septembre 1984 à Edimbourg*, ed. Peter France and Anthony Strugnell. Edinburgh: Edinburgh University Press, 1985.
Suleri, Sara. *The Rhetoric of English India.* Chicago: University of Chicago Press, 1992.
Teltscher, Kate. *India Inscribed: European and British Writing on India 1600–1800.* Delhi: Oxford University Press, 1995.
Thompson, E. P. *Customs in Common: Studies in Traditional Popular Culture.* New York: New Press, 1991.
Tocqueville, Alexis de. *The Ancien Régime and the French Revolution.* Trans. Gerald Bevan. New York: Penguin, 2008.

———. *Democracy in America*. New York: Penguin, 1984.
Trautmann, Thomas R. *Aryans and British India*. Berkeley: University of California Press, 1997.
Trouillot, Michel-Rolph. *Silencing the Past: Power and the Production of History*. Boston: Beacon Press, 1995.
Tuck, Richard. *The Rights of War and Peace: Political Thought and the International Order from Grotius to Kant*. New York: Oxford University Press, 1999.
Tucker, Robert C. *The Marx-Engels Reader*. New York: Norton, 1972.
Tully, James. "Rediscovering America: The *Two Treatises* and Aboriginal Rights." *An Approach to Political Philosophy: Locke in Contexts*. Cambridge: Cambridge University Press, 1993.
Vartanian, Aram. "From Deist to Atheist: Diderot's Philosophical Orientation 1746-1749." *Diderot Studies* 1 (1949): 46-63.
Venturi, Franco. *The End of the Old Regime in Europe, 1776-1789*. 2 vols. Princeton: Princeton University Press, 1991.
Voltaire. *Letters Concerning the English Nation*. 1734. Oxford World's Classics. Ed. Nicholas Cronk. New York: Oxford University Press, 2009.
Watson, Tim. *Caribbean Culture and British Fiction in the Atlantic World, 1780-1870*. New York: Cambridge University Press, 2008.
Wecter, Dixon. "Edmund Burke and His Kinsmen: A Study of the Statesman's Financial Integrity and Private Relationships." *University of Colorado Studies* 1.1 (1939): 1-113.
Weitzman, Sophia. *Warren Hastings and Philip Francis*. Manchester: University of Manchester Press, 1929.
Wellman, Kathleen. "Physicians and Philosophes: Physiology and Sexual Morality in the French Enlightenment." *Eighteenth-Century Studies* 35.2 (2002): 267-77.
Whelan, Frederick. *Edmund Burke and India: The Political Morality of Empire*. Pittsburgh: University of Pittsburgh Press, 1996.
White, Stephen. *Edmund Burke: Modernity, Politics, and Aesthetics*. Thousand Oaks, Calif.: Sage Publications, 1994.
Williams, Eric. *Capitalism and Slavery*. 1944. London: Andre Deutsch, 1987.
Williams, Raymond. *The Country and the City*. New York: Oxford University Press, 1973.
Wilson, Arthur M. *Diderot*. New York: Oxford University Press, 1972.
———. *Diderot, sa vie et son oeuvre*. Paris: Laffont, Ramsay, 1985.
Winch, Donald. *Classical Political Economy and Colonies*. Cambridge: Harvard University Press, 1965.
Wollstonecraft, Mary. *A Vindication of the Rights of Men in a Letter to the Right Honourable Edmund Burke: Occasioned by his Reflections on the Revolution in France; and, A Vindication of the Rights of Woman: With Strictures on Political and Moral Subjects*. Ed. David Lorne Macdonald and Kathleen Dorothy Scherf. Orchard Park, N.Y.: Broadview Press, 1997.

Wolpe, Hans. *Raynal et sa machine de guerre: L'Histoire des deux Indes et ses perfectionnements*. Stanford: Stanford University Press, 1957.
Yaeger, Patricia. "Editor's Column: The End of Postcolonial Theory? A Roundtable with Sunil Agnani, Fernando Coronil, Gaurav Desai, Mamadou Diouf, Simon Gikandi, Susie Tharu, and Jennifer Wenzel." *PMLA* 122 (2007): 633–51.
Yeats, W. B. *The Collected Poems of W. B. Yeats*. Ed. Richard J. Finneran. New York: Collier Books, 1989.
Young, Robert. *Colonial Desire: Hybridity in Theory, Culture, and Race*. New York: Routledge, 1995.
Yule, Henry, A. C. Burnell, and William Crooke. *Hobson-Jobson: A Glossary of Colloquial Anglo-Indian Words and Phrases, and of Kindred Terms, Etymological, Historical, Geographical and Discursive*. London: J. Murray, 1903.

Index

ability/talent, 74–75, 77–78
abolition of slavery: Burke on, 234n18; commerce and, 40–41; in France, 152, 155–56
absentmindedness of British Empire, 7–9
absolutism: commerce as liberty and, 34–35, 40–41; *Histoire* seen as critique of, 36, 52, 54
Academy of Letters, 42, 58
An Account of the European Settlements in America (Burke), 2
administrators, 23–24, 201n35
Adorno, Theodor, 19, 90–91, 181, 182, 183–87
Advancement of Learning (Bacon), 91
aesthetics, 11, 175, 201n35, 202–3n57
affect: Adorno and, 185; in *Histoire des deux Indes*, 14–15; importance of, 175; principles of colonization and, 46–47; role of, 47. *See also* anger; hatred; *ressentiment*; revenge
Africa: anger against Dutch in, 49–52; Cape of Good Hope, 158; depopulation of, 27
agriculture, 62
America: compensation for in the East, 18, 162–74; as creole nation, 205n76; formulation of law and, 165–66; French monarchy compared to, 87–89; India and, 168, 170–71; as place of settlement, 18; population of, 242n109; revenue from, 172–73

American Revolution: Burke on, 163; Burke's support of, 87–89; compared with events in India, 170–72; significance of, 133
analogies, political, 170–72, 174–76
ancien régime, xix–xx, 48, 87–89, 198n12. *See also* French monarchy
The Ancien Régime and the French Revolution (Tocqueville), xix, 69
anger: despair and, 60; against Dutch in South Africa, 49–52; against English in Jamaica, 54–60; exploration of, 14–15; in *Histoire*, 51–52; against Portuguese in Goa, 52–54; role of, 47, 52–54; as self-hatred, 53; as sign of complicity, 57–58. *See also* hatred; *ressentiment*
animals, 39, 94–95
anthropology, 29, 41–42, 44–45, 50–51
anticlericalism, 24, 32–33, 35, 50, 80
anticolonialism: Burke and, 15; in Burke's writings on India, 134–37; contradictions/inconsistencies of, 155–56; limit of, 176; moral arguments and, 40; scholarship in, 182; Toussaint and, 177–81
antithetical pairs (oppositional pairs): administrator/philosophe, 23–24; colonial knowledge/Enlightenment universalism, 2; Diderot and Burke as, 9–19; Enlightenment/postmodernism,

xx; French Revolution/*ancien régime*, xix–xx; *haine/douceur*, 63–64; North America/South America, 26; old colonies/new colonies, 25–26; in *Supplément*, 30–31
apocalypse, language of, 141
Appadurai, Arjun, 189
Arendt, Hannah, 188, 237n42
Ariès, Philippe, 116
Aristotle, 124, 229n65
arithmetic reason, 78, 89–96, 101–2, 105
arriviste class, 116
Asad, Talal, xvii
asceticism, xvii
Auckland, William Eden, 149
Aufklärung, xv, xvii, 187, 188
Aurangzeb, 7, 8f
Austen, Jane, 113

Bacon, Francis, 91
ballast, 83–84, 86
Bandung Conference, 184
banking/finance, language of, 95, 124–25
barbarians: blacks & free people of color as, 159; Europeans as, 55, 219n47; Foucault on, 213n47; Jacobins as, 160
barbarism: attributed to slaves, 152; of English, 55, 58
Barnave, Antoine Pierre, 139, 142, 145
Baudeau, abbé de, 13
Baudelaire, Charles, xvii
Belley, Jean-Baptiste, 18, 150–53, 151f, 207n93, 239n64
benevolence, 33–34, 122, 153
Benfield, Paul, 167
Bengal famine of 1770, 6
Bengal Judiciary Bill (1781), 136, 166
Benjamin, Walter, 44–45, 202n57
Les bijoux indiscrets (Diderot), 28, 201n36
The Black Jacobins (James), 177, 180
blackmail *(chantage)* of the Enlightenment, xvi, xxii, 183, 189
blood, images of, 48, 55–56, 60, 138
bodies, 29, 201n36; female, 232n3
Bonaparte, Napoleon (Emperor Napoleon I), 40, 45, 141–42
Bougainville, Antoine de, 32, 201n31
bourgeoisie/burghers/monied interests, 16, 91, 96–98, 118, 119–21, 127
breeding, 27–37; consensual colonialism and, 14; consent and, 27; *doux commerce* and, 27–28; *Histoire des deux Indes* and, 32–37; *Supplément au voyage de Bougainville* and, 28–32. *See also* interbreeding
Brown, Christopher, 139–40
burghers. *See* bourgeoisie/burghers/monied interests
Burke, Edmund, 76f, 129f, 164f; *An Account of the European Settlements in America*, 2; ambivalence of regarding empire, 7–9; anticolonial thought and, 15; colonial knowledge and, 2, 3–4; conservatism of, 70–71; conspiratorial strain of, 96–97, 115, 128, 227n39, 241n104; contradictions/inconsistencies of, 78–79, 85, 110, 168–69; *Correspondence*, 109; death of, 11, 114; departure of from Parliament, 126; Diderot and, 10–11; examination of works of, 15–18; as founder of modern idea of nation, 101; friendship with Francis, 135, 231–32n88; Gordon riots and, 238n45; imperialism critiqued by, 70–71; interest of in India, 113–14; lexicon of, 15, 74, 176; movement of writings of, 175–76; Orwell and, 237n42; *Philosophical Enquiry into the Origin of Our Ideas of the Sublime and Beautiful*, 28, 76; prophetic voice of, 84, 115, 132, 139, 234–35n19; Raynal and, 10, 69–70; reliance of on idea of nature, 81; reputation of, 70; Scottish thinkers and, 80; self-characterization of, 84–86; sexual difference in works of, 28; "Sketch of a Negro Code," 139–40; speaking on behalf of oppressed, 135, 153; works known for, 10. *See also* Burke, Edmund, letters by; Burke, Edmund, speeches by; India, Burke's writings on; *Reflections on the Revolution in France* (Burke)
Burke, Edmund, letters by: to Charles-Jean-François Depont, 225n18; to Claude-François de Rivarol, 70; to Fitzwilliam, 126, 128; "Fourth Letter on a Regicide Peace," 147–49; to Henry Dundas, 234n18; as illustrative of colonial knowledge, 2; to John King, 238n48; "Letters on a Regicide Peace", 18; *Letter to a Member of the National Assembly*, 121–22; "Letter to the Sheriffs of Bristol", 162, 164–65, 174; to Loughborough, 128–29, 130, 131, 135, 136; to Mary Palmer, 153; to Philip Francis,

135–36, 162–63, 165, 225n18; "Second Letter on a Regicide Peace", 156–61; to Sir Hercules Langrishe, 126, 128, 130; to Sir William Jones, 136–37; to William Windham, 140, 144
Burke, Edmund, speeches by: female bodies in, 232n3; as illustrative of colonial knowledge, 2; "Speech on Bengal Judicature Bill," 166, 167; "Speech on Conciliation with America", 172–74, 235n21, 242n109; "Speech on Fox's East India Bill", 82–83, 111–12, 116, 164–65, 231n86, 231n87; "Speech on Restoring Lord Pigot", 18, 166, 167–72; on St. Domingue, 137–39, 140–43
Burke, William, 113, 162–63

cabals, 96–97, 115, 172, 241n104
Caliban (Shakespearean character), 160
calico, 72
Camden, William, 235–36n26
cannibalism, 146–47, 160–61, 210n20, 221n84
cantons, creation of in France, 83, 87, 89–90, 94
Cape of Good Hope, South Africa, 158
Cap Français, Hispaniola, 140
capital cities, 33
Carnap, Rudolf, 185
Casas, Bartolomé de Las, 27, 57, 155–56, 200n25
celebrity: Rousseau as, 122
Chakrabarty, Dipesh, xxii, 182
Chatterjee, Partha, 145, 182, 246n39
childhood/children, 116–17
Christianity: *ressentiment* and, 212n39
Church: Diderot's views on, 32–33
circularity (circular movement): of idea of revolution, 102–3
citizenship: granted to free people of color, 235n25, 236n39
civilization: commerce and, 34–35, 234n18; imitation and, 38–39
class: Burke's thoughts on, 75–79; French Revolution and, 97–98, 119–20; intellectual class, 120–22, 123, 131; of officials in India, 97–99, 116; planter class, 142, 143–44, 145, 150–52, 154–55. See also class mobility; feudalism
class mobility: Burke's fear of, 16; East India Company enabling, 74–75; French Revolution/India connection and, 86–87; miscibility and, 217n22; revolutions and, 75–79. See also miscibility
class on probation, 77, 116–18, 127
clergy, 32–33, 80. See also anticlericalism
Clive, Robert, 12
clothing/veiling, language of, 125
Cobban, Alfred, 101
coffee, 13, 72, 141, 217n12, 235n24
"Coleridge" (Mill), 9
Colley, Linda, 119
colonial difference, rule of, 145
"Colonial Governmentality" (Scott), xvii
colonial guilt, 111–12
colonialism: aestheticism and, 201n35; cunning of history and, 98–99; debates on in Parliament, 2–3; despotic governance and, 58; *douce colonisation* and, 35; freedom and, 93–94; humanitarianism and, 59; imperious attraction and, 37; literary study of, xxii; modernity and, xvi, 98; narrative of as fairy tale, 63, 64; sexual attraction and, 37. See also anticolonialism
colonial knowledge: archive of, 2, 36, 233–34n11; Burke as illustrative of, 2, 3–4; colonial dominance and, 136–37; effect of on European thought, 110; universalism and, 2, 78
colonial occupation: French Revolution as, 87–89, 93–97
colonies: arithmetic reason and, 89–93; barter/swapping of, 4–5; distinction between, 195n20, 199n18, 220n62; as subordinate concern, 72–73
colonies of the rights of men, 94–96
colonists/settlers: *ancien régime* compared to, 87–89; consensual colonialism and, 14; national character and, 33; as natives, 165, 171
colonized, the: response of, 14–15
colonizing impulse: linked with reason, 90–92
commerce: abolition of slavery and, 40–41; aestheticism and, 202–3n57; breeding and, 27–28; civilizing process and, 34–35, 234n18; *douce colonisation* and, 34; manners and, 79–81; rights of men and, 146; role of, 47; St. Domingue and, 235n24; views of, 202n55. See also commodities; trade
commodities: circulation of, 201n32; coffee, 217n12; East India Company's

270 / INDEX

monopoly over, 6; global network of, 2, 13; human bodies as, 29; produced by St. Domingue, 235n24; rights of man compared to, 142; social contract compared to, 72–73
La Compagnie des Indes (French trading company), 6–7
compensation in the East, 162–74; Burke's articulation of, 17–18; Jacobinism and, 157, 161; in letter to Philip Francis, 162–63, 165; in "Letter to the Sheriffs of Bristol," 162, 164–65; in "Speech on Bengal Judicature Bill", 166, 167; in "Speech on Conciliation with America", 172–74; in "Speech on Restoring Lord Pigot", 166, 167–72
complicity, xv, 3, 14, 52–54, 57–58, 182, 186
concatenations, political, 18, 174–76
conceptual limit, 36, 44–45, 110, 177
conquest: critique of violence of, 200n25; France as having experienced, 16, 87–89, 89–90, 107, 131–32, 157; narratives of, xx–xxi; slavery and, 58
conscripts of modernity, xvii–xviii, xxi
consensual colonialism, 23–45; breeding and, 27–37; commerce and, 40–42; as conceptual limit, 44–45; Diderot's conception of, 14; *douce colonisation* as, 26; in Guam, 62–65; in *Histoire*, 32–37; imitation and, 38–39; as product of hatred of dominance, 181; traveling philosophes and, 42–44
consent, 14, 24, 27, 34, 45
constitution, British, 89–90, 130, 174, 220n54
constitution, French, 133, 138–42, 145
contagion: of Asian despotism, 100; Jacobinism as, 88; language of, 142, 227n39; Nabobs as, 74
Cormier, 146–47
Correspondence (Burke), 109
"Corruption of the Portuguese in India" (chapter in *Histoire*) (Diderot), 52–54
cotton, 142
créoles, 39, 205n76
the crowd, 106
cunning of history, 98
custom, 79–83; Burke on, 92; commerce and, 79–81; cosmopolitan sympathy and, 82–83; explaining Burke's contradictions/inconsistencies, 110; formulation of law and, 166; nature and, 81; prejudice and, 123. See also manners

"Dangers Which Threatened Jamaica from Within" (chapter in *Histoire*) (Diderot), 54–60
Danton, Georges Jacques, 155–56
Darnton, Robert, 13, 203n65
Daston, Lorraine, 113
the dead, 73–74
Deane, Seamus, 105
"Declarations of the Rights of Man," 142, 145
decolonization, 19, 179
delegitimization of state's use of force: Indianism and, 17, 130
democracy: tyranny of number and, 89; virtue and, 212n44
Democracy in America (Tocqueville), 26
Depont, Charles-Jean-François, 113, 225n18
depopulation: of Africa, 27; of New World, 58
Derrida, Jacques, xxii, 36, 206n85
"Description of the Mariana Islands. Singular Qualities Observed There." (chapter in *Histoire*), 60–65
despair, 60
despotism: in colonies, 171; colonization of New World and, 58; defined, 102–3; East India Company and, 7; fear and, 212–13n44; French Revolution and, 99–101; oriental, 3, 99–101; population and, 101–5; rights of man and, 146
Dessalines, Jean-Jacques, 180
Dialectic of Enlightenment (Adorno and Horkheimer), 90–91, 184
Diderot, Denis: aestheticism and, 202–3n57; contributions of to *Histoire*, 25, 198n12; death of, 11; genres used by, 13–14, 36; liberal imperialism and, 14; marriage and, 200n28; prophetic voice of, 41, 47, 56; relations with Burke, 10–11; response of to events of era, 11–12; universalism and, 2, 3–4; voice of in *Histoire*, 40; works known for, 10. See also Diderot, Denis, works by; *Histoire des deux Indes* (Raynal)
Diderot, Denis, works by: *Les bijoux indiscrets*, 28, 201n36; "Corruption of the Portuguese in India" (chapter in *Histoire*), 52–54; "Dangers Which Threatened Jamaica from Within" (chapter in *Histoire*),

54–60; *Encyclopédie*, 3, 13–14, 24; "Etablissements des Hollandais au cap de Bonne-Espérance" (chapter in *Histoire*), 46, 48–52; examination of, 12–15; *Mélanges pour Catherine II*, 38–39; *Observation sur le Nakaz*, 38; *Political Writings*, 25, 37; "Principles Which the French Should Follow in India, if they Succeed There in Reestablishing Their Esteem and Presence", 23; "Le Privilège de la compagnie, sera-t-il renouvelé?" (chapter in *Histoire*), 46; "Reflections on the Good and Evil Which the Discovery of the New World has Done to Europe", 23; *Réfutation d'Helvétius*, 35. *See also Supplément au voyage de Bougainville*

difference, xxiii, 94–95, 145, 165, 174

Dirks, Nicholas B., 111, 233–34n11

Discourse on Inequality (Rousseau), 24, 42

Disraeli, Benjamin, 77

divine providence, 164–65, 166

docility, 39, 44, 62–63

dominance, colonial: consent and, 14, 24, 34, 45; orientalist scholarship and, 136–37

double advantage, 15, 64–65

double anxiety, 77–78

douce colonisation (soft colonization), 26, 33–35, 44, 62–65. *See also* consensual colonialism

doux commerce, 27–28

Driesch, Hans, 185

Dubois, Laurent, 145, 235n24

Duchet, Michèle, 36, 40, 49, 56, 198n13, 222n87

Dupont, Pierre-Gaëton, 145, 238n48

Dutch settlers, 48, 51

East India Company: acquisition of territory by, 7; Burke's position on, 115, 166–67; as colonizers/ruling through conquest, 107; as despot, 83, 100; as empire, 129; extraction of revenue from, 173; history of, 5–6; justice and, 135; merit and, 74–75; parliamentary oversight of, 168. *See also* East India Company officials; Hastings impeachment trial

East India Company officials: class of, 97–98, 116–18, 131; as Jacobins, 120, 135–36; miscibility and, 118–20; private trade done by, 5–6; youth of, 116–17

education, 117, 121

empire: Burke's ambivalence regarding, 7–9; East India Company as, 129; hating of, 181–90; Jacobins and, 157; justice and, 115; liberalism and, 45; management of difference by, 165; natural order bypassed in, 77–78; revolutionaries operating as, 93–94; tropical, 156, 159–61; as unifying force, 174; universal, 157, 165. *See also* colonialism

encyclopedic impulse: colonial power and, 92; cultural singularity and, 14; Diderot's defiance of, 36; Enlightenment universalism and, 2; governance informed by, 23–24

Encyclopédie (Diderot), 3, 13–14, 24

England/the English: anger against in Jamaica, 54–60; barbarism of, 55, 58; barter/swapping of colonies by, 4–5; colonial possessions of (and Jacobins), 157–58; constitution of, 89–90, 130, 174, 220n54; importance of governing India well to, 231n86; Indianism and, 126–27; miscibility in, 75, 78; others of, 105–6

Enlightenment: ab-use of, 189; blackmail of, xvi, xxii, 183, 189; critiques of, xv–xvii, 90–92; divided views of, xxii–xxiii; heritage of, 188–89; invocation of term, xv; pluralizing of, xv; postmodernism and, xx; progress and, 187; radical *vs.* moderate, 4; reclamation of, 180; worth of, 49–50

Enlightenment reason: Adorno and, 186

enthusiasm, 79, 123, 128, 140, 144, 208n3

envy, 96, 166, 241n98

Essai sur la manière de perfectionner l'espèce humaine (Vandermonde), 32

"Etablissements des Hollandais au cap de Bonne-Espérance" (chapter in *Histoire*) (Diderot), 46, 48–52

ethnography, 29

Eurocentrism, xvi

exchange, language of, 158

fairy tales, 63, 64

Falstaff (Shakespearean character), 1–2

the family, 106–7, 140

Fanon, Frantz, 183, 237n42

fear: Adorno's, 184; of consequences of abolition of slavery, 155; Diderot on, 23; of French control in West Indies, 148–49; of imagination, 113;

inspired by Haitian Revolution, 134; of Jacobins, 109; of loss of empire, 167; of man of color in National Assembly, 149–50, 154–55; of men of ability, 77–78; of modernity, 105–8; as spring of despotic governments, 212–13n44; of transformation of society, 15–16; of youth running empire, 116–17

feudalism, 80–81, 97, 98; language of, 5–6

Fitzwilliam, Earl (William Fitzwilliam, 4th Earl), 126, 128

Foote, Samuel, 12

Foucault, Michel: on *Aufklärung*, 187, 188–89; on barbarism/savagery, 213n47; on Kant, xvi, 187; knowledge-power linkage and, 181; on modernity, xvi–xvii; pastoral power and, 173; population and, 222n86; on sexuality, 28; on ship metaphor, 84

four-stage theory of development, 80

"Fourth Letter on a Regicide Peace" (Burke), 147–49

Fox, Charles James, 76f, 129f, 137–38, 143, 164f, 237n40

France: abolition of slavery in, 152, 155–56; barter/swapping of colonies by, 4–5; Burke's description of, 142–43; as cannibal republic, 160–61; as conquest of Jacobins, 16, 87–89, 89–90, 107, 131–32, 157; constitution of, 133, 138–42, 145; as England's other, 105–6; as enslaved, 147–48; as ill/sick, 121; India and, 15–16, 107, 112; intellectual class in, 131; invading St. Domingue, 180–81; Jamaica and, 59; miscibility in, 119–20; monarchy of, 87–89, 100–105; necessity of invading, 158–59; New World colonies and, 163; as piratical, 149; redistricting of, 83, 87, 89–90, 94; Spain allied with, 148, 154; St. Domingue entangled with, 235n24; wealth of, 103–4; as weightless, post-revolution, 86; West Indies and, 147–48. *See also* French Revolution

Francis, Philip, 164f; on apathy of British public, 114; fortune amassed by, 5; friendship with Burke, 135, 231–32n88; Hastings trial and, 240n88; letters from Burke to, 135–36, 162–63, 165, 225n18; letter to Burke by, 233n7; William Burke and, 162

Franco-Spanish treaty of 1795, 148

freedom: associated with colonialism, 93–94; deferring of, 188; imitation and, 38–39; instinctive drive toward, in Mariana Islands, 61; models of governance and, 169; runaway slaves and, 56; of slaves on St. Domingue, 141. *See also* liberty

free people of color: citizenship granted to, 235n25, 236n39; defending rights of republic, 150–52; political rights granted to, 142; property rights granted to, 146

French army: invading St. Domingue, 180–81

French monarchy: Burke's defense of, 100–105; compared to America, 87–89; compared to Asian despots, 100–101. *See also* ancien régime

French Revolution (1789-1799): American Revolution and, 87–89; *ancien régime* and, xix–xx; appropriation of culture of, 177–79, 180–81; Burke on, 15–16, 71–75, 87–89; class and, 86–87, 97–98, 119–20; as colonial occupation, 87–89, 93–97; despotism and, 99–101; English responses to, 99–100; Glorious Revolution as unlike, 75; Haitian insurgents and, 179; India and, 71–75, 85–86; manners and, 80; property and, 78; "Second Letter" on, 156–57; Tocqueville on, xix, 69; Toussaint and, 177. *See also* revolutionaries

Furet, François, xix–xx, 112

Furniss, Tom, 81

future anterior, 42, 44, 206n85. *See also* prophetic voice

gender, 28–29, 104, 232n3. *See also* women
generations, 60, 73–74, 156
genres: Diderot's use of, 13–14, 36
geographical morality, 108
geometric reason, 78, 89–96, 101–2, 105
Gibbon, Edward, 52
gifts: European thought as, 194n35; gift economy, 31, 32; rights of man as, 138, 141; success due to, 103; usage of term, xxii
Gillis, John, 117
globalization, 13, 44–45
Glorious Revolution (1688), 75, 118, 127
Goa, 52–54
Goethe, Johann Wolfgang von, 65–66
Gordon, Daniel, xx
Gordon riots (1780), 144, 237n44, 238n45
Gothic elements, used by Burke, 95, 221n84, 221–22n85

Gouly, Marie-Benoît-Louis, 152
governance, models of, 165, 169, 171–72
great chain of being, 174
Grimm, Friedrich Melchior, 25
Guam, 60–65
Guha, Ranajit, xx–xxi, 182

habit, 124, 229n65. *See also* custom
haine. See hatred
Haiti. *See* St. Domingue (Haiti)
Haitian Revolution (1791-1804), 133–61; French revolutionary culture and, 179; progress and, 187–88; significance of in Burke's thought, 17–18. *See also* slave revolts; St. Domingue (Haiti)
Halhed, Nathaniel, 114
happiness, 62–65, 169, 202–3n57
Hartog, François, xvii
Hastings, Warren, 76*f*, 164*f*; acquittal of, 126; appointment as governor-general, 6; as embodiment of Indianism, 122; fortune amassed by, 5; Nandakumar and, 232n5; as scapegoat, 107–8, 112; as shorthand for abuses in India, 7. *See also* Hastings impeachment trial
Hastings impeachment trial: effects of, 114–15; inconsistency of Burke's views and, 85; Indianism and, 129; *Reflections* as respite from, 10, 16, 113–14; significance of, 111–12
hating empire properly, 183, 186
hating tradition properly, 19, 183
hatred: Diderot on, 23; *douceur* and, 63–64; empathetic (on behalf of colonized), 48; of empire, 181, 183, 186; expressed in *Histoire*, 47; as grounding of critical thought, 66; justice and, 15, 47–48; properness of, 183; *ressentiment* and, 212n39, 221n81; at self, 53*See also* anger
haunting, language of, 47, 48
Hegel, Georg Wilhelm Friedrich, v, 98, 99, 183, 223n99, 243n1
hegemony, 24, 45
Heidegger, Martin, 183
heterosexuality, 28–29, 31–32. *See also* sexuality
Hindostan (Hindustan), 26, 162, 164–65, 171, 174. *See also* India
Hirschman, A. O., 97
Hispaniola: historical counterfactual fantasy of, 159–60. *See also* St. Domingue (Haiti)

Histoire des deux Indes (Raynal): affect in, 14–15; anger in, 51–52; Anglo-French rivalry reflected in, 8*f*; anthropological method and, 41–42; arguments against slavery in, 40–41; breeding and, 32–37; Burke and, 69; Diderot's contributions to, 12–15, 25–26, 198n12; as *écriture fragmentaire*, 36–37; globalization and, 44–45; internal contradictions of, 35–37; organization of, 61, 209n11; pathos in, 51–52; Pocock on, 211n30; principles of colonization and, 9; revenge in, 47; rhetorical techniques used in, 55; scholarship on, 198–99n13; style of thinking revealed in, 3; wealth in, 27. *See also* anger; *Histoire des deux Indes* (Raynal), chapters in
Histoire des deux Indes (Raynal), chapters in: "Corruption of the Portuguese in India" (Diderot), 52–54; "Dangers Which Threatened Jamaica from Within" (Diderot), 54–60; "Description of the Mariana Islands. Singular Qualities Observed There.", 60–65; "Etablissements des Hollandais au cap de Bonne-Espérance" (Diderot), 46, 48–52; "Le Privilège de la compagnie, sera-t-il renouvelé?" (Diderot), 46
historical counterfactuals: double advantage and, 15; *Histoire*'s dependence on, 47; Hottentots and, 51–52; regarding Anglo-French rivalry, 159–60, 161; regarding Burke's position on India, 135; regarding Hispaniola, 159–60; regarding Mariana Islands, 64–65
history: imperial, xx–xxi, 195n20; limitations of, 215–16n90; need for, 65–66
History of Sexuality (Foucault), 28
Hobbes, Thomas, 117
Holland, 35, 158
Horkheimer, Max, 90–91, 184
hortatory mode, 40, 51
Hottentots (Khoikhoin), 48, 49–52, 209n8
House of Commons: as ballast, 83; Burke on power of, 74, 127; Burke's contempt for, 227–28n48
House of Lords, 83
humanism, commercial, 79–81
humanism, Marxist, 182
humanitarianism, 40, 49, 59, 153–54
Hume, David, 125

imitation, 38–39, 62, 204n73
immanence, xviii, 45, 91
immanent critique, 183
imperial compensation. *See* compensation in the East
imperious attraction, 37
India: Burke's interest in, 113–14; compared with America, 168, 170–71; compared with France, 15–16, 107; compared with Germany, 219n47; feudal class and, 98; focus on native gentry of, 135; French Revolution and, 71–75, 85–86; geographical data on, 82–83; imperial rivalry in, 7; importance of good governance of, 231n86; insubordination in, 167–69; manners/commerce and, 80–81; modernity in, 110, 131; as outposts managed by European residents, 18; pastoral power in, 246n39; revenue from, 172–73; violence in, 136. *See also* India, Burke's writings on
India, Burke's writings on: anticolonialism of, 134–37; cosmopolitan sympathy and, 82–83; Europe and, 225n13; European social transformations and, 71–75; justice and, 115; shaping notion of Jacobinism, 110; St. Domingue and, 134; writings on France and, 112
India Act of 1784, 6
Indianism, 126–32; affecting Asia, 127–28; affecting England, 126–27; breakers of law in India as makers of law in England, 17, 74, 127, 131; Burke on, 109; defined, 17, 230–31n80; delegitimization of state's use of force and, 17, 130; as greatest evil, 128–29; Hastings as embodiment of, 122; Jacobinism and, 128–29; language of contagion and, 227n39; mixing of classes and, 116–21; planters and, 154–55; political concatenation and, 176; in "Speech on Fox's East India Bill," 116. *See also* Jacobinism
inheritance: as ballast to vessel of state, 86; House of Lords as validation of, 83; merit and, 74–75; social contract/partnership and, 73–74; virtue and, 78–79. *See also* property rights
injustice: progress of, in Jamaica, 59–60; of slavery, 58. *See also* justice
instrumental reason, 90–91, 93–96, 105
insubordination: in America, 170–72; Burke's response to, 18; in India, 167–69

intellectual class, 120–22, 123, 131
interbreeding: antislavery movement and, 40; arguments for, 39; biological grounds for, 44; fantasy of, 33–34; as imagined solution to colonization, 32, 33. *See also* breeding
inversion, 55, 58
Ireland, 105, 107, 126, 128, 130

Jacobinism, 119–25; Burke's understanding of, 16–17, 134–35; components of, 123; as contagion, 88; as greatest evil, 128; human nature and, 112; Indianism and, 128–29; Ireland and, 128; modernity and, 123, 175–76; Parliament and, 148, 154–55; political concatenation and, 176; prejudice and, 17, 123–25; Quebec Bill and, 137–40; Rousseau as embodiment of, 122; "Second Letter" on, 156–61; shaped by India writings, 110; St. Domingue and, 144–45; as threat of rights of man, 140–44; view of human nature by, 107; violence and, 17, 18, 144–45. *See also* Indianism; Jacobins
Jacobins: as barbarians, 160; black, 150, 154; as colonizers/ruling through conquest, 107, 131–32, 157; description of in *Reflections*, 120–21; peace with, 157–58; racial other and, 154; West Indies as cost of defense from, 157–59
Jamaica, 54–60
James, C. L. R.: Adorno and, 183; on French soldiers, 236n31; modernity and, xviii; on Robespierre's radicalism, 243n3, 244n14; scholarship and, 182; on slogans of revolution, 177; Toussaint and, 19, 177–81
Jesuits, 26, 199n21
Jews, 154
Jones, Sir William, 114, 136–37
justice: doing justice to Indian language/literature/people, 136–37; East India Company and, 135; empire and, 115; hatred and, 15, 47–48. *See also* injustice

Kant, Immanuel, xvi, 24, 177, 187–88
"Kant on Enlightenment and Revolution" (Foucault), 187
Kaviraj, Sudipta, xviii
Khoikhoin (Hottentots), 48, 49–52, 209n8
knowledge. *See* colonial knowledge
knowledge, production of, 182

INDEX / 275

land: as perilous to Europeans, 159; procurement of, 199n21; revolutionaries' relationship to, 106; as source of wealth, 29; as the way a society remembers, 90
landed interests: as ballast, 83–84; monied interests and, 119–20
Langrishe, Sir Hercules, 126, 128, 130
language, figurative: of apocalypse, 141; of banking/finance, 95, 124–25; of clothing/veiling, 125; of contagion, 142, 227n39; of exchange, 158; of feudalism, 5–6; of haunting, 47, 48; of light/illumination, 92; of lost opportunity, 159–60; of the monstrous, 148; of nautical/maritime images, 83–87; of piracy, 149
law: breakers of in India as makers of in England, 17, 74, 127, 131; formulation of, 165–66; undermining of, 130–31; universalism of, 78
Lawrence, Jacob, xiii
leisure, 75–76
letters by Burke: to Charles-Jean-François Depont, 225n18; to Earl Fitzwilliam, 126, 128; to Henry Dundas, 234n18; "Letters on a Regicide Peace," 18, 147–49, 156–61; *Letter to a Member of the National Assembly*, 121–22; "Letter to the Sheriffs of Bristol", 162, 164–65, 174; to Loughborough, 128–29, 130, 131, 135, 136; to Mary Palmer, 153; to Philip Francis, 135–36, 162–63, 165, 225n18; to Sir Hercules Langrishe, 126, 128, 130; to Sir William Jones, 136–37; to William Windham, 140, 144
liberal imperialism: consent and, 14
liberalism: contradictions of, 169; empire and, 45; Marxism and, 49; morality and, 40; Parliament and, 241n104
Liberalism and Empire (Mehta), 4, 182
liberty: abstract, 241n94; commerce as, 34–35, 40–41; granting of to formerly enslaved, 155–56; morality/manners as bridge to, 140; slave revolts and, 56–57. *See also* freedom; rights of man
light/illumination, language of, 92
literature, Oriental, 136–37
loans given to East India Company, 6
Locke, John, 27
lost opportunity, language of, 159–60
Loughborough, Baron (Alexander Wedderburn, later, 1780, 1st Baron), 128–29, 130, 131, 135, 136

Louverture, Toussaint, 19, 178f; as conscript of modernity, xviii; Enlightenment and, 180; as figure for decolonization, 179; language of Enlightenment figures and, 177, 189; Raynal and, 207n93; rumored to have read *Histoire*, 45
love, 173, 185

Macbeth (Shakespeare), 141, 235–36n26
Madras Council, 167, 168
manners: as bridge to liberty, 140; Burke on, 92; commerce and, 79–81; explaining Burke's contradictions/inconsistencies, 110; formulation of law and, 166; working against universalist thinking, 3. *See also* custom
Mansfield Park (Austen), 113
Mariana Islands, 15, 60–65, 215n85
Marie-Antoinette, 136, 232n3, 233n7
marriage, 119, 140, 200n28. *See also* breeding
"Marseillaise" (song), 179, 236n31
Marshall, P. J., 111, 114–15, 134
Marx, Karl, 99
Marxism: critique of liberalism and, 49; in East, 185
Marxist humanism, 182
May, Gita, 11
Mehta, Uday, 4, 182
Mélanges pour Catherine II (Diderot), 38–39
Mémoire sur la Situation de Saint-Domingue (Cormier), 146–47
merit, 74–75, 77–78
The Merry Wives of Windsor (Shakespeare), 1
Metcalf, Thomas, 3, 154
métissage, 27, 31, 119, 227n41. *See also* breeding
Michelet, Jules, 219n47
milk, 13
Mill, John Stuart, 9, 10, 12, 232n5
Millar, John, 80
Milton, John, 142–43
Minima Moralia (Adorno), 19, 181, 186
miscibility: of burghers, 16, 118, 127; East India Company officials and, 118–20; in England, 75, 78; miscegenation and, 217n22; of races in colonies, 141
Mitchell, L. G., 146
modernity: asceticism and, xvii; as attitude, xvi–xvii; Burke's response to, 16; class and, 98; conscripts of,

xvii–xviii; *douce colonisation* and, 35; fear of, 105–8; Foucault on, xvi–xvii; in India, 110; Jacobinism and, 123, 175–76; in revolutionary France, 106–7, 131. *See also* modernity, colonial
modernity, colonial: Burke's arguments against, 16; Burke's fear of, 109; European modernity and, xix, xviii, 17, 132; in India, 131
monarchic governments, 212n44
money, 86, 103–4
monied interests. *See* bourgeoisie/burghers/monied interests
the monstrous, language of, 143, 148
Montesquieu, Charles de Secondat, 55, 156, 165, 212–13n44
Moors, 154
morality, 33–34, 40, 108
Morley, John, 11, 50
Morocco, 149
Muhammed Ali (nawab of Arcot), 167

The Nabob (Foote), 12
nabobs: as contagion from East, 74; as example of breakers of law becoming makers of law, 17; origin of term, 5–6; Parliament and, 172
Nandakumar, 135, 232n5
Nandy, Ashis, 117
Napoleon I. *See* Bonaparte, Napoleon (Emperor Napoleon I)
National Assembly (France): Belley in, 149–53; Burke on power of, 74; education and, 121; ruling of on free people of color, 142, 143, 236n39; slavery and, 142
national character, 33, 106
native customs, 50
native readers, absence of, 51
native resistance, 135–36, 145
natives: as children, 117; consensual colonialism and, 14, 62–63; future anterior and, 44; as scandalous, 111; settlers as, 165, 171; stereotypes of, 31
natural order, 75
nature: arithmetic reason and, 94–95; custom and, 81; French Revolution and, 75; politics and, 148; slavery and, 56, 152; in *Supplément*, 30–31
navigation skills, 64–65
Necker, Jacques, 102, 104
Nietzsche, Friedrich, 65–66, 182, 212n39, 215–16n90, 221n81, 244n18

North, Frederick, 2nd earl of Guilford (known as Lord North), 76f, 164f
North America: depopulation of, 27; South America and, 26
nostalgia, 44
Novalis, 71
novelty, 120–21

O'Brien, Conor Cruise, 139, 225n13, 234–35n19, 237n42
Observation sur le Nakaz (Diderot), 38
old colonies/new colonies pair, 26
oppositional pairs. *See* antithetical pairs (oppositional pairs)
oppressed, speaking on behalf of, 18, 135, 150, 153
oriental despotism, 3, 99–101
orientalism, 14, 24, 182
Orientalism (Said), 23–24, 92
orientalist scholarship, 136–37
Orou (character in *Supplément*), 29, 30, 31, 32

Pagden, Anthony, 26, 200n25, 220n62
Paine, Thomas, 88
Palmer, Mary, 153
Pandora's box, 138, 141, 146, 235n25
panoptical images, 34, 92, 104
Parliament: Burke's departure from, 126; fear of Indianism in, 127; fear of Jacobinism in, 148, 154–55; influence of over East India Company, 6; liberalism and, 241n104; nabobs and, 172. *See also under* speech
parodies, 29–30
partnership, society as, 72–73
pastoral power, 173, 246n39
pathos, 51–52
Paulson, Ronald, 100, 102
peace with Jacobins, 157–58
pepper, 72
philosophes: commercial, 40–41; doubles of, 23–24; figure of runaway slave and, 56; Orou as, 31; traveling, 42–44; universalism of, 3
Philosophical and Political History (Raynal), xviii
A Philosophical Enquiry into the Origin of Our Ideas of the Sublime and Beautiful (Burke), 28, 76
Physiocrats, 29, 49, 86
piety, 188–89
Pigot, George (Baron Pigot), 167–72

piracy, 149
planters/planter class, 142, 143-44, 145, 150-52, 154-55
Plato, 30
Pocock, J. G. A.: on bourgeoisie/burghers, 97, 118; on *Histoire,* 211n30; interpretation of *Reflections* by, 103; manners and, 79, 92-93; pluralizing of Enlightenment by, xv; on transmission of language from France to England, 123
political analogies, 170-72, 174-76
political concatenation, 18, 174-76
political economy, 49, 79
Political Writings (Diderot), 25, 37
Polverel, Etienne, 141-42
Pondicherry, India, 7
population: abstraction of, 93-96; aestheticism and, 201n35; of America, 242n109; breeding and, 44; in consensual colonialism, 14; the crowd and, 106; despotism and, 101-5; *douce colonisation* and, 27; Foucault on, 222n86; in *Histoire,* 32-37; representation based on, 96; as wealth, 27, 29, 222n87
the Portuguese, 52-53
positivism, 91, 184-86
postcolonial thought, xix, xvi, 182-83, 204n73
postmodernism, xx
power: Burke on, 127; colonial, 92; knowledge and, 181; monopolization of by state, 168; pastoral, 173, 246n39
prejudice, 17, 123-25, 229n62, 229n65
Price, Richard, 77, 86, 102, 242n112
primitivism, 35, 184
principle of equivalence, 91
principles of colonization, 9, 37, 38-39, 46-47
"Principles Which the French Should Follow in India, if they Succeed There in Reestablishing Their Esteem and Presence" (Diderot), 23
"Le Privilège de la compagnie, sera-t-il renouvelé?" (chapter in *Histoire*) (Diderot), 46
progress, 102-3, 117, 187
property: as how a society remembers, 90; inheritance of, 73-74, 78-79, 83, 86; monied interests and, 119-20; virtue and, 78-79; vulnerability of, 77-79. *See also* property rights

property rights: Burke's plan to reform slavery and, 140; free people of color and, 146; in Guam, 62; lack of in Mariana Islands, 60-61. *See also* inheritance
prophetic voice: Burke's, 84, 115, 132, 139; Diderot's, 41, 47, 56

Quakers, 26, 199n21
Quebec, 137
Quebec Bill (1791), 137-38

race: Belley on, 150-53; Burke's reflections on, 153-54; citizenship and, 236n39; climatic harshness of tropics and, 159; fear of mingling of, 141; in India vs. America, 168, 171; republican ideals and, 150-52; Rousseau and, 206n86. *See also* breeding; free people of color; natives; slave revolts; slavery
Raimond, Julien, 142
raja of Tanjore, 167
rationalism: Burke's critique of, 72. *See also* reason
rationality: of native societies, 31, 50
Raynal, abbé de: Belley portrayed with bust of, 151f, 207n93; Burke and, 10, 69-70; on Diderot's contributions to *Histoire,* 25; principles of colonization and, 38; Toussaint and, xviii; Toussaint portrayed reading, 178f
reason: arithmetic, 78, 89-96, 101-2, 105; as counterweight to property, 86; instrumental, 90-91, 93-96; linked with colonizing impulse, 90-92; practical, 162, 165, 226n29; prejudice and, 124-25
"Reflections on the Good and Evil Which the Discovery of the New World has Done to Europe" (Diderot), 23
Reflections on the Revolution in France (Burke): Asian despotism in, 100-101; Burke's self-characterization in, 84-85; circumstances of composition of, 10, 16, 84, 113-14; as concerned with England, 127; double anxiety in, 77-78; Hastings trial and, 10, 16, 113-14; India writings and, 71; Jacobins in, 120-21; keywords of, 74; miscibility in, 119-20; prejudice in, 124; sexual difference in, 28; on social contract, 72-74; St. Domingue and, 145-46
Réfutation d'Helvétius (Diderot), 35

regicide ambassador, 149–50
Regulating Act (1773), 6
relativism, 30, 35, 108
religion, 26, 32–33, 35, 40, 212n39. *See also* clergy
Religion within the Limits of Reason Alone (Kant), 188
representation, 24, 96
Republic (Plato), 30
ressentiment: Adorno's use of, 185; as curable, 63–65; Diderot's use of, 48; against Dutch in South Africa, 49–52; against English in Jamaica, 54–60; exploration of, 14–15; meaning of, 55; Montesquieu's springs and, 212–13n44; Nietzsche's sense of, 212n39, 221n81; against Portuguese in Goa, 52–54; in *Reflections,* 119–20; slavery and, 55. *See also* anger; envy; hatred
revenge: anger and, 15; call for against Portuguese, 52–54; call for in Jamaica, 54–58; expressed in *Histoire,* 47; rights and, 57–58
revenues from colonies, 172–73
reverence for state/social contract, 72–74, 130–31
revolutionaries: appropriation of culture of, 177–79, 180–81; as colonizers, 93–97; as despotic, 102; identified with modernity, 106–7
revolutions: defined, 102–3
Rickert, Heinrich, 185
rights of man: as abstract, 96, 146; Burke on, 78, 133; commerce and, 146; despotism and, 146; in West Indies, 138–44
rivalry, Anglo-French: abolition of slavery and, 155–56; barter/swapping of colonies in, 4–5; in *Histoire des deux Indes,* 8f; in India, 7; "Second Letter" on, 156–61; slave trade and, 59; West Indies and, 147–48
Rivarol, Claude-François de, 70
Romans, 93
Romilly, Samuel, 100
Rousseau, Jean-Jacques: Burke and, 3, 72, 121–23, 228n59; as embodiment of Jacobinism, 122; on imitation, 39; modernity and, 106, 107–8, 122; racial views of, 206n86; transparency of, 228n56; traveler/philosophe pair and, 24; on travelers, 42–43
Rule of Property for Bengal (Guha), 182

Russia, 38

Said, Edward: on geographic clarification, 225n14; knowledge-power linkage and, 92, 181; on *Mansfield Park,* 113; scholarship enabled by, 182; understanding of orientalism by, 14, 24
savages: Adorno on, 184; association of term, 55; Foucault on, 213n47. *See also* barbarians
scandal, 111
Schutztruppe, 185
Scott, David, xvii
"Second Letter on a Regicide Peace" (Burke), 156–61
Second Treatise of Government (Locke), 27
secrecy/cabals, 96–97, 115, 241n104
Seeley, J. R., 7, 111, 195n20
settler colonialism, 173
settlers, 14, 87–89, 165, 171
sexuality: as analogy for colonization schemes, 1–2; colonization and, 37; commerce and, 27; heterosexuality, 28–29, 31–32. *See also* breeding
Shakespeare, William, 1, 235–36n26
Sheridan, Richard, 129f
ship metaphor, 83–87, 220n54
"Sketch of a Negro Code" (Burke), 139–40
slave revolts: in Jamaica, 54–59; in St. Domingue, 137, 139, 140, 236n31. *See also* Haitian Revolution
slavery: abolition of, 40–41, 152, 155–56, 234n18; Burke and, 139–40, 147–48, 235n21; as contrary to nature, 61; freedom from on St. Domingue, 141; impracticality of, 49; National Assembly and, 142; *ressentiment* and, 55
slaves: humanity of, 152
Smith, Adam, 41, 80
social contract, 72–74, 112, 130–31
Social Contract (Rousseau), 72
socialism, 185
social transformations: Burke's fear of, 85–86, 109–10; commerce and, 80–81; natural order and, 75; *tabula rasa* view of humanity and, 107
Sonthonax, Léger Félicité, 141–42
sovereignty, 2, 7, 170–71
Spain: alliance with France, 148, 154; colonialism of, in Mariana Islands, 60–65; Hispaniola and, 160–61; New World colonies and, 163; as province of Jacobin Empire, 157

"Speech on Bengal Judicature Bill" (Burke), 166, 167
"Speech on Conciliation with America" (Burke), 172–74, 235n21, 242n109
"Speech on Fox's East India Bill" (Burke), 164–65; British interests in, 231n86; description of Company officials in, 116; phrase "total revolution" in, 231n87; sympathy in, 82–83; as theatrical, 111–12
"Speech on Restoring Lord Pigot" (Burke), 18, 166, 167–72
Spivak, Gayatri Chakravorty, 189, 208n5
the state: formation of, 6; forms of, 222n86; as partnership, 72–74
St. Domingue (Haiti), 133–61; Burke's speeches on, 137–39, 140–43; Burke's writings on India and, 134; commerce and, 235n24; defense of by blacks/free people of color, 150; freedom of slaves on, 141; French army invading, 180–81; Jacobinism and, 140–45; as producer of coffee, 217n12; *Reflections* and, 145–46; significance of in Burke's thought, 17–18; slave revolts in, 137, 139, 140, 236n31
Stoler, Ann Laura, 119, 227n41
structural oppositions. *See* antithetical pairs (oppositional pairs)
Sublime, the, 104–5, 112, 230n77
sugar, 13, 62, 141, 235n24
Suleri, Sara, 111–12
superstition, 50
Supplément au voyage de Bougainville (Diderot): antithetical pairs in, 30–31; breeding and, 28–32; circumstances of composition of, 25; doubles/pairs in, 23–25; *Encyclopédie* and, 13–14; feminist reading of, 200n28; genre of, 29–30; sexuality/gender in, 28–29; style of thinking revealed in, 3; wealth in, 27
the Swiss, 38–39
sympathy, 82–83, 175

tabula rasa, 107, 123, 131
Tahiti, 30–32
Tancred (Disraeli), 77
terror, 153, 160–61
theater, 111–12, 122, 240n88
third-worldism, 19, 184–85
time, xx–xxi, 44, 73–74
tobacco, 72
Tocqueville, Alexis de, xix, 26, 69

Toussaint Louverture. *See* Louverture, Toussaint
trade: rights of man compared to, 142; social contract and, 72–73; with two Indies, 1–2. *See also* commerce; commodities
trading companies, 5–9. *See also* East India Company
tradition, 19, 183, 188–89
transparency, 122, 123, 125, 228n56
travelers, 23–24, 30, 33, 42–44
tropical empire, 156, 159–61
Turkey, 101
tyranny of number (numerical representation), 77–78, 89–90

United Company Merchants of England, 5. *See also* East India Company
universalism: Burke and, 78; colonial knowledge and, 2; Diderot as illustrative of, 2, 3–4; models of governance and, 165; planter class threatened by, 145; race and, 153–54; singularity of culture and, 82

Vandermonde, Charles, 32
vanity, 122, 123, 141, 228n53, 228n59
vengeance. *See* revenge
Versini, Laurent, 35
vessel of the commonwealth, 83–87, 220n54
A Vindication of the Rights of Men (Wollstonecraft), 28, 88
violence: arithmetic reason and, 92; Diderot's call to, 51–53; Fanon's defense of, 237n42; by former slaves, 54–56; Haitian Revolution and, 133; in India, 136; Jacobinism and, 17, 18, 144–45; in Jamaica, 59–60; self-perpetuation of, 59–60
Virginia, 26, 162, 164, 165, 171
virtue, 78–79, 212n44, 229n65, 233n7
Voltaire, 26, 199n21
Voyage autour du Monde (Bougainville), 32
vulnerability, 77–79, 89–90, 112

wealth: Burke's discussion of, 103–4; happiness and, 64–65; India as producer of, 173; population as, 27, 29, 222n87; representation of, 96–97; spreading of, 40–41; wisdom as, 125
Wealth of Nations (Smith), 41
West Indies: climatic harshness of, 159; containment of Jacobinism and,

157–59; imperial rivalry with France and, 147–48; rights of man and, 138–39, 140–44; slavery in, 234n18. *See also* Jamaica; St. Domingue (Haiti)
"What Is Enlightenment?" (Kant), xvi, 188
Whigs, 75, 79, 230n70
Wilson, Arthur, 25
Windham, William, 140, 144
wisdom, 74, 75–76, 125
Wollstonecraft, Mary, 28, 87–88, 221n84
women: Diderot and roles of, 200n28; ownership of, 29, 30, 32. *See also* gender

youth, 116–17, 121, 159

www.ingramcontent.com/pod-product-compliance
Lightning Source LLC
Chambersburg PA
CBHW030435300426
44112CB00009B/1010